From Dust to Snow:

The African Dream?

Lydia and Wilfred Ngwa
(Eds)

African Renaissance Ambassador Series

Copyright © 2006 Lydia and Wilfred Ngwa

All rights reserved. No part of this publication may be reproduced, stored in a retrieval system or transmitted in any form or by any means, electronic, mechanical, photocopying, recording, or likewise, without prior written permission from the editors.

Disclaimer
While the editors have tried to ensure the truth, accuracy and consistency of the material in this book, they specifically disclaim, and assume no liability or responsibility for the use of this book, reliance on its content, whatsoever, nor do they assume any liability or responsibility for errors, misinterpretations, or any inconsistency contained, and specifically disclaim such, as well as disclaiming any other possible liability premised upon reliance or use of this book. For anonymity, some of the authors have chosen to use pennames.

50 percent of the proceeds from the sale of this book will go to the non-profit organization African Renaissance Ambassador Corp.

Published and distributed electronically by African Renaissance Ambassador Corp: Visit www.AfricanRenaissanceAmbassador.com

ISBN: 978-0-6151-3703-2

Dedication

To The African Renaissance[1] and
In memory of the numerous Africans who have lost their lives in the pursuit of a dream abroad.

---

[1] 'I dream of the day when these: the African mathematicians and computer specialists in Washington and New York, the African physicists, engineers, doctors, business managers and economists, will return from London and Manchester and Paris and Brussels to add to the African pool of brain power, to enquire into and find solutions to Africa's problems and challenges, to open the African door to the world of knowledge, to elevate Africa's place within the universe of research,… education and information' – *President Mbeki, at the African Renaissance Conference*

Acknowledgements

As Africans living in Europe and the US, we found ourselves in a unique position to interact with many internationals (mostly other Africans) coming for studies, asylum and work. This book would not be possible without the willingness and openness of these people to share their experiences, however joyful or painful; our foremost thanks go to them.

We also greatly appreciate all those who have facilitated our transition and survival in different countries and cultures far away from home. Just to name a few: in Germany: Leipzig English Church, Prof. Lynnda Curry; in the US: University Presbyterian Church in Orlando Florida; nothing is better than a wonderful church family to help you survive living away from home; in Switzerland: Arlette Flueckiger.

Special gratitude goes: to Dr. J. Adibe (Adonis & Abbey Publishers, London) for helpful suggestions. Also, many thanks to those who reviewed stories in this book, including: Jessie Atogho Ekukole (Editor in Chief, English Language News, CRTV Radio), Peter Suh-Nfor Tangyie (Principal, GBHS Santa), Professor Bole Butake (University of Yaoundé), Ayu'nwi N. Nebafusi (University of Buea), Chemuta & Margaret Banda (President & Mrs, Human rights Freedoms Commission, Cameroon), Charly Ndi Chia (Editor-In-Chief, The Post Newspaper), Prof Kenneth Ngwa (Wabash College, Indiana).

We thank God for inspiration, wisdom and strength.

Lydia and Wilfred Ngwa

Contents

Foreword	9
Intromission: Why do Africans leave their beloved continent?	11
From Dust to Snow: Hitler's Nightmare	15
America, here I come!	44
Studying in Nobel Prize Country	61
Where in Texas is Nigeria?	73
From Dust to Snow: From Charles Taylor to Pat Robertson?	80
'The African must survive'	86
A refugee in Love	93
The Diary of an Asylum-seeker	98
From Dust to Snow: From HIV Negative to HIV Positive?	110
The DV lottery: A path to modern slavery?	116
Re-entry Shock	123
The Canadian Skilled worker program: Brain Drain or Brain Circulation?	127
Europe: Heaven on Earth?	133
Nightmares of Baghdad	148
The Burger	153
An African in white skin	158
An African falls on his feet	161

America: The good, the bad, the ugly	169
My graduate school experience in the U.S.	190
Living as a Muslim abroad	204
When East Meets West	209
A graveyard for Christians	221
There is no place like home!	228
Footprints in the snow	241
Germany versus Macedonia	249
Asylum in South Africa	265
At the mercy of a white man	271
Deleted 'Scenes' (Experiences)	285
The African Dream	298
The African Anthem	310
Country index	311

Foreword

The saying that the world has become a big village is no longer a cliché. In Africa, the latter half of the twentieth century saw the emergence of a new trend: the desire to escape the perils of Africa by traveling to the West. It seems many Africans had come to the conclusion that if only they could land in a Western country, they would solve all their problems. You could call this the "African Dream Hypothesis." But, like in Science, Arts and the Humanities, every hypothesis has to be tested before it becomes law or norm.

In *From Dust to Snow: The African Dream?* This hypothesis is put to the test. The book chronicles the true life experiences of Africans who pursued the dream into the West. With different levels of self motivation, apprehension, courage, fear, determination, and ultimately different levels of expectations and fulfillment, the contributors in this book search for their dreams and reopen the question about the character and quality of the African dream. In the end, and irrespective of what might have been their original expectations prior to traveling, many of the stories suggest a profound transformation in the travelers, as they review their presuppositions and assumptions regarding the countries they traveled to, and, thankfully, their own home countries. A new sense of African patriotism begins to emerge. But it is a patriotism that fully recognizes the pluralistic world we live in, and emerges and grows from a sense of self respect and respect for others.

"Travel and see" is not only a popular saying; it is a wise saying. But since not everyone gets to travel (literally Form Dust to Snow), the metaphorical and intellectual component of the journey is encapsulated and portrayed to the reader in these compelling stories. We learn some good lessons by reading what others have seen through their travels. In and through the eyes of those who have traveled, readers of this book get to see the west, and most importantly they get to see Africa anew.

There are books you can read at your own pace. There are other books that inspire you to read more and seem to create the pace for you. *From*

Dust to Snow: The African Dream? is in the latter category. It is a captivating piece of work, but more importantly it is a much needed resource for Africans who are thinking of their future, and are considering overseas travel as one of the good options. It is also a resource for Africans who have traveled abroad and are thinking of the return home as a critical factor in their search for the African lifestyle. The cross-cultural elements in the stories make the book useful for those seeking to live and/or work across cultures. Ultimately, it is useful for all people, not only Africans and Westerners.

We encourage you to read this book, and recommend it to others. *From Dust to Snow: The African Dream?* will entertain all, educate all, and inspire many.

Delanyo and Elizabeth Adadevoh
(President and Mrs, African Leadership Foundation)

Intromission: Why do Africans leave their beloved continent?

 President Clinton:
"One of the great minds of the Information Age is a Nigerian American named Philip Emeagwali. He had to leave school because his parents couldn't pay the fees. He lived in a refugee camp during ... civil war. He won a scholarship to university (in the USA) and went on to invent a formula that lets computers make 3.1 billion calculations per second. (Applause.) Some people call him the Bill Gates of Africa. (Laughter and applause.) But what I want to say to you is there is another Philip Emeagwali – or hundreds of them – or thousands of them – growing up in Africa today... You never know what potential is in their mind and in their heart; what imagination they have; **what they have already thought of and dreamed of that may be locked in because they don't have the means to take it out.**"

'Africa, my Africa,
Hear our cries.
Hear your dispersed children turned
New World ghetto dwellers...
Africa, my Africa,
Mother Father Africa,
Even in America
Dada sings freedom **wake up**
Songs for you--
Neither century
Nor distance
Not even our own demon
Ignorance
Can deny you
Still live

In the center of our days.'

Those remarks by President Clinton in Africa in 2000 and the excerpt from the beautiful "Poem for Africa" by reputable African Diaspora poet Mwatabuh Okantah set the cue for what you will experience next.

But first take a look at Africa compared to the rest of the world at night:

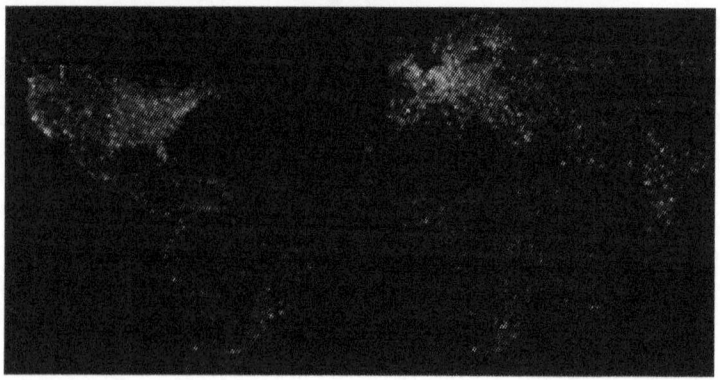

Yes, it is very dark in Africa. Why? Is the perception reality?

First, let me introduce myself: My name is Fako Kilimanjaro, alias FK. I am an ambassador of the African Renaissance. I will accompany you through this book. Together we will travel the world in a few hours, experiencing what Africans go through abroad, with illuminating perspectives from Asians and Westerners. I will introduce you to the contributors: asylum seekers, students and the employed. We will try to answer the questions: 'What is happening to Mother Africa? Why is it still dark? What does traveling abroad have to do with the darkness? How can Africans abroad and non-Africans help to dispel the darkness? Is traveling and living abroad the African Dream or is it a Nightmare? Is there another dream? What do you know about the life of Africans living abroad? What are the caveats? Why should you as an African or non-African care?

Verily, there is another map I would like to show you, but I believe you will trust me without actually seeing it. It's a map highlighting where the big world news organizations focus. The map shows that there is minimal coverage on Africa. And you will soon see what Africans in Diaspora think about this minimum coverage. It seems like the world does not care.

There is an African saying that 'Children are their mother's cane'. At a time when Mother Africa (the origin of modern man) seems to need the support of her 'cane', some of them (Africans) are migrating to western countries, while the others (non-Africans) apparently don't care. According to the International Organization for Migration (IOM), Africa has already lost one third of its human capital and is continuing to lose its skilled personnel at an increasing rate, with an estimated 20,000 doctors, university lecturers, engineers and other professionals leaving the continent annually since 1990. The sad thing is that most Africans go to Europe and America and seek asylum, and as you will see later in this book, this can be worse than being diagnosed with HIV/AIDS today.

The whole enigma, interestingly, seems to be a repeat of history. Around the 13th century BC, according to the biblical story when the first major Exodus from Africa happened, it was a mixed group of Israelites and others leaving Egypt voluntarily (?) for the Promised Land, far away from Africa. During the Slave Trade, Africans left involuntarily to Lands far from their continent. Today, history is ostensibly repeating itself, as innumerable Africans are leaving their continent voluntarily (?), to Europe, America, and Asia, countries far from their beloved continent. The brain drain is a nightmare! A Deputy Executive Secretary of the Economic commission for Africa predicts that if nothing is done urgently, Africa will be empty of brains in 25 years. The thought of this sends a chill crawling up my spine. It would be suicidal. "By failing to offer greener pastures for its own intelligentsia, Africa is committing suicide." says Professor Edward Ofori-Sarpong Pro-Vice Chancellor, University of Ghana at Legon

In summary, Africa is fast depleting its intellectual resources, and most of the West apparently doesn't care. So you may rightfully ask: "What is bad about moving from one continent to another? The imagery adopted to describe such migration is that of moving "From Dust to Snow." The irony is that, while snow is a natural occurrence of nature that cannot be avoided in western nations (and so must be adapted to), dust is a hazard that can be transformed and eliminated for most rural communities in Africa (and so does not have to be adapted to). Hmmm. So what is the solution? Here is a clue. History can also repeat itself in a positive way. Remember the biblical creation story. In the beginning the Earth was covered in darkness, then ...?" The on-going transformation of South Africa evidently comes to mind.

Am I suggesting something? It's not me. It's the experiences we are about to go through. At the end, perhaps, you and I will agree on what needs to be done. Perhaps, as a Westerner, you will care (The experiences provide a look from outside, a series of snapshots on you by those who have not taken your cultural assumptions for granted. It provides an opportunity for host readers to become aware of the perceptions that help nourish or hinder the development of good relationships in an increasingly global society.) Perhaps, as an African, you will remember the African proverb that 'A Prince is a slave when far from his kingdom'; perhaps, as African or non-African, you will better appreciate the African saying: 'Children are the mother's cane'. As you go through the experiences with me, let's consider possible solutions for the looming 'suicide' threatening Mother Africa.

The first 4 'experiences' will be from students: two from Europe and two from America:

Chapter 1

From Dust to Snow: Hitler's Nightmare

"The overwhelming majority of people in our country are open to foreigners." ... "We Germans have and will continue to have a duty to resolutely combat any form of anti-Semitism, racism and xenophobia." – Angela Merkel, German Chancellor

[FK: Chancellor Gerhard Schroeder approached Adriano's 'gravestone' in Dessau (East Germany) slowly, and with a sober expression. He bent low to the photograph of the round-faced African-born family man and placed the wreath, rearranged the red, black and gold ribbons before standing in respectful silence.

On the night of his murder, Alberto Adriano - who had lived and worked in Germany for more than 20 years - had been celebrating a forthcoming trip to Mozambique. He would have basked in the admiration of his village: returning home, no doubt bearing lavish gifts and undreamed of wealth. Instead, his family received a simple wooden coffin from Germany containing the disfigured remains of their son, aged 39. This was a very symbolic act by the German Chancellor, to pay his respects at the simple 'shrine' which now marks the murder scene. We have seen German leaders do this before; but usually marking the victims of the more distant past, at concentration camps, or massacre sites. Yet, in an age when symbolic acts say it all, the message was clear: Germany will not repeat the past - except maybe in education?

Did you know that over 100 years ago half of all people studying abroad were attending German universities? In those days, Germany was a world-wide magnet for education and research. The German system of education has a long tradition and a good international reputation. Today, in the ranking of the most attractive countries for foreign students, Germany lies in third place. Despite the language barrier, foreigners like coming to Germany to study.

From Dust to Snow: The African Dream?

In the first 'experience', three African brothers: Fu from Cameroon, Tsuwi from Kenya, and Bayene from Ethiopia make a monumental decision to leave their families and beloved African Continent to the same destination in Europe, a city in former East Germany plagued with xenophobia. They soon realize that studying abroad is more than just studying abroad. It's an incredible adventure you must be prepared for. Are you prepared? The adventure begins:]

Fu: The idea of travelling abroad is actually a pipedream for someone from a poor African family like me. Mum and dad had to dig very hard and deep into the ground in order to feed and educate us.

As a child, I liked reading a lot: I read a lot about Europe and the US. I immediately realized that those born in Europe and the US were 'lucky' to have been born there because they had more privileges, and opportunities. I began to wonder how God chose where someone is born. What had Europeans done that Africans could not do? Permit me say that, at the time, I did not think about any advantages Africa may have over Europe and the US. Can you think of any?

Interestingly two things really ignited my resolve to pursue this 'pipedream' of going abroad. One of these was what I would call the Einstein stigma. I had read about Albert Einstein. His seventh-grade teacher virtually assessed him to be a fool. The teacher concluded that Albert "would never get anywhere in life". In hindsight, it is unlikely that the problem was Albert's inability, but more likely his circumstances. You see, I believe that opportunity manifests ingenuity. We all know what happened when Einstein's circumstances changed, when he had the opportunity. I realized that you may be a genius, but if you do not have the opportunity or right circumstances to manifest your ingenuity, you may appear to be a fool. I am very sure that many African geniuses have died undiscovered because of the lack of opportunities. Africans are actually Einstein-stigmatized in two ways. I will tell you about the second way in a moment, but the first way is the lack of opportunities to manifest. As I grew up, I dreamt of an Africa producing the next genius of the 21st century, an Africa with the Harvard, and Oxford Universities of the world. I dreamed of an Africa where African children like me would have the same opportunities like those in Europe and the U.S., an Africa that could produce the Einstein and Shakespeare of the 21st century. You would call them Siyanda or Vutomi, or perhaps Fatola or Kofi.

An additional motivation to travel abroad came from an unwonted source, a score I had to settle with the Germans! Growing up, we learned by oral tradition that when the German explorer, Dr Eugen Zintgraff, visited my village Bafut in 1889, he committed two breaches of etiquette. He, in lese majesty, seized the drinking cup from the Bafut Chief, Fon

Abumbi's hand and drank from it. As if that was not enough, he irreverently insisted on calling the Fon by his princely name 'Gualem'. This open display of disrespect was interpreted in Bafut as a deliberate attempt by the German to belittle the Bafut "King". Furthermore it is said that Zintgraff foolhardily fooled the Fon and the Bafut people into believing that his sunglasses (which they had never seen before) were his duplicate pair of eyes. He would, then, leave the glasses in Bafut and travel somewhere else and the people would think they were being watched by him, though he was not physically present. When I heard this story, a desire was born in me to square this up with the Germans, Zintgraff's descendants. How could he have belittled and disgraced my forefathers like that?

I had a score to settle! But first I had to get to Germany. And how? That was the 4 million CFA franc question! Exactly the amount of money I needed to show I had in a bank in order to obtain a student visa for Germany. Where would I even begin to look for such an amount of money? There is an African saying that enthusiasm is the window to opportunity. Perhaps my passion and enthusiasm to travel abroad would provide the window to the opportunity? Even with all the efforts by my whole family to put together money, selling our farmland and borrowing from a local Credit Union at huge interests rates, we only succeeded to raise about half of the amount I needed for a bank statement. Two Swiss ladies, Carolin Huber and Gertrud Ernst, who were friends of my mum, working in Bafut at that time, seeing the situation, finally came to our rescue and offered to lend us the other half – an equivalent of about three thousand euros. I imagined I would pay back the money when I was in Germany.

Finally I got the visa in 1999. It was a miracle! It was the biggest day in my small family's life until then! Dad got the fattest chicken in the compound, roasted it himself, and bought palm wine from East End (a local store) for the nuclear family to celebrate! I felt on top of the world. I now had the opportunity to meet Zintgraff's great grandchildren! A new dawn was breaking in my life. Now, I had just eight days to relish the fact that I finally succeeded to get the visa, prepare for travel, and also begin to prepare my mind for the challenges that awaited me in Europe! I would be taking on Zintgraff's very own, remember? I was of course grateful they offered the possibility. Zintgraff had not waited to be offered the cup. He had seized it! Boy, I was looking forward to this challenge. I had to show Zintgraff's people we were not that foolish.

Soon the day for my family send-off arrived. My friends came, my extended family and well-wishers. Prayers were said for me, committing me in the hands of God, who alone knew what awaited me in Europe. I was advised never to give my passport to anyone, to always pray and

God would keep me connected to my family over the miles, never be involved with drugs, to work hard, etc.

Work hard? I had a problem: the German language. My lectures in the international Physics studies program in Leipzig would be in English, but I would definitely need to know German to interact with the society, to be able to work, to pay back the debt and to support myself, and to help my family and friends to come and join me in Europe (of course not to stay permanently)! A knot of fear of what awaited me formed in the pit of my stomach and was not going away. Second, no one would be waiting for me at the airport in Leipzig. I did not even know where I was going to spend my first night. I hoped I would arrive when the student's secretariat (Studentenwerk) was still open. Besides, do you know how much money I had on me? I owned just about the equivalent of 150 Euros, which would have to pay for registration formalities in Germany, and initial food and board. I thought that when I arrived, the borrowed money I had blocked in the bank would soon be at my disposal. But I had another think coming. Anyway, hey, I did not have anywhere else to get more money.

My flight was from Yaounde-Nsimalen at midnight, with, the then, Swissair via Zurich to Leipzig. My dad came along from Bamenda and it had been particularly hard to say goodbye to my momma and aunt Teh. My two sisters were also there with one of my brothers and friends. Three car loads (cars of family friends of course) went to the airport and some friends who had no space had to go home. We arrived at the airport in time for check-in and eventual boarding. I wore a second-hand overcoat bought by my sister, Akwanwi, from Mokolo market from the bale sent over from Europe, and a firsthand Paco Jeans trousers and shirt. I looked like Neil Armstrong before his take-off to the Moon, ready for the unknown, yet apprehensive – very. Finally it was time to say bye. I hugged everyone, trying to hide the tears streaming down my eyes.

After passport control, I met another barrier where they asked me to show my visa, which I did. They asked me where I was going, as if they could not read the visa. I said, 'Germany'. They asked me why, and I said for further studies. One man laughed as if that was the funniest thing he had ever heard. 'Studies?' He exclaimed in French! 'Everyone says he is going for studies.' Cameroon is bilingual. It was not that these guys could not read or understand English. I immediately knew they wanted me to give them money, call it a bribe. For what? Search me! Most of them believed those who travelled abroad had to be rich. They did not know I was just a poor little guy who had experienced a miracle. In any case, it was not right to give them a bribe. I prayed silently.

'Yes, I am going to study; it is on my visa.' I replied. The woman near him laughed even louder. This was more annoying. Other passengers, especially foreigners, kept passing by and heading for the plane. I knew it was a few minutes to take-off, and here I was with this lady trying to ruin it all. She asked me what my occupation was. I said I had graduated from the university two years earlier, and had been a teacher. She asked for my national ID. I said I did not have it on me. I had left it behind, and I told her I thought my Passport was enough. She asked me to show her my degree from Buea University. I pulled it out of my carry-on, even more worked up. She looked at the English attestation and burst into laughter again, waved at her colleague to come and see what I was showing. She made clear she had never seen such an attestation before! Now, my blood was really pumping and an artery was in danger of bursting. I controlled myself with enormous difficulty as more people passed by. Just suppose the flight took off without me! Huh! I could not just imagine. I had heard about people who got sent back just when they were almost getting on to the plane. You could have heard my heart beating and been shaken by my fluttering nerves. I prayed silently again.

    Amazingly I found a second wind. My body raised the 'threat level' to code red, which gave me tons of courage. No, even if I wanted, I could not give them a cent from the 150 euros, and you could say that again. That was bribery. It was wrong! I patiently explained to the lady that the attestation had to have been genuine for a thorough German Consular officer to grant me the visa. She realized my composure had changed, and noticed the quiet, cool, unmistakable thundercloud undertone in my words. She recoiled all right! She mumbled something about not being sure about me. I remained quiet. Then her colleague shrugged and went away. She too, apparently realizing she was now 'a loner in the Sahara', gave back my passport reluctantly. Phew! And this was just the beginning. I was still in Cameroon, nowhere closer to Germany

    I sat by the window. I noticed the sexy hostesses, and understood why James Bond felt attracted to them. The demonstration about safety was enjoyable for the choreography of it. I spent more time admiring than understanding the stuff they said. After that, I watched pop-eyed as the screen showed the ever increasing altitude, ground speed, temperature outside and the position of the plane and destination temporally. 'Amazing!' I thought.

    Then I thought about those I was leaving behind. When would I see them again? The knot in my stomach grew bigger, and as the plane began to level, I swallowed despondently. I did not know if I would ever see them again. I did not know if the fact, my dream to travel abroad was now real, implied the reality in Europe would be like my dream. I shut my eyes, and told my self: Life or Death, Europe here I come!

From Dust to Snow: The African Dream?

****

Tsuwi: At long last we were on the runway waiting for clearance to take off. The aeroplane started racing down the runway, and in a few I could see the lights of Nairobi town below me. What a wonderful experience to disobey gravity. Then reality suddenly struck: we were airborne cruising at some hundreds of kilometres per hour at close to 30000 feet above the sea level. They say above sea level, but I was thinking about the solid ground below, not the sea. "What happens if something goes wrong and we suddenly plunge into the Sahara desert?" I thought anxiously. Then my thoughts drifted to the months leading up to this flight.

It had been a long wait since the news of the DAAD scholarship had come two months earlier. I remotely knew that after my graduate studies, I would proceed to Germany for my Doctorate. My colleagues at Kenyatta University had looked at me with admiration when they got word of my won Scholarship while relatives and friends were happy that I was travelling abroad to a land of opportunity. I smiled a bit because I concurred with my relatives' opinion. Another broad smile jolted me to reality.

"Oh! I am sorry", I apologised. The KLM hostess must have been standing there for quite a while. She asked me, "What will you drink sir?" I asked her what she had in stock. As she listed the contents of her cart, I tried to make up my mind about what to drink. I ended up taking water. I was not sure whether there was an extra cost or not. I sipped the water carefully waiting for her to return. After a few consultations I gathered that every meal and all drinks (then) were complimentary. I promised myself not to let the hostess down again.

We arrived in Amsterdam at 6.30 a.m. local time. I had never bothered about *local time* in all my life. The pilot had announced something about the time but I didn't understand. I did not have a watch anyway. We were three from Kenya on the same plane. We were on the same journey, and headed for the same destination, because we had the same scholarship. We found our way through the airport to the next terminal. We were again off the ground at 8.30 a.m. to Frankfurt. Frankfurt airport seemed large and confusing. We ended up in a police office presenting our tickets for the next flight. The police knew we were lost and directed us to another door. Another lost guy joined us, who understood German. He was to take a train to Dresden while we were travelling by plane. We depended on his knowledge of the German language, because he claimed to have learnt the language for a while at the Goethe Institute in Nairobi. We made our way through the door the policeman had pointed to, and we took a lift two floors up and ended up in a small train station. 'How can these guys have trains that move through buildings at the airport?' I wondered. Our train friend left us there. We then also boarded an airport train and alighted at some point that looked vaguely familiar. We took a flight of stairs and were back at the arrival lounge. We were going round in circles! After a few consultations with some English-speaking travellers, we made our way to the appropriate terminal.

By 1.00 o'clock in the afternoon we were in Dresden airport, our destination. It was then that I realised we were really conspicuous. The rest of the passengers looked all the same to me. I told my Kenyan colleague in my mother tongue, "Fughakiyehu vikara", translated: "We are alone now". He smiled in agreement. We waited for our luggage, which appeared after a while. Then we followed the other passengers through the exit door dragging our bags behind us. The police stopped us.

"Now what?" I muttered aloud to myself. I thought, "But the rest of the passengers had passed unchecked! Why is this policeman so keen on us?" We were requested to place our bags on a conveyor belt in a language we could hardly understand. Gesticulation was now the mode of communication, though of course the policeman was articulating some audible words though incomprehensible to us. We moved out to the bus stop and removed the papers with our directions. There was a bus that had a number corresponding to the one on our papers. We boarded it and before long we were told to get the tickets from a machine outside. At the machine, we read the instructions carefully before touching it. How can a person get tickets from this metal standing here? I thought. The bus driver called out to us. We bought the tickets from him. I produced the only 100 € note that I had, hoping that it was going to be enough. It was, with plenty of change left over. As the bus moved, we rested our nervous eyes on the papers again to tell the driver our next stop. We announced it as soon as we found it. He smiled; we frowned. An old couple helped us to understand after a terrible struggle with the English language. I came to learn that it was actually the last stop of the bus.

At the bus stop, the elderly couple alighted together with us and explained to us how difficult it usually is for first time visitors to find their way. The man narrated how it was for him the first time he visited Kenya. He told us how he enjoyed seeing the animals in the parks and game reserves. I felt comforted to meet a stranger many miles away from home, who knew and enjoyed visiting my homeland. The old man kept on talking, while for all this time his wife's right hand was tucked in his left hand. A train arrived and the old man explained to us that it was called a tram, just like it was in our papers: Tram 7 towards the city. We bid farewell to our old couple and boarded. 'What a pleasant people they are', I reflected. On the tram we looked for a ticket machine. We found one but could not operate it. I asked a young couple, in their 20's or so, who understood and spoke English well enough, if they could help us.

"You should be able to get a ticket by yourself. I cannot help you!" the young man shouted. "Thanks" I said, greatly disappointed and looking for where to hide from the attention. I longed for the helpful old couple. I turned around to break the bad news to my colleague. I then noticed a lady who looked African seated two rows away. I sighed with relief knowing that help had arrived. Unfortunately, she spoke French. Nonetheless, I spoke in English very slowly, heavily punctuated with gestures and explained to her that I wanted a ticket. She said nothing, but instead demanded money from me for the tickets. I displayed all the coins I had for her to pick what was necessary to make this transaction complete. She picked two coins and retrieved two tickets from the machine. I was really grateful.

We alighted at the Goethe Institute stop, scanned the buildings in search of the appropriate sign somewhere, but to no avail. My friend made enquiries from an optics shop. The lady came out of the shop and showed us the building that housed the Institute. We had actually been standing opposite the Institute. Now what?

****

Bayene: My name is Daniel. My English is not very good, because in Ethiopia we speak Amharic. Ethiopia was not colonized!

I travelled to Germany on the 5th of August 2002, and the reason was because I got the chance to study there. I did three years of college, in Ethiopia, and obtained a diploma. If I stayed one more year, I would have had a Bachelor's degree in accountancy. Well, before travelling to Germany, I was already well informed about the country, by my family and by Germans I had met in Ethiopia.

As it is known, it is very hard to get a visa in Africa unless you are a rich man or a family of politicians. But the way I got a visa is very amazing, because I had no problems throughout the processes. I can say God is the one who did it. Actually, my family and my sponsor had prepared all the documents that were needed according to German law. The only thing I did was to get my passport, to prepare the documents for my studies, and request the visa. So, I succeeded. Over all, what I learned from my visa experience is to be patient, to have hope and to feel free, and to be confident at interviews. Of course, also to give all your processes to God before you start. The day I got my visa in my hand, I was very excited, and my family and I thanked God for His work. At the same time, I felt a strange feeling, because I was on my way to leave my home. On this day, I felt the 'poorness' of my country had made me to leave.

After I received a visa, all my family started preparation for my trip. They got foods, traditional clothes, gifts and so on. Also, after I received a visa, I did a lot of preparations for my trip, like buying a ticket for my flight. I also took medications, like vaccines against any transmissible diseases that may exist from my country. My family prepared a party for 'thanksgiving', and they invited a lot of friends, relatives, pastors, choirs and neighbours. We sang together, we heard the word of God, and we worshipped Him for His work. At the end, they blessed me and advised me, 'Not to forget God'. I started crying, when one of my aunt's sons gave me gifts and said to me that he couldn't accompany me to the airport for my flight. Well, I cried because I loved him so much. Well, in the evening there were also guests. All of them were pastors and my grandfather's friends. They prayed for me. They blessed me, and on this night my grandpapa gave a gift in front of those pastors and others and said: 'I will give you a precious gift, which doesn't pass away, but which gives you a good principle for your life and helps you to overcome all problems in the strange country.' He gave me a small Bible, which is easy to carry, and also a small cross. He said to me, 'Do not forget God, the One who died for us, be with Him, worship Him.' He said this and gave me one proverb from Joshua 1: 5-9.

After the guests left, we started to pack and to arrange my things, but I can say most of our family members seemed sad. My grandpa is the one who wanted to make the atmosphere nice by giving some words. But most of them didn't feel okay, especially my grandma and my big brother. Well, I had a hard time. On that night, I couldn't sleep. I started to shed tears. It was one of my hardest days in my life. The only thing I said was that, 'God help me to see all of my family again without any problems'.

In the morning, every one started to cry. We had a morning prayer together, and started to say bye to those who didn't want to accompany to the Airport in Addis Ababa, where I was to take the Ethiopian airlines.

My mother, my little sister, and some of my relatives didn't want to go there. Actually, I cried, and my Mum said to me, 'Be strong my son, God is with you.' Then, we left. Well, from all, it was hard for me to say my grandma and grandpa bye. Anyway, I was forced to say to them 'bye' in the airport. Then, I left. I was very sad. I wished I had not had this opportunity. I had a very bad trip. I started to read the Bible on my way and saying to myself: 'I will go back home after I join the university.

There is no problem; God is going to help me.' I wanted to sleep, but I couldn't. It was really a very bad, sad day for me.

When I arrived at Frankfurt airport, I was very amazed because it was hard for me to find any black men. All the people around me were whites. I also faced discrimination for the first time in my life. At the gate, I met 6 policemen. They said, 'Can you show us your 'pass'?' After looking at it, 'How long you stay?' I said, 'It depends on my study.' 'How long?' they repeated. I said, '5 to 6 years.' They said 'uhhhhhhhhhh!' It made me feel so unwelcome. The way those people who work there (at airport) treated me – I washed my mind, and it made me to hate them.

At embassy, I had lied (not a good thing) that I did not have any relatives in Germany, but a sponsor. At airport, I was accompanied by my aunty – sponsor. I complained about the way they treated me at airport, and other Ethiopian families said this is normal.

On the other hand, I was very pleased to see the fastest train travelling at 145 km/h, because that was also my wish to see it in my country.

I was very tired and also had a problem with climatic change a little bit.

****

Fu: Finally, our descent to Leipzig was announced and I fastened my seatbelt. A short while later, I was standing on the passport-control queue. The passport controller looked me up and down the way a dog eyes an alien, and took a long scrutinizing look at my passport. I was the only black-man on the flight, and so this procedure did little to quieten my nerves. I waited apprehensively. He called a colleague who also took a long hard look at it, as if it was the first time they had seen a German visa on an African's passport, as if he could not read. It reminded me of the incident in Yaoundé. One of them spoke into his walkie-talkie, apparently to a hidden operator for sometime. Finally, he handed me my passport, a red-faced grin pasted across his bird-like face.

I collected my luggage, glad everything had arrived safely, and followed the sign **'i'** for information, praying that I would meet someone who spoke English. The lady I met at the information desk spoke English, and said the bus to Leipzig Centre was every 10 minutes, and it would cost me 10 DM. She said the bus stop was right out front, which I found easily.

When we arrived at Leipzig centre, I mustered all the knowledge of German I had, and politely asked the driver where I could find Goethe-Strasse where the Studentenwerk (with the foreign student's office) was. He pulled out a little map and marked a spot on it. *'Blistering barnacles!*

Here we go!' I told myself nervously. Now I had to muster all the knowledge of map reading I ever learnt in geography class some 7 years ago. I said *'Vielen Dank'* and dragged my 40 kg bag and carry-on out of the bus. A step of faith into the unknown!

Luckily enough, Goethestrasse was pretty near by and I got there panting like a pregnant woman up a flight of stairs. I dumped the heavy luggage in the waiting room and took my carry-on containing all my important documents along with me to the fourth floor. My very first time to ride a lift! It was around 3:30 in the afternoon and I only found one office open. The lady I met Frau Klimmek was very nice, welcomed me snugly and recommended I spend the night in a Youth Hostel. She spoke so fast that I did not understand everything. She again marked a location of the youth Hostel on my first Leipzig map, and wished me a pleasant first evening in Germany, telling me to return to her office the following day. I wondered how much the hostel would cost!

Back downstairs, I realized I could not carry the heavy bag with me in search of the Hostel. I left it right there, and went off map reading. It contained foodstuff, like plantain chips, garri, roasted peanuts, etc, and my clothes. I trudged off too tired to think or even realize I could buy a tram ticket and take a tram to a stop near the hostel. I would have to speak more German, or listen for descriptions I would not be able to decipher! I had heard Europeans never stopped to help, and that Germans expected you to speak German in Germany. So I walked from one street to the other. It took me about an hour and a half of walking, sweating and map reading to finally locate the hostel. With the tram, it could have taken me only 15 minutes. I could have also called a taxi but I had to save every cent I had. The hostel was not so expensive, just like the Frau K had said. It was 40 DM (20 Euro). I was going to share a room with an unknown person.

I was so exhausted I barely dumped my stuff and climbed into bed. I was not hungry! I was just anxious not knowing what awaited me the following day. Sometime later, my roommate, an American returned. He grumbled something about my shoes stinking, and I got up and transferred them to the bathroom. Such a welcome! The following morning he introduced himself properly and apologized about his welcome. He said that he was in Germany for a gospel crusade and had had an exhaustive day. I said I understood him, and that I would have felt the same if I met someone's stinking shoes after a tough day. Apparently to make up, we prayed together as I told him about my mission to Germany and he gave me his telephone number to call if I needed help and showed me a tram stop, helped me buy a ticket, and put me on the tram. That was the first encouraging thing that had happened since my arrival. I had not even called home to let them know that I had arrived.

From Dust to Snow: The African Dream?

I returned to Goethestrasse. Luckily for me, my bag was still there in the hallway! Frau K directed me to another office where I was matriculated and asked to return with my new address after I get a room. To matriculate, I needed my passport with the student visa; I also needed health insurance, passport size photos, and my original admission letter. The lady in charge of housing got me a room at Tarostr. 12, one of the student hostels. But if this solved my accommodation problems it landed me in to a quagmire. I was given 2 forms (Scheins), one to take to the caretaker (Haumeister) of my hostel and the other for paying my caution and first months rent, after which I was supposed to take the receipt to another office to finalize my housing contract. I needed money for the caution, but I had barely under a hundred euros left while the caution was over 150 euros. So I would urgently need the money I blocked in the bank before travelling. I needed a bank account opened for the money to be transferred to it. I walked to the Commerzbank, while keenly observing my new town. The bank officer who attended to me was the prettiest girl I was to see in Germany for a long while. She was blonde, and she could speak English too. I was impressed. If I had any ideas about this lady, they quickly disappeared like a fist that turned into an open palm, when she told me I needed to bring my registration form (obtained from the town hall) in order to open the account. Huh? Yes, but wait a moment. I needed the money, in order to pay my caution, in order to get my house contract, in order to be able to register at the town hall!

That was the most depressing moment of my first whole day in Leipzig. How was I going to solve this problem? I walked 'home' feeling like my stomach was full of sawdust. For the first time, I missed home. There was nobody to talk to about my situation. No one just to listen! When I got home, my neighbour's door was open. I knocked shyly to introduce myself. It was another pretty lady but she looked cheap compared to the one in Commerzbank. However, her South-American boyfriend whom she introduced right now probably thought better.

That night I did not sleep. I had no one to turn to; I could not even call home, as that would be spending more money, which I did not have. In the morning I went back to the lady in charge of housing. I did pause to wonder why women ran most offices in Germany. Later I was told it was due to the fact that many men had died during the Second World War.

The lady said all she could do was send me to another hostel where people with my sort of problem were sent. After some phone calls, she directed me to another hostel at Nürnbergerstrasse 48. She said I could return to Tarostrasse after I get my money. That cheered me up a little, because I had liked my room. I did not know I was never going to have again it! The room I was put in at Nürnbergerstr. 48 contained 50 beds and reminded me of a dormitory in PSS Mankon. I was going to pay 50 Deutch marks for it per month, and those 50 beds meant I could practically have 50 roommates with accommodation, or rather, money problems like mine anytime. It was a pretty big hall but I was the sole occupant for the first night.

Before going there my neighbour in Tarostrasse and her boyfriend, gave me my first cooking pot, which to me looked like a dish compared to our giant cooking pots back home in Cameroon. She also lent me 100 euros to help me pay the caution fees for my house. This underlined how kind she was. I did not know how long it would take after opening a bank account for the money to be transferred from Cameroon, so I gladly and very gratefully accepted the loan. I promised to return the money as soon as I got my money transfer, but even that was not going to happen.

Two days later I got my visa extended! But the lady at Commerzbank, whom I was told to my pleasure would be my bank account advisor, told me that it would take at least 2 weeks for my first month's transfer of about 500 Euro to arrive. That was disappointing!

Three days after I had arrived, I finally got to buy a phone-card and called home. I got some chiding from my sister. Everyone had been worried! I thanked God for helping me that far and began to get used to my new environment. The first day at school I met other students from Turkey, Libya, Russia, Korea, Macedonia, Guatemala and of course Germany.

Then one evening as I returned to my 50-bed room, I met Akuma, a Cameroonian from Mankon, a village that had supported Bafut in the war against Zintgraff. He was studying medicine and was very kind. He eventually lent me about 300 euros to help me pay for the basic necessities to start with. He also showed me around, and gave me tips about shopping, where to find cheaper phone cards etc. After more than a week of living on chips, garri and patched peanuts, I finally ate my first real meal in Akuma's room.

About three weeks after I had wired my new account number home, I got the first money transfer to my account. I was so happy that day and gratefully returned Akuma's money. But when I went back to get my room at Tarostrasse, some other lady in charge had given it away. This left a bad taste in my month as I sensed prejudice. I however think, I was not justified to think that way. It was probably just that the whole idea of East Germans' xenophobia plus racist tendencies made me very sensitive. Another room was arranged for me at Nürnbergerstrasse 48, coincidentally next door to Akuma. The rents were less than for Tarostrasse because Nürnbergerstrasse was an old dilapidated student hostel. I had lived in that 50-bed room alone, though once someone did come there. He was African but had come with a fat German lady almost twice his age, who must have eventually hoisted him over to her apartment.

In case you are wondering, I did go back to Tarostrasse to return my former neighbour's money, but never succeeded, even after several visits and notes in her mailbox. They just vanished into thin air, or maybe they travelled to South America. Then more culture shock came along, including part II of the Einstein Stigma.

****

Tsuwi: We were given a short interview. The lady interviewer asked me, "Have you learnt German before?" "No", I said.

The interview was over. I was given some forms to fill, which I did gladly. After a few minutes a Mercedes Benz taxi took us to the hostel.

"Wow, these guys use Benz as their taxi!" I told my friend. "*Ni ulaya kuku!*"(We are abroad now), he answered.

Mercedes Benz is a car that is used by the privileged few in Kenya. As a taxi, I imagined they would have a higher charge rate per minute than the ordinary taxis. More so, they are not stationed at every corner of the town but only outside expensive hotels, and of course, a few at the airport. "Anyway, no cause for alarm", I thought. "Cars are one of Germany's biggest exports, particularly the Benz. Just as we use coffee and tea locally in Kenya while the rest is exported, the Germans are doing the same with the cars."

Our second day at the Institute was filled with welcome speeches and meeting other new students who had come from far and wide: China, India, Cuba, Brazil, Russia, Japan, Australia, South Africa and many other countries. Deutsch was now inevitably the language of communication. In the evening we met our Kenyan colleague who had travelled by train from Frankfurt to Dresden. He told us how difficult it had been for him to change trains with luggage at different stations. He told us how he had not bathed because "there was no water in the taps". We explained to him that there was actually water only that it flows out when the tap is lifted up a bit. He had turned the tap clockwise and anticlockwise without lifting. Poor guy! Anyway, before I discovered, I had also struggled with the taps for a while.

Learning German in German was unpleasant for me at first. The first week passed without me having accepted that I could understand German when taught in German. Our teacher never bothered to repeat things for me in English. At some point she even asked me to forget

English and use German. This she repeated, later, when I had performed poorly in one of my tests. Eventually, I agreed with her. At the beginning I used to construct sentences in English in my mind and then translate them into German. It always resulted in a grammatical catastrophe. I now know that it does not make a good impression, when one addresses a respectable person with *Du* instead of *Sie*. I solved the *Du / Sie* dilemma, but did not know that more dilemmas in the language would emerge that, up to now, I have not been able to get through.

Learning in a multicultural ensemble proved fun and provided me with the opportunity to understand humanity, at least to some extent. At the institute, the whole world was represented: Asians, Africans, Europeans, North and South Americans and Australians. People are basically the same, though they may have different personalities, have prejudices over others or amongst themselves and also stereotypes that are most of the time inaccurate. This was reflected in the way we interacted with one another at the institute. Jon, an Afro-American born in Miami and raised in New York, told me how difficult it was to cope with the other two Americans at the institute from California because of his African descent. Alex, a South African who became a close friend, came to my room on a Saturday morning and complained bitterly about how a group of Mexicans had ignored him at a get-together party. He told me how bitter he was, recalling fresh memories of Apartheid. In a class discussion, a lady from Chile told us how a budding friendship had ended abruptly after she disclosed her nationality. She said her counterpart was European. Why is it so hard for people to learn to accept others? We all have shortcomings.

After six months of learning the German language, I was now ready to listen and practice German language on the streets and at my research station. Of course for those of us who would do research, we had already been told that we should address our professors with *Sie* and never *Du*. It paid off well because when I first addressed my professor as *Sie*, he said I know and can speak perfect German.

I searched and found a flat in Leipzig with no difficulties. Everything is on-line, unlike at home where one may have to look in the newspapers or knock on peoples' doors and meet house agents asking for vacant rooms to rent. The registration paperwork at the university and the foreign office was done at exact times as specified. After three weeks, I was a registered member of the town and university as required by law. I found the efficiency very commendable. The police seemed to have no business with me, unlike in Dresden where I was required to produce my passport five times in six months, twice by the same policewoman. Was it because Dresden is close to the border and so strict checks have to be put in place? If that were the case, then I could not figure out why I had to produce my passport on the train to Hamburg. Once I travelled to Hanover and went out with a friend (also from Kenya). He forgot to carry his passport, and we had to walk with the police some 300 m to his hostel. We reached his room on the third floor. We looked like criminals with policemen red hot on our heels. One of the students from the hostel asked my friend in a shocked tone why the police were with us. He answered sarcastically: "*Wir sind Kriminellen*", translated: we are criminals. One of the policemen immediately refuted that. They stood at the door and the passport was brought to them. After a few checks, they thanked us and apologised. By that time, I was beginning to wonder why it was very necessary that the police had to check *us* every time they saw *us*. What a life abroad!

My wife finally arrived to join me and it was good to begin experiencing things together in this new town. She went through the small wonders that I had experienced six months earlier: trams, weather, punctuality, a new language and different foods. She didn't find the weather to be friendly for a long time though. With temperatures swinging from 2 to 10 degrees Celsius, early on that summer, it was too cold for her.

Naturally, any person would like to fit into the society they find themselves in. However, it is not always easy, especially when one comes from a society that is extremely hospitable to strangers. Consequently, you may misinterpret questions you are asked. For instance, I was asked the following questions on several occasions with few variations: What is your name? Where do you come from? Why are you in Germany? Was it necessary for you to come and study in Germany? Will you go back when you finish your studies? At some instances we were asked whether we were refugees! Eh! These questions sometimes leave me wondering whether they are asked in good faith.

The summer proper arrived. It was another sunny season for me just like the other years spent in my country enjoying an unlimited supply of tropical sunshine. The difference here was that the sun would shine as early as 5 o'clock in the morning and I could take a walk at 10 o'clock in the night and still have enough light. For my German friends, however, this was a unique time of the year that had been planned for since the previous summer. One summer afternoon, I walked through the park adjacent to my institute. What I saw was not new, but it was a bit puzzling. Having grown up in a tourist town along the Kenyan coast, I had seen many tourists lying on the beautiful beaches, scarcely dressed, enjoying the sun for hours. I never imagined I would see the same in the middle of the park with no beach in sight. Along the beaches, it is taken a step further. It is not uncommon to find whole families basking in the sun in their 'birthday suits'!

Meeting other people from Africa has always made me feel that I am not alone. At some time in the summer, many people from different parts of Africa gathered in the park and partied, thanks to the Jamaa Africa organisation. I realised that there were in fact many Kenyans married to Germans. Indeed, there are many Germans genuinely interested in Africa and African issues. Every person who comes to Germany has a purpose. It may be long-lived or short-lived. There is always one thing or another that one can learn from another person regardless of his/her religion, financial status, family background or race. I am in Germany because I want to obtain my Doctorate in Physics and nothing more. A seemingly perfect health insurance system, and powerful research laboratories are but a creation. One needs just a little bit of sanity to realise this. Poverty is relative, while riches are a creation of the mind. Absolute poverty is non-existent.

Here are some reflections on life in Germany by my wife, Alice. The first most striking impression one gets when one arrives in Germany is that there is a highly efficient and effective system that organises day-to-day activities. For instance, the transport system is such that the trams, buses and trains are most of the time 'on time'. Rarely, does one experience delays. The streets are very clean with hardly any litter and one even finds it difficult to litter since there are numerous bins at strategic points throughout the town.

However, this organisation takes a little getting used to. It is usual to make appointments for everything: seeing a doctor, meeting a professor and so on. But do you need an appointment to have your bicycle repaired? This also follows for social encounters. You are met with coldness when you drop in without notice. This makes one really nostalgic for the structure at home when you can call on your friends at any time and still feel welcome.

The familiar Sunday scene of people from all walks of life streaming to church is indeed rare. The society is largely secular and one's faith is considered 'private'. Most of the old magnificent church buildings are a buzz of activity not with worshippers but with tourists. In fact some of the churches have been reduced to museums with no active worshippers.

There are a few shocking things that one has to adjust to. For example, just because you have come to an affluent society does not mean that you have automatically made it in life. The truth is that the cost of living is very high and one needs to have a good rein on one's finances.

There are also comforting aspects to life away from home. For instance, the conscious realisation that poverty is universal. It is very surprising at first, to find some people begging on the streets and others scavenging through the bins.

Unemployment is a very real problem, although the well-established social welfare system makes life bearable.

In spite of many warnings and apprehensions about racism and discrimination, most of the people are friendly and ready to help when one needs assistance.

Here are some tips for brethren planning to travel to Germany. It would be helpful to learn a bit of the language to get by before travelling. The society is largely monolingual and ignorance of the language could draw unfriendliness or even hostility. It is also useful to establish contacts in the new place beforehand, if possible. Life can become overwhelming and confusing when you do not know where to get the right food, where to find a church, doctor, accommodation, where to go and have proper registration and even how to make money transfers. Punctuality is a highly prized virtue. Before travelling, be sure to obtain information about the weather outlook so as to dress appropriately.

****

Bayene: There are a lot of cultural differences that I have already observed: the way they dress; the way the people behave: smokers, small girls and boys kiss on the street, and so on; the way they treat people.

I had lots of problems with filling official forms. At beginning, my aunt helped me, but later I was alone. I even wasted one semester, because I did not know the 'dateline' for application.

The first bad experience I have was on the city train – tram. Normally, they do not check your ticket when you get on the tram in Germany. They just do random checks once in a while. If you are then found sitting without ticket, you are booked and fined. My aunt had given me money for a monthly ticket, but since it was already the 18th of the month, a friend from Morocco advised to just wait the two weeks remaining to the end of the month, and use the money for that month for something else. He said the chance I will be checked was small. I stupidly agreed. In the tram, controllers asked me for my ticket and I pretended I did not understand German, so they brought someone, who could translate to me. They took my passport and booked me, and I paid extra money, 40 euros.

The worst one was the day I couldn't find a place to live. When I just arrived, I lived in a student hostel. But when I missed registering for the semester, I had to look for a private room. I stayed at this time with a friend from China. I found a vacancy notice on a university board, and called. They said I should come. When I went there, the girl who opened the door saw I was black. I like reading expressions and body language, and I saw the girl and other apartment mates did not like me, as I was black. She told me the rent was 140 euros, and that I cannot pay it. Why did she assume I could not pay? She told me this herself! Also, on the notice, they had said the house had furniture. But now, she said no furniture, all to drive me away.

The second time, I called another person and the girl thought I was from Great Britain, so she said, 'No problem, you can come.' I was really excited and told Manfred and Dorit, a very nice German couple who lived in the same building on the ground floor. I had met them in the Leipzig English Church. The following day, I brought my entire luggage. To my surprise, the girl instead sent her friend to meet me outside the building. She said, 'I am very sorry; my friend said to tell you she wants to live alone. I also have a brother who wanted to live here, and she wouldn't give it to him also.' I was stunned for a moment. Then I felt sad, after all my excitement and telling all my friends I had a room. I stood there not knowing what to do. I could not leave, since I could not go back to the Chinese again.

Manfred and Dorit, who know my aunt, were very sorry for me and asked me to stay with them. I insisted I would love to pay, and to make me feel better, they accepted I pay 55 euros a month. Later, I moved to my own place.

The advantages in Germany are a lot of opportunities, of course, if you have money. You need money to start off with. Because I had no money at one point, I could not pay for Internet. Then, I was in Interdev, and I had no password to the university computer centre. There is access of the technology, but you need money.

I also like the security in supermarkets, because it is a big problem in our country. In my country, there are no cameras, so guards follow you.

I also like the Xmas preparation in Germany, and the yoghurt. The problem is only materialistic tendency. In big churches, only a handful of old people. However, in the Leipzig English Church, I found a wonderful community. I love the fellowship there, and the Christmas service there. Another good thing is, you meet a lot of people from different countries, and you can learn their culture, the way they think, and so on. I don't have many Deutsch friends, but many from Japan; but when they go back, I stay alone. It is hard to have a true stable friend.

Other disadvantage is that you can have problems just because of who you are, because you are black, as at airport. Many people have negative aspects towards black people. One day, I stood at the tram stop and overheard a mother telling her son I am from Africa, in a negative way. First, because I am black does not mean I am from Africa. Second, I pray God for the day we will be proud to be from Africa.

They also treat old people very bad. I remember, one day, two elderly women trying to catch the bus had heavy luggage several metres from the bus stop. Deutsch youths passed, no help. I offered to help them, and they were very happy and thanked and thanked me.

Also the dressing problem: You will see a professor dressed in a sweater torn under the armpit, while in Africa people try to get money to buy nice clothes. In Germany, unless very official, people do not care how you dress.

I do not like the food in Germany. They eat bread often. I prefer black bread to the white bread; Black bread is more nutritious. I miss the food in Ethiopia, especially the Ajara, which goes with some sauce and lots of chili that would make the European stomach ache. You pay so much money for junk food here. With 8 birr – about a euro, I would be able to feed my stomach well for a whole day in Ethiopia, but in Germany, you need about 2 euros to eat one meal in student refectory.

My advice to those planning to go abroad is that, 'God bless our country, so we do not have to travel abroad because of circumstances'.

****

Fu: My first observation was the fact that foreigners I met seemed to group together. You would see another African across the street you did not even know, and you would do everything to greet him/her. When I shared this with someone, he said it was the same in Princeton, NJ, in the U.S., an affluent neighbourhood with few African-Americans. There, the African-Americans seemed to demonstrate similar unity, usually greeting one another across the aisle while shopping. Is it a way to survive the contrasts between races, social layers?

Of course, even before any thing else, you have to survive the language contrast in Germany. A good thing was that the courses in my study program were offered in English. But I needed German in order to interact with the society. One day I bought Dusch Gel (shower gel) from the supermarket thinking it was body lotion. I had never used shower gel before in my life, so the difference was not easily obvious to me. Each time I showered, using soap, I used the gel to oil myself! As a result, I would turn white after a few minutes. This was puzzling to me, and went on for many days. One day, I decided to read over the German written on the gel tube. I was startled when, from my German-English dictionary, I realised it was shower gel!

When I told Akuma about my experience with the shower gel, he laughed and said he had an equally frightening one about showers. When he just arrived in Germany, and was doing his German language course in Magdeburg, he had wanted to take a bath, but did not realise that community bathrooms on each floor where separate for male and female. (Maybe he did not understand the German?) He went into the female community shower, which had a row of open-showers (no curtains between them). He had just begun to shower when a German girl came in, rightfully, to also take a shower. If she was surprised to see Akuma in the female bathroom, she did not show it. To Akuma's utmost shock, she undressed completely and stepped under an adjacent shower, a hands length from him. Akuma scrambled half-nakedly out of the bathroom!

I also had to adjust to a few things: for example, getting used to eating with a knife in my right hand and a fork in the left hand. This may sound trivial, but you can get really embarrassed. Also, after a month in Germany, I realized how bushy my hair had grown. The few barber salons for African hair were relatively expensive, at least 10 euros per cut compared to about 25 cents back home. Thieves! I bought myself a hair-trimmer set and started practicing to cut my own hair. You could well imagine how my first shaves looked!

Through the turmoil of the 20th century, Germany has emerged as a powerful, confident nation, and with the memory of the wall that divided Berlin into east and west, continues to be the driving force towards greater European integration. The German people enjoy a reputation for accuracy, precision and efficiency – words often used to describe their excellent cars – although an equally enduring image is of lederhosen-clad Bavarians hoisting beer steins at Munich's famous Oktoberfest. People are very independent, and a sister may not even know where her brother is. I soon learned not to ask about peoples' families. I remember hearing that a man died in his apartment and the skeleton was only discovered 5 years later on the sofa! The time estimate was figured out by calculations from the calendar and his stopped watch. No family member had noticed his absence for 5 years! All his bills were paid directly from his bank account! I could not believe it!

Due to the unemployment in Germany, the embassy requirement for a bank statement was for my own good. This would permit me to concentrate on my studies. My 3 months per year work permit would then only help me to supplement the monthly transfers. Well, I had borrowed the money for my bank statement. So, as soon as I began my studies and was more settled, I began my job search. I managed to convince the ladies at the student job office that my knowledge of

German was good enough. I landed my first job, to dig a trench around the wall of someone's house, a job I would never have dreamt of doing in my own country as a degree holder. I worked really hard for DM 12 (6 euros) and hour, until I could not stand up straight. Since I could not really speak German, I avoided unnecessary conversation. This meant I would just keep working and working. Each day I returned very tired and could not study, even having to skip classes for about a week. When I converted the money I earned to francs CFA, I was very happy.

I often found a job, often a tough one, say at a building construction site (called Baustelle in German), where I did not need to know much German in order to transport building material, break down walls etc. My first experience at a Baustelle was particularly hard. The chief foreman, not to mention the workers, spoke very fast in a type of guttural Saxony dialect mixed with real German. I often had to guess what they meant when they spoke to me. They had very bad manners too. They would fart noisily, as if the air they released were some prized perfume. At lunch someone would belch loudly, as if this gastric function was something of musical value, and he would not think to say excuse me. When I shared this with a friend, he commented about the shocking experience he also had in Kiel. One day he was waiting for the bus at the bus stop. In front of him was a middle-aged German. Suddenly and without warning, he farted loudly - 'puah puah puah', followed by a smell, which would have made that of rotten eggs seem appetizing. My friend said he could not have believed his ears if his nose had not confirmed. He was so shocked, and wanted to express his displeasure to the German with a punch, or at least say something violent to him. However, due to the shock and his language handicap, he opened and shut his mouth trying to find the right words violent enough for the occasion. The only words he found were from his African village dialect. So he spoke sharply at him the equivalent of 'You farted in front of me?' The German just stared back surprised. Later he got to know that not all Germans behaved like that. The 'educated' and travelled ones had better manners.

Then I met Manfred, considered the most infamous German in Leipzig by foreigners. He began by telling me he had a lot of stuff in his basement that he did not need, and brought me an old window blind, a used frying pan, old plates and cups and newspapers every other day. I wondered why he was so 'unprovokedly' nice to me. One day, I told Akuma about him and he exclaimed, 'Manfred! Be very careful! He is interested in you!' 'Interested in me?' I asked my eyes growing all round. Akuma laughed at my ignorance. Then, what he meant dawned on me. I was appalled at the prospect. At that time, the only time I had ever heard about a homosexual was in the Bible – where it is condemned, and novels. And now... 'But how can that be?' I asked. 'He told me he has a wife and kids!' Akuma laughed at me again. 'Sure he does, but he is bisexual.' He told me horrendous stories of how Manfred always exploited Africans sexually. I was dumbfounded. So that was why he had been giving me those things and visiting me at funny hours. Back home, it is normal for people you know to visit you without warning, and I had considered Manfred a friend until then.

Then one day it happened. He met me in the corridor as I came back from my bath after a hard day at Baustelle. I was tired and hungry. He had a full roasted chicken with him, huge tempting bananas and some bread. Just what I needed! He greeted me pleasantly, and asked if he should come in so we could eat together. I hesitated, but my curiosity and watering mouth got the better of me. Was Akuma really serious? I was an adventurous and very hungry man. So I ignored Akuma's warning. He stepped in to my room grinning expansively, and shut the door with the heels of his shoes.

After we had eaten, he pulled out 2 cans of Hasseröder premium beer from the cloth sac he always carried. He offered me one. I refused, saying I would prefer my glass of orange juice. Then without warning he made his move. The student rooms in Nürnberger hostel had a single bed, a reading table with one chair, and a kitchen table. Room 20 where I lived had the additional bonus of having a washbasin. Any guest I had, normally, sat on the chair while I sat on the bed. Before I could realise, Manfred was sitting on the bed besides me. Luckily enough, I always dressed up in the bathroom after a shower. I was wearing the type of shorts Mr. Bean wore when he went swimming, and a white Afro-vision T-shirt. As he closed in on me, the phone rang. My girlfriend in the U.S was on the line. It was almost like in the movies; rescued by the phone at the right moment. I quickly moved to the table, sat on it and lifted the receiver. The look on Manfred's face told me plenty. It was the look of a dog that just got a fat juicy bone snatched away from its mouth.

I kept talking to my girlfriend while enjoying Manfred, who was now subjected to a patience exam he would definitely not pass. He failed all right! After about one and a half hours (– never underestimate Manfred!), his patience wore out, and he reluctantly picked up his sac and old newspapers to leave. I continued my phone conversation as if he were not there. If he understood some English, as I know he did, he would have realized to whom I was talking. I did wave cynically at him when he reached the door. If I had fun seeing him go this time, it wasn't fun when he struck again.

Again this time, he met me in the corridor, as I came back from the kitchen with some food I had warmed up. This time he offered me some newspapers and walked into my room, un-invited, saying there were some job offers he wanted to show me. He was clearly exploiting the fact that he knew I needed a job on the side to support me while I studied. Again, it happened so suddenly I was taken aback. As he showed me the job offers, I suddenly felt his hand on my shoulder. I tried to move away immediately, but he grasped me firmly, while muttering that he thought I was very sexy and had nice buttocks. He brought his smelly mouth towards mine, mumbling repeatedly that he loved me.

'He loved me! He loved me?' He was shorter than me, and old enough to be my father, and so I underestimated his strength. He forced me down on the bed, his foul tongue lapping at me. I realized I had to react powerfully, if I was going to get out of this unblemished. I believe God gave me the strength. I pushed back at him with all my might. Finally, I overpowered him and shoved him out of the room, throwing his newspapers after him. I told him to go back to his wife and kids, and warned him to lay off my track or that of my African brothers. He scurried off like a dog caught stealing. Later on, I heard that despite heeding to my threat never to try me again, he did continue exploiting other Africans. Especially easy prey were the much younger Africans who came to Europe directly from high school, apparently overwhelmed by the day-to-day responsibilities they now had to carry without any family member to support them

Probably the best experience I had in Germany was on the day of the award of my Master's certificate in front of the physics and geo-science faculty in October 2000. Normally Germans don't hold a graduation ceremony; but I represented the first student from the international physics program to graduate. I was in the University newspaper the next month. For me, I felt really good to have survived working and studying so successfully, and with such an exquisite grade.

Also, in a way I had proven myself. I had shown Zintgraff that we were not foolish, that we could even do better. I had overcome the Einstein Stigma II, a feeling most blacks identify with: At the universities, you always have to prove yourself before you earn the respect from your white schoolmates or co-workers. Unlike Jews (who not even Hitler dismissed as savages and sub-normally stupid), blacks are assumed stupid until proved clever. This is a terrible handicap for Blacks to carry, being often regarded as, at best, retarded or delinquent, and at worst, as wild and savage. I remember a fellow Nigerian colleague quit the program because he felt 'handicapped' and 'undermined'. This notion was enhanced by his lack of computer skills. It is useful for Africans planning to travel abroad to invest sometime preparing, for example, learning basic computer skills. A friend shared how one day as he worked over-time (as a computer database expert in a company in Kiel), the cleaning lady (a German) came in and was so shocked to find him sitting there, even dressed in a suit and tie. She turned red and exclaimed 'Was machen Sie hier?' (translated: 'What are you doing here?'). My friend was amused to see her so red. Perhaps she was wondering what a black man would be doing there on a computer, while she was instead cleaning. He said he gave her a nonchalant smile, and showed her the fingers of both of his (black) hands: ten minutes for her to clean up and leave the office. She cooled off immediately. In the next days they became great friends, and she respected him as the angels respect God.

Interestingly, in Poland I had a different look of the stigma. As an African visiting Poland in 1999, for an excursion, I enjoyed mini-stardom during a visit to a high school in Zlotoryja. Three colleagues and Dr. Pluta, my physics professor, accompanied me. The previous evening, we had agreed I would be the one to make a speech on our behalf. Unfortunately, when my professor came to pick us up from the hotel, I had just gone to take a dump. I had MTV on, so I could not hear them knocking on my door for us to go. Emptying my bowels took longer than I expected, and by the time I went down to the hotel lobby, my colleagues had left since they were running late for the high school rendezvous. 'No!' I told myself. I was not going to miss out on this one. I had to do something. I could see the girl at the hotel lobby liked my looks or maybe was just fascinated by my colour. Either way, I had her attention, so I switched on my charm. A few polish words later with one of the cleaning girls at the hotel, it was arranged for someone to walk me to the high school, as it was not far. At the school, someone showed me to the class where Dr. Pluta and my colleagues had just gone.

When I strolled into the classroom, hands in my overcoat, everyone rose to welcome the tall intelligent handsome (they just noticed) African who studied physics. I was a rare apparition in the lives of the students in this small town. I was maybe the first one with colour to visit the school. I mean, it was unbelievable how much of a stir I was creating! I enjoyed the moment and made an old speech of mine I'd once made to my high school students in PSS Mankon, and the effect was tremendous. Something about 'Physics is a subject, which required three things for success: The first thing you should do is to work hard; the second thing you must do is to still work hard. If you forget the first two things, you must not forget the third thing – work hard!' This drew a huge applause.

But that was only the beginning. We managed to break free from the high school; but not before the news men got onto us! At one moment, I genuinely wondered what the fuss was all about. The maximum turning point was when we went to the Gymnasium no. 2, where Dr. Pluta's wife taught. There, we addressed pupils, and answered questions they had been preparing all week. I had to show them where Cameroon was on the map of Africa. I signed autographs. Yeah, you heard right. I felt like a celebrity! It is so funny, thinking back, how this could have been so, just because of my colour. I also had a camera with me, so I took pictures of myself being taken pictures of. It reminded me of children in the village in Cameroon, excited when they see a white man. Here it was happening also in Europe.

Somebody once told me Polish girls are sensational. While in Poland, I gave this person full marks for that. It's a bad idea to go to Poland for a honeymoon! Even if you are from Africa! The following day we drove to Karpacz, famous for the Shneekopf. There we ran into a party, organized by some Polish youngsters. That is where I ran into Polish girls. They were pretty elated to see us (I mean me), and they asked us to join their party. I was surprised at the girls' attraction to me. I noticed one particular girl, who worked for a bank in Wroclaw, and danced with her several times. Soon one Polish boy pulled me to a quiet corner and beseeched me to leave his girlfriend, this girl, alone. I was bemused by the prospect, as he looked real scared I was about to woo his girl; but he was wrong. I was like a gigolo, freely flowing with terminal velocity – The effect of the beer probably, or maybe I underestimated my charms. All my comrades expected me to get off with at least one 'catch' that night, but I let myself disappoint them. It was actually good I had phoned my to-be fiancé in the U.S. that evening before running into this party.

Let me mention here that, one feature of being a boy or bachelor in Europe is that you are basically free to date whatever girl you want away from the curiosity and watching eyes of family or friends as compared to the situation back home. What I find disgusting is the fact that many African students going after white girls, to as they say also taste white meat, often pretend they are African Americans, in order to score better with the girls. In my case, I did not have to lie in this way. But perhaps, this is unique to me?

In Spain: The idea that people often under look Africans can be exploited. I have exploited this many times. Here is an example. During my PhD studies I had to deliver my first international science conference presentation in Granada Spain in 2003. They had a competition for the best student presentation. My Professor asked my colleague and me to enter the competition. I noticed I was the only black man in the whole conference. I even moved from hall to hall to see if I could find another. I asked myself where all the blacks in the world were? Maybe one would come on the second day? No, this only made me more nervous. My colleague and I met another student from Germany who said she was always very nervous, beginning from the day before the presentation! That made me feel better for a while, to know I was not alone. But wait a moment! She was white and she was nervous. I was the only black man there, so how was I supposed to feel? It occurred to me then that I was going to represent all the black people in the whole world at the conference. I would be the 'teacher' in an auditorium of white men. I would enjoy this.

Finally on Wednesday, at about 3:40 p.m. my presentation was announced. During my talk, I could see the surprise written over the faces of the audience. They could not believe the good stuff I was spewing. After my talk, people remarked it was impeccable. I felt really good but did not think again about the contest. I immediately returned to the Hotel, bought myself a good meal, and started noticing Spain for the first time. Granada was very beautiful. I later visited the Alhambra and the El Generalife. What I hated about Spain was the fact that the people did not bother about English. You either spoke Spanish or saw a tourist guide. As I waited obliviously for the results on the conference presentation, I had the opportunity to notice how other Cameroonians in Spain were faring.

It was around the end of the Spanish football season. I watched with so much pride how Samuel Eto'o helped Real Mallorca lift the football trophy. He then flew immediately to France for the finals of the Confederation Cup (during which Foe lost his life). In his absence, as Real celebrated, his name was headlines all over. The Cameroonian, the Cameroonian! Football!

This, however, is not enough to dispel racial abuse against blacks. Eto'o has been the target of much racist abuse. To his credit, he has not remained silent. After he scored in a match against Real Zaragoza, the crowd started to monkey chant. Eto'o responded by imitating a monkey. Interestingly a white team-mate of his (ignorantly) joined in the monkey dance goal celebration! The Monkey chant thing happened again in 2006 when Eto'o even threatened to leave the pitch.

In Getafe in February 2005, as the players made their way into the stadium, scores of fans rushed up to the wire fence and shouted 'nigger, nigger' at Daniel Kome, a Cameroon midfielder and Getafe's only black player. In fact, he was the only non-white face I saw - except Zinedine Zidane and Roberto Carlos. For some bizarre reason, even during the warm-up, Kome was to be seen training on his own, away from the rest of the squad.

Anyway, back to the conference story, some days later, I met my professor down the corridor, and the first thing he said was, 'Congratulations, you won a prize at the conference!' I just could not believe it! Not that my presentation was not good. But I think the surprise element worked to my favour. You know, as a Blackman, I think you are given a '−10' even before you walk up the stage (or in general have to prove yourself). So if you score as equally well as the whites, you actually wind up with 10 more points. This gave me a lot of courage and confidence in my PhD work.

After my Master's program, I had four professors campaigning for me to do a PhD with them. One actually encouraged me to apply for a German State Scholarship. I liked the idea better than signing a contract. With a scholarship, I was freer and it was better for my CV. I remember very clearly the day I went to the lady who was in charge of scholarship applications to get application forms. She told me it would be very difficult for me to get the scholarship, adding tacitly 'Because you are from Africa'. I enjoyed the expression on her face when I submitted my application file and she saw my grade, and even more when I actually came to claim the scholarship award. I had been selected second, and probably first foreigner to secure that particular scholarship.

In Germany, I also experienced that, even if you have an international driving license from Africa, you needed to learn more to cope with the Autobahn and the more developed traffic regulations and roads. Beyond the license, the main problem in Germany is not buying a car, but maintaining it. Interestingly, Germans really encourage the use of bicycles. The problem is that you cannot use them in winter. One reason for encouraging their usage is to reduce pollution. I was surprised to find many Professors used bicycles. However, Africans in Germany run a brisk trade with second-hand cars. They have carved their niche particularly with Toyotas, because of the availability of parts in most African countries. As to abandoning your studies for the car business, I can only say you can do one or the other but hardly both successfully. Most students who go for business just renew their student registration every semester and then disappear. At the end, they leave a negative impression with the Universities. Then, the next Africans are even more stigmatized. Africans can change the negative impression in Westerners minds by avoiding such negative actions.

Other Westerner's impressions are not negative at all. They are perhaps just cultural. In Zurich, I attended a wedding where I was the only African. Everyone thought, since I was African, I could play drums better. So they asked me to play drums during the wedding party. I did what I could.

To conclude, let me say that 'The biggest trouble with traveling abroad, as an African, is that even if you travel abroad, you're still an African.'

The million dollar question, I was often asked in different western countries was if I would eventually return to Cameroon? I often replied by saying that I have more use back home in Africa than in Europe. The trick is to plan well so you can establish the means to help your own people and live reasonably when you go home.

[FK: In any case, Fu Bienkaa successfully completed his doctoral work in 2004 with a summa cum laude at his PhD defence. Fellow African brother Julius Tsuwi followed suit on October 11, 2006. Fu is currently a faculty member in UCF, Florida. Julius returned to his home country Kenya with Alice, amidst mouth-watering postdoctoral options in Canada, Germany and the U.S. Bayene is still studying in Germany.

Education has indeed greatly opened up the former Eastern part of Germany and Hitler would have a heart attack if he saw the Germany of today. "Those who went abroad during the World Cup, as I did, sensed that an entirely new view of Germany had developed. Now it's important to continue implementing what became visible to others in everyday life.", says Gerhard Schroeder (Former German Chancellor) after the 2006 FIFA World Cup in Germany. Schroeder, was recently appointed head of an anti-racism group. Thank you Germany for the opportunities you give Africans and for the willingness to do more.

And now an experience from America:]

Chapter 2

America, here I come!

*'I stood and stared in disbelief,
In shock at what I heard...
If this is it, I'm not sure I want to say
America here I come.'* – Wilfred Mbacham

[FK: The Asana family's move to the U.S.A. was a far unexpected reality, and a long dream come true. The immediate family is made up of two parents (Festus and Jenny) with four children (Lydia, Elizabeth, Emmanuel and Ruth). The experiences in the U.S. constitute a memorable landmark in the life of each family member, and the memories linger on in confirmation of the statement by their Dutch friend Rev Blok that "Africans have a long memory." Here now are the Asana's versions of 'Coming to America'.]

Festus' story
My vision of modern America started in the early 1960s, when I entered secondary school, Cameroon Protestant College (CPC) Bali. CPC, the second oldest institution of its kind in our nation, was an ideal institution and till today I am still proud to be associated with it, because this school gave me a sense of direction, character, and vocation. It was the springboard for my future academic pursuits, and there I saw the windows into the world. On the teaching staff were Cameroonians from various regions, Dutch, Germans, Swiss, French, and American missionaries and Peace Corps volunteers.

They were the years of the Kennedys and Martin Luther King Jr. I still have fresh memories of the visit of a big group of white and black Americans (the Crossroaders). In my mind's eye, I can see the stage on which they stood and sang, "We shall overcome", in the school assembly, to the great admiration of the staff and students. The American Peace Corps volunteers taught us American writing, American literature, and we became used to the American accent "coming through the nose." I even picked an American pen pal Barbara Z. from Nebraska with whom I corresponded for ten years (1964-1974). All this American influence left a deep positive mark on me, but coming from the family of a 'poor' pastor and being the first of many children, I did not at that time dream of ever crossing the Atlantic Ocean. In fact, the largest body of water I knew then was the Mezam River. With our school not far from the Bali airstrip, we saw small planes land and take off every week, but I considered them reserved for a class of people I would never get close to.

The years rolled by, and I became a pastor of the Presbyterian Church in Cameroon after completing my studies at the Faculty of Protestant Theology, Yaoundé, an ecumenical and international institution whose dean then, the Rev. Dr. David, was American. Memories of the assassinations in the United States lingered, but the Americans I met always impressed me as very civilised and democratic people. I began to nurse the possibility of continuing my studies in the U.S. after teaching at the Theological College Nyasoso for some years.

In 1983, I had admission and scholarship grants in two schools – Princeton and Harvard. I chose Harvard University where my friend Victor had helped me with application procedures and was a student at the time. That year, the Rev. Dr. I. Elang, who had earlier returned from the University of Dubuque in Iowa, took over from me as principal of the Theological College. He gave me my first orientation on life in the U.S. One of the most interesting points was the warning that a door marked 'restroom' does not lead into a room where you can take a rest. It indicates a toilet! This was most useful for someone arriving at an airport or institution expecting to see signs for toilets. One of the problems I had was what type of clothing I had to take along. I could not fathom what life would be like, and could only stretch my imagination from pictures I had seen of people and scenes of Europe and America. My shopping was rather scanty since I could not afford much anyway.

My departure from Cameroon was no big issue, no send-off party, no publicity, no convoy, and no crowd to see me off at the airport. It was painful to part from my dear wife Jenny, leaving her with three little children, the youngest of whom was just three months old, in a small rather unsafe house near the Presbyterian Church, Ntamulung in Bamenda. It was August 1983, and the morning was bright. My senior friend (my "big" to use our secondary school appellation), Mr. Paul Ato, was on hand to drive me in his car to the bus stop. As I waved my family goodbye and got into the car, I would see the peculiar look in my daughter Elizabeth's eyes seeming to ask, "Where is my father going to and when shall I see him again?" Her eyes seemed to pierce through my heart, and I felt like coming back, but I persevered and held back my tears 'like a man'. On the seven-hour bus ride to Douala, I daydreamed as my thoughts remained in Bamenda.

Arriving in good time to catch my Swissair flight to Zurich, I realised that I was now getting into the unknown. I changed planes in

From Dust to Snow: The African Dream?

Zurich with no problem, but in New York I missed the plane for Boston. Our earlier flight had been delayed, and when my suitcase came out, the handle had been torn off. Within an hour another flight was arranged.

When I came out at Logan airport in Boston, there was nobody to receive me. Because of the delayed flight, my friend Victor who had offered to pick me up on behalf of the University had returned home. I was really scared. I had a few dollar bills on me but no coins to make a phone call. Even if I had coins, I had not mastered how to use a pay phone. I went up to a young police lady and explained my dilemma. Her immediate polite and kind response deeply impressed me. I refused to expose my ignorance to her; so I read the instructions on the phone, made a few attempts, and the ten cents coin brought home my friend's voice. Within an hour, we were hugging each other. "America, here we are!" our hearts seemed to be saying. Even though the green plantains and fresh groundnuts I had brought for my friend's family were confiscated by American customs, we were just happy to see each other.

For the first semester, I lived with Victor, his wife, and two little boys in their small apartment. Victor gave me my first orientation, and I was initiated into American foods gradually. It took time to get used to the new life style of rushing, and to get my bearings. I got lost a number of times before getting used to even the apartment where we lived. I prayed for that first semester to end, so that I could have my independence and make my own discoveries.

During a reception given by the Dean of Harvard Divinity School, I came across a gentleman by name Charles Busch from Texas who was to become a very special friend to my family and me. Charles introduced himself to me, developed instant interest in me, and later gave me very useful orientation from the angle of an American. I still remember that he was the one who taught me how different American coins are referred to (e.g. quarter for 25 cents). He accompanied me to the post office, the famous Harvard Square, various shops, and introduced me to Chinese restaurants. He got funds to buy me a very good complete and new winter outfit (boots, jacket, gloves, muffler and cap). Till today he remains one of the closest American friends my family has.

When I finally moved to Harvard Divinity Hall, the oldest university dormitory (room 24) in the U.S., it was an historic experience for me. My first shock was that boys' rooms were not separated from those of girls, and everyone used the same toilets and showers without discrimination. At first, I often felt embarrassed. Soon I got used to it and we lived like family. The second thing I had to get used to was the fact that sometimes my American friends never meant what they said. For instance, many people said things like, "We'll get you a winter coat", which I hadn't asked for, but they were just 'trying' to be 'nice'. We cooked in turns in groups and whenever it was my Kenyan friend's and my turn, our American friends almost 'cut their tongues', because we cooked very delicious and spicy meals, which were always appreciated for their African taste.

I had to learn early that in America one must work hard, because the song "Everything's free in America", by Trini Lopez, is the biggest lie. You only get what you work for! I got a campus job with the Harvard University Police Department as a security guard, and it turned out to be a very useful job for me in various ways. I did most of my school assignments at work, as I worked in quiet science laboratories and other quiet buildings with time to read and write between rounds. My orientation and interaction with the functioning of the Harvard University Police made me smart and security-conscious till today. I was able to earn enough extra money to buy air tickets for my wife ands children to join me a year later.

One particular night at Divinity Hall is memorable for me. I was to travel to the Niagara Falls on the U.S./Canada border with a group of international students for a Christian University conference organised by the Friendship for Overseas Students (FOCUS), a ministry of the historic Park Street church in Boston. I had to complete and submit a term paper the morning of our departure, so that a friend could type and hand it in to meet the deadline. The evening before our departure, I put on my pyjamas and sat up in my room reading and writing. Without succeeding to lie on my bed, I soon saw the sun rising. The night was over without me blinking. I took off my pyjamas, got ready for the long Greyhound bus ride, and we left for one of the Seven Wonders of the World! I had heard about the Niagara Falls in a Geography lesson in 1965, and at last I had the chance to 'experience' it.

I saw my first snow in 1983. Back in Cameroon, we had seen pictures of snow and sang songs about snow, but could never fathom what it really looked like, how it fell, or how people coped with it and got rid of it. I was in the home of Jon and Kathy Wood in Connecticut where I had been invited for Thanksgiving, a historic American holiday in November. We still have a picture of me carrying in my arms, little Lauren Elizabeth, their first daughter, in the snow. It was a thrilling and indescribable experience!

I had known Kathy many years back in Yaoundé when she served with the Summer Institute of Linguistics (SIL), working for some time with the Pygmy tribe –the Bakas. Back in the U.S., she got married and the Wood family has since had deep ties with the Asanas. While in the U.S., most of our Thanksgivings were spent with the Woods who are indeed a true Christian family to us. The second beautiful experience of heavy snow for me was the same year in December at Stony Point near

New York City, where I was invited to spend Christmas with a few other international students. The following Christmas, my whole family was there for the same experience and more, as we were taken to New York City to see the decorations on Christmas Eve. It was awesome!

Till today I refer to the one year of absence from my family as 'the longest year in my life'. From my bedside, I could dial Cameroon any time, but my wife and children did not have easy access to a phone, so my habit was to write a letter to Jenny every Sunday on a regular basis. Unfortunately some of the letters would delay along the way, and she would sometimes receive three at a time, and sometimes go for three weeks without receiving any. We had no access to e-mail back then the way we do today. When Jenny and the children finally arrived, a beautiful apartment awaited them at 18 Peabody in Cambridge, Massachusetts – a Harvard University housing estate. I had vowed not to enrol in a doctoral programme, if I didn't succeed to bring my dear wife and children to join me in the U.S., and God heard my prayer. The harmony of my family was for me more important than a string of degrees.

Jenny's story

It was made known to me that my children and I would join my husband in the U.S. one year before we finally left Cameroon. So, psychologically I had been preparing my mind to leave Cameroon throughout that year. Even so, when the time for us to leave drew near, there was a lot of anxiety in me. I tried to picture what America looked like. I fantasized it to be a place where there was no grass, but all tarred. I kept picturing beautiful houses, all story buildings, well built roads and so on. Of course, there was the anxiety of meeting my husband from whom I had been separated for one year. The two girls' anxiety was mostly to meet their father whom they missed a lot. Our son was just three months old when their father left, so did not know his father unlike his sisters.

My main reason for going to America was to join my husband, Festus. But I left Cameroon already on a student visa to study at Lesley College, Cambridge Massachusetts.

Obtaining an entry Visa to America was not a problem. Lesley College, which was a well-known University in the Boston area, sent me a Form I-20, which facilitated the acquisition of the visa at the American Embassy in Yaoundé. With my stamped passport in hand, my focus now turned to our departure. My mind was pre-occupied with the fear of the unknown. How was I to travel alone with three kids? How would such a long journey in a plane be? What type of food would we find there? Which type of clothes should I have sewn for the children and me to wear on the journey? What should I carry along? The excitement of reuniting with my dear husband took away some of my fears.

Finally the departure day proper came. We left for the Douala airport, where we met my brother-in-law, Gustav, who had come from Yaoundé to see us off. After checking in our luggage, we all engaged in such warm lively conversation that nobody paid attention to the announcement inviting us to board the plane. It was just a few minutes before take off that a Good Samaritan came and asked us if we were travelling by Swiss Air. When we said yes, he informed us that boarding had been announced. We all panicked. How was I to carry three kids, in addition to my hand luggage and go through the customs fast? We quickly said goodbye, but my brother-in-law decided to escort us as far as he could before being stopped. The customs officers were unhappy because they had questions to ask but there was no time. For example, "You are going to school in the U.S., and taking along three kids; how will you manage with them?" Of course, they had to let us go fast or else the plane would have taken off without us. God led us through. Gustav carried Eli and held one bag. I carried Emma on my back, holding Lydia's hand and dragging another bag. Gustav was allowed to go right to the plane. As soon as we were well seated, the plane took off, which meant it had been waiting for us. Thanks to God!

After the plane had been in the air for about an hour, one of the kids asked me, "Mama, is the plane not moving?" Being her first experience, she must have forgotten the take off shock, and since the plane had attained cruising speed and height, it glided along with people moving freely in the plane. She must have expected turbulence or some other sign of movement. Lydia and Eli quickly made friends with the hostesses who took them round, answering their questions and even taking them to the cockpit.

We were served a snack of chocolate, which we all enjoyed; then, came time for lunch. We were served four trays of a fish meal. The children looked at it and refused to eat. I returned three trays, and opened one for myself. When I tasted it, it was saltless, no pepper, no 'maggi', no oil. In fact, it was tasteless. I couldn't eat. We had failed to indicate that I was travelling with kids, so they had no kids' meals. We managed with the snacks and drinks till we arrived in Germany.

We changed planes in Zurich, Switzerland. It was not an easy task, but we managed to find our way to the other end of the airport, where we were to board the next flight to Stuttgart, Germany, where we were to be picked up by our friend, Rev. Thiefeld, to spend three nights with him and his family before moving on to the U.S. We came to a place where we had to go down "moving steps" (escalators). I stood there really scared out of my mind. While I wondered what to do, a man offered to take the hand of one of the kids. I fastened Emmanuel on my back with a large towel, hung the bag on my left shoulder, and held Elizabeth's hand. I had been watching people step on the escalator. I gathered courage and stepped on it, dragging Eli along and holding fast to the rails of the escalator. Now as it was rolling down, I watched very keenly to see how the others stepped off. I stepped off dragging my daughter along, and took a deep breath not believing we had made it. I saw our friend waving on the other side of customs. My face brightened and my heart lightened at the sight of a familiar face in the midst of strangers, new things, and foreign sounds, including the German language. I told the children, "Look at Rev. Thiefeld!" We all smiled and waved back, eager to get through customs. As we hugged in greeting, I felt great relief in my heart, and I thanked the Lord for seeing us through the first part of the journey.

At the end of our stay with them, Mrs Thiefeld drove us back to the airport, where we took a plane first to Zurich, then to Boston, U.S.A.

On arrival at Logan Airport, first while still in the air, as the plane was descending, I looked out of the window and all I could see was water, water everywhere. I held my breath and prayed. Let me explain something to you now. I come from the grasslands of Cameroon. Unlike those from the coastal region who grow up swimming and fishing in the Atlantic, I have never had reason to get comfortable with the sight of large bodies of water, let alone being in them. As such, it was only natural that, for a second, my greatest fear was that we would land on water, as I saw no land in sight. I came to discover that Boston is on the coast, and that Logan airport is just near the Atlantic Ocean, which separates the Americas from Africa.

We finally touched down safely, on land. As others rushed to disembark, I took my time, secured my baby on my back, and we moved out into the airport building. As we went through the customs, I was told that the single form I had filled on the plane was insufficient. I was asked to fill-out three more forms, one for each of my children. As I struggled to complete them, I suddenly heard somebody shouting out with a loud voice, "I know you, your name is Jenny; your husband is Festus! I am his friend working here at the airport. He has asked me to help you." You can imagine my relief. We greeted each other and he helped complete the forms for me. Due to the delay, my dear husband was restless, panicking and thinking we had not come. Thank God he came to pick us up with some dear friends, Charles and Susan.

With the help of the friend who first met us, we claimed our luggage and moved out to meet Festus in the waiting room. On seeing us, he jumped up, rushed towards us, and hugged us tightly. Our joy at being reunited was more than words can describe. Meanwhile,

America, here I come!

Emmanuel was still on my back. Anxious to carry his baby, Festus stretched his hands to carry him. Emma screamed and hung on my neck tightly, almost strangling me with all the strength his little 15-month-old body could muster. His father was deeply disappointed that his own son did not know him, but knew it was a natural reaction; all he needed was a little time. It was a few minutes before we snapped out of our own little reunion world and greeted the friends who had come with Festus. We set out driving to my new home in Cambridge, Massachusetts.

On the way I noticed that the trees had no leaves. Wondering why they were all dried up, I asked my husband. He told me that they shed their leaves in preparation for winter. Well, that did not make much sense to me since I had not yet understood the different seasons in America. It was only later that I understood it was characteristic of the season for leaves to fall off the trees, in the fall (autumn). The other thing that caught my eye on the drive home was that I saw people walking on the streets, putting on heavy jackets and "blankets". On enquiring, I was told that it was because of the cold temperatures. Of course, we felt it; the African attires the tailor had made for us before we left were too light for the cold.

Upon our arrival at what would be our home for one year, in Harvard University housing at 18 Peabody, my husband took out his keys and opened to a first floor apartment. We all entered and felt the warmth of a home. I felt the satisfaction of accomplishment, having made it to an unknown land with three kids. It was not a big house compared to what we had at home. In fact, it was rather small. It had two bedrooms, a parlour with a kitchen attached to it, a bathroom and toilet. There was a couch in the living room, which when you sat on it, sank really low. Festus later on told me he had picked it on the street just outside his door. I had my reservations about the apartment, but knew my husband had done nothing less than his best to prepare for our coming. After visiting other homes, I realised ours was more inviting than most of them.

I had to start school immediately, so Festus took me to my campus. Every place we went to looked just like the place we had just passed. The buildings were quite similar. We went to the registration office and fulfilled the registration requirements. My husband accompanied me on the bus to school for one week and came to pick me up, showing me all the important places and things in the area like bus stops, which bus to take, where to shop and so on. So my transition was a piece of cake.

Matriculation day came. I went alone. I met other international students, and started making friends straight away. We were lectured on security and what we needed to know about the campus. We were shown around the campus. The buildings, especially, the library, classrooms, refectory, and offices, and the international office were key points of interest. I paid for my health insurance, a new concept to me, through the school.

For our five-year stay in America, I had a lot of different experiences. Many of them were funny to others, and looking back now I may agree. However, some of them took me unawares, others annoyed me, and still others just plain terrified me. One of these experiences occurred during an evening poetry class with a guest lecturer. As usual we sat in a circle on the floor. The lecturer brought in a big bag and put it besides her. Then she said, "I am going to present a snake and we shall explore it and see different ways of analysing it as poetry." I thought I did not hear her properly. She then unzipped the bag and started to bring out a big snake. My goodness! A live snake right before my eyes! I jumped up, went into the other room, beckoned to a friend signalling her to bring me my bag. I used another door to get out of the building, and started running home. Fortunately, I still had enough rational to remember to take the bus. I told the story to my family and they laughed and thought it was funny, but for me it was an escape from death. I may have a heightened phobia for snakes even for a Cameroonian, or African in general for that matter, but where I come from, most snakes are poisonous or can strangle a person to death. For this reason, most of us believe the only good snake is a dead snake.

The second was an encounter with neighbours. It all started after our one-year stay in Cambridge. My husband graduated from Harvard University, and had admission into Boston University to continue with PhD studies. We had to leave our apartment, and so we were in need of a new apartment to live in. We tried calling many apartments listed in newspapers for rent. For each one we called, the answer was: "Sorry it has been taken." After many tries, we realised that it was because we were not Americans, so the people were not sure we would be good tenants. On a Sunday, just a day before we were to start paying a $25 per day fine for not having moved out, my husband and I decided to fast and pray for a house. We had started packing in faith. At church, friends opted to do the calling for us that day with their American accent. They took my husband to their home. Later that evening, they found a good apartment for us, which we all liked. It was in an all white neighbourhood in Arlington Massachusetts (One of the reasons we did not look for an apartment in the heart of the city was because we did not like the school system there, and there was some talk of racism there). We moved that Sunday night, in the rain, into our new home, a two family house with another family in the basement apartment.

After about two weeks, our children saw some children playing across the street in front of their house. Lydia our first daughter told her two junior ones to go and play with them. I was quite anxious, but I did not reveal it to our children. As soon as they started to cross the street to meet their "new friends", their grandmother saw our "strange black kids", coming towards her grandchildren. She rushed down, calling, "Tommy, Erin!" She flung open the door, pushed them in, and banged the door closed behind her. Our kids stood there demoralized. I quickly shouted out of the kitchen window from where I was watching, "Lydia, come in! One day you will play with them." When they came in, I comforted them by saying that we were not yet known in the neighbourhood and so they should only play in our yard. It did not take long before our neighbours' children, the same children from the incident, started coming over to play with our children. Thank God for child-like hearts. The relationship soon grew, and the children soon started coming into our house. When they saw that they were well received, they continued to come to play and watch TV and videos with our children. They also loved our Cameroonian foods, and we started doing things in common with their single mother and grandparents who lived upstairs from them. We did car-pool to drop off and pick up children from school, baby-sat for one another, and exchanged gifts.

Some of the very touching things that same family did for us included the following: When my husband went home for his research during winter, the grandfather would come over to shovel the snow from our driveway for me to be able to drive out. They took care of us in Festus' absence, especially, as I was expecting our last child, Ruth. When I gave birth, the grandmother provided most of the things for our baby, like a car seat, clothing, and all the love of a grandmother. In fact, by the time we left, there were a lot of tears because it was hard to separate. When Lydia was returning to start secondary school in PSS Mankon, Cameroon, one of the gifts the children's mother, Maura, gave her (for her good work of taking care of her children both in school and at home) was a beautiful gold necklace. It is good to maintain a good relationship with your neighbours.

Some more funny experiences: While still back at home in Cameroon, my husband wrote and told me that he had bought a comforter. When I read that information, I took a deep breath. What was a comforter? What type of thing had he bought to comfort him? Despite my curiosity, I decided to wait and see. Two days after we arrived, I asked, "Where is the comforter you bought?" He showed me a warm bedcover. When I told him what I had thought, we both laughed and he said, "You thought I bought a girl to keep me comforted?" Americans call the thick warm bedcover a comforter.

A few days after our arrival, one evening Festus asked us, "Can we have hot dogs for supper?" "Hot dogs, no, thanks!" was our immediate reply. We did not find out what hot dogs were before saying no. It did not take long before hot dogs became the children's favourite.

One evening, Festus' friends came to welcome us. One lady kept uttering, "Oh boy!" With my narrow thinking, I thought she was making that expression only when my husband said something. After they left, I asked my husband why the woman was saying "Oh boy". He explained that it was a common expression in America, which did not mean much. I told him I thought she was calling him her boy.

As far as living in America was concerned, there were two sides to the coin: disadvantages as well as the advantages. Living far away from home, no matter how glorious the place might be, one will always be a stranger. It was not easy for us to adjust in a foreign land where we had no family, coupled with a strange culture, where people keep to themselves and seem to live for themselves for the most part. If not of our church family, The First United Presbyterian Church Cambridge, we would have been left to ourselves. Thank God my husband was there before we went to America. He had made some good friends who stood by us: helping us with babysitting, showing us around, and getting us around from time to time before we got our car. When we were at home for too long, we were very lonely. News on TV was very scary, always news of murder, kidnapping, drug related shootings, demonstrations by racist groups like the Ku Klux Klan, and skinheads.

There were advantages. I will mention a few. In education, there are good school buildings, fewer kids in each class per teacher, and many opportunities for all to learn. In security, even though there were gruesome crimes, America had a good security network. If you were in trouble and called the police or fire department, in a short time there was an officer there to help you. I remembered that not long after we arrived, my husband instructed us on which numbers to call if there was a fire or an unwanted person around. One evening, while he was at work, the smoke detector went off. I got very confused not knowing which of the many neighbours to contact. I called the fire department. They told me to set-off the fire alarm for the entire apartment building, which was extremely loud and would signal everybody in the big building to rush out. Even though I tried to tell them that there was no fire, they insisted; that was the only thing that would get them there to turn off the smoke detector. So, I set off the fire alarm. I was so frightened by the loud sound of the alarm, I took the children and we ran out forgetting to take the keys. The door locked after us, and I stood outside wondering how we would ever get back in. The tall apartment building emptied, the fire truck arrived and the firemen asked for the keys. I told them they were locked in. They took out their master key and opened the door to my surprise. Of course, they discovered that it was a cockroach that had entered the smoke detector and made it go off.

Medical care was good though very expensive. Once you paid your medical insurance monthly, in poor as well as good health, you always got good medical attention when you needed it. I was fortunate to have given birth to our last daughter, Ruth, there in Boston at Brigham and Women hospital. It was a difficult birth, but since I was in the hands of experts who cared, I was well attended to.

Economically, I believe that when a country has good road infrastructure, communication is easy and business grows. There are good shopping centres where one can buy just anything you can imagine. Everybody took their work seriously and worked quite hard. You earned money hourly. A lazy person cannot survive out there. On the whole there were many opportunities there.

Our children had their own share of difficulties. Being the only black children in their classes, they faced some sort of segregation for some time. Lydia, especially, went through some hard times with handling this issue, being a very outgoing child. During recess, the other kids would keep away from them, and so they were lonely and sad. It took our prayers and support to help them overcome it. Thank God our children were well-mannered, smart kids. In a short time our yard became a gathering place for the neighbourhood children. Later all three of them were elected class captains by their respective classmates.

Lydia's Memories

Life is really something. The more I try to figure it out, the more I realise I can't. More so, I don't believe I am meant to. God's path for me is the best. That trip to the U.S. with my Mom and siblings many years ago was my introduction to the world outside my home country. Too bad I do not remember what was going through my six-year-old mind at that time. I know my siblings and I got lots of Swiss chocolate and got to look into the cockpit. I do not remember the stopover in Germany, but I do remember the kitchen had a really nice smell. I now imagine it to have been a mixture of freshly brewed coffee, and freshly baked chocolate cake dusted with white sugar powder. Don't ask me why. Pictures tell me we, the kids, were thrilled to see our dad again and to receive welcome presents from dad's friends. I remember our first home had a tiny backyard, and we had an Indian family as immediate neighbours. My first school in Cambridge was racially diverse. My best friend's name was Sarah, a Caucasian girl.

In Arlington, I remember starting third grade in the lowest reading group but moving to the advanced group before the year was over. I was able to be part of all the different crowds and moved between them with ease. I was right up there with the nerds when it came to spelling bees, and math tests. I got along with the boys, maybe because I was good at gym. I was often invited to the sleepovers of the popular crowd. When it was my birthday, I got them all together!! I was often the teacher's pet, but managed to do that without being hated by my classmates. Many a time after dinner, I would get a phone call from one of my buddies, Terence, with the question, 'What did we have for homework?' Oh, I loved to read and made full use of our school and public libraries. I would get so lost in books that I couldn't hear anything else going on around me. I particularly liked Nancy Drew mysteries.

My parents were great about helping and encouraging us to integrate into American life, but we were taught that our home was Cameroon, and we would return. It was unheard of at home for children to address adults by their first names. When a child casually greeted my mom with 'Hi Jenny', she wasted no time in kindly but firmly telling them to address her either as Mrs Asana or Aunty Jenny. Her children of course did the same for all other adults. Mom and dad spoke our native Bafut to us sometimes. I respect and thank them for this, for when we returned home, particularly in the village, we were able to at least understand and could soon make ourselves understood to our grandparents. We could not speak the lingua franca known as Pidgin English, and our English was so heavily accented that it was difficult for others to understand us. At home, children learned to help out at home at an early age. Mom was not going to make an exception in our case just because we were in America. It was even more imperative in the U.S. for our family that we the kids were disciplined and helpful, because both Mom and Dad were full-time students with part-time work. The notion of house help as we had always had at home was unthinkable in our new life. Of course, I sometimes thought some things weren't fair. I was after all, a normal kid. For example, when my baby sister was born, I could not play on the school softball team that year. I had to help with my sister.

I believe we were once in danger of being kidnapped. It was a warm summer afternoon. My siblings, two other kids and I were out in our front yard. I was the oldest of the lot at age 10. A man walking by our unfenced lawn stopped, smiled, and greeted. We chirped innocent hellos and went on playing. The man offered us candy in a friendly manner. Before any of the kids could accept, I told him we didn't want any. He stood for a few more minutes as if interested in our game. He then asked if anyone wanted to go with him to get ice cream bars from a nearby store for all of us. As I started to tell him we were not allowed to talk to strangers, my mother calmly questioned what was going on from the upstairs kitchen window. Just then Mary, whose kids were playing with us, came out. She (not so calmly) demanded to know what the man wanted. He defensively said he just wanted to buy the kids ice cream.

"Our kids don't need ice cream from you. We have enough right here at home!" my mom called out. Our neighbour blew her lid, "You better stay away from our kids, mister! Leave them alone before I call the cops!" "Go ahead," he challenged. "All I did was to offer them some ice cream."

My mom kept her eyes on us, while Mary went in to call the police. Mom tried to engage the man in conversation to keep him there, but he cunningly slithered past our lawn, then the next house, and the next, before ducking around the corner. Within minutes a patrol car arrived. The police pair combed the neighbourhood but the man was nowhere to be found, just minutes after he had been in front of us. The police returned and questioned us further. It was believed the stranger might have had an accomplice parked around the corner waiting for him to appear with an unsuspecting child, who thought he/she was going to get ice cream with a nice new friend. Such a child may then have ended up having their picture on a milk carton months or years later with the words 'Have you seen me?' above it.

Those five years of my childhood spent in the U.S. have contributed significantly to who I am, and how I view the world around me. I was a daring and inquisitive child. I was often able to try things out or seek out answers to my questions in that setting in ways I may not have been able or allowed to do at home at that age. Growing in a predominantly white environment and being counted among the best in most of what I did gave me self-confidence, boldness, and ease with people that are different from me in every possible way. Now, I am able to respect others as fellow human beings without thinking for a minute that their colour or upbringing alone makes them superior or inferior to me, a view some uneducated people at home share with some sometimes educated but nonetheless narrow-minded Westerners. Partly due to my multicultural experiences, I desire to encourage love and appropriate respect amongst the rainbow of peoples of the world.

[FK: The Asana family returned to Cameroon in 1989, where the Rev. Dr. Asana has served in many positions in the Presbyterian Church in Cameroon (PCC). As of 2006 he was serving as PCC Synod Clerk, and as a leading committee member of the World Council of Churches.

To cap off the story in the U.S. let me now introduce you to a poem by a Harvard student who lived just around the corner from where the Asanas lived, but did not know it. The poem captures life in America in a remarkable way. Enjoy]

From Dust to Snow: The African Dream?

It's the land of milk 'n honey we are told,
Where streets glimmer and glow
With intentions kind and gentle.
This land of freedom 'n some fifty states
Carries with it the pride and price to pay,
The rigor, the riches and reward
For the hard working, the pure in spirit.
May we cherish before we perish
The labor of a people
Forged and formed by destiny.
I will to where "In God we trust".
That day I'll say, good Lord
America here I come!

Towers and ramps and winding streets,
Oh Boston what a maze.
The haste and half-baked smiles
Were hard to catch up with.
The stench smell of burnt gasoline
Few friends on whom to lean.
I'm here to study hard,
I said in self-motivation
America here I come!

Hay you man of Africa!
Oh no! I come from Cameroon.
How come you made me out?
The way you dressed, ya walk 'n talk.
At the Marriot for lunch, shall we?
A lunch to welcome you,
We'll split the bill in half.
It will be time well spent.
I smiled then ground and pondered,
Is this for real "The promised land?"
America here I come!

I stood and stared in disbelief,
In shock at what I heard.
With potluck lunches and BBQs
"No meal" you are told "is free".
All that's news are bad bed tales,
A shooting, an arson
A rape or child abuse

America, here I come!

You walk the streets in town
Your hat and heart in hand.
Streets smartness rewards your fight
Anger is voiced as F.Y.A.
A million acronyms and abbreviations.
Information sharing is not gossiping,
Or keep your stories and privacy.
Humble not and market yourself
And favor not or bribe your kind.
But networking and lobbying we must
And in so doing by gentle persuasion.
If this is it, I'm not sure I want to say
America here I come.

No I'll take up courage and say,
America here I come!
To make the best of what I can
I'll take mistakes for some I'll make.
I'll pick up values and some I'll give.
America here I come.
I'll fly with your eagle
But walk with my lion.
I'll make myself a better me.
In objectivity and in judgement
America here I come

"My choice weapon remains the pen, not the sword
But courage I must to skin the cat another way.
I'll stitch in time to save nine
And earn a penny by saving one".
America here I come
I'll make haste but not break my pants,
Prove myself I will not do.
Whether I fall, I'll rise
Whether I rise, I'll further rise
Succeed I must, succeed I will
America here I come!

Wilfred Mbacham, Harvard University, Boston, MA

[FK: Professor Mbacham did not only succeed, he made Africa proud at Harvard by his excellent performance. He is presently a faculty member at the University of Yaoundé I and also founding president of the Fobang

Foundation. He is also holder of a Bill Gate's foundation Malaria Research Fellowship.

Professor Mbacham says: "You know, for someone who was born in Africa, came to the United States, and was not attracted by all the opportunities that are there, I felt I had to return and make things happen back here. I am satisfied because I have been able to touch the lives of many people. Money for me wasn't the ultimate happiness, and just by being persistent, the money is starting to come. We will continue to push as far as our energies permit and hope that there are other people who will take over. If African researchers can just persist and do good work, they will be noticed by the funders. This is what Africa needs, not a brain drain to the West, leaving Africa to suffer. "]

Chapter 3

Studying in Nobel Prize Country

'When the dog decides to meet the goat, his friend, he must be prepared to eat grass with it.' – African saying

Nothing is more frustrating than graduating from the university only to find you still dependent on your parents and family members. Years go by, you get older, yet you are hopelessly at the same spot. The situation is made worse where the Bachelor's degree is fast loosing ground in Cameroon. Go anywhere to look for a job, if you could be given the opportunity to go through the application before the interview, you realise there is just no need for you to show up at the interview. Why? The number of applicants with Master's degrees far outweighs applicants with Bachelor's degrees, which is your own circle.

This is the situation I found myself in, after graduating from the University of Buea. I could not support myself, let alone family members who put hands together to see me through my university studies. To salvage this situation, I needed a degree higher than the Bachelor's. Could I not get this Master's degree in Cameroon? Yea, I could, but one thing, however, pushed me to apply for a Master's degree program in Sweden – free education in Sweden. Motivated by this, I assembled documents for a Master's degree program at the Umeå University in Sweden.

I got the admission, and the next step was that of obtaining a visa. I assembled the documents necessary for a Swedish student visa for international students. Barely two weeks after forwarding my documents, I got news from the Swedish consulate in Douala that my visa had been approved. Was this news! Just then I saw the brightest of futures I have ever imagined for myself in my life. I was feeling on top of the world. I longed for a very close one to break the news to. I rushed back to end-of-tar Longla, but did not meet Henry in his room. Down I darted to the common room, where I saw him at the far end playing cards with Genesis in the midst of rowdy and excited supporters. I drew near and called out, 'H-e-n-r-y!' He knew immediately that I certainly was up to something great, for he could see the word 'excitement' written all over my face. "What's the matter?" he asked, as he came up to me bumping into the chairs that obstructed his way.

From Dust to Snow: The African Dream?

I took my time breaking the news to him, enjoying every word that tumbled out of my mouth. As is almost the normal tradition of Cameroonians, we went for a drink, accompanied by our pal Genesis. Watch out! I said we went for a drink, but it later on turned out that we went for drinks, for I could hardly tell how I found myself on my bed the following morning. How I got home, God alone knows. It occurred to me the following morning that I seemed to have made the send-off party when I was still about a month or so before take-off. One thing I could not have forgotten to do, as excited as I was, was to thank the Almighty for the new door He opened in my life; I was determined to make just the best out of it.

The one month I had before taking off seemed like an eternity. At last, it was August 21st 2002; my flight was scheduled for 10:00 p.m. that day at the Douala international airport. I will hardly forget this day in my life. It rained fit to drown a duck. I had last minute items to shop for that day. I returned to the house totally wet. We left the house at about 8:30 p.m. for the airport, though I was advised to be there by 6:00 p.m. That same afternoon, as I was taking off from Buea for Douala, Roseline said to me: "Robby, I can imagine how you will cry at the airport for leaving your loved ones behind." I told her, "If you think I will let gold go for the price of tin, then you've got to have your head examined." Why should I cry when taking off to greener pasture? I saw then just no reason why I should. I went through the checks and all was o.k. It was close to take off time. As I fastened my seat belt, it suddenly occurred to me then what I had left behind: my family, and loved ones. I now could understand why my elder sister and brother had to shed tears at the airport. I did not know if or when I will ever see my loved ones again. As the plane roared down the runway, I gave no thought of the challenges that lay ahead of me, all I knew was – I was finally off, heading to my long dreamed land.

Though I had Umeå as my final destination, I could not head straight to Umeå without making a stop at Göteborg, the second largest town in Sweden. I was picked up at the Göteborg airport by one of my two best friends (Nche and Denis, popularly known as Dr. Bush). These guys, who had been in Europe a year before me, laid a red carpet for me. The welcome party was a gesture that remains permanently stamped on my memory. My one-week's stay in Göteborg in the company of these two guys was a short period in my life I'll hardly forget. We took the town to pieces, as we visited snack bars and major sites and tourist attractions in the city. We rounded up the festivities of the week with a visit to the most popular nightclub in town.

My brief stay in Göteborg went a very long way to greatly strengthen the wrong and very stupid impression I left Cameroon with about Europe – the impression in every other person's mind back in

Cameroon who has not lived the experience, that Europe is a bed of roses. In fact, I left Göteborg with this impression deeply rooted in me that I found it pretty difficult to believe I was still in Europe following the predicaments, which awaited my arrival in my town Umeå. I hit Umeå at Martina's hour (11:30 p.m.) and was picked up by a friend and former classmate of mine in the University of Buea, whose name I withhold. It turned out that things were hardly to be the same in Umeå as they were in Göteborg. I could hardly bring myself to believe that I was in Europe then. The situation presented itself far worse than in Cameroon. I guess it will be proper if I begin at the beginning with my experiences in Umeå.

By the time I arrived the house, I was hungry enough to eat a horse. Unfortunately, my friend had been busy the whole day and could not find time to prepare something, even though, he knew I was on my way to Umeå. In the morning we paid a visit to the supermarket. It was splendid, I must admit. I was particularly attracted by one shelf, a shelf with very beautiful and highly appetising apples. I pushed aside my friend and reached for one. This, I polished on my sleeve before sinking my teeth into it. The attempt made by my friend to stop me was in vain. He was just too late. Before he could realise, peristaltic movements down my oesophagus were following the first bite of the apple. I noticed then that I was a point of attraction in the supermarket. All eyes were on me. What is wrong with that? I asked myself. Is it not normal that we 'taste' oranges, mangos, guavas back home (in Cameroon) before buying? It dawned on me then that I had changed environments. This did not in any way stop me from finishing my apple. The deed had already been done, and I knew it would even be more stupid if I stopped eating it. I equally noticed one thing in the supermarket that sent a cold chill crawling down my spine; prices of commodities were nonnegotiable!

Why this cold chill down my spine? Honestly, I had very little money on me comparatively. I relied on picking up a job, but was that something easy to get? Within a few days, not very much was left of what I considered in Cameroon to be a very huge sum of money on me. My own share of the one-month's rents made away with about a quarter portion of my dough. I saw my money fast dwindling away like the morning mist. Worst of all, no job yet! After a month, I could hardly say I had any money left on me, and to be frank, my friend was the I-don't-give-a-damn-about-your-situation kind of a friend. It meant nothing to him whether I ate or not. To say I found myself in a fix will be making one of the world's greatest understatements. I noticed my difficulties were fast narrowing into a crisis, and yet no job. After two months, if I could be allowed to consider the apartment I shared with my friend a state on its own, then I will be very right to qualify that the state was facing an economic crisis. Did the "head of state" care? A chronic economic devastation plunged in when I could no longer meet up with my own contributions to the "national budget". The "head of state" sent me on exile. Little did I know my expulsion from the "state" would turn out temporally good for me! In my new "state", for the first few days, I found things very contrary to the first. The "head of state" here was a compassionate guy and a former secondary school classmate, but he had gotten entangled with one Swedish girl who was equally of the go-jump-into-a-lake-with-your-crisis type. I soon found out that my friend was equally at the mercy of this girl and had no voice in the house. Any decision the girl took was final. I considered this pure madness. Within a week, my situation in my new "state" was not any different from the first. I had to move, and move fast; otherwise, I would have been on board the next flight to Cameroon.

Amidst my predicaments, vis-à-vis my academic challenges, I must proudly say here that if there is one big thing I did achieve in Sweden, it is my education. Thank God, He made me hold steadfast to it during the turbulent moments. Anybody who has lived the experience will agree with me that this is the most tempting moment to damn the education thing to hell. If I did, which I almost did, then I would never have stopped regretting the whole of my life. Things finally got well cemented thanks to Ethel, a Cameroonian sister in the chemistry department of the University of Umeå, who helped me pick up a job. It was not only a job, but also one that paid well. Then, I was able to move into my own student flat, able to pay my bills, and be "head of state" in my own "state". Thank you Ethel!

Wait a minute; I guess I did skip quite much of my first experiences in school. The first thing I got from my program coordinator was my key to the computer labs. Here I noticed something that later on became of top importance to me – free Internet! This was something hardly within reach in Cameroon at the time. I found it difficult to believe the fact that I was exposed to the net 24 hours on 24. As I mentioned earlier, these free services became of prime importance to me for I could sit in front of the computer the whole day without feeling bored. The computers, I must confess, became my prime console. Most of my difficulties and frustrations were buried on the keyboard. Honestly speaking, the computers became my greatest companion – no friends, no relatives, what a style of life indeed!

The situation was made worse by the fact that the Swedes are a very reserved class of people. A typical Swede sitting next to you will never start up a discussion if you don't start one. Imagine living with a neighbour you may never set eyes on! It is six months today since I moved into my new student flat. Each time I slam my door, my neighbour's dog barks. For these six months, I have never seen this dog or its owner. From this, one can see how lonely it can be. They prefer to spend time playing with their pets, rather than finding time to sit and chat with friends. One other outstanding characteristic of Swedes is self-centeredness, and from the few other Europeans countries I have been in, I can say without loss of generality that this is equally a typical characteristic of most Europeans. Imagine finding yourself in a society where nobody gives a damn about his neighbour. One thinks only of oneself. This is very contrary to a typical African society, where my problem becomes automatically my neighbour's problem.

It becomes very frustrating if you leave from a country where Christianity is the talk of the day, and suddenly find yourself in one where it is almost impossible to hear that word pronounced for almost your entire lifetime there. If you live in Sweden and end up in paradise, then you must have had a very sound Christian background back home. I will not be very wrong if I say here that not up to 2% of Sweden's population knows the word God, let alone live according to His ways. Don't get me wrong. Ask any Swede if he/she is a Christian, and he stands there staring down at you the way a farmer examines a prize bull. It is rather unfortunate that each major section of the city has a church building that could contain lots of people. But get in there on Sundays during official worship hours, you find almost all the seats empty. One thing beats my imagination till moment. Is Cameroon really preaching religion or Christianity? With Cameroon's large religious population, how can one explain the fact that Sweden which is almost void of religion and hence Christianity is far more advanced in almost everything than Cameroon, which has over 70% of its population being "followers of Christ?" What are the hallmarks of true spirituality? Is it reciting the Holy scriptures from cover to cover? Is it the singing of hymns, the wearing of splendid robes by the clergy, carrying the Bible under the armpit and declaring unlike persons sinners? Are men of God more spiritual because of the genuflection and respect from the lowly, the poor, meek and gullible? Can spirituality be bought and can titles (Reverend, Elder, Bishop, Father, Chorister, Deacon, just to name a few) and church going lay claim to it? My dear Cameroonian and African brethren, what spiritual food are you preparing to sustain you in the great world beyond after this life's brief jamboree? I pray your answer be that of a true Christian, a true child of God. Again don't get me wrong. I did not just bring this in for the sake of preaching. Honestly speaking, the few Swedes you meet in church, who are Christians are examples of children of God. Is it not therefore better to have a few who are true Christians than a mass dancing left and right with no reasonable destination?

Every coin has its reverse side. There is one striking good aspect of a typical Swede that will live in me the rest of my life – honesty. A

From Dust to Snow: The African Dream?

Swede sees no reason why he should steal or lie and equally sees no reason why you should lie. They tend to believe whatever you tell them, and they give you that confidence and trust unless you abuse it. I guess a typical incidence here will better substantiate the point. One day, I misplaced my wallet and phone on campus. In the wallet were three thousand five hundred Swedish crowns (approximately 350 euros). When I discovered later that I had misplaced these items, I dialled my number. My phone never rang. I came to a conclusion after several trials in vain that the person who picked them up must have turned off the phone. About four days went by; all attempts I made towards recovering the missing items came up to a blank wall. I finally gave up all hope towards recovering those items. One week went by. On the 8th day, after classes, I decided to stop and check my mailbox in school (each student has a departmental mail box). In it, I found a well-sealed envelope addressed "SURPRISE", no name on it. I felt the items inside. They were hard. Despite the fact that my name wasn't on the envelope, I tore it open. Inside I found my wallet and phone. Astonishingly, the contents of the wallet were intact; no penny was missing from it! My phone was however off as I had predicted. When I turned it on, it blinked red, indicating that the battery had run down. It occurred to me then that the phone's battery had certainly been down by the time I had dialled, and so the call hadn't gone through. I stood there, dumfounded, not thinking about anything in particular. Minutes crawled by, and by the time I came back to myself, I realized I had been standing there for close to ten minutes. The sixty thousand dollar question now is: "Would you and I have equally returned those items to the rightful owner if we picked them?" The answer lies in our consciences. This trickles one other incidence into my grey cells, which I will equally recount.

During our very first week in school, some Spanish friends of mine and I went visiting in the city centre and got to a museum. Just at the entrance of the museum, you have a coffee boiler, where you take coffee if you want to, and then place five Swedish crowns there. There was no attendant, just a matter of the conscience again here. Funny enough, there was enough money there such that if your money needs change, you just pick up your balance and walk away. One guy on our team took the coffee and left without paying. The other team members reminded him that he had not paid for his coffee, and guess what he said? "I guess I have a lot of conscience, otherwise, I would have picked some money there, added to the coffee and left." Suppose such a guy had come in contact with my phone and wallet, would I have ever recovered them?

There is equally one other striking aspect of Sweden – top security. To be honest, I feel more secure in Sweden than in my home country. I could move about very freely at any hour of the night without fear of armed robbery or ambushing. There is of course no reason why a Swede should get involved in such activities. What initiates a majority of persons to get involved in robbery is poverty and hunger. Swedes enjoy social allowances. An average Swede will never complain of hunger. They have the basic necessities needed to sustain life.

Duty consciousness. Enter any office in Sweden and you are treated like a king. It wasn't until I came to Sweden that I knew that a worker in any office is the servant, and the customer the king. This is very much contrary to the situation back in Cameroon, where when you enter an office, nobody gives a damn how long you stand there. The worker makes himself very comfortable in his revolving chair feeling like a king. Moreover, in Sweden services are rendered to customers on first-come- first-serve basis. How are services rendered to customers back home? The order in which you are served in an office in Cameroon depends on the type of "studs" you have in that office (that is your personal relationship with the workers). Those with iron studs are served first, irrespective of when they arrived. Unlike the situation back in Cameroon, before you earn a single penny in Sweden, you must have toiled hard for it. A civil servant in Cameroon goes for about three weeks of the four in a month without passing at his/her job site, yet at the end of the month he gets his full salary and nobody queries him/her. This is weird, and is direct stealing from the state. I know it will be a big puzzle to many Cameroonians to learn that a female minister in Sweden was charged with a very heavy fine and dismissed from her post just for the fact that she used a state credit card to buy napkins for her child. Somebody is certainly saying, "Just napkins and she was fired?" Of course, yes. If nothing is done after buying the napkins, then tomorrow it is certain that she will use the card to buy a baby bike, then gradually to her own bike, and finally to a car for herself. It is therefore wiser to stop this theft at the preliminary state before it goes worse. How many such incidences are sanctioned in Cameroon? Just coming late to work in Sweden, you answer a query to that, let alone staying away from work without permission. What a well-organized and balanced system indeed. No room for laziness. Gender equality is about a hundred percent. Here, a woman does just anything that a man could have done, and contributes equally to nation building. About 52% of Cameroon's total population is made up of women, and what level of development do we think we can attain if the voice of the majority (that of the woman) is not listened to?

The technological differences are innumerable. Sweden is so technologically advanced such that machines tend to do almost everything. Get to a fuel station, you find there is nobody to attend to you. You just slot in your card and pump your fuel yourself.

Having had my feet planted firmly, I decided it was time to know places in Umeå. My first target was to know how club life in Umeå looks like. I started at the famous nightclub in town. Unlike the club in Göteborg, where there was provision for security, there was none here. I elbowed my way through the teeming crowd to the bar, where I ordered a glass of cider. I asked the bar attendant to add some cubes of ice; this he did. I paid for my drink, and moved to the farthest end of the bar in a good position to give myself a clear view of the club. I pulled up a stool, climbed on it and leaned back against the wall. I wasn't really in dancing mood, especially, as I wasn't with my pals. I sat there for as long as I can remember, while sipping my drink gradually. Then something happened! I felt a warm touch around my arm. I gave myself some seconds to consider the touch. One thing was clear; from the warmth of it, I concluded, and of course rightly that it was a feminine touch. I turned slowly in the direction. My eyes met those of a blond, her hand still holding my arm. She was quite a beauty, I must admit, with perfect symmetry. She flashed on a smile as bright as a neon sign that sent hot sensations crawling up my spine. "Hejsan", I said in Swedish. "Kan vi danser", was her response. I climbed down from the stool and what followed next was a nightmare that will live with me for as long as I live.

The dancing progressed smoothly, and she was an excellent dancer, I must equally admit. After about two minutes or so, I felt another touch on my arm. Unlike the first, this one was a cold grip, one that conveyed the fact that something was certainly wrong. I spun around immediately, equally trying in vain at the same time to free my arm. "What do you think you're doing?" came a roar from a tall muscularly built ill looking figure of a man with a bullet shaped head perched on a very long neck. It wouldn't be wrong to conclude from first sight that this guy was fit for the ring. I glanced up; my eyes met a pair of others. From the look of them, the man appeared to have been drinking a lot that night. He certainly was drunk, I concluded. He dragged me out of the bar to a dimly lit corridor that offered a variety of smells, from stale garbage to unwashed bodies. He produced a key from his pocket, opened a door, and ordered me in. This I did obediently having registered the door number in my mind; in case things would turn out rough, I would have to call for help. I had my cell phone with me.

We walked into a room that smelled of fornication. Without another word, he gave me a slap that sent me crashing down the floor. I fought my way back to standing. The door burst open and the blond rushed in. I stole a glance at her, a mistake, a very terrible mistake, for this guy sapped me the second time. Believe me, when this guy saps you, you stay sapped. I drifted into a world full of stars and bright lights as I went crashing down the floor again. Thank God, my stay in my new found galaxy was very brief. As I was recovering, I saw this moron approaching me with the word 'kill' written all over his face. Immediately, I did the most intelligent thing I have ever done and will possibly ever do in my life. I apologised. "I'm sorry," I said, even though, I knew pretty well that I had done nothing wrong that warranted an apology to this freak. I noticed then the powers buried behind certain words. These words suspended the punch from his hand in mid air, as if stopped by some powerful magnet. Contrary to what I thought he would do, he flashed on a smile showing a pair of white teeth and a lot of gum. When this guy smiled, he looked handsome. He extended his hand with fingers that looked more like rods than real human fingers. The fingers appeared as though they were placed under a powerful electron microscope. I hesitated for a moment and then extended mine. He grabbed it; my palm completely swallowed by his, pulled me up and released me. I stood there like a stone man, while my heart did rock n' roll. The blonde was nowhere to be found. I figure she must have escaped the frightful sight of the scene. Without a word again, this maniac grabbed me by the hand and conducted me through the crowd to the bar.

Without asking my choice he ordered two beers. I wasn't in drinking mood, but to please this beast in man's clothing, I was left with no choice. We sat there for about five minutes without a word from either of us. I looked at him and wondered what was cooking up behind that dangerous mind of his. He appeared to be speaking to himself, for his face was full of contours, resembling that of a mathematician faced with a challenging mathematical problem. I found I was close to laughing. Immediately, he looked in my direction. I hid a grin behind my glass as I 'zipped' from it. He finally broke the silence, and as if reading my thoughts he said, "Thinking I'm nuts?" My heart somersaulted, for the cold look in his eyes was returning. Then something again happened, my chance of escape! He got up and walked across the bar to the far end. My gaze followed his direction. What I saw brought a smile to my lips for the first time since I came in contact with this lunatic – I saw the blonde talking and laughing happily with another guy, equally my height and build. "He's got his next victim for the torture chamber" I quipped to myself. I abandoned the drinks, snapped my jacket, picked up my face cap, slapped it on my head, and bolted out of the club. I squinted, glancing back time and again to see if this bully was after me as I legged it back to my room, my heart missing a beat each time a tall figure came into sight. I scarcely slept that night.

The following day, a very bright Saturday afternoon, I went down town and entered a café where I ordered a hamburger and a cup of

From Dust to Snow: The African Dream?

coffee. My eyes roamed around the room. Seated at a table in one corner was this maniac, together with the blonde. I turned to dash out of the café. "Don't go", the guy ordered. I stopped, determined in my mind that none of what happened last night would repeat itself. He left his table and walked up to me. I turned slowly and my eyes met his directly. "I'm sorry, very sorry", he said. "I never knew what drove me crazy last night", he continued. "Never mind, it's okay," I said while boiling inwardly with anger and rage. By this time, the blonde had crept from their table up to us and equally immediately apologised. They invited me to join them at their table. This I did. He signalled the waiter and ordered fruit juice for us. In the course of drinking and discussing, I learnt this bully was a German and the blonde a Swede. It was of no surprise to me learning that this guy wasn't a Swede. His behaviour did not in any way reflect that of Swedes, who are a peace loving set of the human race. From when I left this funny couple that bright Saturday afternoon till now, I've never met either of them again. It is my greatest prayer never to.

Do those in Europe lack anything? When somebody in Europe tells his/her friends back home that his time has come to come back home finally, those back home think he must be nuts. This I know pretty well, because I used to think the same way. What are you coming back home to do when you have everything out there? Have you ever imagined yourself spending years without seeing the dearest persons in your life? How do you expect to be happy when all those to make you happy are thousands of kilometres away from you? The greatest illness I face out in Europe is homesickness. I miss my family and friends that much that it takes me almost a quarter of my earnings a month for phone calls to Cameroon, as an attempt to be closer to my dear ones. You will never know how valuable something is to you until you are robbed of it. It meant nothing to me just to sit back there in Cameroon, chat with friends and have some fun together. Out in Europe, those gatherings are not there. Even if there are, they are very rare. I guess one thing that greatly contributes to the lack of this togetherness out in Europe is the fact that life out in "bush" is like a rat race. You just keep running from one thing to the other until at the end of the day you realise that you have forgotten to eat. For example, yesterday it wasn't until about 7:00 p.m., when I smelled onion being fried in my neighbour's room, that I realized I was hungry. It is not a strange thing to hear someone either in America or Europe complaining of time. When I was back there in Cameroon, I would often ask whether these guys out here wanted God to have made their own day to be 28 hours. Even so, this will still not be enough. I stated somewhere before that when I just arrived in Sweden I could sit on the computer 24 hours on 24. I know it will greatly surprise people back home that I now live with the internet in my room yet am unable to check my mail for a whole day!

The general notion back home is that once you've had your visa, it is the end of hard times, the end of misery, and the beginning of a completely new and happy life for the individual in particular, and his family in general. On the contrary, I must remind you that it is not the end of the journey. Rather, to me, it is just the beginning of yet another hard task that lies ahead. Before long, you come to realize that you've just walked out of an old set of problems into a completely new set of problems. At this moment, you do not need to sit, fold your arms and wait for things to happen – they never will. You have to make things happen. You must think and think deeply. A man is the product of his thoughts; what you think (that) you become. Honestly, hard work pays out in Europe, and in order to succeed, it takes an ability to set your priorities in the right order. Life is nothing short of a nightmare if you start by misplacing priorities. The worst mistake many often make is to let the system "consume" them. You will hardly be able to find your way out of it if that happens. What then becomes of those you left back home expecting quite much from you? If one could be able to put in the same amount of efforts put back home in an attempt to succeed in life, then you will sail through greatly.

The beginning is always rough, no doubt, but the end justifies the means. I am sailing through my academic work here excellently, and therefore, I say it without mixing words that my objectives and expectations out in Europe are met. I give thanks to The Almighty for this.

It will not be very appropriate, if I should conclude without a word to my African brothers who are thinking of travelling to Europe for one thing or the other. It is no bed of roses. To those who already have comfortable and well-paid jobs, you stand to regret for the rest of your life if you make that mistake to leave the job and travel out to "hustle". By the time you realise, and make up you mind to go back home, it might just have been too late for you. To those who find themselves in a similar situation to the one I had before leaving, remember that we are living in an era experiencing changes at an astronomical rate. The lazy and the slow have no future in this era. You must therefore try to keep pace and stretch your head above the rough tides, lest you be swept along. For those within this circle, I will not discourage your travelling abroad. However, remember you have to face just a lot of odds especially at the beginning, some of which may include: language barrier, racism in some cases, loneliness. When the dog decides to meet the goat, his friend, he must be prepared to eat grass with it. To those who are already out in Europe, we envy this place because the citizens contributed their various quotas to make their country what it is now. We must therefore bear in mind that we have to take home the knowledge gathered to help build our respective countries and make it a better place for future generations.

Robinson Mukwanka

[FK: While in Sweden, Robinson unfortunately, lost his brother and sister within a period of one year. He dedicates this contribution to their memory. He completed his Master's studies and got married to the beautiful Fanny. Robinson moved to Idaho in 2006 for a PhD program.

As Sweden is home to the world's most revered award, the Nobel Prize, we hope Robinson and the other African scientists in Diaspora can bring Sub-Saharan Africa the Nobel Prize in a Science Discipline.]

Chapter 4

Where in Texas is Nigeria?

'Within every African American lies a pure African – one whose blood lines are not "diluted" by interracial integration or rape committed by whites during slavery – a DNA signature strong enough to link African Americans back to their specific ancestral home in Africa'. –Chicago Sun-Times.

It all started in June of 1998. I had just graduated from secondary school in Benin City, Nigeria, and it was time to start thinking about my future. The most important decision was already made for me – I would be going to university abroad. My older sister had just left for a university in the United States, and my parents decided I would follow suit. However, this is pretty much where their assistance in the decision-making process stopped. Handing over the reins to me, they informed me I was chiefly responsible for my admission, reassuring me they were always there for advice and money (oh so important!); but the ball was now most definitely in my court.

So, here I was, a youthful 16 years of age embarking on the task of charting my immediate future. Seeing how young I was, it was decided I would wait a year before departing for the university. I had one year to make it work. The following 6 months were a whirlwind of online applications, S.A.T exams, recommendation letters and essay writing. Once I had sent in all the necessary application documents, I was finally able to take a breather and reflect. "I'm going half way across the globe, without my family!" When I was younger, I had lived in the Netherlands for a while with my family. My father's job had taken us there. However, this would be different; I would be embarking on this journey as an adult of sorts, left to experiences and deductions of my own, devoid of the sheltering presence of my parents or immediate family. I was excited, eager; I wouldn't let myself think of any negatives, at least not yet.

The letter of acceptance arrived early in 1999. I would be going to the University of Texas at Austin. Now, I had to get a visa. I called the American embassy in Lagos, and set up a visa interview. At this time, there were several stories of rejections coupled with words of advice about what to do on the interview day. I simply committed it into God's hands and didn't think much about it. The day before the interview, I made the trip down to Lagos with my mum, who was my chaperone and moral support. Some more prayers and a good night's rest later, I was in the American Embassy waiting for my number to come over the loud speakers. After a substantial wait, I was called and made my way over to the interview window. "What do you intend to study?" the consular officer, a lady, asked. "Physics," I responded. That appeared to surprise her. However, she ensued to ask the standard questions for financial support papers, admission letters, I-20, and the like. "Have fun in Texas!" And with that, she returned my documents with an appointment to get my visa at a later time. Evidently my prayers were answered! My visa interview went by without a hitch, and now all that remained was the countdown to departure.

My departure date was set for the first week of August in 1999, since I had to attend Orientation at the university during the second week. The months between my embassy visit and my departure were spent between working (I had a job), packing, and saying my goodbyes. Some were emotional, like the goodbye at my church, while others were light-hearted and jovial. Thank God, my mom was accompanying me on the trip. She was going to help with the initial settling down process, including assistance with things like opening up a bank account (At the age of 17, I wasn't yet considered an adult in the U.S). My first real sense of departure occurred when I was flying out of Warri to Lagos. My family and some friends gathered at the airport to wait with me before I had to leave. With mixed feelings of sadness and anticipation, the goodbyes were a little awkward. It was the first time it really sunk in that I was leaving. The departure from Lagos was a lot easier; I went to sleep on one side of the world, and would be waking up on another.

I arrived in Houston, Texas, in the first week of August. Going through immigration was easy enough, no big shocks. I was tired after the long trip and wanted to go to bed. Once we were through, our host was there to meet us at the baggage terminal. Chatting, we made our way to the exit. As we stepped out into the Houston atmosphere, it was then I got my first of many American surprises. It felt like I had stepped into a blanket of hot moist air. The air was so thick, heavy, and hot that I almost took a 'double-take' to make sure we hadn't been duped into thinking we had ever left Nigeria. That was my first taste of a Texan Summer! Apparently, August is the hottest part of the year in Texas, and Houston is legendary for its humidity.

After a short stay in Houston, we made our way to Austin. In Houston, we had lodged at our host's residence. In Austin, we had no host; so, we spent the few nights before the dorms opened in a youth hostel. This was an interesting experience. A youth hostel is not like your typical hotel; actually it's not a hotel at all. Essentially, it's supposed to be affordable accommodation for people making transitional stops, or

Where in Texas is Nigeria?

people making backpacking trips around the country. It was here that I made my first acquaintances. They were about 7 of them in total; only none of them was American. They were all foreigners like me. It turns out we all had something in common. We were all going to be attending the University of Texas at Austin that fall (during the semester starting in August), and we were all temporarily lodging in the youth hostel while waiting for more permanent accommodation. The represented countries were quite diverse: France, Spain, Ireland, Australia, England, Romania, and of course Nigeria. We had several engaging and educational discussions. From the youth hostel, I went to the dorm. After my mom helped me with some shopping and moving into the dorm, she said her goodbyes and then I was on my own.

My time in the dorm was my first real encounter with a bunch of Americans. All the girls on the floor were Americans including my roommate. The time at the dorm was fun, and an experience in learning about the American culture. The dorms are a really good way to spend your first year. Being on campus, you're right next to all your classes. In addition, there are a lot of activities on campus that are put on for residents, so you get to interact with and meet a lot of people.

Some of the more memorable first experiences in Texas were when some painfully ignorant Americans asked me some of the completely 'absurd' questions. It was soon to be my conclusion that the average American did not take an interest into affairs of the outside world. Being August 1999, Nigeria had just transitioned in May from a military dictatorship to a democratically elected cabinet. The swearing in ceremony of the new president was covered by several news leaders including CNN, and had in its attendance several prominent leaders, many Americans amongst them. By this token, I was sure that at least some Americans were a little aware of where Nigeria was located. This was not to be reflected by some of the questions I had about Nigeria in the early months following my arrival. By far the most amusing was the question posed by an individual, after I had just revealed that I was from Nigeria. "Oh Nigeria - really? Where in Texas is that?" And then, there were the questions that were so stereotypical that you thought they could only be asked in the context of a film. "So do you all live in trees?" "You have Internet in Nigeria?" "Are there wild animals playing in your backyard?" After a while, I started having a little fun with them. In my response to the last question, I answered, "Oh yes, there are several varieties of animals; only my parents won't let me play with the lions, because they think it's too dangerous." The individual's eyes brightened at my response. Eagerly he quipped, "Really?" I smartly responded, "No." His face fell instantly. I then spent a few minutes trying to explain to him that Nigeria and most of West Africa have mangrove vegetation as opposed to the safari friendly savannah vegetation that a lot of people think is synonymous with Africa, when in actuality that type of vegetation is mostly in the eastern part of the continent.

Another interesting experience occurred due to my particular circumstances. Like I mentioned before, I majored in physics. In my department, not only was I one of the few girls, but also I was the only person of colour. This fact was never apparent to me per say, and it was never highlighted in an awkward manner. However, the fact that it was by no means the norm was evident in my experience with trying to get a job in the department. The method I chose in looking for a job was to simply walk around the department and knock on doors, asking the professors if they had any positions available. Although the first time around I had little luck, my awareness of my complexion was heightened. During my interactions with the professors, I observed a general look of confusion mixed with surprise on their faces. It was as if they were puzzled to be seeing a black person (the fact that I was a girl didn't help either) approaching them for employment. Don't misunderstand me. There was nothing negative about their actions. It was just apparent that there was an element of disbelief in their reactions. Even in my fourth year in the department, I was still surprising some professors. During a departmental ceremony in which they were presenting some students with certificates, the time came when it was my turn to receive my certificate. After the inevitable butchering of the pronunciation of my name, I went up to receive my certificate. As I was receiving my certificate, the president of the department who was presenting the certificates blurted out, "You don't look like a physics major." I simply responded with a knowing smile.

The historical past of the United States has made it a country with interesting demographics. As a result of the slave trade, there is an African American race in the country, albeit a minority one. Normally, as an African, when I visit a foreign non-African country, it is apparent I am a tourist or foreigner. However, because there is an African American race in the U.S, it is not immediately obvious that I am not an American citizen. Instead, it is often assumed that I am just a member of the Black American population. However, in the midst of this apparent connection, apart from our common heritage, there are a lot of differences between native Africans and African Americans. Unfortunately, these differences have often led to the creation of a gulf and not a bridge between Africans and African Americans. On my campus alone, there were several forums to address the issues of this friction between the African and African American communities on campus. It is not that there is necessarily a sense of animosity between the two groups, but more a lack of the sense of solidarity.

During my participation in these forums, I formed the opinion that the friction between these groups is due to the lack of education, and therefore, tolerance for the differences in cultural background and experiences. There is a different psychology an individual possesses when he is part of the indigenous race, as opposed to the psychology he possesses when he is part of a subjugated minority race. Understanding this, in my opinion, is crucial to understanding the reason for different outlooks on the same situations. Oftentimes, the friction between the groups is a result of compounded frustration, because one party could not understand the behaviour of the other party. This might seem surprising, since surely, other ethnic groups do not always understand each other's behaviour, and yet do not have a resulting frustration directed towards each other. Nonetheless, the difference is that in the American environment, Africans and African Americans are often lumped into one larger group – 'Black folk'. Hence, there is an involuntary identification issue. One community's actions reflect on the group as a whole; hence, the frustration when one community acts in a manner that is contrary to the expected behaviour placed by the other group, irrespective of whether the acting community is behaving in a manner according to its culture and its experiences.

In addition to the contrasts between the African and African American cultures, I also observed a more general contrast between the African culture and the American culture as a whole. Differences in codes of conduct, in interactions with individuals older than you, and in the amounts of exposure to adult material experienced by youths were apparent, even after the initial months following my arrival. However, in the midst of these differences, similarities were observed.

[FK: Ms Chieze Ebeneche represents an ideal and rare combination of beauty and brain vested in the same body. She holds a B.Sc. in Physics from the University of Texas at Austin. As of 2006 she is a PhD student in the same institution.

Lady C's experience raises the important question: Why do Africans and black Americans often fail to forge relationships in the classroom and the workplace. Here are some opinions:

'They blame nationality, ethnicity, culture, economics and education.'

'Many black Americans (like Americans) are ignorant about Africans. They share comic Eddie Murphy's joke that Africans "ride around butt-naked on a zebra". A black person once asked me if I knew Tarzan. I told him, "Yes, he is my uncle." A lot of African-Americans were taught that Africa was nothing more than just a primitive, backward jungle from whence they came.'

From Dust to Snow: The African Dream?

'Africans have picked up whites' fear of blacks. "Our perception of African-Americans is that they are a race of people who carry guns and are very, very violent."'

'Africans admire the American struggle for civil rights. Yet, when some come to America and discover black is not so beautiful, they insist on maintaining a separate identity. African Americans are surprised about that: "You don't talk or dress black!"'

"When indigenous African people come to the United States, they adopt an attitude of superiority... about individuals who could very well be of their own blood."

'Some African customs, such as female circumcision, shock Americans. Other traditions have been forgotten, or, in the case of Kwanzaa, invented in America.'

'The women's liberation movement has barely caught up to Africa. That's why I think many unions between African men and African-American women don't tend to last. Most African-American women are like, "I'm not going to put up with the notion that you are the absolute head of the household".'

"We are baffled by African Americans' unwillingness to take advantage of America's many opportunities and their willingness to blame most problems on race. "In 1990, the median household income of an African immigrant was $30,907, according to the Center for Research on Immigration Policy in Washington, D.C. That compared with $19,533 for black Americans. Africans who immigrate to the United States come largely from the educated middle class of their countries. The research center reports 47 percent are college graduates and 22 percent have a professional specialty. Only 14 percent of black Americans graduate from college."

"If you visit Nigeria or Ghana, the masses of the people are locked in the same circumstances as poor African-Americans. Both groups seem content to do nothing other than what they are currently doing. The denial among Africans comes from living in a place where all the bodies that surround them look the same as they do. That makes it easier for them to fail to see that the folks who are controlling the whole economy of Nigeria are the oil barons - and they don't look anything like (black) Africans."

'African Americans appreciate their heritage more than Africans do. We have to convince them to preserve the slave dungeons in Ghana or to continue the weaving of the kente cloth. Tours to Africa are booming. Feeling rejected at home, many middle-class African Americans turn to Africa. But in the final analysis, culture won't free you. Any ordinary African will tell you a dearth of culture is not the source of our affliction.'

"We're faced with a situation where 3 to 10 percent of the total trade in Africa happens in Africa. The rest is exported from Africa. The future of all black-skinned people centers in Africa. That is our birthright and someone else has it. The struggle we have to make lies in undergoing a 'new birth', and this time we must not forget to keep our birthright. We must do that together, African and African American, all Africans.'

Interesting don't you think? Before continuing with more student experiences, let us now try asylum and refugee perspectives from Europe and North America. Again we will have 2 from Europe and 2 from the US.]

Chapter 5

From Dust to Snow: From Charles Taylor to Pat Robertson?

'Now why is a freedom-loving, God-fearing man such as Pat Robertson signing on the dotted line with Taylor...?' – The Washington Post

Kamatehun, Liberia (September 2001)

Zizemaza, commander of the "Jungle Force" of Charles Taylor's Armed Forces of Liberia (AFL) pointed at us and said: "You Gbandi people are the brothers and wives of the dissidents. We'll kill any Gbandi person we see." Turning to his soldiers, he said, 'So kill them!' Then thirty or so people, including my Father and Mother, were tied with rope and put inside three houses. They begged, but the soldiers slapped them and told them to shut up. We heard the "pa, pa, pa" of the gun. Then the soldiers lit the houses on fire; and so ended the lives of my Mum and Dad.

Orlando, Florida (July 27 2006)

[FK: *It was one of the rare evenings when John would be home earlier than 10 PM. He had two restaurant jobs at Olive Garden and Boston Market. He worked seven days a week from 6 am to 10 pm. Now, he and his family were having rare quality time together as they watched the movie titled Dreamer. It was kind of awkward for me to break into their quality time at this point, but they were expecting me. The movie Dreamer is inspired by a true story; John, Esther and their three adorable kids had an inspirational story of their own to tell me. John also had a very powerful message for first African female president, Liberian President Ellen Johnson Sirleaf, and for the American people.*

A scrumptious aroma came from the kitchen that made my mouth water. My enzymes were telling me I could really use some of that food. I noticed that they now had a new TV and DVD player. The sofa and loveseat was also newer than the ones I saw the last time I visited them. You could tell they were now relatively settled in Orlando. John told me they had not bought any of it. It had been given to them by goodwill Americans and their caseworker.

From Dust to Snow: From Charles Taylor to Pat Robertson?

A few moments later I was munching some of the delicious food Esther had prepared while John told me their story. It was parboiled Basmati rice drowned in some type of thick palm-oil-saturated yummy peanut sauce.]

I lost both parents in the Liberian Civil war: I was among hundreds of thousands of the Gbandi Liberian Refugees who fled to Guinea to escape the civil unrest. My wife and kids went ahead of me, and, as a male, I was forced to join the LURD (Liberians United for Reconciliation and Democracy). When we said we could not fight, they beat us and rammed me repeatedly with their rifles. You can still see a scar and indentation on my head. It sometimes still makes my head hurt, even now.

One night, some of us escaped into the bushes. We were in the forest for 3 nights and you can imagine what we were eating. Then we trekked on foot for a long long distance through countless checkpoints, where armed groups stripped us of our personal belongings and forced us to pay bribes before allowing us to pass. The UN High Commissioner for Refugees (UNHCR) provided newly arrived refugees with shelter, food, and other basic assistance at transit centers in southern Guinea near the Guinea-Liberia border. UNHCR eventually transferred us further inland to established camps.

I was lucky to have escaped with my wife Esther and 3 children. We lived in the Kouankan camp, housing more than 32,000 Liberian refugees in the Nzerekore area of southern Guinea's remote Forest Region. We the Gbandi people had been targeted for our perceived support of the LURD. LURD had been formed in 1999 by Liberian refugees in West Africa led by Sekou Conneh, and was supported by Guinea from the outset, and allegedly received the tacit support of Britain and the United States.

The International Rescue Committee (IRC) in collaboration with UNHCR helped to settle us at the Camp. Later, we were moved to the Kountaya camp in Guinea. They tried to train some of us to teach the children in the Camp. I was awarded an Attestation of Volunteer Services and a Teacher's Training Certificate that qualified me to teach children at the Refugee Camp. I was originally a primary school teacher while in Monrovia.'

'In the refugee camp you are living outside of space and time, you have no roots, you have no past, and you don't know whether you have a future. You have no voice, you are not a citizen, you have no papers, and sometimes you haven't even got your name. You have to pinch yourself to reassure yourself that, yes, I am alive, I am me, I am a human being, and I am a person.'

From Dust to Snow: The African Dream?

Our hope was the resettlement program. I prayed day and night to be selected. Each day, for what seems like an eternity, families like ours would sit in shaded doorways at the camp, sheltering from the brutal midday sun – girls plaiting each other's hair or women laboriously preparing meals – all of us were aware of the special 'buses' to America, Australia and Canada, but especially America. At the entrance to the camp, the camp Administrator would scrawl updated camp statistics on a large blackboard in his office. Some of the big white letters were of people who had just left the camp and the African Continent all together, either to Australia, Canada or more likely, to the US. Those who resettle in America have the right to call for relations through the US' family reunification program. I had my wife and 3 kids with me and if I were selected for the USA, we would automatically go together. I prayed even harder.

I was classified as a victim of torture, and the US-based NGO, Center for Victims of Torture (CVT) counseled us and referred us to the UN resettlement program, which after verifying our story, would have to decide whether to resettle us or not. Imagine our joy when they did! It was a huge celebration in the camp for our family.

Our Departure from Conakry was on 13 September 2005. The flight to the US lasted 18 hours via Brussels. At Newark, we were given an authorization for political asylum in the US. We connected to Orlando, Florida, and arrived on the 14 of September. Elizabeth from the Catholic Relief Services was waiting for us at the airport. She was very welcoming.

Then the culture shock began! Beginning with the car seats for children: our three kids had to be properly strapped in seat belts and infant car seats. Elizabeth explained she could not drive if all were not wearing their seat belts, including the children! I liked that! I realized soon enough that in America, you have to abide by the rules or laws and there is minimum discrimination. All are equal before the law. That was not how it was in Liberia.

Arrangements had been made for accommodation for us for the first 7 months. After that, we were supposed to be responsible for our rents. That was our first big shock! We could not imagine paying so much money just for rents: $780 for a 2 bed-room apartment. And they planned to increase the rents! A job had been arranged for me at Olive Garden. It was agreed that I would pay 151 dollars a month for three years to repay our travel fare to the US. They gave us food stamps for our food. We were educated about the importance and availability of preventive healthcare – seeking regular health services before a problem arises in order to avoid worse problems in the future. We realized we needed health insurance, which was very expensive. And there are many fellow Americans suffering from this. Thank God we were granted Medicaid.

We met some Jehovah's Witnesses, who, decided to help us with shopping, and donations to help us settle. They also invited us to their Kingdom hall. Church definitely would help our trauma and fears, but I often had to work on Sundays even before getting the second job. The Jehovah witnesses said they did not celebrate Xmas. This was surprising to us, and we were suspicious of the 'church', and stopped going. Later, Esther and the Children started going to the University Presbyterian Church in Orlando, after meeting another African couple, who took them there. It is a predominantly white congregation, but we liked it there. Esther and the kids were picked up and dropped off after Church.

Traditionally in Liberia, educational infrastructure existed mainly in the capital city of Monrovia, with more limited educational opportunities in the rural interior of the country. Schooling was severely disrupted by more than a decade of recurring fighting, as well as repeated periods of flight by those seeking refuge. Though I am educated and can speak English well, my wife, like most Liberian refugees coming to the U.S., has a more rural background and can not really speak English though she understands well. She has been learning fast. Our eldest son himself had experienced multiple disruptions in his education with the wars and movement. In refugee camps, educational exposure was limited. In the US, arrangements had been made for him to attend an elementary school not far from where we now live. Esther stayed home with the other 2 kids

Everyday, I trekked about one and a half miles to work, which was nothing compared to the feats I accomplished in Liberia. We had no car, and it would save us some money, anyway. If I converted 1 dollar, it was about 50 Liberian dollars, and that could do a lot. It brought great joy just by sending home 30 dollars by Western Union.

Some things we had to get used to as parents in the U.S. were the lack of a communal network of support, like extended family for raising children. Even in the refugee camp, we had such a communal spirit. So, Esther had to take care of the children pending a possible job. In America, you are encouraged to be very hard working. Now you understand part of the reason why I work so hard with two jobs. There is another important reason I will tell you shortly.

Computers are still a mystery to me. We missed that evolution for the many years in the refugee camp. It was so amazing when a family friend helped me create an email address. It all still seems like magic to me.

From Dust to Snow: The African Dream?

When I was granted asylum, I was told that after I pay the airfare, at some point, I have to decide whether to return to Liberia or to stay permanently in the U.S. The decision is already made, and I have a plan.

I believe that every African abroad, who has had the opportunities they have, must do something for their home countries. Otherwise, you would have betrayed our mother continent. We have that responsibility. In Liberia, I would be mocked at, if I returned there without having done something to contribute to my country's development or helping create the same opportunities, I have had here, for fellow Africans at home, so they do not necessarily have to be forced to travel abroad as I was.

I work so hard because Esther and I plan to build a house of six bedrooms, each with a toilet and bath. We plan to establish a business to help provide jobs for other Liberians and to support our children to have a future in Liberia. To President Ellen, I say: 'Fight hard to erase bad practices in Liberia. Encourage Liberians abroad like us to come back. Foster equal treatment and opportunities for Liberians like in America; no molestation, promote peace, make education affordable in Liberia, as it is in America (free up to high school, at least)! Make Liberia free and green again. Encourage investment by foreigners in Liberia to create jobs and opportunities and convert our natural resources to wealth for the Liberian people. I have heard that Tele-Evangelist Pat Robertson repeatedly supported former War Lord President Charles Taylor in various episodes of his 700 club program during the US' involvement of the Liberian Civil War in June and July of 2003. It is alleged he even had an 8 million dollar investment in a Liberian Gold mine. We really need such support from America. However, this time: President Ellen, you have to ensure Liberians benefit from this. Create the conditions for investment for sustainable development.'

I wish to thank the American people especially for giving my family a future. Remember that Liberia was founded as a Republic in 1847 by freed American slaves. We Liberians may distinguish ourselves from one another by whether we are descendents of Americo-Liberians (the original American freed slaves), or whether we trace our heritage to one of the 16 indigenous groups traditionally located outside of the capital city of Monrovia. We are often conscious of last names as an indication of one's ethnic heritage. While the American Slaves descended from Africa, Liberians also descend from America, so in a way, America is like a second home to me.

According to the brilliant PBS documentary "African American Lives" hosted by Harvard scholar Henry Louis Gates Jr., Oprah Winfrey — one of the richest, most influential and most popular people in the world — originally descends from Liberia. So Oprah is really like my sister in the African sense. In fact, every African American can be linked to their specific ancestral home in Africa. So they are our brothers and sisters.

No doubt, Oprah seemed specially connected to the new Liberian female president when she hosted her on the Oprah Winfrey show. To me, President Ellen Johnson being the <u>first female</u> African president signals a rebirth of the continent, the beginning of a new era.

[FK: Between 2003 and 2005, the US Refugee program (USRP) resettled more than 8,000 Liberian refugees in the United States. It's funny how history has a way of repeating itself. From John, I learned that: first, Africans (slaves) came to the US, then the freed slaves returned to Africa (they founded Liberia), and then John was forced to leave Liberia for the US again, and now he plans to return to Liberia again. The sad truth is that we hardly learn from history. Hopefully, truly Africans will return to the world stage, the way they inspired ancient civilization.]

Chapter 6

'The African must survive'

'Even for the "lucky souls" (asylum seekers) who, after years of uncertainty, have been granted the right to remain in France, life is far from rosy; they soon realise that life in France, even with the proper documents, remains difficult.' – Jean-Marie Volet

[FK: *'The woman at the rear of the Air France flight to Kinshasa was still screaming as we taxied down the runway at Paris Charles de Gaulle Airport. Hemmed in by French police officers, she pleaded to be allowed off the aircraft. As the plane took off, her screaming subsided to a low whimpering. This was a failed asylum seeker being sent back forcibly to her country of origin, the DR Congo.*

Throughout the European Union, there are hundreds of people in a similar situation - nervously waiting a one-way ticket back to the Congolese capital, Kinshasa. Although Africa's bloodiest conflict has cost an estimated four million lives since 1998, many EU countries judge it safe to send failed asylum seekers back. The situation in France is worse in some ways. Asylum seekers do not have an easy ride, and for most of them, it ends up as a personal tragedy: more than 80% of the applications are eventually rejected and the asylum seeker expelled. If Jonathan knew this, he may not have gone to France.:]

Whether from the Cape of Good Hope in the South or from the Sahara in the north, whether from the Great Lake Region in the East or from the Mount Afadjato region in the West, 80 percent of Africans coming to Europe have a completely false idea of where they are going. "I'm going to the land flowing with milk and honey, I'm going for greener pasture, I'm going to the land of roses". These are a few of the expressions that prospective emigrants always use before leaving Africa. What euphoria! It doesn't take up to a month after arrival for it to dawn on them that they were building castles in the air. I will limit my experiences to Singapore, and Malaysia (where I have stayed and had the opportunity to interact with many Africans), and France (where I applied for asylum).

My departure to Singapore was in April 2002. I was going for studies towards a terminal degree. The program was to start in June of the same year. I least expected that I was going to a land where the people were scared and suspicious of any person with black skin. At the airport, I was harassed and interrogated as a person standing trial for a felony. The verdict was immediate: "We are allowing you to stay for one week, after which you go back to your country and come back in June when school starts."

'What was this?' I asked myself. Isn't it absurd shuttling from one end of the planet to the other and back in less than two months?

I decided to move to neighbouring Malaysia, where I thought I would wind time before coming back for the program. To my greatest dismay, I met a thousand and one Africans: Congolese, Liberians, Nigerians and so forth. There were about two hundred Cameroonians, all Francophone. They were very excited to meet me. "Il traduira pour nous et notre mugons" they told themselves. "Tu es dans quels business?" one asked me. I was lost. Guess what! They were all 419 men. When I made it clear in unequivocal terms, "I can't do it and I will not do it", they started making a mockery of me. They gave me names: mboot (useless man), njimbo (sucker), and etc, etc. "Tu vas mourir ici" they told me, meaning, "You will die here".

It was a common saying amongst the Africans: "darkie must survive!" Africans in Malaysia referred to themselves as 'darkie'. Without the possibility of making a genuine penny, they resorted to all sorts of means to survive: 'faymanism', 419, dating old and haggard women, etc. 'Sampa' was the most common, where guys had to walk scores of miles a day to the 'hither land' to hawk. If you were lucky to be caught by a kind police officer, he would spare you from going to jail, but would make sure all items you were selling were confiscated, as well as all the money on you.

The system persisted like this, until the Malaysian government sent out their best and most rugged police officers to track down all Africans: old and young, fat and thin, short and tall, staying legally or illegally. All Africans were arrested indiscriminately. With the myth that all Africans use black magic, these police officers became extra tough. As if to confirm this myth, Liberians who had been hardened by a decade old civil war and narrowly escaped death themselves, fought gallantly with police officers even in the ratio 1:10, punching until the last breath in them was insufficient to continue before yielding to arrest. Some Nigerians being so smart, even after being arrested, still 'snuck-off', while others bought their way through. Cameroonians talked until almost becoming fire-spitting dragons.

The story did not end there. I planned to prove my compatriots wrong, by showing them that one could still make it without resorting to crookery. On a bright Wednesday morning, I dressed very well and moved to town (Kuala Lumpur) to scout for something to do. After a while, a flashy car stopped alongside me. I did not need to look a second time at the man sitting behind the wheel before concluding he was a gentleman. We exchanged pleasantries. He gave me his phone number and said I could call him if I needed help. After his departure, I took a deep breath of relief and thought, 'Oh, God sent somebody to me'. I did not want to expose my desperation to him, so I waited and only called after two days. We made arrangements to meet, but I could not find the place we had agreed on, since I was new in town.

The next day, I called again and he said he had waited three hours before leaving. We arranged another meeting. He arrived early. After we had discussed for some time, he repeated, 'how, how, how, how?' I was scared, and thought he might be insane. Behold, the help he talked of in previous days was not the help we know and use in the queen's language. He said, "But you said something." "We have been conversing for long, what are you talking of?" I asked. Without mixing words he said, "You know I love black men. I want to f**k you." I was taken aback and stammered, "Is—is—is that the help you want to give me?"

He was even more surprised than myself, and asked me whether I had never done it before. He did not give up so easily. He tried to cajole me by telling me what he thinks are the advantages of being gay. He even went as far as proposing that he would give me money. When I finally narrated the story to a group of Africans, a Nigerian man came in with his own story showing a lot of remorse. He began by advising those present. He said, in life it is not good to be too wise or too greedy. According to his story, wisdom and greed are antonymous. He said a Malay man had wanted to spend the night with him, and had offered him a hundred dollars. He had insisted on three hundred dollars. They could not strike a deal, so the man left. Unfortunately, it was that very night the great police raid took place and he, the Nigerian, spent three weeks in jail. He said, if he had not been greedy, he would have been in that man's house and would not have been arrested.

Later I found a means (which I am not allowed to reveal for some reasons) to get to France. There I applied for asylum. Entering the French chapter of my adventures, a friend told me he became aware it was truly a developed country just at the Charles-de-Gaulle International Airport in Paris when he landed. His awareness was not as a result of the well-constructed airport or the multiple aircrafts landing and taking off every few minutes. His awareness stemmed from the precision and dexterity with which his luggage was stolen, no traces allowed. He confided that if it had been in Africa, he would have been more careful. He said he thought in Europe, where there is plenty, no one cares to steal. When my dear friend finally entered the town, and saw how Africans were dragging their belongings up and down because they had no place to stay, he became happy. He said the robber really helped him because he wouldn't have been able to drag his suitcase around the way others were doing, and at the same time he would not have wilfully thrown away his belongings.

In France the greatest problem Africans face is finding accommodation. Even the French have it tough renting a house, not to talk of owning one. The French claim to be a socialist state where the government wants to provide services to all and sundry. Unfortunately this is very impossible. Africans with irregular residence status have many options to choose from. You either decide to sub-rent a house, if you are able to pay for it that is, break into an abandoned house, sleep at train stations or in cars, or present yourself every night at a police station where you are transported to a place where you can spend the night before moving back to the streets the next morning. Most guys here, being very courageous, prefer the option of breaking into an abandoned house and making it their home where they will at least feel "free".

This leads me to a story a Nigerian boy narrated to me. One night he struggled all through to get a place to sleep. Finally he located an abandoned car. He broke the windscreen to open the door. Realising it was just after midnight, he decided to walk around and return at about 3 am, so he could sleep for a few hours before morning. On his return, there was an Algerian boy deep asleep in the car. He was furious, and determined to evict the other young man from the car. The Algerian could only speak Arabic, and the Nigerian could speak only English. They could not understand each other. This resulted in a manly fight, which lasted about an hour. In the end they used signs to make an arrangement in which they shared the car. This guy said when he got up the next morning, he looked worse than a 'mechanic'.

More than fifty percent of the Africans in France have no residence permit. This means they either have an illegal status, or have a temporary permit renewable every three months. Both situations disqualify you from almost any good thing you can think of: accommodation, work and so forth. If you do anything, the first question the police ask is "les papiers?" (Your documents?) If you apply for a job the first question is "les papier?" A Malian immigrant told a police officer, "Je n'est pas neé avec les monsieur" (I wasn't born with them sir). Because of the importance of this document, the lines you meet at the French administrative office in charge of issuing residence permits (carte de sejour) will, immediately, remind you of the lines of voters in the first ever free and fair 1994 elections in democratic South Africa.

The transition from dust to snow can drastically change an African in Europe. The exploitation by Africans of other fellow Africans seems to be very much en vogue. It is often said that a drowning man will grasp a snake as a saviour. The senior Africans, who have been there longer, use the desperation of newcomers to their advantage. They make them work for mean wages; some don't even pay. The only live fight I ever witnessed was between a Congolese boss and a Nigerian worker. This fight could only be compared to that of Mike Tyson and Evanda Hollyfield. The only differences were that they were not in a ring, there was no referee, and no rules were stipulated. The reason for all this was that the boss had bossed his worker at work as well as his salary to the extent of not paying him at all. In the end, he was subdued during the muscle flexing and he agreed to pay his worker's salary.

It's unfortunate that in France, as an African, you are considered foolish or unenlightened until you prove otherwise. The people do it in a way that, if you are not intelligent yourself, you may not realise it. A friend of mine from Mali helped his counsellor fix some things on her computer to the amazement of her colleagues who rained praises on him. They praised him so much because they had not expected someone like him to do such a thing.

You know Africans are very daring, courageous, and malignant as well. Guys can do anything if it is to their advantage. There is a centre in Paris called CHAPSA. This place is in a hospital, and used as a centre for psychiatric patients. At the same time, people who don't have accommodation are lodged there in the night and allowed to go the next morning. You register before going in, and a sheet of paper is given to you. A dear compatriot kept jumping into buses and trains without paying. Whenever he got caught, he gave the CHAPSA registration form to the controllers who would then conclude the man was a psychiatric patient and would let him go. He narrated a story that while on a bus, having not paid as usual, the controllers came in with police officers. Everyone showed his or her bus ticket and when it was his turn, he shook his head continuously not responding to the questions he was asked. When asked to present his identification papers, he handed over the CHAPSA paper. After looking at the paper, he heard them talking in low tones: "Il est fou". (He is mentally unstable/an idiot). He also said to himself, "On vera qui est le vrai fou" (We'll see who the real idiot is). The officers handed his papers back to him and left. He prided himself, saying they were the real idiots. Achebe says, since you have decided to shoot without missing, I have also decided to fly without perching.

While sitting in a suburban train here in Paris, I witnessed a quarrel between an African lady and a French young man. It resulted from the fact that the lady sat on the same seat as this boy. She was the third person to sit on a seat meant for three. When this boy was about to get off, he spat on the girl's face. What I saw was not the action but the reason behind the action.

The African must survive

At some point I visited Alice, my fiancée in Germany, who had also applied for asylum there but been rejected. This was during Xmas 2003. While we were there with a family, which was hosting us that time, we entered the American Diversity immigrant Lottery program. Just two weeks ago, having completely forgotten about it, I got a letter telling me I had been selected! I looked around the dovecot I lived in. There was no one I could hug or kiss or skip around with. So I jumped and jumped, rolled on the bed, did a headstand and shook my feet in the air; and of course, I called Alice to break the news. It was almost unbelievable. It was time for me to tie the knot with Alice once and for all. Then she would also get a green card. Were our asylum lives about to come to an end? We got married in October 2004, in France. It was a wonderful occasion, though most of our family could not be there.

Dear brothers and sisters and prospective emigrants from Africa, beware that you are leaving the dust to meet snow, be prepared to meet a thousand and one other unexpected changes.

[FK: An emigrant in France laments that "Il ne se passe presque pas de jour sans que je sois victime de quelque chose parce que je suis 'couleur d'ébène' noir charbon" ("Not a single day passes without me being harassed in some way because I am Black".

According to the Guardian Unlimited, in August 2006, French police stormed the biggest squat in France, evicting hundreds of West African families from a squalid, disused hall of residence. Up to 1,000 squatters, including 200 children, many from Ivory Coast, Mali and Senegal, had been living crammed into 300 small rooms with improvised wiring, poor sanitation and damp. But only half were asylum seekers or illegal immigrants. The rest had legal status to remain in France but, support groups said, they could not find housing because of racism and discrimination. Most of the squatters had jobs, some men worked as security guards or builders, many women as nannies and cleaners for families in Paris. The Red Cross had to help the evacuated families in makeshift tents. Ghislain Thierry, an electrician, had lived in the squat for 18 months, sleeping on a mattress in a shared room. Born in Cameroon, he had been in France legally for 12 years, attending school and then university. "I have a decent job and enough money to rent a flat. You'd think I would be able to find a roof over my head without having to live in a squat, but not in France. I experience racism every single day, in every aspect of my life." Amadou and Kaloja, a young couple from Mali, also legally living in France, shared a room with their one-year-old son, who was born in Paris. They left the squat with no possessions but a handbag and a bag of nappies from the Red Cross.

From Dust to Snow: The African Dream?

Mariama Diallo, who runs a local women's support group, said the conditions inside the squat "tested the limits of human endurance". She added: "When I come out, I scrub myself but I can still feel fleas. The place has never been fumigated. You can't breathe from the smell of damp, leaks and decaying building. It's nauseating. I see children covered in rashes, kids with allergies or asthma, but what can their parents do?"

The local council requisitioned 350 hotel rooms to house about 800 squatters. Those with residency permits could then apply for social housing. Illegal immigrants were to be taken to holding centres before being deported.

At the time of the population census in 1999, around 3.3 million foreigners lived in France, equivalent to 5.6% of the total population. The percentage of foreigners has remained relatively stable over the past 25 years. The largest group of foreigners living in France is Algerian. Other important countries of origin are Morocco, Turkey and sub-Saharan Africa. However, immigration from Asia, primarily from China, Pakistan, and India has been gaining increasing importance.

According to the book, 'France Means Business, Enterprising, Innovative, Surprising', France is undoubtedly the single most attractive country in Europe and a world leader with enormous potential.]

Chapter 7

A refugee in Love

"Our chiefs are killed...The little children are freezing to death. My people... have no blankets, no food...My heart is sick and sad...I will fight no more forever." – Chief Joseph

[FK: While we Africans have been liberated from colonialism, we have to liberate ourselves from war with ourselves. When Malcolm X demanded justice and equality for African-Americans, for them to be respected as human beings (not animals), he said blacks first had to love themselves. We Africans need to love ourselves in order to prosper and avoid situations as this one of Deng.]

It began at dawn with a big explosion, followed by a rain of bullets from automatic guns blasting at the hut in which I lay, jerking me to my feet. Impulsively, I screamed, calling for my mama. I heard frightened yelling coming from across our neighbour's hut. I ran barefooted into the outer room of the hut. There I found my mother, sprawled on the living room mud-floor. Her blood had made a wet spot around her head, as it gradually soaked into the floor. Her eyes were wide open in an eternal stare. Horrified and confused, I fled barefooted into the woods. Hundreds of frightened kids and women were running in all directions. Machine guns rattled all over drowning out my laboured breath, as I scuttled through the thickets. Thorny bushes scratched welts on my arms, but I sprinted on, my heart pounding.

Together with the others, we trekked hundreds of miles on foot through the hostile East African desert for about two months across to Ethiopia. I was just 9 years old. Older boys, like me, looked after the youngest ones. Many of us died of starvation. Some died of thirst, even after drinking urine. Wild animals attacked some. It was traumatizing to watch vultures feed on the bodies of our fellow humans.

It is a miracle how I survived the tortuous trip. Finally, we arrived in Ethiopia and were put into refugee tents. We waited in western Ethiopia for months in a refugee camp in Panyido, living at first on kernels of corn we cooked over a fire. I grew weaker and weaker, and weaker. I missed my family in an indescribable way. It had really dawned on me that my mama had been killed. I mourned and buried her in my mind. However, until now, I do get nightmares! And what about my papa? I often dream of him, hoping he is still alive somewhere. I also dream about our huts, drums and going out into the fields with the cattle.

Finally, conditions were rife for aid to reach us. The International Red Cross started bringing canned sardines and salads. We gobbled the food, our first substantial meals in months. But just when we were getting into some sort of refugee rhythm, war also broke out in Ethiopia. Chased by tanks and armed militia, we frantically tried to cross the River Gilo, where thousands drowned, were eaten by crocodiles, or shot. Again I survived. Together with fellow survivors, I walked for more than a year back through Sudan to Kenya. We reached the famous Kakuma refugee camp emaciated, and dehydrated. On the trek, more people died from gunfire, lion and crocodile attacks, disease, and starvation. We often had to eat leaves, carcasses of dead animals, and mud to survive. The survivors were like a family.

In many ways, life in the camp at Kakuma was like that in any other Sudanese village. The youth lived in clusters that served a family-like function. Soon, months turned into years. We lost our baby teeth and grew into young men. Most of us were male, but there were a small number of females amongst us. One of these was a Fulani girl called Salimata. Salimata had extremely raw African beauty. Because of her beauty, she got the attention of the male aid-workers who clearly did not hide their interest in her. But Salimata had character.

I remember the day I won her attention. I ran into a scene where an aid worker who headed our division of the Kakuma camp was molesting her. I fell in love with her immediately I saw her. I hated the aid worker immediately I saw what he was doing. I almost killed him. She was really something. The incident would later cost Sali a lot. Food rations were greater than in Ethiopia, but far from adequate: 3-1/2 kg of wheat flour, the same in corn flour, and a quarter kilos of lentils every 15 days. Sali had the possibility to get more, if she showed some more sexual-warmth towards the aid workers. She did not. She told me her virginity was sacred, and that God meant her for the man she would marry alone - nobody else, even if she had to die. The fact that she was a refugee would not compromise that. I was awed by her principle. I loved her even more.

We studied daily together, reading world history in outdated texts, practicing English. My best companion was Sali. I loved reading the history books and wondered why history kept repeating itself, sort of. There was still much tyranny in African countries as recorded in the past history books. Why did we study history if no one learnt the lessons? I promised myself I would specialise in African history, and would do something to change things.

The UN Refugee Agency, working in collaboration with the U.S. Department of State, agreed to resettle some of the refugees in the US. Fear gave way to hope when I enrolled in Kakuma's cultural-orientation classes. The majority were taught by African aid workers who knew America only from textbooks. 'This is how winter feels,' they said, passing around chunks of ice. 'This is what you do in an emergency,' they said, calling out the numbers 9-1-1. They spoke of relatively strange concepts to us: rent, payroll taxes, car insurance, etc.

I was very lucky to be selected in one group of to-be- resettled refugees. Unfortunately Sali was not selected. Was she paying the prize for being 'recalcitrant'? It hurt. It hurt so badly, to leave her with those 'wolves'. I promised her I would do everything to be reunited with her soon. It was not easy. Did refugees have a right to be in love, to choose whom to love?

At last, I boarded a plane for the first time in my life and watched my world disappear: the dusty hot refugee camp and the friends who replaced a family I no longer remember, and most of all, my Sali. Sali had replaced my dead mama; and now, I was loosing her again. Was I ever going to see her again?

I arrived in Boston, Massachusetts, shocked by the unfamiliar coldness of winter. The International Rescue Committee matched me with three other boys as roommates. The unfamiliar environment and the snow terrified us. Church groups brought us winter clothes from their own closets, and Christians offered to drive us to the grocery store where we learned to buy pre-cooked chicken and bread. We had difficulties cooking because we were not used to using a stove or microwave. When we cooked, we ate in the same big plate in remembrance of eating together from a calabash as kids before the war. During the first few weeks, we huddled in the cramped quarters of our apartment. We spent our days playing games we had learned at camp, and talking about Africa. It was at least consoling to have one another and the opportunity to work and study. When the trauma of the past surfaced, we offered consolation to one another. When 'survivor guilt' surfaced, we prodded one another to stay focused and make something of ourselves. But it was really difficult for me. It was really difficult for me to feel grateful for being alive while at the same time feeling intense sorrow for those who had not survived, including my mum and perhaps my father.

Refugee officials, having no birth certificate to go by, assigned us a January 1st birth date and estimated our ages. We all looked forward to going to school. With the support of a Church in Boston, we were finally enrolled in a public school. Parentless, one of us proposed and we adopted the quote "Education is my mother and my father". My dream like those of many of the other boys was to get a high school diploma, a college degree, and then return to Africa. This was an ambitious goal that made me start working 70 hours a week. Besides I would want to save to marry Sali. It would be the equivalent of several cows for the dowry. I hoped my papa was still alive somewhere. It would be great for him to welcome Sali as his new daughter. I was hoping Sali would accept to marry me. I thought of her, a beautiful young virgin, with character. That was the real African woman. That is how our mothers taught us to live.

My favourite book in the Bible was Song of Songs. I meditated on it day and night. I was in love. I wrote to Sali every night. I put the letters together to mail at the end of the week. As soon as I started working, I sent money to her regularly. I asked her to leave the Kakuma area and enrol into a school in Kenya. I missed Sali so badly; I would sneak away from my roommates and cry. Was a refugee allowed to be in love? What did I have? Each day, I prayed and made plans hoping she would be able to come to the U.S. some day. Sometimes, I could not sleep and had to write to her. I felt disoriented, and in love.

Given that some of us were really intensely black, we could be spotted a mile off, like an oasis in the desert. Word spread around about us, and though we found friendship and counsel from other students, African and American alike, I often felt really angry at times when Americans joked or used insensitive slang. The first time I got really mad was when an American said: 'Wassup homie?' I considered it an invective about my homelessness rather than just a greeting.

The first day I got really ticked for real was when a white American girl said, 'I don't want to sit with that monkey.' It made me work even harder to show I was better than most of those who eyed me with a sassy look. We Sudanese started segregating ourselves, and not sitting with students who were not refugees, or who were white. Sometimes people looked contemptuously or sympathetically at me because I had a different skin colour, like I was so different, like I was dirty, or something. They always thought my English was not right. Sometimes, students would move away at lunch when I sat down. Other students would tell me to sit elsewhere. It happened many times and I really felt homesick. Homesick? Where was home? So I threw myself into working and studying really hard. When I was not in school or sleeping, I was at work in a fast food restaurant. It was difficult to do all this and still have good grades, which only prospered the notion, held by some, that Africans are stupider, only more athletic. In fact when they heard I was from Kenya, they thought I would be a great long distance athlete. I personally think this is racist nonsense. I vowed I would work had to show that I was intellectually superior; at least in History. Later on, I started winning more respect and I made some American friends. I was studying History, as I always wanted, hoping I would be able to help all Africans learn from History.

One shock I had in America was that I could not understand why - despite the big talk of the American dream - there are still many homeless miserable people in America. It was far from the perfect world we had dreamt of in the Kakuma. The American dream takes all you have to achieve it; but it is at least good to have the opportunity to use your gifts.

Is there an African dream too? The starting point will be to learn from history, stop the wars and power mongering. Perhaps we can come up with an African constitution, which can also influence the policy of governance in the different African countries. Perhaps it can be agreed upon to make sure a President or head of government in any African country does not have more than two terms in office. Perhaps, it is not a bad idea to set up an African security force analogous to the FBI, which could intervene in States where coups or rebels surface. We can create opportunities for Africans in our respective countries. We can be the same as America, but even better. We have the potential. We have strengths, which instead of exploiting, we have turned into weaknesses. We have lots of natural resources, like in the Democratic Republic of Congo (the richest piece of land in the world); we have African attributes Sali reminds me of.

There are more than two million of us lost boys. Most of us still suffer survivor guilt. The only way to overcome survivor guilt is if we can do something to help prevent what happened to us from ever happening again. Recently, I watched with dismay what was happening in Darfur. We have seen this before in the Rwandan genocide. We even experienced it ourselves, as lost boys. But alas, we did not learn from these. My dear brethren, lets learn from history. Maybe that is one of the greatest lessons I have learned as an uprooted (refugee) African living and studying history in America. I see in the American history a nation that turned the corner, and repaired her mistakes. Like America, Africa can also make it. Let's begin the revolution today. The first step is to believe we can do it, as I believe I will see Salimata again, someday.

[FK: Dak Deng, is a Lost Boy from the Nuer ethnic group of Sudan. He was finally able to marry Sali. However Dak never got to see his father again. Perhaps he is still alive.

We really need to STOP THE WARS in Africa. We need to extol the greatest virtues of Africans: LOVE and Brotherhood!]

Chapter 8

The Diary of an Asylum-seeker

'Asylum seekers are not looking for an asylum, just for a good place to live.' – Anon

[FK: Forced by circumstances beyond their control to seek a life outside their home countries, prevented from entering legally and from working, denied a fair hearing by the asylum system, excluded from health and safety protection at work, kept from social care and welfare, vilified by the media and therefore dehumanised in popular imagination, the hopes and dreams of asylum-seekers for another life are finally extinguished. Cases of death during forced deportations continue to abound: 1) the 31 year old Cameroonian, Christian Ecole Ebune, died in Hungary. At first, the pilot agreed to take him on board, but when he continued to shout and protest, the pilot refused to go through with the deportation. Ebune was then taken into a service corridor away from passengers where, it appears, he was beaten and his feet wrapped with tape. When one of the officers noticed that he was unconscious, the airport emergency physician was called. Ebune could not be revived! 2) 27 years old Samson Chukwu died in Switzerland during the second attempt to deport him. Chukwu's death by suffocation was provoked by the position in which anti-terror unit officers placed him.

Should I continue? There are other cases of the same thing happening in France, Austria, Belgium, UK and possibly Germany, as we will see in the following diary of Ignatius Bakia.]

After my advanced levels, I wanted to continue my education in Cameroon. However, the word 'Bush-faller' had just come into fashion. I started to look for a way to travel to 'bush', or rather to 'fall bush'. The slang 'bush' comes from the Cameroonian youth who are struggling to make their lives better, and simply means overseas. Hence, a bush-faller is one who travels overseas. I am not sure what motivated this choice of language. Life in Cameroon after the few years of economic lapse was extremely difficult, and since a high percentage of the population depends on agriculture, it was extremely hard for the common citizen. Fraud, bribery and corruption became normal activities among civil servants. It was survival of the fittest.

The diary of an asylum-seeker

My father was a local farmer, who fortunately left the CDC, Cameroon development cooperation, and cultivated his own cocoa plantation, managing with 28 workers. I knew very well he could sponsor my trip to 'bush'. So I went to him one Sunday evening with my mother besides him. 'Father,' I began, 'I want to be a bush-faller.' I went on to explain to them what I meant by bush-faller. My mother was in support of my idea, but dad disagreed completely. I went to God in prayer. I wrote to the University of Michigan, in the U.S. The application forms and information package were sent to me. I took a neat sheet of paper and began to jot down the most important requirements: a birth certificate, national identity card, passport, my certificates – Ordinary and Advance level GCE. I opened a file in which I placed all my documents. I named the file 'Bush'. While waiting for a response from Michigan, I went to the U.S embassy to find out information about schooling in the U.S. From the United States Information Services office, I obtained 14 steps to study in the U.S. Back home I started going through the 14 steps.

One day my father brought a big envelope with U.S postage. It was from Michigan. I told my father the contents of the letter, and he realized my seriousness to be a bush-faller. I brought out my bush file. He saw for himself all the documents necessary for travel. "Delay is not denial," a preacher man once said. By this time I had a passport without a visa. My father called me and asked how much money I needed. How to get the money was the question on the table. I estimated the sum of 2.5 million CFA francs, about 3750 euros. The money came from my own portion of our cocoa plantation on the basis of a pledge.

I had a friend who told me he knew a man working at the American embassy who could process my visa for me quickly. I met the man, and he told me that before he could start any work, I would have to deposit the sum of one million CFA, and promised me a three-month wait for the visa. I told him that if he wanted to do my job, I would give him a deposit of five hundred thousand francs. While he was looking for the student visa, I was also busy looking for a business visa. In a short time, the business visa came first and I decided to grab this opportunity and use this visa.

The long awaited day came, the day to fall-bush. At the time, I thought it was for good that I was leaving, not for good. My post of general supervisor on my father's farm was ended. My family was anxious to bid farewell. My briefcase was well arranged like that of a real business tycoon, but I alone knew the affair behind my business visa.

I left home successfully, although at the airport I gave bribe, which is normally called by the immigration officers 'cola nut'. This process is also common amongst the police, gendarmes, and the army who squeeze bribes out of taxi drivers and clandestine drivers even when the particulars of their cars were okay. It is a nasty habit, and a cankerworm that has eaten into the bone marrow of the society. Even top officers make it extremely difficult for those who want to be honest to be promoted.

Though I flew with Air France, France was not my destination. So in Paris, I had to take a train to the Bundes Republik Deutschland (Germany). I had heard things were better off in Germany, the world's third best economy. But I did not know where I would end up. At the Köln train station, I was stranded, as the person who was supposed to pick me up did not turn up. As I sat somewhere, I observed a high degree of police patrol, and I remembered stories about the German police and the Gestapo; the thoughts brought me to my feet. I decided to leave the train station immediately. I took an underground train to an unknown destination, and dropped out at the end-stop. I carried my bag on my shoulders. By this time, it was dark and cold. Even the clothes I wore could not stop the cold penetrating my bones.

At the cry 'I go die with cold', I raised my head immediately and saw a black figure approaching me from the other side of the road. I approached him immediately, and expressed my problem to him. He rather asked if I knew an asylum centre. I responded negatively. 'Do you have money with you?' I had only 3 DM, which he took, and bought two bus tickets directly to the asylum centre. He advised me on what I should tell the police. 'By the way, do you have your passport on you?' he asked. 'If you are controlled, and the passport found on you, they will seize it and you will be deported. So if you have your passport on you, give me.' So, I made the first biggest mistake in Europe. I gave him the passport, and he promised to return it the following morning. I even gave him my return tickets to Cameroon, since I had paid for a round trip, which is typically cheaper!

At the police station, my application for asylum was being processed, and I was given shelter in a small cabin. While in the cabin, I saw ducks swimming. The following morning, I realized I had slept in a stationary ship. Meals were to be given to me thrice a day. The following morning, I was interrogated by the police, who carried me in a container lorry. The lorry was partitioned into sub-sections, which could take around 50 persons without you knowing or seeing who your next neighbour was. No one explained where they were taking me. It wasn't until I reached their office that I knew. Passport size photos and fingerprints were taken. During this time, I did not know where I was. I felt like a captive, and I began to wonder if it had been a wise decision to leave home. I felt like the lost son in the Bible. Later on, I was given a train ticket and map to go to Halberstadt.

The diary of an asylum-seeker

The word 'Halberstadt' means half-city. There, a military camp used during the Russian invasion had been renovated and turned into a transit camp for asylum seekers. From my knowledge of map reading and picture interpretation, I had learnt in school, I was able to 'pilot' a group of 15 others, both men and women going to the transit camp with me. In Halberstadt, we walked into the hands of the police again. We registered, and were given a temporal hall where we spent the night. Like my friends, I was given a nylon bag of food: 4 loaves of bread, 1 sardine, a plastic cup, knife, fork, spoon, butter, sugar and honey. The worst of all was the pillow, blanket, bed-sheet, foam, and the bed itself. I thought that all these things were the things from concentration camps used by Hitler.

The next day we had medical checks, AIDS test and x-ray photographs. My AIDS test was negative. However, I had chest pain and consulted three doctors. Each of them was interested in 3-4 syringes of blood. When I did the simple arithmetic, I had lost almost a litre of blood since I arrived there. Meanwhile, I was still feeling pains despite the tablets they gave me to take. Now I was sent to a special clinic for lungs. Here too, I lost a good quantity of blood. I was sent to a ward of tuberculosis patients containing Vietnamese who seemed totally sick, body soul and spirit. Just as I entered, one of them coughed like a car engine with a low battery. I almost caught the next plane home, but where was my ticket or passport? The mistake I had made was beginning to haunt me, and rightly so, because it was going to cost me untold misery in the impending weeks.

I told the doctor that I neither smoked nor drank alcohol; I asked how I could be so sick that they were putting me amongst such TB patients. He said, 'From the polluted air.' I imagined the air in the ward would be far more polluted! I was not convinced, but I had no option other than to summit myself calmly to the 'hospitality' agents.

I was in the hospital for a month, no contact with anybody. Even my new friends who came together with me from Halberstadt did not know my whereabouts. Before taking me to the theatre, the doctor brought a consent form with a series of question for me to go through and sign. I was on the stretcher like someone who was going to go through a major operation. After doing other small tests during the day, nothing was discovered. Then the doctor said to me, 'Mr. Man, you are ok. We have found nothing.' Then I asked myself why this special clinic? Were they interested in my blood? Why was the doctor in Halberstadt, after the x-ray, so serious, as if I had a life threatening disease? Were they interested only to use me for experiment? Only God knew their plans and intentions. I had no immediate answers.

From Dust to Snow: The African Dream?

One week after I came back from hospital, I was called up for an interview about my asylum case. The interview did not last for long. They rejected my asylum case (which I had based on religious persecution). After spending four months in the transit camp, I was transferred to Harbke, in an isolated place. This too was an old military camp used by the Russians, on the boundary between West and East Germany. From here, we had to trek 3 kilometres to reach the nearest supermarket, or where to collect money. In short, the camp was just like a pivot carrying many long invisible chains. You were like a grazing goat with a rope on the neck. These invisible chains that held many of us could really be felt. Some of my friends went mad beyond repair by any doctor. Some turned into chain smokers; some became chronic alcoholics or heavy drug dealers, and sex slaves. To relieve the stress, most of us compromised our moral values to the whims and caprices of German women, and even nymphomaniacs. When a German woman realized you were unable to deliver 3 to 5 'rounds', then you were of no use to her. I made a decision that I would never succumb to any of these women. Some asylum mates were lucky at times to either buy a passport and travel to England or the U.S, or woo these women to marry them.

The main pipes carrying water at the camp were coated with rust. After heavy demonstration, the administration took a look into the matter. Certain adjustments were made, like recoating of the pipes with paint. At the camp, you cooked what you liked and no one planned your meal for you. Everyone had his or her pot, plates, etc, which was necessary in the kitchen.

One day, when I was ill, a doctor said to me, 'Germany has good and strong drugs and even if you are sick you will get well.' He said so because he knew what they were gaining, if not blood, the organs like kidneys, especially, when a refugee died. This was not just speculation. There was a boy who had gone through deportation procedures. The authorities failed to expel him forcefully from the country, and this boy later fell ill. He himself was not aware of the illness. He went to the social office for the health department to issue him a notice, called in German a Krankenschein, which would enable him as a refugee to consult the doctor. In the process of obtaining the notice, he collapsed and was immediately rushed to hospital. As he was undergoing treatment, the doctor asked him to sign a document so they could change his blood. Meanwhile, the boy talked to some white patients in the ward who had been there for 5-6 years waiting for organs. So he thought, if their own citizens had been there that long waiting for organs, what more would a black refugee like him hope for? Could it be that the doctor wanted to kill him, and get parts for other white fellow citizens? He had nobody in Germany who would even realize he was missing. How could the doctor

The diary of an asylum-seeker

tell him all his blood and organs were not good? If that were so, there was no need living. During this time, the news about Doctor Death in Britain who murdered over 200 patients was rife. As this guy thought of this, he decided to detach everything from his body and left the University clinic. The boy lives right to this day. The story taught me a lesson as a refugee.

On my part, I went to the foreign office to report my lost identity. I was asked to bring 4 passport size photos. I gave them the photos, and was rewarded with a deportation paper as my ID. Due to fear of deportation, I changed towns. I used a friend's passport, a British passport he had bought, for 2 months working as construction-site-helper, and paying 20 percent to the boy. Then I bought mine with the money I had been saving. It was also a British passport, of an African-Jamaican-British; one parent was from Nigeria and the other from Jamaica, but he had been born in England. I don't know if he had died, or whether the Nigerian who sold it to me had stolen it. We knew most whites found it difficult to distinguish Africans on photographs. The guy, whose passport I had, even resembled me a bit. I was only afraid to use it in case it had been stolen and he had reported its loss, and police were watching out for it. I rented my own place and started working.

Normally as a foreigner, British or Cameroonian, I had to report myself to the foreign office. A three months visa was given to me to look for a job. I had a job, but was really afraid because of the passport. I decided not to report back to the foreign office after the three months expired, although I was paying tax, health insurance, rents etc. I had no problems moving around the city. One day, after my work permit had expired, I had a job opportunity at the Hanover Expo-2000. Now, as a British passport holder, I needed to report to the foreign office to obtain a residence permit to allow me work for an extended period of time. Since life was getting difficult, and I had to pay for housing, transportation and health, I decided to take the risk to go to the foreign office, especially, as it had worked before. Besides, the police had controlled my passport a few times before and there had been no problem. But, that was my second big mistake. I was arrested at the foreign office.

I spent 24 hours in a cell, and was brought before a judge. I was charged for staying illegally in Germany, and for using a false passport. The prosecutor requested deportation. They found out my real identity, maybe because of my fingerprints taken on the very first day I had requested asylum. They had, somehow, also found my long forgotten Cameroonian passport. Since I could not pay for a lawyer, they provided me with a lawyer. I had to choose any one I preferred from a list. I picked a very healthy looking man as my defence lawyer, but the prosecutor won. I was kept in a prison for 4 months, and later transferred to a deportation camp. Here I spent 5 months. The authorities carried me 2 times to the airport, first to the Berlin Schönefeld airport, and then to Frankfurt international. Each time they were unsuccessful for some reason.

After sometime, for a third time, they decided to deport me via Frankfurt airport. This time was my death warrant. This was a day I thought I would live no more. It was a day of disgrace in my life. Before my deportation, I was taken to a prison instead of a deportation camp. I spent a week there, before the cops drove me to the Frankfurt international airport. We left around 11 p.m. to arrive Frankfurt the following day around 5 am, in time to catch the early Air France flight. On the way to Frankfurt, I had both my legs and feet chained. At the Frankfurt airport, I was handed over to the immigration police who kept me in a cell. I was ordered to remove all my clothes, and stood naked in front of 6 immigration policemen. I was asked to bend so they could inspect my anus, and one dipped his fingers into my anus. I could not explain why he was doing so; maybe he was satisfying himself by fingering me, as he wore gloves. 'What are you looking at?' I protested. He ordered me to shut my mouth, and that he was doing his job. Later I thought they could have been checking for drugs.

Then, I was ordered to raise my feet. He looked under my feet but saw nothing. Since I had grown some hair, one of them patiently gave himself work as if he was searching for lice on my head but also apparently found nothing. Lastly, I was ordered to raise my hands as they concluded their inspection. Meanwhile, my clothes and shoes had been passed through the inspection machine, and nothing was found. After putting on my clothes, they bought a large belt like the one given to winners at boxing matches; only, this one looked very vicious. It carried two accessory smaller ones on the left and right, which could be pulled forward longer, and backward shorter. On the heads of these small belts were handcuffs. I put both hands into the handcuffs, and the belts were pulled behind and fastened with my waist carrying the larger one. Then at the middle of the mother belt, just lying perpendicular to my vertebral column, was another handcuff. The function of this was to raise me up if I tried to fall down. Both of my feet were also chained.

Since it was during winter, I was covered with a winter jacket so that nobody could see how I was being rough-handled. After doing all this, a bus driver was asked to bring the bus close to the door. They formed a circle around me and marched me off, so to avoid the situation from the camera. After handcuffing me this way, both hands, both feet and waist it was still not enough. Two policemen held and kept bending my head, pressing it downwards so I could not turn or look left or right. From my left and right, I could at least still sense that two policemen were also bending my second and third fingers, and the fifth cop was holding the handcuff on my waist. As I climbed into the plane, helpless and weak but courageous in soul and spirit, my whole body was chained. I felt like no cell could move. One hostess was not pleased at the way I was being handled. We occupied the last 4 seats. The way I was chained did not permit proper circulation of blood. I felt excruciating pain both on my feet and hands. I asked the policeman sitting beside me if he could release the chains and that I was feeling pains. He told me to hold on till the plane left the ground.

By the time the plane was almost full, I was unable to bear the pain anymore. I remembered the case of one African who died in the plane being escorted by three Austrian Aliens Police officers who had been given the order to deport him. In so doing, they used adhesive tape to tie him to his seat, and to seal his mouth as well as partially seal his nostrils. He suffocated. This African brother was a victim of racist policies. Now it could be my turn.

I started crying for help in German, 'Lass mich los! lass mich los! Die Kette tut mir wehr!' (Release me! Release me! The chains are hurting me!) Everybody in the plane stood up and watched, as I was struggling with the police. Immediately the pilot came and intervened, and asked the police to take me off his plane.

This was how I was freed for the third time from deportation. Now, instead of carrying me back to the deportation camp or freeing me, they carried me back to prison where I spent weeks before I was taken back to court. You can imagine my nightmares. By this time, the immigration police had filed their report in court stating that I fought them. A woman from the foreign office also wrote an application to the court, stressing that I must stay in prison until I was deported. She went on to say that from the time I was previously released from the deportation camp I should have left the country voluntarily.

Despite the torments, I still had the courage to overcome the immigration police with full confidence. The hellish treatment they gave me gave me courage. I defended all these allegations before the judge. The statement of the immigration officers was not taken into consideration, due to my explanation to the judge about their brutality, and the pains they inflicted on me. The report from the pilot concluded the whole interrogation. He had sent a fax to the court. Coming to the question of the woman working at the foreign office, I defended myself clearly before the judge. I explained that from the day I was released from the deportation camp, I was released on the basis that I was ill. Secondly, the prison had found no reason to keep me. I had been released to enjoy half freedom. I continued, 'I came to your office from the day of my release when you gave me a deportation certificate as my travelling ID, on which you clearly stated I had no right to leave without permission. How then do you explain to the court that by now I should have left the country? Did your deportation certificate even allow me to go to a neighbouring State? I could not leave the country due to the law you imposed on me. You respect the law of your country, why do you want me to disrespect it?'

The woman was unable to defend or answer my questions, because she had centralized her argument on the report that she had prepared and passed to the judge. 'What happened at the airport?' the judge asked me. I described in detail how I had been brutalized, and rough-handled. I explained how, in the plane, I finally could not bear the pain and shouted for the other passengers to rescue me, and how the pilot intervened and I was carried off the plane.

The verdict was out, and I was released to continue to enjoy my half-goat-like freedom. If I left my State and happened to be controlled in another German State, I was to be fined 40 euros with a warning. This law restricting my movement is called Residenzpflicht, and does not permit refugees to move freely in Germany. The law becomes a strong law in poor States of Germany, because it brings income to the State, whereby, there you are compelled to do the social work with a payment of 100 euros a month. Many refugees point out that Residenzpflicht, in addition to many other laws, does not only restrict their rights, but also marks them as 'not equal' or 'different', 'less important' and 'weak', in comparison to Germans. Some refugee organizations compare Residenzpflicht with the former laws of the South African apartheid system. I may not leave the county to which I have been assigned, and am obligated to live in the refugee housing that has been assigned to me. Nowadays, you can apply for permission, with 4 euros, to leave your region for a period of one to five days. This is just to hinder the free movement of asylum seekers.

There was another incidence that almost extinguished my life. I was returning from the wedding party of a fellow African one very early morning. At the tram stop, three Nazis saw me. They started shouting, 'Nigger, Nigger, komm hier wir machen dich tot', meaning 'Nigger, Nigger, come here we will kill you'. I also retorted, 'Weiss Weiss Schwein, ruhe!' meaning 'white white pig, quiet!' One of them was so worked up he came over and pushed me three times, and went on to give me four solid blows with his fist. I used the method of non-retaliation. I fully knew that if I retaliated roughly, his people, who were racist, would persecute me, especially, as this happened just a few weeks after I had been released from prison. So what I did was: I handed over my cell phone to a friend who called the police. The good thing is that the police come swiftly, compared to what happens in Africa. When the Nazi saw the police, he wanted to escape. I proved to him that not retaliating did not mean I was weak. I held him strong, and his two friends came to his rescue. But it was too late. As the police came, his two friends had to escape while blood oozed out of my nostrils. The police caught him and took him for interrogation. I was put into an ambulance. Although I was bleeding visibly, the ambulance doctor asked me whether blood was coming out of my nostrils. I retorted bitterly, 'Can't you see that my shirt is stained with blood?' On his medical statement, he still never stated that blood was coming out of my nostrils. He wrote that I had swellings on my face. Even the x-ray photo I took was not in the report. The x-ray burns I am still carrying will remain a mark to remember as long as I live. They had left x-ray scar burns on the left upper part of my chest. From the medical side to the police side, I was taken for questioning. The policeman who questioned me was a skinhead, just like the Nazi who had fought me.

I waited for 3 full months, and no letter came from the police or from anywhere, not even from the Nazi to say sorry for what he did. I used my own initiative and wrote a letter to the police commissioner, who responded directing me to a state prosecutor. The state prosecutor sent a letter to me to appear before court. It would be good to be in court as an accuser and not an accused. When I told my lawyer, he was very reluctant to push the case. I think he was working hand in hand with the foreign office to expel me out of the country, and had just been a window dressing. He probably saw this as another opening that could instead make me stay longer in Germany, so he never wanted to show up for the case. However, I fought the case myself until a compensation fee of 800 euros was given to me. My pleasure was not from the compensation fee, but because justice prevailed, which is a good thing about Germany.

After collecting the compensation fee, I went to my lawyer to explain how it all went. He told me then, to my surprise, to bring all my documents and that I had been cheated. I brought my case file and gave it to him, whereby he filed a letter to the Nazi. The Nazi accepted to pay 400 euros additionally. Up to this day, the lawyer has never given me even a quarter of the money. Meanwhile, he very well took my bank account number three times. I allow you to conclude for me.

I took my own initiative again to write to the Nazi and his lawyer. His lawyer responded, asking me to contact my lawyer. The duck had already swallowed the worm! I had been exploited and cheated because I was a mere refugee anyway. It is really an experience! The white man cannot say all blacks cheat, nor can the black man say all whites cheat. There is a Cameroonian saying that 'Fools are food for the wise, but once in a while, the fool may have his chance over the wise. A dog has its own day'. So, don't treat brothers and sisters, even of different colour, refugee or non-refugee, like fools; but treat everybody as he or she is, and do not exploit or violate someone's basic rights.

Today, so many years after I left Cameroon, I am still under Residenzflicht, waiting that someday I shall have a change of fortune. After three failed deportations, the German authorities are probably giving up. Unless something dramatic happens again, I think they will leave me in my chained state till I make a wrong move or leave voluntarily. In the meantime, it is so torturing to stay at the asylum home and have nothing to do, so you are compelled to take the 100 euros per month work offer, or work in black at your own risk. Some African student-friends help get me work, and I work on their behalf. Recently, I was almost caught again when I was working in another city. I have also tried a distance-learning course on computers in England, and even successfully completed one level and have a diploma for it. At least, it keeps me busy.

I also have another German girlfriend. The previous one I had only exploited me sexually. She said she would like to help me by marrying me, but first she had to complete her divorce proceedings. After two years with the same song, I dropped her. I like the present girl a lot, and would even love to marry her. She is quite pretty, but I am afraid to loose her by bringing up the issue. I know a lot of asylum mates who have ended up marrying rather fat incompatible women more than 2 decades older than them, just to get off this psychological quagmire. My former girlfriend was such. I heard a Kenyan committed suicide, by jumping from the 5th story of his German girlfriend's flat, after the girl started dating another boy, thus dashing the Kenyan's hope of ever getting married to her and having 'papers'.

Believe me; it is so hard to live without plans and without any sense of direction. I have given up hope of ever seeing my family again. Once in a while, I send money home from the little I save. I sometimes consider giving myself up for voluntary deportation. I would be better off in Cameroon. What chills me is what happens after deportation. I have decided to adapt a 'don't care' condition. I have numbed myself. It helps me at times, but how can a man live without hope?

[FK: We cannot possibly understand what Ignatius Bakia is going through. In New York a groundbreaking scientific report by Physicians for Human Rights and the Bellevue/NYU Program for Survivors of Torture showed that refugees seeking asylum in the U.S. who are placed in jail-like detention centres suffer a myriad of physical and mental consequences. The report said amongst other things that: detained asylum seekers suffer extremely high levels of anxiety, depression and Post Traumatic Stress Disorder. The already poor psychological health

The diary of an asylum-seeker

of asylum seekers worsens the longer they are detained. Ignatius has been like this for more than 5 years already. Can you imagine what will become of him? Do pray for asylum seekers.

We will now look at the experiences of African 'workers' abroad. A study, conducted by the Pollution Research Group at Natal University in South Africa, says that a third of all skilled professionals in Africa have left to pursue careers in the West. But how, really, is life for these professionals. How is it like to work abroad? First, here is an experience to transition you into the experiences of workers. Living as an illegal immigrant?]

Chapter 9

From Dust to Snow: From HIV Negative to HIV Positive?

'HIV does not make people dangerous to know, so you can shake their hands and give them a hug: Heaven knows they need it.' –
Princess Diana

[FK: Imagine you are sitting in the waiting room of the British Embassy waiting for the Consular officer to tell you whether your visa has been approved or not. Your heart is somersaulting like that of Carol Yager trying out for the Olympics. In the internal turmoil you quietly pray for a positive decision. Now, imagine you are sitting in the waiting room of a hospital awaiting your HIV/Aids test results; you are sweating like a whore in church. In both of the preceding cases, the decisions or results can be life-transforming. Which of these situations would you prefer to be in? In hindsight, you may actually prefer to be found HIV positive than to have a positive decision for your visa. Now you must be thinking I should have my head examined. You are right. How could I possibly prefer to be HIV positive than to be granted a visa?]

My parents were very poor, and I had to depend on goodwill extended family members to complete high school. After high school, I was an ambitious teenager, brimming to do nursing, to travel abroad, to marry a well-to-do husband, to be respectable in society. Little did I know!

Six years ago, I got into a Medical School to do nursing, after a hard struggle. Usually, to get in, one would have to bribe the officers in charge of the final selection process, even if you passed the exams. Shortly, after that, I got married. Then, I thought my dreams were coming true. Little did I know!

While in Medical School, I decided to carry out a voluntary HIV/AIDS test. I can never forget the day the doctor told me my results were positive. I could not believe it. At that moment it was like I was the first person to ever have such an infection. I felt like the world was coming down on me, but the Doctor asked me not to be discouraged. I could not accept the diagnosis, and told myself it may have been a mistake. I was so afraid to tell my husband. I stayed for a year without telling him. I chose to reject the results in my mind. Then, I was involved in an accident, and had to be infused with blood. The test was done

From Dust to Snow: From HIV Negative to HIV Positive?

again. The results were given to him, but he did not show me. Instead, he went and showed them to my brothers. Well, I knew, but feigned ignorance. From then I started suffering rejection from family members, friends and my husband. Those are the times when you know who really loves you in this life. It is exactly because of the fear of rejection that I had not told anyone. However, I am really sorry I did not.

I hung on to complete my medical course. I then got a position to work with the medical staff of the Presbyterian Mission. It was now very difficult for me, because screening was done before any recruitment. I suffered from emotional stress for months. My life was shattered, like the twin towers on September 11. Usually when something is shattered, stress has no further impact on it, right? That was not the case with me. I felt useless in the society, in life. I had lost all the things I used to dream of, my studies, career, my husband, hope, etc. Many people waited for my death. Fortunately, I joined an organization, which fights against AIDS called GTZ. I started giving testimonies for payment to keep up with my treatment. However, the treatment was so expensive that I could not afford it with the little money given to me after each testimony. I stayed for another year without treatment, just living by God's grace. I did voluntary work in a treatment centre for HIV/AIDS where I met many patients.

Then I felt like I had a new call. I had to pick up some of the pieces and start afresh. I called a few of the patients, to start a Help Association to share our ideas about the common problems we encountered. We registered the organization and many people began to join the group to gain knowledge on how to live with this situation. The association has up to 60 persons now and every one benefits from the small grant being given.

I realized HIV/AIDS was not the end of life, that acceptance is the first crucial treatment to it. I realized I could become useful in my community as a consultant. Any new case came to me for advice. I counseled patients on how to cope and live again. Because of the stigma, many people adopted the refusal status I had earlier adopted myself. My organization made HIV visible by giving testimonies, home visits to sick ones, taking care of orphans, etc. The organization offered capacity building and income generating activities to help members to be self-employed (since no one wanted to offer us jobs). We were bracing ourselves for when the little grant would run out. Good nutrition and drugs are part of treatment. All of this made many people come out of their shells and joined the fight.

Then, I decided I would stop living from day to day and start dreaming again. Let me seize this opportunity to say that anyone, who finds herself in this situation, should not be discouraged. HIV does not kill. You can kill yourself, but not the virus killing you. People even doubt my testimony when they see me and how I look physically. I learned that it is never too late to learn. Since my other dreams had been broken, my traveling abroad dream resurfaced, and was even more attractive now: a change of scene and a fresh start. I heard that in Britain, even illegal immigrants got free HIV/AIDS related treatment. I would love to go there. But how was I going to ever make it abroad?

From the formation of the organization, I learnt many things like project writing and abstract writing. This was to design projects to look for funding to help the organisation. I had no opportunities for Britain, so when I heard of this University program in Abu Dhabi, UAE, I wrote an abstract, and it was accepted. They would provide me with a partial scholarship to pay for my accomodation, and feeding. They processed my visa for me, to come and share my knowledge with the students there. I would also be able to study. I started dreaming big again. Besides, going abroad would make my family proud. Perhaps this would square up some of the disgrace my HIV status may have brought to all those I love so dearly.

The preparation for my trip was so stressful. I had no body to support me financially otherwise. My flight was with Kenyan Airways. It was a long and tiring trip. I did not know that a plane gallops, so it was my first big shock. There were too many clouds, and it was a very old plane, and very noisy. I also felt lonelier than an HIV/AIDS patient. My friend, I had to travel with, had left earlier due to my financial difficulties. I looked forward to arrival. We finally touched down in Dubai at about 2 am where no one welcomed me. I had to find my way by myself from Dubai to Abu Dhabi, which was a journey of more than two hours.

I took a cab and paid a whooping $50. I did not know there was a bus going to Abu Dhabi for 4 dollars. At that time in the night, and alone in the car with the driver, I was very much afraid. Thank God I arrived safely.

Abu Dhabi UAE lies on a T-shaped island jutting into the Persian Gulf from the central western coast. Over a million people live there with about an 80% expatriate population, amongst which are many Africans. The opulent Emirate Palace puts the United Arab Emirates firmly on the tourist map. Costing more than £2 billion to build, it is the most impressive resort ever to be built in the Middle East, and the most expensive hotel in the world by some counts. There is always a good moment to remember, like spending five days in the Emirate Palace, which is so beautiful, and the Rotana (a Beach Hotel), meeting 'friends' from all over the world, sharing ideas and experiences on culture and studies. There were over a thousand participants present, but only four Africans; we felt like water in the Sahara.

From Dust to Snow: From HIV Negative to HIV Positive?

I soon realized that there is a lot of stress in every thing you want to do in UAE. Beginning with the visa policy, you are only allowed one entry. Many people prefer to have a visa and stay without food. Housing is another issue; it is not easy to have someone staying alone. Because of the expensive housing, people always stayed as a crowd, two to ten people per flat. Another issue is about finding a good job. This depends on connections, which most Africans do not have access to. Sex harassments abound. When you enter a taxi, the driver starts asking for sex and for how much; it is said that all African females are 'business ladies'. You would be in your room, and someone would knock on your door looking for sex ladies.

All of UAE looks artificial, apart from the air you breathe. Even artificial rain has been used in Abu Dhabi. The artificial rainfall helped alleviate dry spells that had lasted for days. The rainmaking efforts helped bring the temperature down from 47 degrees Celsius!

As far as culture is concerned, and from what I have seen, a Dubai national woman is not allowed to do any form of business, even shopping. She is discouraged from working. She would have to touch men she barely knows, which is forbidden in the traditional Islamic culture of the United Arab Emirates (UAE). Among UAE nationals, it is generally considered inappropriate for women to speak to men they are neither married nor related to in public. Most, if not all government universities are single-sex. But contact with male worker colleagues is increasingly seen as acceptable. In the night, the society frowns upon young women who are still out after 10 pm. During the day, every part of the body is covered with clothes, except the eyes (to see). Some females even cover the eyes too with a veil. Moreover, they are very shy to strangers.

Another culture shock came with the food. Back home, okra is used in making draw soup. But in UAE, it is cooked whole and eaten as salad. I could not believe it. The first time this happened, I decided to go to a Chinese restaurant. On the menu, I found a very colourful dish of panzani. I chose it. When it was served, I could not eat what was served. It looked far less appetizing than it had seemed on the menu, and sure enough, it was as tasteless as boiled cabbage, as sticky as a gecko's foot, and as slimy as if it contained ground okra. I dejectedly decided that, in UAE, all food had okra. As if that was not enough, I heard about corn fufu and was excited I had finally found something similar to food at home. Instead, I found out it was a type of fufu call semolina fufu. I did not like it by one bit, and stayed for about a month without really eating. However, now semolina is my best meal. I also came to discover what I had also always seen in magazines and TV, the hamburger! Finally!

From Dust to Snow: The African Dream?

One funny experience was when I saw an eraser, and thought it was chewing gum. I had never seen such erasers before. I told the friend, I was with, that I did not like gum or sweets but that she could eat it if she wanted to. She was shocked that I could ask her to eat an eraser! Yew! How does an eraser taste?

When my university program in Abu Dhabi finished, I went to Dubai. I thought milk and honey flowed there. I stayed in a hotel, with no friend – nobody to direct me. I was full of stress. When I visited the cyber café, I met a Kenyan guy who asked me not to go back to my country, that I could make my life happy in Dubai. I thought about the struggles back home and figured I could give it a shot in Dubai. So I followed the Kenyan's advice.

Later on, I got a small-time job. I made a friend and started staying with this friend. My visa was about to expire. I asked my boss to support my visa change. She refused, and I had to go into what is called < OVER-STAY>. Before I could save any money, my over-stay was 'heavy'. I now had to work to be able to pay the over-stay charge of $1000 dollars. This was not easy; I still cannot afford it. I worked for sixteen hours for a hundred dollars per month.

While in Abu Dhabi, I had applied for a scholarship to go to Canada with another HIV positive friend. It came out successful, but now I had no money to go back home and get my visa to travel to Canada. I pleaded for help from family members and friends, but no help came my way to pay my over-stay penalty. I had to miss the opportunity.

In general, many Africans travel to the western world (though UAE is sort of the confluence between East and West) to look for greener pasture. When they reach, life is not worth what they thought it was, so they are forced into activities that will make them to have money. These activities are categorized, and if you are not learned in some, you will not do them. The most pronounced ones are the Nigerians and Cameroonians. The 'back-dollar' business is being practiced by all, both learned and unlearned. It's the way to the fast buck. About 75% in Dubai do the back dollar business, and only about 25% are involved in other activities like cargo handling and working in the city. Most of them are in jail. Every blessed day that God gives, they are going to jail. Why? Because their business is illegal, and an individual cannot manufacture money. It is a form of stealing, and sometimes violence is part of it, maybe between the Mogul and the boys or amongst the boys fighting over the 'loot'. In this case, the cops always come in to intervene, and on the long run these Africans find themselves in the jails. Hundreds of them are presently there, some in the hospitals with handcuffs on them. This is due to a low level of education and also frustration to meet up with the demands of life, and the expectations they had before leaving Africa.

The girls have their own struggles too. Since wages at times are too low, they tend to walk the streets. They say it pays more than spending a whole day working maybe for 5 dollars. Streetwalkers may get up to a hundred dollars per day. Every girl in Dubai is a beautiful one because there are a lot fewer girls present compared to the number of men. That probably contributes to why girls go in for hanky panty. The girls like the 419 guys, because they (guys) make quite a roll, and settle them (girls) with huge sums too. The belief is that a girl can never stay without the help of a boy in Dubai. This is common with the Nigerians. Some go to Nigeria and tell girls the good aspects of Dubai. When they accept to come to Dubai, they say, 'Ok, I will sponsor you and at the end you will give me (maybe) 15 to 20 000 dollars.' When the girls arrive in Dubai, and do not find a good job to do to return this money, they have to walk the streets. In the process, some girls may be deported. The drug business is the most lucrative in Dubai. Though there is a lot of dough in it, if caught you are coolly awarded a jail term of 25 years.

That is Dubai. The Africans who make it here are those who have a good level of education, and are determined. My most difficult experience is when my visa expired. I was so afraid, even to visit the Pharmacy for any consultation. The worst came when my sponsor asked me to leave, but I did not have money in hand to go for the visa change. That was really the beginning of more stress. It lessened when I was told that many people stay without visas. So I had the courage to stay without a visa.

At this moment I really like to go back home, but no means. I left home thinking I would get what I want and go back home. If you are planning to travel, I will discourage it if you don't have a good view of what you want to go and do. In other words, I will try to direct the person not to fall a victim as myself. I miss my family and friends dearly. Dubai is a land of frustration. I pray God will provide me with the $1000 dollars to pay my overstay charge and return home. The organization I founded needs me. I owe them a big apology. Even if I go back with nothing fruitful, my thinking about life abroad will never, never be the same again.

Anabella Nala, UAE

Chapter 10

The DV lottery: A path to modern slavery?

'The man who gives me employment, which I must have or suffer, that man is my master, let me call him what I will.' – Henry George

[FK: Reports show that, for the first time since 1990, more black Africans – about 50,000 legal immigrants (many through the DV) - are coming to the U.S. voluntarily than the total who disembarked in chains of slavery before 1807. New York State draws the most Nigerians and Ghanaians. Do you know which state draws the most Cameroonians? Here is the story of a Cameroonian who won the DV lottery; little did he know he would just be moving from one set of challenges to another.]

One afternoon I had an unexpected letter. It was from the Department of State, Kentucky Consular Center (KCC), Williamsburg USA. As I tore the letter open, I was wondering why I would get such a letter. I knew only a few people in the U.S. and they had not written to me for years. The letter was dated March 16, 2003. It read:

Dear Victor Mbah,

Congratulations! You are among those randomly selected and registered for further consideration in the DV-2003 diversity immigrant program for the fiscal year 2003 (October, 1, 2003 to September 30, 2004). Selection does not guarantee that you will receive a visa because the number of applicants selected is greater than the number of visas available. Please retain this letter and take it with you to your visa interview.

Approximately 100,000 individuals were registered for further processing. However there are only between 50,000 & 55,000 diversity visas available under the FISCAL YEAR 2004 DIVERSITY VISA PROGRAM. Therefore, it is most important that you carefully follow these instructions to increase your chances of possible visa issuance.

Please read and follow the enclosed instructions carefully. ALL FORMS AND CORRESPONDENCE must be sent to the Kentucky Consular Center at the above address. Please notify the Kentucky Consular Center of any change in address, addition or deletion of any family members, and any information, which you believe, may effect your application...

...Please be advised that even though you send all the above listed documents to the KCC, your case may not be scheduled for an

The DV lottery: A path to modern slavery?

interview appointment until a visa number is available. You will only be contacted by the KCC when a visa appointment is scheduled. Please do not call us to check when your case will be scheduled.

If it should be necessary to contact the Kentucky Consular Center by telephone YOU MUST ALWAYS REFER TO YOUR NAME AND CASE NUMBER EXACTLY AS THEY APPEAR BELOW. Your case number should be clearly written in the upper right hand corner of ALL documents and correspondence sent to the Kentucky Consular center.

It ended with my Case Number, PA Name, Preference Category – DV diversity, Foreign State Chargeability – Cameroon, and Post – Yaoundé. This was followed by the KCC telephone number and E-mail address. The necessary forms were enclosed.

Now, not many people get to win a lottery in their lives! Not in this way! I had completely forgotten I even entered and application for it! It was absolutely overwhelming. I was stunned and inactivated for several minutes. I could not believe it. I had the opportunity that could change my life forever. I could not even celebrate. I could not express the joy deep inside me.

Coincidentally my mum was visiting me on that day, together with my little nephew Victor. The moment I blew into the house, she knew something dramatic had happened. I just showed her the letter; words were beyond me. She expressed her happiness really graphically. She picked Victor up and whirled him round and round until he squealed. She even wanted to pick me up too! Of course, she couldn't; my mum's quite little and I'm big; but she gave me a record breaking number of kisses and hugs. It was a great day for the family, but we had to celebrate quietly. We were not ready to let others into it yet.

This was the opportunity the family had been waiting for. My going abroad could open many doors for other family members to travel overseas as well. And it was not just overseas, it was America! I had to do everything to make sure I got all the requirements and did well in my interview. Then my mum suggested I should look for a nice juicy girl and marry, so that some other person could also benefit. I did not have to look far. At that time, I had a big squabble with my girl-friend. With the DV news, she quickly put that behind her and we did a court signing before I proceeded with the DV process. We would do a church wedding later.

I completed and returned the forms. A couple of months later, I got a letter with our interview schedule and the things we still needed to do. The biggest problem I had anticipated was to prove that I had enough finances to support myself and my new wife upon arrival in the U.S., without being a social burden. To fulfil this requirement, I contacted

From Dust to Snow: The African Dream?

a family friend who made an affidavit of support for me. We also had to do medical tests including HIV/AIDS tests.

Finally, we went for the interview. The medical tests had to be done by a US-embassy approved doctor, who would then send the results to the embassy. Because of that, I (we) only got the decision from the embassy after more than a month of suspense! The visas were granted! We genuinely thanked God for the opportunity. Despite our efforts to keep the news secret, a lot of people already new about it before we even organized thanksgiving and prayers in church. I promised myself that though I would be a U.S. permanent resident, I would remain a Cameroonian.

So, at the end of July 2004, the Continental Airlines flight that touched down at Baltimore Airport at 9:50 am had brought us with it. We had had to do finger prints and some paper work at Newark International where they gave us temporary Green cards. They said it could take up to several months before the real Green card arrived. We were going to stay with a family friend for the first couple of weeks. It was the family of the friend who had kindly done the affidavit of support for us.

On the day and time we arrived, this family friend, David, was at work and so we had to take the shuttle from the Airport to the house. It costs 40 bucks. I felt it because we were fast running low on cash; and we had hardly begun! David had told us where to find the key. He and his family (a working wife and one baby, who went to day-care) had a mortgage on a 2-bedroom house. We were going to borrow the baby's room while we tried to search for our own place to live.

Immediately, we realized how tough it would be. We had no car, no health insurance, no credit history, and worst still – no money. Just buying the flight tickets had meant selling the piece of farmland my father had given me. Getting a driving license and a car were the priorities. In the U.S., a car is a necessity in many states! I needed it if I was going to work. On the first morning I woke up, I realized we would have to readjust the ideas we had about the U.S. from Cameroon. David and Theresa were already leaving for work. David said he would try to take permission from work to help drive us around to get one or two important things done. They all looked in a hurry!

A week of psychological torture later, during which David was unable to get a day off from work, he suggested we start doing some things by ourselves using the bus (MTA) service. The first thing would be to apply for a social security number. We would need it for work. So our first stop was the social security office on Security Blvd. It was about 50 minutes away. We had heard that mostly poor people take the bus. We were poor – in fact we had little over 200 dollars now. I had hoped David could save us a few dollars by driving us around.

The DV lottery: A path to modern slavery?

When the bus arrived, we had our first real embarrassing moment in the U.S. We needed exact coins to pay for our fare. We had a 10 dollar bill. We explained to the driver that we did not know we needed the exact amount. It was clear to all in the bus that we were foreigners. The driver suggested we wait for the next bus and look for change. He said he had no change. We painfully and reluctantly offered to give him the 10 dollars just to avoid further embarrassment. Luckily a fellow rider offered to provide change for us. What a relief it was!

David offered me his bicycle, and I began riding around searching for apartments. It was very difficult to ride in Baltimore! David helped to make some calls. Thank God, one apartment complex was giving an August special for a one-bedroom apartment. The administrative fee was waived and it would cost us 510 dollars including washing and drying machines, water and sewage. David offered to pay the first month's rent for us! God had answered the prayers of all family and friends who had been praying for us!

By the time we moved into the empty 1-bedroom/1-bath apartment on Saturday with David's help, we needed jobs and fast! We did not have what to sleep on, and we would need to eat. David got us a Coleman Queen Raised Airbed and Pump from Kmart. We got an old table and 2 rickety chairs from David which served as all our furniture. We carried one chair to the bedroom at night and brought it back to the sitting room during the day. Theresa lent us 2 pots, 2 spoons, 2 knives, two forks and two plates for cooking and munching. That was going to be it for the next weeks.

The job hunt was tough! We had been issued social security numbers while waiting for our cards. Maryland is considered to be the State for most Cameroonians in the U.S. In fact many people had told me not to go to Maryland. They said there is a lot of gossip there and so on. You know what! In hindsight, I would still have come to Maryland! It was a Cameroonian brother in Baltimore who helped to provide us with the first job for my wife Irene. She would be picking tomatillos in his vegetables shop, and helping out when there were many customers. However, this Cameroonian brother paid Irene only 4 dollars per hour (below the minimum wage). We took it because it was better than nothing. True, I think he exploited our situation since he knew we were very desperate. His wife had spotted that Irene was pregnant and, as I will show you below, it meant we were in a more desperate situation.

The biggest problem for a new immigrant in job searching is that employers often look down on the qualifications you bring from Cameroon. They are partially right because, coming from Cameroon you lack the technological adeptness that is often required in the U.S. Even with cleaning jobs, the cleaning equipment is more sophisticated than at

From Dust to Snow: The African Dream?

home where you can use your hands to mop the floors without raising any eyebrows. Your work experience from Cameroon needs to be weighted for an equivalent here in the U.S; this often means you don't get the job! So, you have to start small. Get a small-time job like I got. I got a job as a guard at a hotel. Guards, who are also called security officers, patrol and inspect property to protect against fire, theft, vandalism, terrorism, and illegal activity. As an unarmed guard, there are no special educational requirements, though most require that you would have left US high school (have O-levels). The main requirement is to have a driver's license. I would be paid $20,320 a year before taxes. In Cameroon you may think this is a lot of money, but after paying for your bills you are virtually left with nothing. At least I had gotten a job from which we could guarantee our daily bread and then gradually move on. Hallelujah!

One aspect of culture shock for me was the squirrels. I first took real notice of them one day when I took Theresa for a walk in the park. I saw this squirrel climbing into a garbage bin in the park. It was very healthy. That was good meat! It would save us some dollars if I caught it. I imagined how good smoked squirrel would taste in a bowl of pepper soup. As I started towards the squirrel, I remembered the movie I had watched about 'Ukwa in London or something', in which he caught a bird in the park and was hauled by the police. Was it also unlawful here? I paused and glanced around. No one was looking. I decided to approach it slowly. It was not even afraid of me! Irene told me she did not think it was a good idea to catch the squirrel. When I stamped my leg on the ground, it scurried reluctantly up a tree. I walked away thinking about bush-meat back home; my mouth was watering and Irene smiled sympathetically back at me.

Winter was soon approaching, and the bicycle would not help then. We needed to get a car in addition to beginning to get things for the baby. I soon realized that most people got cars on credit. It meant they got it financed by a bank and then they paid back gradually with an interest. At first, I thought I did not want to owe anyone. Then, I realized I was in for a rough time in the U.S. When I finally decided I could owe somebody, I realized we had no credit history, so no one wanted to lend or lease anything to us, including a car. I got rejected over and over again. It was traumatizing!

That just added to the toughest one yet! How would we manage without a car when the baby arrived? More importantly, since none of our jobs provided health insurance, it was a nightmare for me how we would be able to pay for child delivery. We could not even afford to be ill. Without insurance, it would cost us at least $4000 if we had a midwife do a home birth. Was it that expensive? Yes, it was a real nightmare for me.

The DV lottery: A path to modern slavery?

I tried to get a job which would provide insurance for my family. As I grew more and more frustrated, I considered more and more to deliver the baby myself. How did our mothers in the village do it before hospitals came? David suggested we apply for Medicaid. After many visits to Medicaid offices, they told us they would only support after the baby was born. They said we had a unique situation having just arrived in the U.S. Finally we found a Cameroonian midwife from the church we attended who offered to help with a home birth for free with no string attached. You see why I said Maryland is therefore not a bad choice after all! There, your Cameroonian brethren who know how tough things can be can help you.

It was a very difficult situation for us. We decided to do that. If there was any complication with the birthing process, we would just call 911 and say the baby came too fast. It was very risky, but we finally did it like that and it worked! God was so good to us. We then took the baby to the hospital, and then she was covered by Medicaid.

To be able to get a car, I took a second job. I was guard from 10 pm till 6 am. I worked in a restaurant from 8 am to 4 pm. I had little time to do anything else. I then understood why many of my friends in the U.S. had hardly communicated with me. There was hardly any spare time!

In 2004 Proudfoot Consulting announced the findings of its annual productivity study, which showed that the historically high productivity rating achieved by the U.S. compared to other countries is driven by longer work hours, not greater efficiency. Proudfoot's findings were based on analysis of more than 1,600 detailed studies representing more than 10,000 hours of work at client projects in Australia, Austria, France, Germany, Hungary, South Africa, Spain, the U.K. and the U.S. According to the study, the U.S. is tied with Germany for most efficient labour force, with 64% of available time spent productively. However, when the longer American work day and shorter annual vacation time is factored in, U.S. productivity lags behind Germany and France. Measured as Gross Domestic Product (GDP) per actual hours worked, France is the most productive country.

Most Africans like me come to the U.S and work so hard, developing the U.S., while our continent is not even at a level where reliable data for such analysis can be collected. I think we all have the responsibility to change this. One of my biggest areas of culture shock was when I realized there was no public holiday on Good Friday! I had to work full time that day also. Well, come to think of it, I got some extra money. But I was shocked all the same. I could not believe America of all countries would not respect such a day.

From Dust to Snow: The African Dream?

One of the happiest days in our lives was when we finally got our first car. It was a used 2000 Ford Taurus. It was a huge accomplishment. Now we can refocus on bringing up the baby. Perhaps we can save up some money and pay for my mum to come and help out with the baby. That's why I am keeping the 2 jobs. I know! It is like Modern Slavery – voluntary slavery! Well, it maybe better in some ways than being a teacher in a private college in Cameroon, as I was 3 years ago – especially as Irene and I hope things will eventually improve when we can get better jobs. There is no turning back.

[As of 2006, Victor and Family are still in Baltimore. Their car recently broke down, unfortunately. It had no factory or extended mile warranty, and so they had to spend all the money they had saved for Victor's mum's trip to repair it. They began saving again. Victor is such a hard-working man!]

Chapter 11

Re-entry Shock

'Home is a place you grow up wanting to leave, and grow old wanting to get back to.' – John Ed Pearce

My name is Benedicta Leero. I have always had an appetite for new experiences, and a different existence. So I decided I would take my first steps to a new adventure. I decided to go away in an organised program, which would allow me to have adventure but also offer a buffer of security and assistance if needed. I left my family and my country Botswana and went to Germany as an au pair.

I had 3 children to look after ages of 2, 5, and 7. The family was affluent. The father was a doctor, and the mother a lawyer. They welcomed me into their beautiful home and I felt very comfortable from the start. I was required to work 40 hours a week, which includes childcare and light housework. For this I would be paid around 180 euros a week. In a way I was not prepared for the work, which involved getting 3 children up in the morning, giving them breakfast, packing school lunch boxes and making sure they were dressed and ready for school, etc. It was not as easy as first thought. Then, I had the rest of the day to do laundry, shopping, all whilst looking after a 2 year old; and then from 3:00 p.m. having the older children back home from school, taking them to swimming lessons, or friend's houses, making dinner, getting them ready for bed.

When I was with the children I realized I had to do my best to protect them. I had read stories about what was expected of au pairs and some of the incidences that had occurred with au pairs. One of the stories was about a brave German au pair who died after being dragged under the wheels of a truck as she successfully saved the life of a 14-month old toddler whose pram had got caught by a commercial vehicle. Onlookers were shocked when the toddler's pram got caught by the lorry's wheels and began to be dragged under the chassis. The child's au pair vigorously began to pull the pram back and was assisted by a passer-by, but the young German girl was dragged underneath the truck and died later from head injuries. Miraculously, the 14-month old baby escaped with only minor grazes.

I also heard about the experience of another au pair in the U.S. found guilty of second-degree murder of an 8-month-old. It was alleged that the au pair violently shook the baby and bashed his head against a hard object, causing a head injury that led to his death. The au pair was allegedly upset because her employers had imposed a curfew, cramping her lifestyle. All these stories made me particularly alert in carrying out my duties.

One of the main disadvantages of living in Europe is nature itself. The weather is terribly different from that at home. Winter and autumn can be depressing; it is dark and cold. So it is very important to have friends, especially, friends used to that kind of weather. Barriers in communication can make it difficult to socialise. I had a lot of foreign friends and they hardly spoke English, and we had to communicate in German, which none of us was good at. It is very hard to express yourself when you cannot say what you want because of the language, and it really pains not to be able to say exactly what you want to say. Well, according to my experience, the cultural differences made the language even more difficult because I could not say anything I wanted to my friends, since when I would try to say something, a joke for instance, it would be misunderstood. Once, I found myself in a very tense situation, in which I had to explain a joke to someone. Well, I concluded that all my friends were very sensitive and I had to choose my words carefully, when I talk to them. This sometimes made me homesick. I started missing my friends with whom I could talk about anything I wanted.

When I lost my cousin, most of my friends wondered "Why do you have to grief so much for a cousin. I retorted, 'Are you guys not so close to your own cousins?' Living far away from home, I always feared what would happen if there were an emergency at home. My contract as an au pair said I should be able to live for a full year without going home. Even when my cousin passed away, I had to mourn her abroad. This was not only because of my contract; it was also very expensive to fly home for the funeral. I always had this in mind because life is full of surprises. When I heard a telephone ring, I would pray that it was not to deliver bad news.

One thing that also made me know that I was not home was that I was the centre of attraction when I took the children out for a walk. People would look with curiosity and ask: 'Are these your children?' (Come on! I am black and the children white!) At times we would go out to swim at public pools, and I would feel, and in fact see that a lot of people stared at me; like spears pointing at me, and I felt it even with my back turned. Well, whether they were looking with admiration or whatever, it was just too much to take lightly.

Well, being in Europe had its advantage. Well, it is technologically developed. It is very rare to have an electrical power outage or no water. The rate of deaths caused by public transportation seems to be only two percent the rate in my country, Botswana. Also public transportation is very reliable. Rates for crimes: theft, rape, you name it, are lower than those in my country. I mean the way things are run is great. For example, the police do a very good job. Simple crimes like wrong parking and speeding are well monitored and controlled such that you hardly can find such things around town.

Well, I can say that I did not expect much when I left home. All my expectations were those people scared me with from home when they said it was a racist country. I did not experience that. I mean, it is of course normal for some white people to stare at a black person. Some are not even German. I had a friend from Lettland who told me that if I visited his home country, I was going to be stressed because they hardly see foreigners, not only blacks but Asians too. This made me realise that I was in a far much better place. But as an au pair, I will say that it was an amazing experience. I was blessed to have had that family despite the conflicts in the process. I will say every family has misunderstandings within the household. Their complaints were reasonable, and mine were also reasonable to them.

I had a really great experience. I recommend being an au pair to anyone considering this. I have made a lot of friends from across the world: Philippines, Poland, Spain, Russia, Peru, China, to name a few. They want me to visit them and want to visit me too. This world is smaller. No one can be lost in it. If you are yourself, not trying to be someone you are not, you can make it internationally. I hope to go back to Germany, one day, to further my studies.

Going back to Botswana was very hard. I was baptized at the Leipzig English Church the day before my return. This church I had worshipped in had a great fellowship. I cried as I hugged good-bye. I cried even more while hugging my jovial adorable loving godmother Prof. Lynnda Curry. I was going to miss the fellowship and love shared by the church, which had a wonderful multicultural mix. In fact it is a unique church to find in the eastern part of Germany.

My flight back from Berlin was via Johannesburg to Gaborone. While I experienced culture shock coming to Europe, I did not expect to, when I returned. So it came to me as a huge surprise. No, I never imagined I would experience "Re-Entry Shock". By "Re-Entry Shock" I mean the opposite of culture shock – in reference to all the adjustments you'll have to make when you return home. Adjustments? At home? People expect going home to be the easy part, but in fact it is also a challenging situation. You've changed a great deal while you have been in Europe, perhaps more than you realized. And things at home may have changed as well...or they may seem shockingly the same, as if your friends and family stood still for a year while you zoomed off to the other side of the world and had this life-changing experience.

The first two weeks at home were awful. Everything, my friends or family did, seemed unimportant compared to what I could tell or do. The same thing went for my school. It was hard returning there. And while I felt all this, I missed my European family, church and friends more than anything, that life I had enjoyed so much suddenly disappeared.

When I got home, there were strange new stories and many people were very excited. Some of my old friends had moved; some were very excited to see me again; some expected presents from abroad. Some people, I knew, had gotten new jobs or fallen in love or had babies; all this in one year. I showed the pictures I had taken in Europe to nearly all those who came to visit. I listened to their ahing and ohing. But soon I became just part of the society. Many times I found myself saying "That's not how we do it in Germany". I would sometimes wonder how the au pair who replaced me was doing. Was she loved more than me? Did my host family miss me?

Chapter 12

The Canadian Skilled worker program: Brain Drain or Brain Circulation?

'As the traveler who has once been from home is wiser than he who has never left his own doorstep, so a knowledge of one other culture should sharpen our ability to scrutinize more steadily, to appreciate lovingly, our own' –Anon

[FK: It was not until the early 1600's that the first named African arrived voluntarily in Canada. Multilingual Mathieu Da Costa was a free African man who acted as a translator for Samuel de Champlain with the Aboriginal peoples on Canada's east coast. However, the largest early group of Africans to enter Canada did so as enslaved people – involuntarily forfeiting much of their history, heritage, culture and power.

One of the most significant pillars of Canadian life is the extensive social security system. Access to medicine is open to all for no charge; there are government-sponsored job and self-employment training programs; free libraries and community centres fill the streets of every city, and the unemployed, disabled, retired and disadvantaged people receive social assistance. However, Canada is one of the few countries in the world whose population rate is actually falling: there are more people dying than being born, and the Canadian population is steadily getting older. The Canadian government reacted to this looming crisis by creating the Skilled Worker immigration program. In this program, people with college education and experience in medium - to high-level white-collar professions can come to Canada as Permanent Residents. To qualify as a Skilled Worker, a person has to show at least a college-level diploma and several years of work experience, and reach a certain number of "points". Many Africans have seized this opportunity as with the DV lottery program of the U.S.

So, today the Canadian skilled worker program has inspired a new wave of African immigrants into Canada, and one may ask if they are arriving voluntarily or involuntarily. Furthermore, how is the Canadian experience? What is its impact on developing countries in Africa? The Fatolas share their experience:]

Travelling abroad became an issue during my second year in university. It became a matter of whose family had enough resources to send their loved ones abroad. I actually needed to participate in an exchange program; my graduation from the university depended on it.

My family and I decided that the best program for me, as a person studying a foreign language, was to stay with a German family. This would enhance my German language learning. We decided on the "Au-pair Program".

Thus, the numerous visits to the German Embassy began. First, to obtain information about the requirements for obtaining a Visa for the kind of program I was interested in. It was at the embassy that it first occurred to me that a lot of people really wanted to leave Nigeria for "Greener Pastures". There, I noticed that people would go to any length just to get a visa to travel out of the Country. You could virtually hear conversations, like someone telling others how and what lies should be told, and all that could be done in order to obtain a visa.

We began communicating with the organization that was in charge of the au-pair program in Germany. That was a heart-wrenching experience for me, because of the poor postal system. It took about two years to get all the necessary papers together after many visits to the embassy. At last, I got the visa in late December 1993, and departure date was set for the 14th of January the following year.

As the day of my departure approached, there was excitement in the air, partly because I was the first amongst us children who would be leaving the country. But the excitement slowly turned to anxiety. I started to think of what awaited me, and what would be expected of me in my 'new family'. My heart was torn between the benefits of going and the pain of leaving my safe abode and people I knew and loved. I was engaged to a lovely guy at that time, who happens to be my Husband and the father of my two children. At the time of departure, amidst family and friends, I felt like a lamb that was being led to the alter. There were prayers said, and words of advice given by well-wishers. Departing from my fiancé was the most difficult thing. There were so many tears, and then the hour finally arrived, and there was no turning back.

At about 6 a.m. on the 15th of January 1994, I arrived in Duesseldorf, Germany. The first thing that stuck out to me was the fact that I was the only black person I could see. Even though I am a light skinned African, I felt as dark as charcoal. And then, there were all these eyes staring at me, and I remember feeling as though I had fallen out of space and had landed on the wrong planet. This particular feeling stuck with me for about ten months.

While serving as an au pair in Germany, I was also studying. During this time, I got married to my husband who had also travelled to Belgium. Our first son Fola was born in Germany. Upon completion of my studies, my family and I migrated to Canada (as skilled worker immigrants) in June of 2003. I tell you, it was a lot different from my first experience back in 1994. This time, we were leaving with "Kind und Kegel", as the Germans would say, i.e. with all that we have. This time, the concern was more of whether everything would go as we had planned. How would we survive the first few days in a totally strange land, staying with people we hardly knew? All these "fears", so to speak, soon disappeared on arrival, because it was immediately evident that Germany and Canada were two different worlds.

In Canada, beginning at the Airport, one is almost not noticed. This is not meant in a negative way. It is just because there are lots of like-skinned people around. So, it was almost as though we were back to Africa, and there were (and still are) friendly nods here and there. I remember the Immigration Officer saying to us at the point of entry, "Welcome to Canada! Can I say Congratulations?" He showed excitement and warmth, grinning broadly like Julia Roberts. That really meant so much to us.

Assimilating into the system is not at all as difficult as it was in Germany, - of course, not without challenges. Fortunately we now had experience living abroad in Germany. In addition, our status was different. We were 'Landed Immigrants', who have almost the same rights as the Canadians themselves. We soon noticed that, as everywhere else, the colour of your skin matters, only that it is better concealed here than in Germany.

The most intriguing experience I have had since I came to Canada is the fact that, even though the certificates both my husband and I brought into this Country are from Europe, and not only from Africa, it is difficult to integrate into the system job-wise. It is a sad case here, in Canada, to note that well over 90% of the immigrants are not satisfied with what they are doing for a living. Most people are just working in order to be able to pay their daily bills. Most people have degrees and job experiences from whatever country they are migrating from, and yet, when they apply for jobs here, they are always asked for "Canadian Experience". I keep wondering where one would ever get this, if no company first takes the initiative to employ one.

On the whole, I still feel that here (the Western World) is a better place to be, compared to our country Nigeria. Nevertheless, that is not to say that the ugly picture that some "un-educated and ill-informed" Westerners often paint of Africa is true. There is no doubt, life generally seems to be better in this part of the world irrespective of where one finds oneself, be it in the area of: security, child bearing and child raising, or your dignity as a person. There is a huge difference in all of these things when one compares the two continents.

Take, for example, things that are taken for granted here are things one would actually have to be praying to get in Nigeria. For instance, take the issue of running water or electricity; it is constant here. Yet if it ever happened that one of these things needed to be shut off for some hours, in Canada, we all get panic attacks. But these are things that are being dealt with on a daily basis in Nigeria and many other African countries.

I would also say that there is a different approach to how children are raised here compared to how it is done in Africa. While I tend to favour discipline when a child does what is bad, I still think that there are pros and cons. I am of the opinion that we tend to take it to extremes in Africa. Discipline is done out of anger, and most of the time, it has nothing to do with what the child has presently done. Instead, parents vent their anger and frustration on their innocent children. Here, they are indulged and left to do what they want. If you, as a parent, try as much as to discipline your child, you risk having your child taken away from you by Child Welfare. I have evaluated both perspectives, and I find myself taking a bit here and there, which has helped me to personally strike a balance between the two worlds. Nigerians have traditionally followed the Biblical adage, "Spare the rod, spoil the child," meaning, if you do not discipline a child, you will spoil the child. Physical forms of discipline, while typically frowned upon within current North American society, are common in Nigerian culture and are viewed as necessary to prepare a child to be a good citizen. Corporal punishment is an accepted, even expected, form of discipline for children, and is seen as an indication of good parenting. A rattan switch, or belt, might be typical items used to punish a child, often called "beating". A beating that leaves a mark on a child is not necessarily considered excessive, as it would be by child welfare standards in the Canada. In Nigeria, any adult may discipline a child, including teachers, relatives, and neighbors. Those who do not physically discipline their children are likely to be viewed as spoiling their children. Discipline may also include a harsh tone and verbal reprimands toward a child, which may be considered verbal abuse by some Canadians.

Another traditional form of discipline, which would conflict with Canadian child rearing standards, is the use of ground hot peppers to punish a child. Hot peppers are ground up and made into a powder or paste. This is then applied to sensitive orifices, primarily the eyes or genitals, and may include putting the child outside in the sun to intensify the pain. While it is very painful, it is thought that this pain will ensure that a child does not misbehave, e.g. steal, again. In Nigeria, the hot pepper is ground using a mortar and pestle, which would not fully grind the seeds, the hottest part of the pepper. In Canada, blenders are typically used to grind peppers. If parents use peppering as punishment, this technical change from pestle to blender may unintentionally make the practice of peppering more painful since a blender will grind up more of the seeds

One other thing that strikes me here is the fact that "You" are your own limit. Whether you ever make a way of living a fulfilled life, here in the western world, is totally dependent on you, and not the Government or the society. You, as a person, have the power to take your own life into your hands, and make whatever you want out of it. On the other hand, the reverse is the case in Africa; the government mostly determines what will become of one. You have a few folks at the realm of affairs enriching their own pockets, while the best brains are roaming the streets because they do not have a means of getting what they need to make it in life. Here, in developed countries, hard work is always rewarded, while the opposite is the case in the developing countries.

It is important to highlight the fact that where ever one finds oneself, there will always be challenges in this life. One must keep keeping on, without fainting or giving up on your Dream and Goal. My husband often tells me this - "Where you have been is not as important as where you are. And where you are is not as important as where you are going. Above all, where you are going is not as important as what you do daily to get there". Successful people think differently. That is why they act differently. We all have limitations, but Champions rise above their limitations. Watch against phrases like: "You are not able", "Forget it", "Can't be done", "Impossible". It takes a man that can see the "invisible" to accomplish the "impossible". While I know that there are racial issues, I honestly believe that many are not limited by the colour of their skin, but by the state of their heart. All things are possible to him that believes. Presently, my husband is working with one of the richest companies in the world – the 8th richest. He is well paid, while I am spending quality time with the kids to give them the quality start-off that they need in life.

We are plodding on, and the gates of hell cannot prevail against us.

Derin and Martins Fatola, Toronto, Canada

[FK: So when such skilled Africans take advantage of the Canadian Skilled Worker Program, what happens to Africa? Do Canada and other western countries care? Apparently not, unless they are still to set up a fair system that would address this problem. Recently, there has been growing emphasis on reverse flows of knowledge, skills and money the migrants send home. What was once termed brain drain is now seen

as brain circulation, but this has blurred important issues. The evidence of reverse benefits flowing back to source nations is far from convincing.

In 2000, The United Nations Economic Commission for Africa organized a major conference on brain drain in collaboration with the International Organization for Migration (IOM) and the International Development Research Center (IDRC, Canada). The conference made numerous recommendations to enhance and strategically reverse brain drain (and enhance brain circulation) such as creating a database of expertise in Diaspora. But there is no illusion that even with successful brain circulation schemes, developing countries, especially Africa, will continue to face serious challenges of massive outflow of talent and skill until such time that the socio-economic and socio-political environment improves significantly.

Whether it is the DV lottery, or the British or Canadian Skilled worker program, it is a fact that Africa is paying a big price for the exodus of skilled workers!]

Chapter 13

Europe: Heaven on Earth?

"There are more things in heaven and earth, Horatio, than are dreamt of in your philosophy." – William Shakespeare

[FK: When Sam Ayiehfor was leaving Bamenda for Germany, he and his beautiful newly wed, Geraldine, knew their dream was coming true; finally, one or both of them would be travelling to 'Heaven on Earth', or at least they thought. But how would they reconcile the African proverb 'A prince is a slave when far from his kingdom' and their dream? Were they headed to The Promised Land or To Slavery? Geraldine Ayiehfor recounts:]

I come from an average poor family of five, and my parents are divorced. My mother had to take care of us all, because my father went his way and remarried, forgetting about us. My mother was a mere typist – secretary with a monthly salary of 36.000 FRS C.F.A. ($75). With this salary, and no other support, life was very hard for us.

When I was young, I used to be ashamed of my mother, and I would say many terrible things to her. Worst of all, I kept on blaming her for the separation between my parents. But she slaved to educate us. What more can a child ask for from a parent, apart from education? We all looked up to her for daily bread. From high school, right to the end of my University life, we lived in a house, which had no windowpanes. For food, we hardly had problems with that because we had farms. During holidays, we would help our mother on the farm. The produce was just enough for our stomachs and nothing more. My mother could not afford extra pocket money when we left for school. This meant that we were left at the mercy of others.

While in university, I became so exposed to the world and to so many strange activities and standards. I needed to dress well to school. Life was really hell then. It was here that I started seeing, practically, what it was like to be in Europe. We had friends who talked of nothing more than about their family members in the Western World. The truth is that, these friends were not just talking because they liked the sounds of their own voices. One could see from the way they dressed, the type of beautiful houses they came from; their futures had Europe written on them.

From Dust to Snow: The African Dream?

During special seasons like Christmas, when many 'Bush-fallers' (Africans in the Western World) travelled home to visit their families, one could see them in very good cars, parading the streets of Buea, near the university, with music in their cars turned to the highest volumes. We students called these cars "moving night clubs". It was so beautiful to stand by the roadside and witness them pass by. Their girlfriends and families were regarded as semi-gods, and everybody wanted to be identified with them. In Buea, it was so easy to identify these 'Europeans' – the way they dress, their type of cars, their hairstyles, and the way those from America, especially, talk, walk, not to mention the way they spend money on beer, girls, at nightclubs and hotels. Who would not love to be one of them, or associate with them?

I, out of the hardships of my growing years, happened to have fallen in love with a nice boy then, a neighbour of mine. When it was certain that he had to travel to Europe, he pretentiously looked for a stupid reason and dumped me. In order to identify myself, or at least to also have a friend in Europe, I personally looked for his address, pretending or at least not believing that really he had dumped me, after all we had shared. It was very difficult to get his address. Families are always very protective with the addresses of their children in Europe. When I finally got it and wrote to him, all I got in reply, after the hard struggle, was abuse and a reminder of my lowly breed. It was obvious, he had gone to heaven on earth (Europe) and the difference was clear. No more dealings with people of my type or breed. I wept and felt so bad. I could not believe how travelling to Europe could make all the difference. I felt so bad because he was my neighbour at home, and everyday I saw their house and all the bitterness kept on resurfacing. I knew the only way to get even with him, was also to travel to Europe. When he first came home for a visit, all the girls in our small village wanted him not only for a boyfriend, but also for a husband. By the time I heard he was home, he had already gone back to Holland. I heard all the things he did when he was home. The fact that he did not even mention my name when he was home made it all the worse. I thought every day about Europe and my desire to go there grew more and more.

I envied him and all those who came from Europe. They were just so special, and people adored them so much. I usually went to my room and cried when I saw any of them pass by. I used to ask why God was so unfair. For secondary school, I had gone to the school of the rich (mission schools); it was not easy for me to fit in that group. Whenever I wanted to make a friend, people would look down on me, meaning that I did not belong there. Rich people's children did not want to make friends with those of the poor. The secret is that, most of these rich students had connections abroad in one way or the other. It was not only at school. All the rich people in our small village community wanted their children to associate only with the children of other rich people. Only the children of these rich people could afford going to Europe. They travelled to Europe all the time. I was so unfortunate in that: people who had links to Europe always surrounded me. I had the Prime Minister's daughter as a classmate all through secondary school. Everybody wanted to be her friend, because it was obvious that she would go to Europe the minute we graduated from secondary school.

With all these experiences, and the way things were going on in Cameroon, there was all indication that Europe was the only answer. I was never going to lift my family or my mother up if I did not go to Europe. I sat and prayed to God every day, for I wanted to travel to that heaven on earth. How did I, the daughter of a typist (not even the type who uses a computer, but one who still uses a typewriter), and a taxi driver (not even the one who owns a taxi, but one who loads other taxis at the park for tokens, or when at his best of luck, helps other drivers, in order to get just enough food-money at the end of the month), expect to travel to Europe? I struggled to ask help from some friends, but all they were interested in were their bodily desires. They would not outwardly refuse to help me, but would keep on building my hopes and encouraging me day in and day out, yet no results. When they had the least opportunity, they wanted to have the small money that I could lay hands on for themselves. I tried to contact some people, and requested friends or old school mates abroad to assist me, but little did I know of their own troubles and responsibilities. This went on for so long; I almost, at one point, decided to drop out of school thinking that I would succeed in travelling abroad, if I concentrated more to look for money and pay someone to help me travel abroad. Thanks to God, I did not drop out of university. Finally and patiently, I graduated.

I gave up the useless struggle to travel to Europe and went back to my hometown, to look for a job as a teacher. I knew this was the end of the struggle for my family. 'When we are down to nothing, God is up to something.' Little did I know that God's perfect time had come! It is at home that I met my husband. We are of the same age group, origin, and lowly background. He had just completed from the Fotso Victor University of Technology, Bandjoun, studying Electronics. He easily found himself a job as a computer and electronics engineer, at one good communications centre in Bamenda, our hometown. He found a job quickly because what he studied was very practical. His salary was good enough at the time to keep us up with life. His father had died four years back, and he had two younger sisters and a brother who looked up to him. His mother worked as a primary school teacher, with a salary lower than that of my mother. He, once, wanted to travel to Europe desperately, because he knew Europe was a solution to all problems. He met a friend, who promised to help him. This friend told him that, since he was an Engineer and versed with computer knowledge, he would look for a job abroad for him. This friend deceived him, took the small money he had saved, and vanished into thin air. He was disappointed, so much so that he decided to drop the issue of travelling abroad once and for all. He decided to focus on his job.

When he met me some months later, we were settled and ready to face life as Cameroonians. We got married six months later. A friend of ours who saw how hardworking and dedicated my husband was, offered to help him get a scholarship. Two days after we got married, this friend called from Yaoundé to inform him that he had gotten the scholarship. We could not believe at the moment, because it was so rare for a person to get a scholarship opportunity in Cameroon, and not give it to a relation or family member of his. Of course, there were some strings attached. But really, when God says yes, nobody can say no; and when it is His time, there is no stopping His supernatural provision.

After just seven days of marriage, somebody who was not only a boyfriend, brother, friend or some relation of mine, but my own very husband, someone to call my own, would be travelling to Europe. Words could not explain my happiness. I was crying for him. I was so happy for my husband. He was such a hard working person. He was bound for success whether in Cameroon or else where. At the age of 24, he was already happily married. This is one of the aspects that can show how serious a young man can be. As he hugged me, I was so proud of him.

My husband realized he had forgotten some documents in Yaoundé with our friend. Yaoundé is a journey of about four hours from home, and about three and a half hours drive from there to the Douala International Airport, where he had to board his plane. We had not done his shopping yet. Everybody in the house was rushing up and down trying to see what could be done that morning. I was so uncooperative; I wanted to be by my husband. His mother could not stand by him at those last moments to give her final good byes. She went to her husband's grave, took some ground and gave us to eat. She also gave her son a Bible and we prayed. She left immediately for her farm, while we were preparing to leave for Yaoundé. We could understand her pain. Her eldest son, whom she now considered her husband, was leaving for a far away country. One thing was very certain. Though in pain, she was so proud that her own son was also going to Europe.

My husband, a friend, and I hired a vehicle to Yaoundé to get the documents. Another close friend, Peris, had to go to the Bamenda main market to do the shopping, and then, to meet us at the Douala international airport. I could not go to do his shopping, because since we got married we had not had time together; it was during this journey that we could discuss some important issues.

In our hurry to reach Yaoundé as fast a possible, we met about seven police checkpoints on the way. At each checkpoint, we had to stop and present the documents of the vehicle. There was nothing we could do about it, because instead of traffic lights and road signs determining our pace of travel, normal human beings like us, in the name of security men, were not only determining the pace of our travel, but were slowing it down without concern. At one point, I had to go out of the car and beg by crying and explaining our situation before they could let us go. My husband had given them some money; it was not enough as they claimed, and he had shouted at them. This only made matters worse. They would not let us go until when I started weeping. If we missed the plane, there were so many things at stake here. My husband had just left work for some days, pretending to be sick. If his boss knew that he was travelling to Europe, he could have done all he could to stop him, considering the services he provided for the company. It was better I just started crying, to let the police know just what pain they were inflicting on us. This helped a lot, because they let us go.

We collected the documents and headed for Douala. It was difficult to get to the freeway, because it was the evening rush-hour period. The tension was so much that none of us said a word for a while. Then my husband thought the driver was too slow, and wanted to drive the vehicle. I could not accept, because he might as well have driven so fast that we would never have reached our destination. We met Peris and the others at the airport just in time for my husband to seize his bags and head on for check-in. My husband never had enough time to tell his well-wishers farewell at the airport. He was the last person to board the plane.

In the midst of all the hurrying and confusion, I never had the opportunity to miss my husband, or to properly tell him farewell. I was so afraid he would miss his plane, so much so that nothing else mattered to me. When he checked in, he never came out again. The one thing that I remember him telling me, when he was about to run into the check-in zone, was that I was going to join him soonest. As his plane began to taxi down the runway, I prayed to God, asking Him to take care of him for me. I was ashamed to cry, because my friends, especially Peris, would laugh and imitate me afterwards. As soon as the plane took off, my knees buckled. Peris was just in time to support me as always. That was when I became afraid. It was then that I realised that even though my husband was going for our good, there was no guarantee that he was not going for good (We might never meet again).

Two days later, he rang home to tell us he arrived safely. I was so happy. I felt so important. At least, a part of me had gone to that land filled with milk and honey. Even if I never made it there, I was still so happy. That was when I became bold enough to tell some other friends of his that he had travelled to Europe.

My husband's travelling to Europe started my own days of personal happiness. I was not only a successful university graduate, not only married to a handsome loving man, but also had a Bush-faller to call my own. I could not believe that, as poor as we originally were, my husband could get an opportunity to travel abroad. When I walked on the streets, I felt so important. Parents in our small village community, who never greeted me before, started greeting me warmly. Doors that could never open before to me, started opening. After church services, some people had time to greet us. Children of rich people in our small community, who were of my peer group, started coming closer and being very friendly. This was the first time that our family was being recognised in our neighbourhood, just because one of us had made it to Europe.

My husband called me day and night. It was so wonderful, and that was really when I thought that he was really in heaven. I missed my husband so much, but I was consoled because I knew he was fine. He did not only call, he sent money to me by Western Union. I was so happy to be amongst the selected people who went to collect money from the bank. I once saw my secondary-school principal at the bank. He was so proud of me, when I told him I had come to collect money sent by my husband, who was in Europe. When I looked at him, I saw the respect with which he greeted me.

Even though I was so happy with myself, I was losing self-control. Everybody knew that I was just married, and my husband had travelled, meaning that I had a lot of money. Before I got out of my bed, there was either a family member or friend standing at my door, waiting with a basket of food. They claimed they had come to see how I was doing. Their real purpose was to lay a problem, and ask for money. Afraid to soil my face in front of family, like a stingy wife, I gave away all my money. I spent until I got myself so mixed up. My poor husband was there, sending money as often as he could, or asking friends back home to give me money. At that moment, life was so easy, and I knew I had money that would never end. I kept on spending. Within three months, I had spent a fortune. The worst of it is that, my husband never complained. I struggled to enjoy the life I had missed out when I was growing up. I bought expensive clothes, and wore the latest things in fashion. I was the wife of a Bush-faller!

Four months later, my husband directed me to meet some friends, who would take me to the German embassy in Yaoundé. I made my passport, went and presented myself at the German embassy. They promised to get in contact with me, if they reached a unanimous decision. I never took my husband seriously. He had not been gone for long, and I did not expect to follow so soon. I decided not to go back to my hometown, but to remain in Yaoundé, where I enrolled to learn Deutsch at the "Centre Pilot" Yaoundé. I went to the embassy everyday for the next month, and no response. They told me to go and wait. The problem was that one document was absent from my file. When embassies say they need all requirements to be presented, there is no joke about it. This document was to be faxed from the council hall, in the town of my destination in Germany. I was so worried, and I called my husband all the time. He just told me to keep on checking. Associating everything to bad luck on my part, I stayed on miserably. After all, many friends had told me that it would be impossible for me to travel, when my husband had been gone just a few months. I could not even concentrate on the Deutsch language course anymore. I knew that I was just being delayed because the visa would not be issued. I was in so much pain.

I stayed in this pain for a long time. One Monday morning, I went to the embassy, and there, my visa was given to me. As I held the piece of booklet close to my heart, I started thinking of all what had gone by the past month, and it was a miracle. In tears, I clung to my passport as if my whole life depended on it. I was also going to travel at last! I tried to call my best friend Peris to tell her the wonderful news, but could not get her. I wept the more. This is a friend who means so much to me. I called my family to tell them of my blessing. Was that news! It was wonderful!

On the day of my departure, we reached the airport at about 8 p.m. I headed directly for check-in, because I wanted to see what would be done with the tons of things everyone had given me. When my bag was weighed, two bags were rejected instantly for a start. As I was returning from the check-in zone, my mother-in-law and mama were coming in with their own bags. I just smiled and told them I could not carry those things. They were so annoyed. I carried the two rejected bags out, telling them I had gone beyond the luggage limit. It was then that they could reason. All my bags were repacked. An elderly mother, who was going to Britain, pitied me because I was already crying. She took one of the bags as her hand luggage, since her children had refused her from carrying anything. Because of this confusion, it was difficult for Peris to sort out the most important things. She struggled, first of all, to pack the things people had sent for their families. When she finally succeeded in packing fewer things, the bag was still over-loaded, because parents of friends had sent things that were too heavy. I did not even know the contents, which was dangerous! It was a friend who finally checked-in my luggage, because he works at the airport. I wore three jackets with pockets and things stuffed everywhere in them. I was sweating and crying. It took a long time for my mother-in-law to calm me, because during this period, my cousins and far relations were fighting over some of my valuable possessions that could not be packed.

My father started weeping. My travelling abroad had afforded a brief time of family reunion at the airport. When I looked up into the eyes of my daddy, I did not only see the tears of a father in pain, who was going to miss a nice daughter he never had the opportunity to be with, but also a proud father in tears of joy, sending off a daughter, to the 'promised land'. My last words were, "My God who has brought me this far, will surely take care of us all. Give Him a try, and He will never fail you." They were so shocked the way I personalised God. As I walked away, they were still shocked, surprised, happy, not knowing what to think.

As we were queuing-in at the last checkpoint, two boys were held for alleged fraud of some sort, and they were escorted off the plane. They were not only weeping, but also wailing. They never came back. I felt so bad for them; they had made it to that point!

The plane was not full, and I was so annoyed, wondering why embassies had to refuse people visas while planes flew empty. The hostesses gave us instructions about safety measures. I was sitting by the window. As the plane took off, I looked through the window, and behold, I have never seen such a beautiful sight in my entire life. I saw the town of Douala in the night with all its lights. It was so beautiful, and I felt so happy and lucky to have been placed by the window. I was busy watching, when out of a sudden something happened. It seemed to me as if the plane was dropping, and I felt my heart also dropping, or maybe coming out of my mouth? I almost shouted. I think the plane must have been changing altitude or so. I tried to adjust. I looked at the faces of the other passengers, and they were so calm. When I turned to look at the window again, the sign of lights and the Douala city had vanished. I started praying. When I opened my eyes and tried to look outside again, I saw a large piece of metal outside. It was going up and down. I was so frightened. I tried to focus, and it was only then that I saw that it was the wing of the plane. I pulled down the window shade but could not concentrate. When I opened it again and looked down, I saw something like water. God forgive my soul! I pulled down the shade for good. This window position was now a nightmare for me. I decided to start thinking about the joy in Europe. I promised myself that when I arrived I would start work the very next day, because I had heard that Europe had so many job opportunities. I thought of my family, and Peris. I knew she would join me soonest.

Europe: Heaven on Earth?

Food was served in the plane, but I had no appetite. I was afraid through out the journey, until our arrival at the Charles De Gaulle Airport was announced. This was the longest journey of my life. I opened the window again. When I saw France from above in the early hours of the morning, I breathed again, because I realised I had finally arrived paradise.

As I passed one checkpoint, I was given a ticket for a continental breakfast at the airport. I still could not eat, because I was so anxious to see my husband. The time went by slowly and I was so angry. I kept my heavy handbag in a corner, and went around having a good look at the airport. I did not even care whether that bag was stolen or not. I was already so tired from carrying it.

When I finally boarded my plane for Hamburg, Germany, all I was planning and thinking about was how to meet my husband. When I arrived, some of my luggage was missing. I gave a complaint immediately, and my husband's address was taken.

As I hurried out, to my shock, my husband was not there. He was not there for the next two hours. I have never been so disappointed in my entire life. Little did I know that it was the least of the surprises waiting for me in Europe! The airport at Hamburg was beautiful, but not as nice or as large as that of Paris. There was no way I could ask anybody anything because I did not know Deutsch. At that moment, I knew what a mistake I had made to travel to Germany without knowing the language. When my darling finally made it, he was smiling. I forgot my anger and ran into his arms. It was a wonderful reunion. I have never felt happier. He told me to hurry or else we would miss the bus, and train. I stood there looking at him; he had grown so pale, so shabby. He had not even shaved for so long. I could not believe it was my husband. I felt pity for him from my innermost heart. Before the bus came to a halt, he was already pulling me along. He jokingly commented that my suitcase was too heavy, not even knowing that some boxes were missing. All the same, it was not easy for us, carrying my luggage and jumping in and out of buses and trains. For once, I was so grateful that the other bags got missing. On the way, I discovered that people were always in a hurry. I was so happy because I entered a plane and a train for the first times in my life, almost on the same day.

When we alighted from the train, in Flensburg, it was really cold. It was winter! At the train station, we met some of my husband's friends who were so happy to see me. I virtually begged them to take me home. When we reached their student hostel, he opened his apartment and we all went into the bedroom with his friends. It was all fun the first evening, because his friends kept on asking me questions about Cameroon. I had to plead with them to come the next day. When they finally left, just the look in my eyes demanded explanations. My husband told me that what was really his was the bedroom we were standing in. When I looked around, all I could see was a bed, a wardrobe, a reading table, a bedside cupboard and a small stand, where he kept his books, a very small television, and a laptop. This bed to me could not even accommodate the two of us at once. I did not see where some of my decorations could fit, like the backrests I had brought. I was embarrassed and I felt so bad. My husband understood my shock. I remembered the big apartments that I left home, with no body staying in them. He told me that the apartment was being shared with four other students. He said he had been waiting for me to come before we could look for a bigger apartment, and that I should persevere till the end of the month.

When I unpacked my bags, especially my clothes, the room became very congested. While I took my bath, my husband rapidly cooked something for me to eat, but only after he had shaved and looked neat again. He had to remove foodstuff from my bag, to prepare the meal. This meant that he himself had not been having enough good food. I immediately thought of the money he had been sending home; I felt so guilty. I wondered why he would not use money to go and buy some African foodstuffs. Little did I know how expensive African foodstuff was in Germany! I thought of what my husband might have been forgoing for me. The bathroom, though two-in-one, was very modern. After everything, my warm shower restored all the strength I needed. After our joined supper, we had a nice time like a family! I told my husband about home and all that I had gone through. While we were discussing, the phone rang. It was an agent from Air France; he had brought my missing luggage all the way from Hamburg to Flensburg.

Before I got up the next morning, my husband was off to school. He came just for a few minutes in the afternoon. He came back again only in the evening. Meanwhile, during the day, I decided to arrange the room to my own taste. When my husband came back, I gave him company while he cooked, to familiarize myself with the environment. It was then that I saw the two girls and a boy, who shared his apartment. One greeted, but the others did not even acknowledge my presence. I was so surprised, and when I greeted them, only one responded. I was embarrassed. We ate in the bedroom, because it was to us more intimate and private. We discussed till the morning hours, before sleeping.

The weather did not improve, and my husband kept on saying that when the weather improved, he would take me out to see some places. I later discovered that the problem was not only the weather, but that my husband did not even have the time to take me out. Like a joke, I spent a whole week inside the room, only going to the bathroom or the kitchen. During these days, my companions were the phone, the television, and the Internet, since we had these at home. The friends, who came to welcome me the first day, never came again. They claimed to be very busy. I kept on phoning friends and discussing with them. I thought I could visit all these friends to give their parcels from home personally. My husband said I could travel at the end of the month. With this, I knew I could go round visiting the whole of Germany. When I asked the addresses of those concerned, they were always so sceptical, and in most cases, never even gave me their addresses. I came to realise the simple truth: everybody was afraid of a visitor. It was expensive to host one. Besides, many people who come to Europe through fraudulent means had put their (hosts) friends into serious problems with the authorities. Secondly, considering the size of the rooms that are available and affordable, it is really inconvenient for two people to live in a room, not to talk of a person who is not family.

In the second week, my husband started creating some time for me. He would come home early and take me to the supermarket, where we got our groceries. These supermarkets were the easiest places we could go to, because they were within walking-distance. I discovered that items were very expensive, because I kept on equating prices to my home currency. My husband told me to stop equating, else I would go mad one day.

My husband established health insurance for me. One needed insurance, because it would be very expensive if you went to a hospital without it. At the end of the month, we got many bills: for our insurances, rents, phone bills, and many others. What caught my attention in particular was the phone bill. Attached to this bill was a letter from a lawyer. My husband would be taken to court if he did not pay this bill. The bill was too high. When my husband just got to Europe, the first thing he had done was to get a phone. He did not know the cheapest phone line to install. He did not also know that there are some cheaper codes that could be used in phoning. He would call and we would talk about things that, in hindsight, were not worth the cost. How would we pay this bill? In Europe every body has his or her problems. You cannot ask for help, even from your own mother. If any of these bills were not paid, our names would automatically enter 'the computer' as debtors, which was very dangerous. This could mar the prospects of extending our visas. So we decided to pay all the other bills. Whatever remained, we would use it for the phone bill. We would arrange to pay for it gradually, monthly.

With this situation, I tried what I could to minimise the bills. I just could not afford luxury anymore. All my trips for visiting were cancelled. I personally started going to the supermarket only for necessities. Luckily some of the spices I brought from Cameroon for soup were still available. We were fortunate that the bills for heating and Internet services were included in our rents. This is one of the biggest advantages that students have in student hostels. With the weather so cold, especially during the winter, the heater was on for 24 hours a day. We used hot water for bathing and electricity for cooking.

When we tried to get a fixed phone installed in our new room, we realized the German system is very effective. There are computer records everywhere. When they discovered that we had signed to pay the phone debt at a stable rate, our new line was connected. I stopped calling friends or making international calls. I started spending all my time either sleeping or watching television. I could lie on the bed in one spot and watch television for almost seven hours. Our new room, though tiny, was better. Here, only one other tenant shared the apartment. At least, there was some privacy for us as a couple. Nevertheless, even in this economical room, our problem concerning housing was far from solved. In our student hostel, it was not allowed for two persons to be in one room. Besides it was very tiny. As such, I had to be hiding in this room, because it was my husband who was the legal owner of the room. I used to go out very early when the caretaker was not yet around, or later, when he had gone home; but most of the time, I was indoors. We were fortunate that the other German students did not report to the authorities. Unfortunately for us, the caretaker saw me struggling to smuggle myself out one day. At once, he sent a warning letter to my husband that the housing contract would be terminated, because he was not keeping to the rules. This was a terrible situation for us. If we were sent out of our room, we would have to look for a non-student residential house. It would be more expensive. So I really had to hide until we could afford two rooms. If one student hostel terminates a contract, it would be difficult to have another, even in another town.

The third week, I started Deutsch classes. Even though I was relieved because I met new friends and had assignments to do, to pay my fees also needed money, which we scarcely had. But what could my husband do? How could he go on leaving me at home all the time? Besides, I needed to learn the German language. Now, as a student, I could move around freely in a bus. Before, I could not afford bus services without a student ticket, though bus services are the cheapest. Taxi services were not affordable as they were only on hire bases, unlike at home, where they are the cheapest means of transportation.

It was in school that I met my first friend in Germany, Simonie. In our class, all of us were foreigners, trying to learn Deutsch. Though we all came from different countries, most of us could manage English. It was here that we were able to discuss, as a group, our various problems and difficulties in Germany as foreigners. I discovered that we all faced the same problems: loneliness, joblessness and worst of all, the difficulty of interaction with Germans. Simonie is from Zambia, married to a German. I was so surprised that she had the same problems I had. The only difference we had was that Simonie's husband was employed and was rich. Even though Simonie's husband was rich, she had no real happiness. She had no child, and they virtually had nothing to do with money, apart from bills. The rest of the money, Simonie sent to Africa. She used to send a lot of money to Africa. Simonie tried all she could to satisfy her family back home, yet she could not. She kept on receiving letters from home asking for money. She was always disturbed. This is a poor girl, who had gotten married to an old white man who was very sick, just to make sure her family got a better life. This white man was impotent, meaning that Simonie could not have children in her matrimonial home. She lived such a desolate life in Europe for the sake of her family, yet her family would not appreciate it. When she sent money home, her brothers squandered this money on girlfriends and nightclubs, while she was there not even knowing where a nightclub was located. Her mother's house in Zambia, had become the house of all her relations, and in the process, her mother knew no happiness.

Simonie is not happy in Europe; her brothers are not making any efforts to become independent. All her sisters are getting pregnant daily; after all, they have free food and a luxurious house free of charge. When they manage to write Simonie, it is only to ask for money. Nobody cared to greet her or even ask about her husband. It was so painful. Her sisters and brothers never cared about education. They are not even willing to go to school, even when the money is sent from Europe. This is a girl who has no future to call her own in a foreign land. She tries all she can to make her family at home comfortable, yet to no avail. She grows paler and paler everyday. Even with all the difficulties, Simonie was able to stand firm because she had come to know and believe in Christ. Simonie lives in Denmark, though she attended classes in Germany. Flensburg is in the north of Germany, bordering the south of Denmark. It is only a bus drop from Flensburg to Denmark. I think getting to know Simonie was one way in which God showed me that what my husband and I were going through was just the least of what some Africans in Europe are going through.

The first day I met Simonie, I envied her. She was married to a German! When I came to know her better, I discovered that she envied us instead. She was always weeping on my shoulder. It was so sad. It was from Simonie, again, that I saw that money really is not all that matters in life. As a German's wife, Simonie had a permit to work in Germany, but she still could not get a job. Unfortunately for her, mostly the old rich white snobs of Germany occupy Flensburg. It has automatically become a desert for young blacks who come to Germany in search of a better life.

But Denmark is different. The Danish will prefer to give foreigners jobs, in order to avoid them from begging or pestering them. This is why Simonie and her husband decided to settle in Denmark. For one thing, Denmark has very high salaries but with a lot of taxes. Danish people pay a lot of taxes, especially, on luxury goods like cars, cigarettes and drinks or even chocolates. Between us at the border, I buy my necessities from Denmark where they are cheaper, while the Danish come to Germany to buy the luxuries. Only buying cars from Germany is the same as buying in Denmark. We used to sit at the borders during the weekends and see how private cars are turned into trucks for transporting beer. The rear tires almost got lost beneath, due to overload. I used to wonder what a single family could do with so much beer and cigarettes within a week. These people smoke and drink, as I have never seen in my life. Also, the coast of Denmark is such a wonderful site. This is where most of their new land is being reclaimed from the sea. The sand dunes are wonderful.

Already, by the second month of my stay, we had started receiving mail from home with demands, the same as those I used to see in Simonie's mail. Our own little addition was that, the friend who helped us secure the scholarship of my husband wanted us to help him transport all his family members to Europe. More to that, whenever he needed money, he thought it was normal to turn to us. I was not even working, and I was not sure of a job in the near future. I now knew why parents were so protective of the addresses of their children abroad.

On the other hand, we were feeling so bad. We thought daily of our parents, the loved ones we had left behind. We could not even make phone calls because things were really hard on us. Our first challenge was to live. I thought of my brother Jones. I discovered that he was better off as a teacher with a family at home than I was in Europe. As a wife, my family was expecting a baby from me. Given the circumstances, this was impossibility. In Africa, people are happy to give birth, but in Europe it is difficult. We were barely able to take care of ourselves.

All in all, when I look at myself today and my entire life, it all seems like a miracle. I recall the beginning, the separation of my parents, the hardships and signs of nothingness and no hope for the future. Here I am today, in Europe, very rich with experiences. But one thing is very certain; if we stay abroad, our success is likely never going to materialise. Real success can only be evaluated, measured and appreciated at home; no matter how long we stay, what we do, or how far we go, our home is Africa. Cameroon is our final destination. My husband and I will keep on waiting on the Lord. He is still renewing our strength daily. May He bless you, and we hope you gain something from our experiences.

[FK: Samuel finished his Masters degree and they moved to England for his PhD. Geraldine works for Royal Mail. A very remarkable couple! They still get lots of mail from home!]

Chapter 14

Nightmares of Baghdad

'Joining the U.S. Army as a foreigner can fast-track your U.S. citizenship, but it could also fast-track you to your grave. Don't join unless you really feel it is your calling. Of course not everyone is cut out for the army.' – Tolu O.

[FK: Recently two Marines killed in Iraq have now been awarded US citizenship posthumously. Surprised that foreign nationals are serving in the U.S. military, and even doing the fighting and the dying? You shouldn't be. Shortly before his death, a foreign Corporal wrote a letter to a former high school teacher explaining why he was willing to go to war: "I want to defend the country I plan to become a citizen of." Some Africans coming to the US clearly identify with the above statement. Here is an insider's perspective from a fine young man from Nigeria.]

My parents lived in England back in the 60s. In fact my 2 elder siblings who were born in England are currently resident there. Unlike them, I did not have automatic British nationality. I grew up in Lagos, and so I had to find my own way.

A cousin of mine was an Ambassador in Cuba and said he would help me to come to the U.S. So I flew Iberia from Lagos to Cuba via Spain. From Havana, I flew into Miami. I took the shuttle to another cousin's apartment in Fort Lauderdale.

When I left Nigeria, I dreamed of being an architect. After arrival, I had to adapt to the realities on the ground. It was really tough for me, and I went back and forth between several jobs. I even had a part time job repairing people's electronic equipment when needed. Then, I realized it would be tough to sponsor myself in school.

Things became really tough, and I decided to have a change of scene, and to save on housing. I went to Atlanta, Georgia, to live with an Uncle who only tried to exploit me. He even got me into trouble. He had a car with no insurance and I was caught by the cops driving it. He had assured me the car had insurance. He said he would easily solve the problem. It was only when I realized I could go to jail that I confessed everything to the judge who pitied me and showed me mercy. The point I want to make is that your fellow country men and even extended family can also be very exploitative. Some give you jobs and pay you less than the minimum wage in the U.S. since they know you are desperate.

Finally I returned to Florida and decided to join the U.S. Army. I had always wanted to be a soldier though I was now older than I would have loved to be when joining. The incentive to later pay for my college tuition was also good motivation. Besides, it could fast-track my American citizenship. You can be drafted as a resident alien, when there's a draft, or you can join in the ranks as a foreigner, but you can't be an officer unless you're a U. S. citizen.

I had to do the Armed Services Vocational Aptitude Battery (ASVAB) test. The line scores determine which jobs an individual qualifies for. If you fail to score at least a 31 on the test, you would not be allowed in the Army. There are some exceptions that could allow you a score as low as 26, but don't count on it. I scored 75 and so could be a Finance technician, Legal Services Specialist, and other good stuff. However, there were no more openings for the areas I liked.

I signed a 2 years contract to be a GI. I went to Missouri, Fort Leonard Wood for training. I was there for 5 months and trained in Nuclear, Biological, Chemical defense including basic training in IT which was a handicap coming from my African background then. It was really tough. I was the third oldest. I had to work really hard and lost 7 pounds. I got used to it later.

With the ASVAB score I had, I could choose in what area I wanted to serve. I chose to be an NBC (Nuclear, Biological and Chemical) specialist. An NBC specialist maintains the unit's NBC defense equipment, trains Marines in NBC defense measures and protection, and advises the unit NBC officer on all NBC defense matters. There were not many of us, and I was the only one in my unit. I liked it because I was the only one in my office, and the commander would say I was his NBC specialist. Then we were drafted to Germany.

In Germany our base was in Schweinfurt. I was however rotated to Kosovo (in 2000) for 8 months. There was no threat of NBC warfare there, so I just helped in the supply unit. Mainly patrols were carried out.

Back in Germany, my worst experience there had nothing to do with warfare or security. Many foreign girls love U.S. soldiers in bases in their country. That is very true for Germany. I easily got a German girlfriend. She was a Bavarian from Coburg. She was ready to marry me. When I realized this, I decided to get the record straight with her. I told her I was an African, from Nigeria, though in the U.S. army. To my utmost shock she said 'tchusss' to me, and broke-up with me immediately. By then she was already making plans to show me to her parents. I was utterly stunned at the behavior. How could someone 'dis-love' me just because I was African? I now understood why most

From Dust to Snow: The African Dream?

Africans in Germany pretended to be U.S. citizens. That way they could win the German girls.

While I was still singing the blues, I met a Nigerian girl in Germany. I told her I was looking to settle down and that after my recent experience I would rather have an African girl. But where were the nice African women? She said she had a cousin back in Nigeria who was a born-again Christian and that I should get her instead of a white girl. That sounded like good advice.

I went home to Nigeria to see her. She was beautiful alright, but I had the impression she just wanted to use me to come to the US. She came to our house but would not eat the food, even what she had prepared. I was suspicious. I prayed over the food before I ate each time. The following day, she asked me to buy her a car. Even if she had put juju in my food, it would have been better for her to let the juju work for a week before asking for a car! And she was supposed to be Born-again?

I decided to leave her for the US immediately. This was in 2002. 'When are you coming back?' She asked. I said I did not know. She said if she did not hear from me after six months then she would put the boot on the relationship. To throw her off, I showed her a child and said it was my son. She said she could not take care of a child I had with another woman. That was the breaking point. I told her it had been a joke, but that the joke had helped me reach a decision.

I returned to the U.S. still womanless and looking. I met several African girls. I observed immediately that African girls in the US had changed a lot. They were no longer the humble girls from Africa. I met another Nigerian girl I really liked or even loved. Like the one in Nigeria, she would not eat food she or I prepared. She had all the take-out numbers, and wanted to eat in restaurants. She said cooking was a waste of time and that she could not cook. I guess I was really exploited by her. By the time I broke up with her, I had paid her tuition, paid about $1000 for her car's down payment and knew dozens of different restaurants in town.

Frustrated with women, I re-enlisted in the Army. This time, I was sent to Iraq in 2003 for 5 months. It was one tough experience. Fellow Nigerians in the US army were killed in Iraq. One Nigerian was killed when a bomb, buried in an Iraqi road, detonated near his Humvee on October 28 2004. His company had set out on patrol at eight in the morning, and linked up with another unit to transfer prisoners. He had seen military service as not just a noble calling for a country he loved, but perhaps an immigrant's lucky path to achievement, and status. He had hoped that serving would help him bring the rest of his family, including four siblings and his mother, to the U.S.

Like millions of other Americans who join the National Guard, and many of the young, black men like me, this Nigerian had not been able pay for college. So, he had joined up a few months before September 11, 2001, securing money for his classes, medical benefits, and a life insurance policy. Two years later, he realized a dream by becoming an American citizen. In February 2004, he shipped off to Iraq, after me, joining the thousands of foreign-born soldiers on active duty there.

Back to me, we had many incidences where I was almost killed myself. I think God helped me so many times. We went though many attacks in Baghdad. One day we were lost between Kuwait and Baghdad and were really lucky nothing happened to us. The experience has left me transformed and wiser.

If you really don't like serving as a soldier, don't join the army. I know many of us Africans are compelled to join the army as an easy way to U.S permanent residency or citizenship or because of the benefits such as college tuition. But if those are really just your reasons, I would recommend you not do it. It's not a lifestyle everybody is cut out for. You have to go through some tough times too, like not having breakfast, having to lie on the bare floor in training – even before the reality begins. You are ordered around, and people tell you what to do. I had always wanted to join the army, and it was great to be able to serve in the U.S army in that sense. But till today, I suffer from the effects. I have nightmares of Baghdad. I have recurring pain in my head, so I cannot study at times.

I think in some ways Nigerians are better off at home than living abroad. Many are crazy about America and many fall victim of 419. Already there is a 419 scam on Iraq. You may get an email like this:

I am [Name deleted], a sergeant in the American army, presently in Iraq. During the raid of the Saddam Hussein hideout, which was also where he kept funds and valuables, I successfully smuggled out a box containing $15.5 million, which I have moved out of Iraq through a diplomatic channel. The funds are presently in the custody of a Securities and Finance company in Europe. I want to move the money finally to a safe bank account through a reliable person. If you are willing to assist me in the deal, urgently contact me through this address for further details.
Regards
[Name]

The objective of the 419-letter writer is to persuade you to pay out more and more money to facilitate the transaction. There are cases where American victims have lost hundreds of thousands of dollars through such advanced fees. So beware! In England, Scotland Yard has been probing a multimillion rand fraud - dubbed the 419 scam - following the arrest of six people in South Africa on suspicion of being involved in a Nigerian e-mail and letter scam that is thought to have defrauded hundreds of millions of dollars from victims. Four of those detained were Nigerian, one was South African, and the sixth was Cameroonian.

I think if you have a good job back home, don't give it up to go abroad and start from scratch, especially, because your previous qualifications and experiences may not even be recognized out here. You are better off at home. You also have much better peace of mind.

As a prospective mechanical engineer, I dream of the day when my country would be able to manufacture their own cars. If the politics is right, I would like to go back to my country and invest there and transfer the knowledge I am acquiring here in the U.S.

[FK: Tolu is currently completing a degree in Mechanical Engineering at the University of Central Florida, Orlando. A truly remarkable man with the courage and patriotism Africans need for an African Renaissance.

In the Marines, at one time, out of a force of 175,000, 7,331 were not yet citizens of the United States and 5,416 became citizens after enlisting. Defense officials estimated at one point that there were 31,000 foreign nationals serving in all the service branches, many of whom are now fighting in the Gulf. Even as American casualties are coming home, there are plenty of would-be Americans who'd be more than happy to join the fight if it means they'd have a chance at living better lives afterward. President Bush signed an executive order expediting citizen applications for non-Americans serving in the military as of September 11, 2001. But heed Tolu's warning. The U.S army has some of the bravest men and women in the world.]

Chapter 15

The Burger

'Wood already touched by fire is not hard to set alight.' – Ashanti proverb

[FK: Ask a Ghanaian kid what he would like to be in the future.
'A "burger"!'
'A what?'
'"Burger", like uncle Kwasi, Bra Kwame, Kodjo Papa, Ofa Ata.'
'Why a "burger"?'
'They have money, drive nice cars, and they don't work, wear nice clothes, live abroad....']

My name is Samuel Dodo. I joined the International Association for the Exchange of Students for Technical Experience (IAESTE) in January 2002. I was then a third year student in the Department of Physics of the Kwame Nkrumah University of Science and Technology in Kumasi, Ghana. Little did I know that a lifetime opportunity was just about to come my way! During one IAESTE meeting, the president called me in private and said, "I want you to be a burger. What do you think?" "There is this pending internship in Germany for a physics student. I will like you to give it a try. Come on, I know you can make it!"

For a moment, I was lost in time and space. I didn't know what to say. Perhaps, I would more appropriately describe my state of mind as having mixed feelings. One part of me was happy for such an academic opportunity. But the other half of me wasn't just ready to abandon my dreams of travelling to the States during holidays, to seek greener pastures and return to school when the semester resumes, just as other colleagues were doing then. After I became conscious of having not answered him, I asked, "Where in Germany?" He smiled for a moment and said, "Leipziq". I didn't know that he meant 'Leipzig', which I had never heard of. I had already made up my mind. "No" was the answer on my mind, because I thought he would mention cities like Munich, Stuttgart, Hamburg, Hanover, Bremen, Düsseldorf, Frankfurt or even Berlin. These cities were cities, which I knew were highly industrialized. Not willing to show the disappointment on my face, and to dump his confidence in me, I told him to give me some time to think about it.

I rushed to the internet cafe on campus just after the meeting, quickly typed 'Leipzig' under Google search. I was disappointed again to find out that it is an East German city. Who on earth would go to a former communist city in Germany, which is still under-developed compared to its western counterparts? I asked myself if any African in their right state of mind would travel into the midst of these racist Germans and survive.

No! In fact, no! 'There is no way I am going to spend my money going to this hostile part of the world', I thought. Days and weeks passed, and I was still battling the idea of going to Leipzig. I later found out that, after all, the University of Leipzig is the second oldest university in Germany, and some of my favourite Physicists like Peter Debye, and Gustav Hertz were once at this University. Being someone who liked orchestral music, I told myself, "Why not travel to the birth land of the great Johan Sebastian Bach?"

Finally, I had to talk to my uncle who happens to be a surgeon in Germany. He embraced the idea, so much so that, I changed my mind. I had to borrow $400.00 from a couple in my church, after convincing them that I was capable of paying this money on my return. This was to be my processing fees for the internship. I was not happy about the topic of the internship, because it had to do with Nuclear Magnetic Resonance (NMR), which I knew very little about. I started visiting the library frequently to read more about NMR. Less than two weeks after my documents (which included birth certificate, English language proficiency certificate, course read in the three years of my study, other academic achievements relevant to the subject etc) were sent, I had an acceptance letter from the German Academic Exchange DAAD, and an invitation letter from the Faculty of Physics of the Leipzig University.

I visited the German Embassy in Accra two days after receiving these two important documents, coupled with my passport photos, introduction letter from the Registrar confirming his knowledge of my impending trip, and the required visa fee for a three months standard visa. At the consulate, they asked the purpose of my travel, though it was stated on the document from the DAAD. Panic and fatigue from having to rush to the embassy to have a place in the long queue, which started the night before, could not spare me the chance to speak fluently and smartly. I stammered the letters I.A.E.S.T.E, and later said internship. My feet grew cold, and my face suddenly turned pale with fear. Lots of thoughts were going through my mind at that time. What would I tell my friends if I was not granted the visa? They would certainly make mockery of me; they would inevitably call me names like: "The disappointed Burger". What would become of the $400.00 I borrowed? How would I pay back? I finally managed to master courage and look confident, though the questioning time was over. The consular officer asked me to come and check after two working days. It was a Friday, which means I was supposed to come back on Wednesday. Unfortunately, the tradition of no work on Wednesdays of the Auslaenderbehoerder and the Burgeramt in Germany even applies to all their embassies overseas. The fact that I would have to return in seven days was the last straw, which broke the camels back. I sought the face and favour of the Almighty God in prayer, whom I trusted beyond all possible doubt that He would save me from becoming a laughing stock among my friends. He alone could make my dream come true.

At last, it was Wednesday evening. I could not sleep, and was awake till 02:00 in the morning before setting off from home. I got to the embassy at 04:00, but the queue was already long. I faithfully joined it, waiting patiently till it was my turn. The call of my name woke me up from half-sleep. I quickly pulled myself together, and was ready to face my fate. "God, in your name I go. Let thy will be done." These words were my prayer, just before opening the door of the cubicle in which the consular officer was waiting. With every passing second, my mind was just set on two things. If I were granted the visa, then I would be the happiest person on earth. If not, then I would curse the day I was born, for allowing myself to be lured into this whole burger affair.

Up till now, I can recall exactly what happened in the presence of the consular officer, just before she handed my passport to me with the visa printed in it! I remember very well how overjoyed I was. I called my best friend telling him how happy I was to have obtained the visa.

I didn't have money to obtain the ticket for the flight from Accra to Leipzig. I was left with two weeks to perform any miracle to secure the flight. I visited one uncle to the other with hope of borrowing $800.00 for my ticket. I left all of them with disappointment for their inability to help me. I don't have that many aunties though; but the few I have couldn't help me either. I talked to a travel agency, which helps students travel on credit and pay on return. But this also requires a guarantor with collateral. No one wanted to take such a risk. I eventually had to return to the same couple again for assistance. This couple happens to be the head of the children's ministry of my church. They had to loan me this money again from the account of the children's ministry.

On the 30th of July, 2002 at around 15:00 GMT, I was on a queue at the Kotoka International Airport for the check-in. I had my Lufthansa flight ticket in my passport in my left-hand, my carryon bag, and a medium sized suitcase full of winter and a few summer clothes. My lovely mother, my elder sister and her husband, and my best friend Konadu, were at the airport to see me off. My mum couldn't help it but to continue sobbing, because she was so happy to see her first son travelling abroad. It was difficult to say the final goodbye amidst the tears of joy.

From Dust to Snow: The African Dream?

The breeze was cold and windy at the stairway hanging from the door of the aircraft. I took each step with caution, careful not to disclose that I was a first-timer. It was like a dream, seeing myself in a plane, listening to the safety measures, which ought to be taken in time of emergency. I will never forget the sensation that modulated through my body. The wave, reminded me of the Tsunami earthquake. This was when the aircraft took off from the runway. This made me grip my seat so firmly that my knuckles almost tore though my skin. I forgot I had me seatbelt fastened. The thought of seeing sky-scrappers of twenty, forty or even more floors couldn't let me sleep during the nine hours flight to Frankfurt am Main. I made sure that I requested every kind of food served on board.

Summer's early sunrise over the sky of Frankfurt is a beautiful sight every man aught too see from the window of the Lufthansa aircraft. How I had wished to explore the beauty of this financial city of Germany, before taking the next flight to Leipzig. I was deprived of this, due to security reasons. I rather had just a glimpse of it from the transparent glass of the airport building. As I waited an hour or two in the busy airport, I watched about ten aircrafts taking off and others landing every passing minute.

In the much smaller Leipzig-Halle airport, it wasn't difficult for Prof. Geschke to make me out, because I was the only black in the arrival hall. He called my name as he drew closer to me. I turned, and with a brilliant smile shook his hand. I forgetfully clapped his finger as is the custom in Africa. I was a bit embarrassed when I became aware of myself, but quickly became at ease with his exceptional friendliness. Not withstanding that he is quite old, I decided to carry my suitcase and carryon bag alone though he offered to help. We drove in his car, conversing about my rather long flight from Ghana.

He introduced me to some of his group members, and I was then taken to my office, which I liked instantly because of the wonderful view from the window. We went to lunch that afternoon, and something memorable happened which I would never forget. He handed a menu book to me, and asked me to make a choice. Rather unfortunately, the menu was in German, and I couldn't understand. I didn't ask him to explain the menu to me either, because he was my professor and not a friend. I chose a menu with soup, hoping I would enjoy it. When the food was served, lo and behold, it wasn't what I was expecting. The mashed potatoes and sauce wasn't my kind of food. I turned to the soup hoping it would be a consolation. It was rather worse. I nearly vomited. He saw the disappointment on my face. It tasted different and wasn't that spicy and hot as it would be in Ghana. I was embarrassed. I barely managed to eat, and this compelled him to take me to the grocery shop after the lunch. I prepared something delicious for myself later that evening.

The house in which I stayed was lovely and the landlady and her husband were very friendly. They provided me with anything I requested, and invited me over for dinner occasionally. They even took me to Dresden a nearby city of about 170 km from Leipzig, where we visited the famous castle "Der Zwinger" and some other museums, all paid by them.

One day, I woke up, just to realize that my room was flooded to knee level. It had rained heavily overnight, and this made their drainage system in the house to 'choke'. This was around the same time in August 2002, when the heavy flood in Dresden destroyed so much property. We all had to work in the water to get rid of the water. This made them like me more.

Everybody was nice to me at the workplace, and I even made some friends. I never had any confrontation whatsoever with the people and even till date haven't seen such a thing. The people were friendly where ever I went, at church, at the parks, at the lakeside, in the pubs, sport complexes and even discos. Sooner than I had wanted it, my two months internship was getting over.

I organised a party two nights before my departure and it was very beautiful to see the number of friends I had made in such a short time. The night was very wonderful and emotional as well. Among the people who came for the party was my girlfriend Julia, and Eva my closest friend with whom I spent most of my leisure time. I said my last goodbye to Frank at the airport that early 3rd October, 2002 after we had spent my last night together with his wife Conie. At this point I was sad; I was leaving such wonderful people. I knew I might not see some of them again. I got to Ghana with many sweet memories of Germany as a whole. It was obvious at this moment that my perception about Germany had changed, and I wouldn't allow anybody to call Germans racists.

With the wonderful memories from Germany, I decided to apply for my master's degree program in Germany. I returned to Berlin on 30th July, 2003, after completion of my B.Sc. degree in Physics.

I have been a graduate student since April 2004. I am happy that I considered my friends question, "Do you want to be a burger?"

[In 2006, Samuel married lovely Josephine Ankrah in Berlin Germany, where he is currently a doctoral student.]

Chapter 16

An African in white skin

"He who does not know one thing knows another" – Kenyan Proverb

[*FK: Is culture shock sensitive to skin colour? How does a white person's experience compare with that of a black person in a western country? Debbie goes straight to the point:*]

By the time I was 17, I was ready to leave Kenya, the place of my birth, a place of familiarity, my culture. I wanted to go exploring a new world with new people. Little did I know how different it would be!

I was so excited about going to America. I thought everyone would be really friendly, and really excited to get to know me and learn the exciting experiences I had to offer. I was blessed to have a roommate at the Christian college I attended who somewhat understood my background. You see, she had lived in Africa too. The only difference was that I had lived surrounded by the local people, my friends, and she had lived surrounded by other missionaries. So in a sense, she was better equipped for life in America than I was. My other roommates were totally different and I remember not understanding all the little things they said and did. They were American.

I remember clearly the little setbacks I faced; they didn't seem so little at the time. I remember wearing my 'Born in Kenya' t-shirt with pride one day, only to be stopped by a girl who asked me why I was lying. I was puzzled, as I hadn't said a thing. So, I asked her why she thought I was lying. She told me I couldn't possibly have been born in Kenya, presumably, because my skin wasn't the right colour.

I also clearly remember an English professor singling me out in front of the whole class, telling me that if I spelt any words the British way I would be penalized. Well, with a British father and an American mother, how would I know which words were British and which were American? They were just part of my vocabulary. I felt even worse when my roommates invented 'Debbie's Dictionary', a list of all the words I said that were different, such as: biscuits = cookies (in the U.S.), chips = fries, bonnet = hood (of car), trousers = pants, etc. I began to feel so alone and different. I did try to explain to the patient ear that they were many differences between British English and American English, more than people actually realise, and that it could be very difficult for someone like me.

My first winter in America was very cold, and I remember being scared to walk anywhere for fear of slipping and falling on the ice. The snow, beautiful as it was, was very cold. After a few winters, I began to appreciate the snow, as when it snowed it meant it was too cold for it to rain. I preferred to walk to classes in the snow and only get my shoes wet, instead of walking in the rain and getting cold and soaked. I would never have enjoyed the snow if it hadn't been for Mike, another Kenyan student, who started a snow fight in the street. Ah, the good times!

My greatest bugbear, however, was my complete isolation and rejection by the African-American community at my college. That was so disappointing to me, as I thought they would have been thrilled to meet someone who had actually lived in Africa. All my friends in Kenya were black, and naively I thought I would be accepted the same way in America. It was an incredible shock! I even asked to join the African-American organization, only to be rejected, presumably, because my skin wasn't the right colour. I had never thought on those terms before. I wanted to share my culture with people I thought were like-minded. It wasn't till a few years later, when I became president of the International Student Organization, that the other African-American students finally realised I wasn't an impostor or pretender. Then, I began to make some lovely, valuable friendships that lasted the whole time I was at college.

My saving grace was the international students who I knew were experiencing many of the same things as me. It helped me forge such a close bond with them. My driving force became the urge to educate Americans on the cultures and differences of the International students. I wanted everyone to know and appreciate the differences of others, and learn to accept them for who they are. I would like to think that in the 4.5 years I lived in that small town, Beaver Falls, in western Pennsylvania, I was able to change a few people's perceptions about people with different cultures.

Now, I don't want you to think my time in America was terrible. It was just in the first year or so that I experienced that terrible culture shock and felt that incredible isolation. I learned fast, spelt the American way, spoke the American way, made friends and worked hard. My professors were wonderful, some took me under their wings, and I knew that I could always go to them in times of trouble. Ann was my rock. I knew that any time I had a problem she would make time for me. She gave me the will to achieve; she encouraged me, as I became President of The International Student Organization and editor of its newsletter. I loved showing everyone that it was okay to be different; it was something to be proud of.

So, having spent the first 2 years of my stay at Geneva College trying to fit in, I spent the rest of my time being different and proud of it. What a learning experience!

[Deborah Underhill is presently resident in Birmingham England.
Debbie's experience invokes thoughts of whether skin colour matters. From her case, one can conclude that culture shock is colour blind.]

Chapter 17

An African falls on his feet

'I have been driven many times to my knees by the overwhelming conviction that I had absolutely no other place to go.' – Abraham Lincoln

[FK: *'In order for people to be happy, sometimes they have to take risks. It is true these risks can put them in danger of being hurt.'*
That is an understatement! Let me put it this way: The risks can put them in danger of death. But, Mark Twain once said, *'Sail away from the safe harbor...Dream!'*]

In 1982, I decided to take a risk. I made up my mind to leave my country Cameroon and go abroad to Germany. This decision was not at all an easy one for me. First of all, I could not count on financial support from my parents who were poor farmers. Secondly, I would have to stay without seeing my family for quite a long time, since I could not afford an air ticket to visit my parents and family members. But one does not discover new lands without consenting to lose sight of the shore for a very long time. Third, I was going to a country where everything was new to me, language, culture, people, their way of living, weather, food and many other things. In addition, the fear of loneliness and not being accepted were haunting me. However, you cannot eat palm oil without risking climbing the palm tree.

If you are to survive as a foreigner in a foreign country, you need to be determined, and flexible. I am someone, who can easily and quickly adapt to various situations, but still remain myself. The first thing to which I quickly adapted was the German kitchen. I ate almost everything that could be eaten. I did not refuse to eat any type of foodstuff, even those that I had never eaten before. I was in a difficult situation that did not permit me to refuse any food offered. Let me explain.

Having completed the language course at Blaubeuren and Schwäbisch Hall in 1983, I found myself living without a residency permit. I had no money since all money had been spent on language courses. I had no work permit. Mrs Bandlow and Mrs Riderer (Germans I had come to know) offered me shelter and food free of charge. For four months, I lived in constant fear of being caught by the authorities. The Riderer family was also afraid of being caught and penalized for giving me illegal lodging. I was desperate. Returning to Cameroon without professional qualification was not an option.

When problems come, they come in bundles. At that time, I lost my passport and had enormous difficulties with the Cameroonian embassy, which refused to issue me a new passport. I was without a passport in a foreign country for almost a year. Without any legitimate documents, I could not even confidently walk along the streets. I was not able to identify myself, if something happened to me. Even the numerous telephone calls to the Cameroon embassy, which Mrs Bandlow made concerning this problem, were to no avail. I had no peace of mind, and I could not sleep at night. My nights were spent weeping instead of sleeping. Every now and then I had the feeling that, on going out of the door, I would be confronted by police officers, who would deport me.

At this point, everybody who tried to help me gave up, and most of them advised me to return to Cameroon. I was, however, determined to resist and wait to the bitter end. My return to Cameroon without a profession meant that I would have wasted time and money for nothing. The chances of having an opportunity to study a profession appeared to diminish each day. With the help of Mrs Schwarz, I decided to look for a bank where I could carry out a practical course. If I proved myself efficient, I might be given the opportunity to study professional Banking. It was also not easy to find a Bank, which was prepared to offer me this chance. Mrs Schwarz contacted several directors of cooperative Banks in the area to see if they could help.

After a long period of waiting, I was asked to present myself at the cooperative Bank at Herrenberg on September 9th, 1983. Mrs Schwarz travelled with me to Herrenberg, and I met the bank Director, Hanßmann. The interview lasted about half an hour. Mr Hanßmann asked Mrs Schwarz if she could put her hand into the fire for me. She told him that she was convinced that I was a reliable and honest person, prepared to work hard in order to meet up with expectations. So it was, at last, that I was offered the chance to carry out a practical course.

The opportunity was attached to certain conditions, which I had to fulfil with the authorities before I could start. I had to present both a working permit and a residence permit, a condition that was difficult to fulfil, because I had been in the country illegally for four months. Things became even more complicated, due to the fact that the authorities in Ulm had not been informed of my illegal stay. It was a problem, to convince the officer in charge to backdate my residence permit to June 1983, to bridge the 4 months illegal stay from June to September. Mrs Bandlow mobilized all her contacts with people he thought could be of help, so that I would not miss the golden opportunity in Herrenberg.

An African falls on his feet

Friends and sympathizers made several calls to the District Officer (Landrat) on my behalf. The president in the District Office in Ulm was really hard-hearted, and kept insisting that I should present myself to the public prosecutor and explain how it came about that I had stayed in Germany for 4 months without a residence permit from the authorities. But God can enter the minds of people, no matter how hard they may be, and soften them, if He wants to fulfil his plans. After a long struggle in Blaubeuren and Ulm, the big wonder came to happen: I was issued a backdated permit, thus covering my illegal months in Germany.

It is really wonderful how the mighty hands of God kept protecting me in the critical situation in which I found myself. During this time, without any hope of coming out of this deadlock, I wrote to my parents telling them that if they did not hear from me again, I could be sitting in prison. The reply to my letter came after sometime, with the cry that I should return home immediately. I was, however, determined not to go back to Africa without having reached the qualification I was struggling for. I once more wrote to my parents telling them that there was no turning back, and that I was looking forward to the future, be it good or bad.

With my permit, covering the months of June to September, I was able to present myself to the authorities in Herrenberg in order to begin my banking practicals. Herrenberg is a small town 34 km from Stuttgart.

On my arrival in Herrenberg, I spent the first two weeks with a family at Haslach, a village 3 km from Herrenberg. The lady was a friend of the Riderer family in Blaubeuren, where her husband had been a pastor for some years. It was difficult for me to stay in Haslach without a car. I felt lonely, and above all I had turned into a sort of attraction. As I was walking around, people kept staring at me. In a way, I could understand their reaction, because some of them had never seen an African before.

My practicals were to begin in one of the branches of the Herrenberg Cooperative Bank, which was located at Oberjesingen. As I did not have any means of transportation, I tried together with Mrs Schwarz to obtain a room in this village, but all our efforts were in vain. People whom we contacted, asking if they could let a room to me, were distrustful because I was black. Finally I got a room at Haslach, and travelled to work with a colleague who lived in the same village.

A most terrible thing, which I experienced, was on a Saturday in winter. It was bitter cold, and my colleague, who went to work with me, had a day off. I had therefore to go on foot from Haslach to Oberjeisingen, which was a distance of about 8 km. In cold and frosty weather, which I was not used to, I thought I would never reach the Bank walking in the cold. My blood would no longer circulate, and my whole body felt ice-cold. I had a similar experience later, as I waited for a bus at the bus station at Herrenberg to take me to Haslach. As a result of standing too long in the snow, one of my toes became frozen and gave me a lot of pain, after which, I could hardly wear shoes. At that time, everything seemed to be against me: starting with weather and food, and ending up with people's dialect and their way of thinking.

Apart from a few exemptions, the Suabians in southwest Germany have a general characteristic. When someone is irritated, or agitated, the first word they spoke to cool down their temper was "Scheisse", which means "shit". I never understood the reason why people were fond of using this particular word, although it is impolite. Once, I was invited to birthday party, and most of the people present were non-Suabians, who in very rare cases used this vulgar word. After we had eaten cakes and drank coffee and tea, we sat together in a comfortable circle and suddenly found ourselves in an interesting conversation. I had always thought that whenever one felt relaxed, or something was very interesting, one called out this word "Scheisse". And so it happened! We were all sitting around laughing after someone had narrated a funny incidence. In the middle of the laughter, I shouted out the word. Suddenly, everybody was silent, and they looked at each other with astonishment on their faces. I myself was surprised to see people reacting in this way, but nobody said anything regarding the issue. My main aim of saying this word was to give more fire to the laughter. Silence in the room, after the incidence, made me feel that I had done something out of place. After the guests had gone, I helped my landlady to clear away the teacups and wash them. She asked me if I had noticed extraordinary reactions during the birthday party. I said yes, and asked her why the visitors had reacted in such a way after I had shouted "Scheisse". She then explained the meaning of the word to me, and said it was vulgar, and to be avoided by every well brought up person. She advised me to remove this word from day to day vocabulary.

The month of December is the beginning of the winter in Germany. The word winter for me was a name for European season of the year, but what stood behind this word was unimaginable for me. I remember my first winter in 1982. I was sitting in my room in "Auf dem Rücken", which is the name of the street where I was living at the time, trying to do my German language homework. After sometime, I lifted my head and looked outside. Through the window, I saw how the grass started changing its colour from green to white. I became curious and anxious to know what was going on outside. I opened my window, and saw small white particles, which were falling from the sky. I was totally perplexed and speechless. I stood there behind my window for almost an hour, watching these white particles falling. I ran downstairs to my landlady, and asked her what it was that was falling outside. How was I supposed to know what it was, if I did not ask? Mrs Maier, my landlady, told me that it was snow, and took time to explain to me when winter begins and ends. I had never seen snow in my life. Apart from postcards, it was like a miracle to me, and the experience was simply marvellous. As a schoolboy, I had been told that snow was very cold, and you could become sick from the cold if you do not wear warm clothes. This narration remained within me, up to this historic day, a fairy tale that was being told to children.

With perplexity, I watched the snow falling. I intended to go to town to do some shopping for myself, but the question was how to get to town without the snow touching my head. I thought if snow fell on my head and body, I would fall sick. I did not have an umbrella, which would have provided the solution to my problem. So, I decided to use my handkerchief to cover my head and protect it. Later, I was walking through the street of Blaubeuren with my handkerchief on my head, when I saw a group of young people, standing in the snow without anything on their heads, and even playing with it. I could not believe my eyes! They were really touching this cold substance, which I thought was dangerous to one's health. I stood there and watched them forming snowballs, holding them in their hands and shooting them at each other. I wondered why I was carrying a handkerchief on my head. I took courage, and pulled away the handkerchief. The snow fell on my head, and even remained on it before melting away. The big question now was: would I fall sick after having carried snow on my head? I think this experience with snow is really marvellous for most of us who come from tropical countries, where there is no snow. Most people who have this experience for the first time try to suppress their emotions, in order not to be laughed at.

It was difficult for me to wear warm clothes: I had problems with putting on gloves; wrapping a scarf round my neck gave me the feeling somebody wanted to hang me. I also had to become acquainted with sleeping in a heated room. Also, life in European countries is extremely expensive where you have a contrasting winter and summer. You need different sets of clothes for the winter and for the summer. The cold weather always made me homesick.

Looking back at my first Christmas in Germany, I see myself sitting in my room, lonely, with little to eat apart from bread and cheese. I slept the whole day, and my thoughts were in Cameroon with my family, who would be spending Christmas singing and dancing. During one of my lonely moments, I tried to bring a few lines together about Mr. Loneliness:

Mr. Loneliness, Mr. Loneliness!

From Dust to Snow: The African Dream?

Who are you really?
What are your intentions?
Are they good or are they bad?
Should I give shyness the blame or your invisible power?
Loneliness! Do you know how powerful you are?
You even pursue man till he falls into depression and frustration.
Loneliness, you must finally understand that your power is limited
And man can overcome you.

You might ask who that person is who is more powerful than yourself.

His name is Mr Patience and man needs him to overcome Loneliness.

With time, I began to notice and make interesting observations with regard to the way Germans celebrate Christmas. For most of them, Christmas has a different meaning from what it really represents. Every country has its own customs and traditions, but I find it unsettling that some parents ask their children to make a list of the presents they want to receive, while forgetting to tell them why they celebrate Christmas in the first place. On the day after Xmas, they call Boxing Day, people can exchange presents they don't like with other people through radio programs, Internet, etc. They could also return them to the supermarket.

The way Sunday services are held is very boring, especially, at the beginning when I recalled our African services. In European services, the clapping of hands is almost taboo, not to talk of drumming, although, some youths are experimenting this way of worship. I had grown up without hearing an organ being played in church on Sundays. As I am not a musician, and cannot read the musical symbols, the playing of the organ appeared to be unnecessary. Gradually, because I was ready to learn and understand, I became used to this kind of music.

Although whites and blacks differ, I believe that they belong together. What impressed me amongst the German people was their sympathy and goodwill. Many people gave to help the underdeveloped countries of Africa, which is humane. Many people have the will to help through donations for projects in Africa. There are numerous private organisations, which support different projects in various parts of Africa. It was also encouraging for me, as an African, to see how people in Germany demonstrated and protested against racial discrimination in South Africa in the eighties.

There is the saying that 'In Europe people have watches but no time, while in Africa, people have no watches but lots of time'. If there were a supermarket for buying time in Europe, it would make a lot of money. Everybody is so busy, and no one seems to care for his fellow human. Permanent stress as happens in Germany can sometimes end up in illnesses, which are often incurable despite modern medical advancement. Loneliness multiplies this problem. Even though the life expectancy is higher, people are apparently less happy.

My Mother visits me!

One dream of Africans in the Diaspora is to invite their family to visit them in the white-man's land. My mother was 56 years old when she visited me. When I left in 1982 for Germany, it was an incurable wound for my mum. I remember her weeping bitterly at the airport before my departure. The first two years of being away were a difficult time for her. Whenever she thought of me, she started weeping. I was like the prodigal son who went away from home, his parents not knowing when he would ever return. They did not know anything about what I was experiencing. My mother sensed I was going through some real tough times, so she often wept. She would love to visit me to see how I was getting along. She told me this during her visit in July 1988. Her wish and longing could not be fulfilled because she was too poor to save money for the air ticket to visit her son.

On Tuesday June 28 1988, I arose early as Mrs Schwarz was to collect me in her car to meet my mother at the airport in Stuttgart – Echterdingen. Some friends of mine had also come to the airport to join us. The plane landed 10 minutes behind schedule. As the time for the plane to land was drawing near, I became nervous and extremely anxious to see my mum after 6 years. After the plane had landed and the passengers were pouring out into the waiting room, I was straining my eyes to see her. When I saw her coming, I ran towards her and collapsed into her arms. For a long time she held me in her arms full of joy and satisfaction, tears streaming down our eyes.

On our way from the airport, my mum asked how long I was still going to stay in Germany before returning home. When I told her I intended to stay for another 3 or 4 years, she was very disappointed. She wanted me home earlier. I was very happy with all the things she brought, especially, the African foodstuff, which I had lacked for the past 6 years. I was so happy to eat food prepared with palm oil, which my mother had brought. Eating African food after such a long time felt as if I was rediscovering my African identity, which I thought had disappeared. The first night she spent in West Germany was a very short one, because I was so eager to hear all the news from home.

Working along Stuttgart's main shopping street, Königstrasse, we came across beggars, drunkards, and homeless people, and my mother was speechless. She thought Europeans that she had seen at home represented the European standard of living, which would be characterized by the absence of poverty. She now saw that the way

Europeans live in Africa was not indicative of all people back in their respective homelands. It changed my Mum's thinking that Europeans were all rich and had everything they needed.

On the 30th, Mum prepared a typical African meal. In the evening, we were invited by a group of friends who wanted to meet my mother. After supper, we sang some songs and then conversed. My friends had many questions to ask. They were interested in the types of crops my mother grew on her farm, the well-being of the family, and her feelings seeing her son after such a long time. She answered the last question by saying that it was as if I was lost, and had been found again. My main activity was to translate all that she said from my mother tongue (dialect) into German and vice versa. My mother was very impressed with the welcome these friends offered her. She convinced herself that I had nice friends who regarded me as one of them. Soon she had a very favourable impression of Germans, and thought that all Germans were as nice as the friends she met during her stay in Germany.

The days kept passing and the three weeks were like 3 days to me. Finally on July 17, Cordula Siefert took us to Frankfurt Airport. My mother's visit was the highlight of my stay in Germany.

In my experience, God always showed me his loving care, and carried me through all my difficulties. Today, I am looking back to numerous ups and downs, tears of sadness and joy, and I must say, though the impact was often rather violent, I am glad to have always 'fallen on my feet' in prayer.

[FK: Herr Peter Nebangwa dedicates this contribution to the memory of his parents who passed away in 2004. Today, he works at a bank in Frankfurt. He is one of the founding members of the African Renaissance Ambassador Corporation, an organization seeking to promote the African Renaissance amongst Africans at home and abroad.

It is time for Africans to dream of an Africa, where their children will grow and want to stay.]

Chapter 18

America: The good, the bad, the ugly

'Do not tell the man carrying you that he stinks.' – Sierra Leonean saying

[FK: Each immigrant comes to the U.S with an image of America in his/her mind. An America often reconstructed from Hollywood movies, MTV and glossy magazines, half-remembered history lessons and the Moon Landing, an America of star-spangled banners, dollar bills and Lady Liberty. As soon as the I-94 form is stapled on your passport at your port of entry, reality begins to meet myth head-on. Here is Miranda Musonge's experience:]

For hundreds of years, people from every continent have been coming to the US in search of the American dream. If earlier they came by cargo boats and steam ships, today's African, like me, travels economy class, on mostly European and American airlines via Europe, even when it is shorter to fly directly across the Atlantic. In my case, the flight was via Paris. When I got off the plane in Paris, I could not imagine I was in France! I looked out and saw the splendid buildings along the streets. The roads were so clean, and everything looked so beautiful. In fact, I knew I was in a completely new world.

I had to start adjusting right from France. The first adjustment was with the escalators. I was quite excited because I'd seen them only on television before. Since I hadn't experienced getting on them before, I nearly fell when I first stepped on them. As a result of this first scare, I tried to avoid them every time I had to ascend or descend. In some instances, I couldn't avoid them; I tripped over a couple of times.

Just like the escalators, my first encounter with the baggage carousel (in New York) was fascinating. It seemed like a rattling python, continuously spewing the luggage of hundreds of passengers who stooped to collect. After collecting, I had to re-check-in my luggage for the connecting flight to Los Angeles.

My connecting flight landed on a hot dry day in L.A. As we drove from the airport, I was impressed by the highways so wide that some divided into 4-8 lanes! That was awesome to me. When we reached my sister's house, I was surprised to see that the cars parked along the curb looked beat-up like Kumba-Mamfe cars. Out on the stoop, a bunch of men were sitting hunched over their six packs and a dog was incessantly barking. A homeless man was clanking garbage cans. My sister's home was in a slightly rundown three-family house, and as we trudged up the stairs, bags and all, I wondered with a sinking heart whether this was really America.

Since then, of course, I have learned that America is — like any place — a mix of the good, the bad, and the ugly. Rather than a glittering peroxide Hollywood replica, America is people — tall, short, thin, fat — often very fat, diverse faces and beliefs, cultures and colours — and that's where its true beauty lies. When I say very fat, I am not kidding.

When I got up the following morning, I thought I was in a dream. Come on man! I was in America! As I stood gazing through the second story bedroom window at the American sunrise, lo, I saw a man who seemed like two people put in one. I was glad he could not see me staring because he would have thought I was looking at an alien. He had wild tattoos all over his hands and arms. He wore scary-looking chains and bracelets, and had a very big ring pieced through his nose. The first image I had in my mind when I saw him was that of a pig, an engineered (agric) pig. Just then, two kids came along, even fatter. Compared to them, I was like a broomstick. I had never seen people as fat as these. They had stomachs that overflowed past their waists, with some almost touching their knees! I wondered what they ate that made them so fat. I felt like I could not breathe when I looked at them.

After being in the U.S. for a while, I have come to see some reasons for their obesity. Some Americans eat so much fast food that it is as if they sleep with food in their mouths, eat in their dreams, and wake up with food in their mouth. In addition, because of the technology, they avoid the least activity that would cause them to break a sweat. (I have seen Americans drive to their mailboxes in front of their houses, like driving to a pit-toilet in the village back home). Because of that, fitness studios abound and are big business in the U.S. Still, despite the ongoing influx of diet and exercise programs into mainstream culture, 2005 reports show that the prevalence of obesity and being overweight in the United States has not only increased, but significantly so. Close to two-thirds of adults are either obese or overweight; that is nearly two out of every three Americans!

One thing that probably agrees with the picture of America is the abundance, which goes with waste. I was stunned by the sheer wastage of food, even when there were many homeless people on the streets of Los Angeles. This was particularly worrying at the time when I followed the news on Sudan where mothers had to give their children leaves to eat. Then I really felt angry at the careless throwing away of food. Then I understood why Americans viewed Africa the way they did.

Perhaps the biggest culture shock came when I realized I was on my own as soon as I moved to the University, UCLA. I was totally on my own! No extended family to bail me out. No second cousins or brother-in-law's uncle to give me a recommendation for a cushy job. I was in the driver's seat. In Cameroon you get up in the morning and there are ten people there to greet you and to discuss how you slept. Here, you do not even 'sleep'! When you call someone, you meet an answering machine even on the cell phone.

In Cameroon — it's all there for you: your identity is there for you, your life is there for you, your community is there for you. Over here, everything is what you do yourself. It's a lot of pressure; plus you are now a minority. There is something to be said for growing up in a country where your accent is just right and your skin colour is the only way to be, a place where everyone understands the word Bush-faller. Yes, even the English is different here. When I just arrived, and was greeted by an American 'Wazz up?' I was really puzzled. What did he mean 'What is up?' I did not know how to respond. I felt really paranoid until I learnt from my sister that that was just an Americanism for 'hello, how are you?'

Other issues included holding the door open for someone coming after you. It took a long time to fathom the cold looks I got each time I let go of the door after me! The orderly and polite lines at banks and checkout counters, buses and theatres in America, are something unthinkable in Cameroon.

As a budding woman, I have also learnt while here that even when I reach 80 or 90 years, I will not just abandon attempts at maintaining myself and looking good as most people do in Cameroon. For American women, life doesn't begin or end with a husband. That, perhaps, is one of the biggest cultural differences for women Cameroonians can learn from. Also, the idea of despising women who are not married, as is tacitly done in Cameroon, is non-existent here. I know we girls push the liberty bit in America too much, especially, when we realize we are free to do anything we want, including flying out of town to sleep with a boyfriend, without fear of family opinion. We should rather maintain such moral values as our parents taught us at home.

Overall, living in the U.S., one must transform himself/herself physically and emotionally to survive. You will soon find yourself paying more attention to your weight; you will have to learn to overcome the enormous societal stress – alone: bills, bills, bills, and bills. It was also very challenging as a foreign student to adjust to my American surroundings. During this learning process, I tried to be in contact with the American culture, while remaining connected to my language, traditions, and cultural beliefs. From my experience, it is helpful to become familiar with the International Student Services Office and what they offer for support and information. I also tried to develop social networks and friendships with other international students. I became involved in the Black Student's Alliance. This provided a sense of belonging. I also learned that despite the pressures out in the U.S., it was important to stay in contact with family and friends e.g. via e-mail or telephone calls when possible. This helped to overcome loneliness and homesickness, academic difficulties, confusion with American culture, anxiety, relationship problems, and prospects of depression.

[FK: Miranda is presently a nurse. Though she has attained the American Dream, she wishes she could be able to work in America and live in Cameroon. That is impossible! She wishes there was an African Dream too. Perhaps Martin Luther King's dream can be re-written as: 'I have a dream that one day even the continent of Africa, a continent sweltering with the heat of injustice, sweltering with the heat of oppression, (the heat of corruption, war, poverty, HIV/AIDS etc) will be transformed into an oasis of freedom and justice, and prosperity.']

Chapter 19

Before you travel abroad tips

'Ignorance is the worse form of poverty.' – Arlette Flueckiger

[FK: Preparing to travel abroad goes far beyond the visa requirements: Do not learn this from hindsight. The time is now.]

Akongwi Fusi: Studying abroad is a great experience, but there are critical times to deal with.

The battle began after I completed high school. My greatest dream was to obtain quality education and just like many others would reason, I knew the best place to realise my dream was the western world. I wasn't interested only in going out but was determined to learn a third language. Growing up I had contact with many German family friends, and being a member of the German Club at school, I decided on Germany.

Getting an admission was no problem because my relatives in Germany took care of that. I needed to do an elementary course in German at the Goethe Institute before leaving my home country. I got into this course, and 6 months later, the number of youths struggling to get to Germany increased. The only way for the German Embassy to cut down this population was to tighten the conditions for getting into their country. New laws came flooding in daily. No one knew exactly what was coming up. After fulfilling all conditions, I thought I was free; but no, I had to wait for a year because my money deposit was in a bank in Germany instead of in Cameroon. That way was chosen because my family wanted to avoid complications. More than 50% of the students didn't get a visa because of false bank statements or similar situations. That was the daily complaint. My money could not easily be retrieved, because my signature was needed. It was a whole year before the bank statement was accepted. This year of uncertainty was a nightmare, but I knew the day would come when I would leave Cameroon. Getting through this, my admission letter was no longer valid, and it took me a further 6 months to get one. By the grace of God, I had no difficulties when I finally filed my documents and just four weeks later, I had my visa. I'm really grateful because some of my colleagues are still fighting to get a visa five years later.

From Dust to Snow: The African Dream?

The period after obtaining my visa should have been the best, but it wasn't. For the first time, I was confronted with the reality. I had to leave my family, my home, friends, well-known community, and my country and culture for a country I did not know; a foreign land with foreign culture, people and behaviour. There was also the complicated language and society to deal with. All I thought of while fighting to get a visa was the good life and education I could have in Europe. I spent time asking myself, or rather, dreaming of how things would be upon arrival in Germany. My expectations were very high and I thought of no negative aspects.

My family carried out all the necessary preparations for me, especially putting together foodstuff. A month after getting my visa, I finally set off for Germany. At the Douala International Airport, I thought the world was coming to an end for me. I finally had to leave my family. Just imagine, I wasn't leaving from one province to the next where I could easily go back home. No! I was flying across an ocean, thousands of miles away from home!! I didn't know when it would be possible for me to meet my family again. I shed tears. So it was that, on the twenty fourth of November 1998, I repeatedly bid my family and friends goodbye. I don't know how many times I embraced each of them before tearing myself away to board my 5:00 p.m. flight. I left them all behind for a land where I had no mum, no dad, no brothers and sisters to get on my nerves. How I miss that. My dream was coming true, but would it be what I had been dreaming of? It wasn't!

I landed in Hamburg, Germany and looked forward to seeing my new home for the first time. The only person I knew there was my young uncle. Everything was strange, but I told myself that this was 'Bundes', as we referred to Germany back in Cameroon. I looked around the huge airport, but my uncle was nowhere to be seen. I walked out through the main entrance and met Ray who was there to meet me instead of my uncle. He took me to the train station, bought me a ticket, and I started my one-hour train ride to Kiel. As soon as I got off the train, my excitement resurfaced. There were my uncle and a schoolmate of mine from home.

The weather was bad, really cold. I was exhausted from my eight-hour flight. I noticed that the streets were neat unlike in Cameroon. I looked forward to a big apartment where I could relax and rest, but I soon realised that student life is the same everywhere. My uncle had a tiny room just like most students at home. Although these were the last days of autumn, it started snowing that same evening. Although, I was quite excited, I fell asleep. When I woke up, it was completely dark. 'Oh no, I slept too long' I moaned. The Cameroonians who came to welcome me all laughed. It was still about 5:00 pm, yet dark. This was a surprise to me. I was also surprised that instead of someone taking me to the hotel where I was to spend the night, I was merely given directions. I had to walk 1.5 km through a park. It took me over an hour because I got lost. Thank God for the little German I had learnt at home, which helped me find my way. The fact that the buildings were numbered made it a lot easier than it would have been at home to find a building. I spent my first night thinking of my family.

On my first full day in Kiel, I was accompanied around Kiel to run necessary errands. I had to look for a room of my own, get proper winter wear, learn how to read the bus schedule, register at school, at the town hall and many other formalities; Germany and its bureaucracy! My companion had been in Kiel just 4 months, and we made a great team of two 'fools'. When I was left alone in my room, I thought it was as quiet as a graveyard and the saying 'home is home' rang in my ears. I started life on my own. There was no one to help me make decisions. Freedom, you might say, but I hated this freedom. I still remember how annoyed I used to be when my parents questioned me when I came home late in the evenings. Is it not the dream of every youth to be free? In our youth, we think leaving home is simply a way of getting out of what we think is an intolerable situation. This is not true. I would give a lot to be under my parents comforting control once more.

I went through the first month trying as much as possible to get used to the new situation. Christmas day, my first away from family, was the worst experience I had. Nothing happened. The streets were empty and I remained indoors. Most people seemed to be relaxing from the tiredness of the previous day (Christmas Eve). I tried to make some phone calls but could not get through to Cameroon. I was bitter and all I wanted was to take the next flight back to Cameroon. I was lonely and felt cut off from the world. Just two months earlier, my greatest wish had been to get to Europe, and now my wish was the reverse. These feelings are one of the short-lived problems, but there are other problems that will never be solved so long as we, the black race are in Europe.

On New Year's Eve, or Sylvester as it is called, there were spectacular shows, great fireworks and many other sites and sounds to behold. I went out with a few friends warmly dressed. The weather was terrible, and despite two pairs of socks, I found my feet were still very cold. We tried to keep warm by standing close together. We joined in the countdown, fire works went off, and that was the start of a new year.

Many foreigners encounter problems in Germany, but my honest opinion is that blacks get the worst of them. I think that what Hitler preached is still implanted and hidden somewhere deep within some German citizens. I do not think every German is mean to blacks, but I find it hard to believe, that they will ever consider us their equals. Racism in Germany can be compared to sin. Just as we don't wish to sin, yet do so, most Germans talk against racism but are unable to wipe off the urge to look low on the black race.

Life is generally expensive in Germany compared to Cameroon, though the means of earning money are better. One must get used to the different types of food eaten in Germany with the popular 'Kartoffel' that is potatoes, eaten in all possible forms. Shopping wasn't easy during the first few months. I took hours just to get a few food items. It's very amusing when I think of those days now. It was especially difficult to learn how to use numerous electronic devices for day-to-day life. I felt ashamed at first when I did not know how to use the different gadgets, but realised it was normal that I did not know how to use what I had never used before – like cash dispensers. I then found it easier to ask for help. After these minor challenges were overcome, the real battles began. Foreigners are checked on a daily basis by the forces of law and order. Foreigners are treated as potential criminals and since they are more regularly checked, this is reflected in statistics. Some people and the media interpret and use such data as propaganda, trying to demonstrate a link between foreigners and crime. Even politicians foster stigmatisation, ignoring the fact that such statistics stem from the existing mentality reflected in the legal system itself.

I must earn money to finance my living expenses in Germany, unlike when I was in Cameroon. The bad thing is that many youths back home believe money can be 'harvested' just anywhere in Germany. As a student, I had to make the choice of either being a good and poor student, or a 'rich' one who might never see a classroom. It's quite difficult getting into my course. Just about 4% of the admissions are allocated for foreigners each semester. I can only say God has kept me. When I started my course, there were three other black Africans in higher semesters. Two of them dropped out and just one girl was left. Being a Cameroonian also, she motivated me a lot. After three years there are still just three black Africans in my institute.

My first day of school was 'great'. It was different from where I did my language course and the first meetings were horrible. I was standing on that block, shaking all over, afraid of making a false start, afraid that everybody was watching me. I kept thinking how crazy I was. I understood nearly no complete statement during the first lectures despite six months of German language studies. I just sat there looking dumbly at my professor. It was no fun at all. Many classmates even asked me later if I would cope with my studies. It was a challenge for me, and I became more determined. However, it's not been easy. I encountered situations where I had to sit in a row by myself, or have several empty seats before the next student. I remained the 'African who knows nothing'. There were however some nice students who cared and understood the language barrier. It was difficult to follow up lectures the first semester because everything in my course is 100% in German. Even through I can now speak very fluently, I must keep learning daily. New words come up in Pharmacy, my field of studies, and so every single day there is a new discovery. The behaviour towards me changed quickly when I finished a practical exercise first. Everybody stood amazed. They arrived before me during the next practical session. Although it took me longer than the others, I was determined every single time. As time went on, I grew more and more self-confident. I think I accomplished something. I learned how to cope with difficulties and improved my grades. I remember validating all my courses, and the funniest thing was that I did not need to go to check my results. My mates called to inform me. They were more interested in my results than in theirs.

I thought that after that my problems would be over, but no. I had trouble getting a placement position and lost a lot of time. I had problems with teaching assistants, but the worst of it was when my microbiology professor openly humiliated me the first day I got to his class. Without spending up to fifteen minutes in class, he started picking on me and told me I should not waste my precious time. He said I would never succeed although it was our first encounter with each other. How could he judge me from appearance? His verdict made me hate microbiology, but despite all that, I succeeded. It cost a lot of energy. When he handed over my attestation, he said I had shocked him. I wasn't his first victim. He had caused another African to cry in class. I did my best not to antagonise my teachers and supervisors. I avoided all needless confrontations. In fact, I tried to be friendly. Well it worked in the majority of cases, but not always.

Getting to the students' job office, the best jobs were reserved for Germans. 'Oh well' I thought. 'It is their land. Such phrases as 'accent free German', 'EU citizens only', excluded most foreign students. Once an employer called me for a job, we discussed all that was needed over the phone and I was asked to come and sign the contract. When he finally asked my country of origin, the job was automatically taken away. He told me he would call later for rearrangements, but we all know what that means. Wait for a year, if you like, there will be no other call. I have learnt to deal with resentment. After all, we encounter that in our home countries, and even families sometimes too. So what do we expect of a race that looks so different from us? Here's a tip, remain calm. Rebelling accomplishes nothing; neither does hateful, spiteful behaviour. I remember being so mad about the resentment towards me that I used to say I hate Germans. But what difference would being against them and treating them in like manner make? I came across a Bible passage that touched me and helped me accept people as they are: 'Take care that rage does not allure you in spiteful actions.... Be on your guard that you do not turn to what is hurtful' (Job 36:18-21). It helps to forgive and forget hurtful actions towards you, though forgetting can be difficult. As I tried to implement this in my life, I realised there are many good people among these people. It is worth getting to know them better.

Most Germans know almost nothing about Africa. Some don't even know Africa is a continent. Most Germans don't leave their states, and when they do, the majority drive to Mallorca, Spain for a few weeks vacation. They ask the funniest and most stupid questions you can think of, and many of us here have learned to reply in a similar manner, although they don't realise this. Some ask if we speak Africana in Africa, if we live on trees, how long we've been basking in the sun to get this black colour and so forth. The thing is, I don't believe they are as innocent as they claim. I don't know why this funny stereotype is so popular over here. The craziest questions were:

How did you come to Germany, was it on a bicycle? Do you have cars in Africa? Of course German stations portray only negative things about Africa. The wretched one is always an African!! Germans believe we spend our time fighting wars. Some of these people can really be awful. The question I keep asking is 'Why do we spend so much time learning all about foreign countries, all that happened in history, when they don't even know where Cameroon is situated?' I feel bad because I did not learn the history of Cameroon in school, but can tell you all about German unification and reunification, Italian unification, the partition of Poland, and all about France and Napoleon Bonaparte. We aren't treated well back home by our fellow countrymen, but whites are treated like gods when they reach Africa. Do we deserve this? At home things are not well, outside same. Where should we turn to? How can we cope with this unequal treatment? It has nothing to do with Germany or the western world. We should clean the rubbish we are sitting on at home first. Tribalism is common in Cameroon, and Africa as a whole. Well, I'm no longer overly concerned about whether I'm treated equally. I made the mistake of trying to pay people in their own coins, but it's wrong. Thank God he turned my path. If I am snubbed, I try conquering the evil with good. It can even be fun too. I know we have many diverse habits and values but they can blend into a workable routine.

I think it is good getting through the difficulties we face. I learned a lot and I'm still learning. I wish we could be as honest as Germans. They are conscious of buying their tickets before getting on trams and buses even though they know they might not be checked. I admire this so much and wish we could get this into our systems. There is much trust between the state and its citizens. Can we say so about our country? What do those of us who have the opportunity to experience this life do when we get back to our countries? Do we try to implement those good things or do we get back to sink into our 'destiny'? I have never seen a set of people as direct, clear and orderly as the Germans. Everything is printed in black and white. Funny, just everywhere you find people standing in a queue; big and small, old and young. I couldn't understand it the first day considering the situation back in Cameroon where the 'big bosses' are first attended to. People are treated in Cameroon according to class, but in Germany all are equal before the law!

The one thing Germans should learn from Africans is the spirit of family. I am proud of this. Secondly, I think we need missionaries from Africa to help save many lost souls in Germany. They helped bring Christianity to Africa and now it's our turn to bring it back there. Their faith is too weak! What am I saying? Do they even believe there is a God? I don't know if up to 30% of the population knows the true significance of Christmas or Easter. Easter here means painting eggs, ha ha ha. And you may ask how people with such little faith can be so prosperous, while many Africans with a strong belief in God aren't able to have three meals a day. I can only say God knows why He made it so, and we should not forget that even the most faithful people in the Bible went through one trial or another. Christ Jesus is the best example!

I am happy in any case, that I came to experience another lifestyle, to have maybe quality education despite the odds. Life in all is a struggle no matter where we are. I know all I need to succeed is Christ Jesus, and I keep thanking Him for all. The western world is not a paradise as many of us think before getting there. It might have a good 'charisma', but we shouldn't forget that although roses are beautiful, they still have thorns. It can also be nice back in Africa, and no matter where I live, I know all will be well by God's grace. I have learned to live and cope with every difficulty. There were moments I thought I would give up, but there was a stronger power to hold me up - the power of God! You will succeed too in your own small corner if you trust in God. Father I thank You!!

Germaine and Joe Mbongue: Is it a sin to be born in the Dust? If not, then it seems to be a crime for a person from the Dust to be in the Snow. In your dust my brothers and friends, nobody looks at you as a dusty person, maybe because every body is dusty. I remember what my grandfather used to tell us, how our countrymen used to suffer during the German colonial times in our country in 1884-1916. That time was one of the worst that my people faced, and how? The Germans thought that we were black because we did not wash our bodies well, and that for us to be like them, we had to brush our skin with certain leaves called "sponge leaves", a type of leaf used to wash dishes in the village when there is no modern sponge. They used that to brush our forefathers till blood would come out, hoping that their bodies would become white. Oh God forgive them, because they wanted to change your mystery. The man of the Snow used to think like that in the past, but it is not very different today. Some still think we rubbed something black on our bodies. I can remember one white lady rubbed her arm on mine one day, and then she said she wanted to be sure it was not paint on me. We are objects of curiosity both before children and elders. Some elderly people still think a baby from a black couple living in the Snow should be white. What a fantasy! While we were waiting for the tram at the tram stop, a child told his mum: 'Mama, Look he is black because he did not take a bath!'

However, none of us from the Dust or Snow chose or requested to be born in the Dust or in the Snow. We are either from Snow or Dust because God wanted it to be like that. As a person from the Dust, your skin betrays you in the Snow. You are recognized from far off. You may be intelligent or not, you may have the passport of the Snow, or be married to a woman or man from Snow; it does not make you a man or woman of Snow! You will always be reminded at each level (be it the classroom, office, playground, stadium or even in the church) that you are a stranger; you do not belong to and cannot be accepted in the Snow.

The attitude of the man in the Snow vis-à-vis my Dust is remarkable. Like all his country people, when he draws closer to me, it's to ask me the following questions (i.e. the FAQ): *What is you name? Where do you come from? How old are you?* In my Dust, I know to ask somebody's age, especially, your elder, is lack of respect; but in Germany, a child will ask you how old you are. For me, that was like an abuse for someone I don't know, and worse of all some one younger than myself, to ask my age. With time, I understood that was their way, and was part of their culture.

What are you doing here? From this question too, you will really see their attitude towards students and asylum seekers. At first sight, they all see Dusty people as asylum seekers, and so the question is just to reassure themselves. When you say you are a student, then they treat you with a little bit of respect as compared to their reaction to asylum seekers.

Will you go back after your studies or will you like to stay here (in the Snow)? Your answer to this question is very important to them. When you say you will go back, then they feel good. You need to be there to see the impression on their faces. But when you say you'll like to stay, you can be sure that no one will be your friend.

When you talk with the man of the Snow, 90% of those you talk to will always ask you these five questions. No, to remain in a country where you do not belong, where you are not considered as a human being, where you are all the time between life and death! Ah, no! I will go back to my Dust among my own people who recognise that I am a human being, who know my dignity, and who give me the respect I deserve. The moment the man of the Snow has an answer to all these questions, it's finished. You will not imagine that he is the one with whom you've been talking a while ago. They might even bypass you without saying a word again. Another thing is that they spread news like wild fire. The least thing or information about yourself you give to anyone say in class, before you leave that place that day, all would be aware of your whole life and history. So I preferred not to give certain details about myself, even to my closest German comrade. That's terrible. What annoys me is that, the way we welcome or treat these Snow people in our Dust is not to be compared with the day-to-day life of stress an antipathy in the Snow. In fact, they are being treated in the Dust like gods, while we do not have even the value of a dog in the Snow.

If I were not a Christian, and would give all to Jesus, I would have been a patient now, because of the stress I've been facing both at the university, as well as out of the university. Because I am from the Dust, I am being considered as one who has nothing to offer. I can remember one day at the university, we had to form groups of twos for chemistry practical exercises. Before then, I had sympathised with two German girls whom I considered as friends. Being three, it meant one of us had to form a group with someone else. I saw that my two friends where confused and did not really know what to do. Of course, I understood the two wanted to be together. To make things easy for them, I told them not to bother, and that I was going to look for someone else or be alone. It was painful because anyone I asked already had a partner. So, I went and wrote my name on the list alone. On the next day, when I went to the list, I discovered that one other German girl who did not have a partner wrote her name besides mine. I don't know if she knew it was that black girl, because it was just the first week of school. After the first test and practical class, my two friends were eager to know my results, which of course were good and theirs negative. I could read deep regret on their faces. One finally said that if she knew, she would have been my partner. The other practical sessions where good for all of us, but at the end of the semester, my results were better than theirs. I think they learned a lesson.

That lesson was not only to my two friends, but I think also to my other classmates who wanted to know the black girl's results. That is why I encourage my brothers and sisters who are already in the Snow to make sure we shine especially in schoolwork. Maybe, that will one day make the man of the Snow to know we have no 'Dust particles' in our brains. The truth is that, if in the Dust we could have just half of the facilities one has in the Snow, we would do far better than them. Take for example, the fact that I touched a computer for the first time when I was about 18, while in Germany, children have the possibilities of having toy computers, which is a good thing. How many parents can afford such expensive toys in the Dust? In the primary schools and secondary schools, children already get to know much about the computer. At home they have computers at their disposal. This will take time to be implemented in the Dust; the few secondary schools, which have computers, are private. How many parents can afford to send their children to such schools?

Why should I be living like a criminal when I did not commit a crime, because of my skin? Why should I be looked upon as excrement on the street, train, etc? Why all this? I think till Jesus comes back, these questions will not have an answer. Lord please come back and restore your justice. It is hard!

Before you leave the Dust...

Leaving the Dust to go to Europe, be it for studies or to seek asylum is a big risk, so it is very necessary to think twice before taking that decision. Before we make the decision to Europe (Germany) or USA, it is necessary to fulfil the following requirements, putting aside the admission procedure and visa processing.

1) You need to know the history of the country and the people. A good knowledge of the place you go to will permit you to make the right decision. Unfortunately, many young people do not have the possibility of doing all this, because dad or mum takes care of everything and you really only get involved when there is a document to sign, or when you have to appear for interview. On the other hand, this issue of going abroad has become like an obsession, and people do not care to know where their children are going. All what matters for them is that their children leave home, so they can also have the pride of saying somewhere that they have a son or daughter, sister or brother in Europe.

2) You need to learn the language of the host Country, which in the case of Germany, is more expensive compared to your tuition for what you really want to study. The truth is that, when I arrived in Germany, I was unable to follow the news on TV, although I had studied German for almost one and a half years in Cameroon. I don't want to

mention the cost of transport, legalising documents, and writing the German exam. Although it is expensive, it is nevertheless necessary, because the language is the first tool in any communicative society, without which contact with other people is totally impossible. A good knowledge of the language is also necessary for integration, and especially necessary for students who have to study in this foreign language. The learning process is not very easy, especially for someone who is not gifted, and can take a very long time. I can remember my first lectures at the university; it was like hell. Some young people end up being frustrated because they finally do not cope with the language.

3) You have to learn and know the custom and culture of the country. To learn the custom and culture of the man of the Snow is not something to neglect. I want to share the experience I had with my "friend" Hans. In Europe, we are in a world of globalisation. That's why friendship does not have its original meaning anymore, but a give and take society. But what can you give if you're from the Dust, if not your ignorance and your stupidity? As I talked with Hans, I tried to explain to him the life of the man of the Dust, hoping he will have sympathy and help me one day. But forget! The man of Snow is one who does nothing for nothing (50/50 or even 25/75 in his favour). Before he engages to help the man of the Dust, he knows his gain will be 10 times the amount he put in to help. Take for example, the so-called help they send to our Dust. How much of this help really remains in the Dust? The money ends up going back to them, because the experts come from them. The experts are paid from this money or help; the machines to be used for the work or project or whatever you may call it are bought from them. So how much finally remains? Whatever be the help you receive from him, you must pay in one way or another; 'A man of calculation!' I mean, even in our own land, they treat us like animals! I remember one experience some time in 1995, where I had to train a new survey team in Tanzania. My boss gave me an old Toshiba PC to work with, while my colleagues from the Snow had a PC 95. And here is the thing: I had to train a colleague who had to be my boss later on; someone who did not even have my qualification and many of such things. I felt so humiliated, and asked myself why I had to have this job, which will always put me in contact with the people of the snow. I was nevertheless consoled by the fact that I was suffering for a noble purpose, Bible translation.

All the times Hans invited me to his house, it was to eat cake, and as you know, cake for us is not food. However, because of the respect I had for him, I never complained, knowing that I would eat my grieß when I got back home. I knew, if I were invited to his place for supper, I should not think I would have some rice and stew or jollof rice or dodo and beans like we do at home, but that I would eat bread and sausage, maybe with soup, milk or coffee. The first time I was invited for supper at my friend's place, I ate the two slices of bread on my plate. I thought something better was coming, but it was all over. What a disappointment it was! That was because I was ignorant of his culture. The other times I had to have supper with my friend, I took my normal supper before going to him, so that I would not embarrass him with how I eat his bread. My friend was of course satisfied after 3 slices of bread. Why? Because they are always eating something! It may be carrots, green pepper, chocolate or sweets in different forms. At 4:00 p.m., he has his slice of cake and tea. So it's just but normal that he has a light supper.

One day, he invited me to a "Kneipe" (bar) to share a drink. My pockets were empty (lack of liquidity) but I went because I thought, like in the Dust when somebody invites you, you do not need to have cash on you. I thought he was going to take care of the bills. That was a big mistake I made. We went on the appointed day, and as usual, I avoided luxury. I looked through the menu and ordered the cheapest drink. The evening went on smoothly, and we had a nice discussion together. The time now came for the bills to be paid. The attendant asked if we were paying "together or separate". My friend quickly said separate. That meant he would pay for his drinks, and I for mine. Knowing that my pockets were empty, I felt so ashamed and humiliated, and from then, I decided to turn down any invitation if I don't have money in hand. I asked myself why I ever accepted that invitation. That was a good lesson for me to start asking more questions about the man of the Snow, his culture. For them it's just normal that you pay your bills when you're invited, but for me it was so strange.

Another aspect of their culture, that was a problem to me at the beginning, is their respect for their pets. I thought it was like at home where you could kick a strange dog, which comes around. I was very surprised, when I heard that if I did such a thing, it would be a serious problem with the police. One could even end up in prison. The most upsetting thing about this issue is that, people even prefer these animals to men. I sat one day in the train, and this lady smiled at her dog every now and then, but when she took up her head to look at me, she frowned as if she had a problem with me not even knowing me. I then asked myself how a human being could love an animal more than man.

Another part of their culture and custom that is different from our practice in the Dust is the fact that I must call my friend and make an appointment before visiting her. In our Dust, I could visit my friends or parents when I wanted. I did not need a special invitation, or to inform them in advance. Another thing is that, in our Dust, we do not attach much value to food. What I mean is that, in the Dust, you can even eat cooked food at a friend or relative's house. But in Germany, if you're not invited to eat, then you can forget. I found this practice bad. I think I prefer the Dust, where people give little or no value to food.

One day, I got into the train. Standing besides me was an old woman, who could hardly support herself. I got up and gave her my seat; to my greatest surprise, she refused. I nevertheless stood up, and the seat was empty. As the train took off, she was so shaken that she had to accept the offer I made to her. At that time, she said, "Thank you." It was so funny, that even the people standing around laughed. Did she really need to prove strong? Another reason for such behaviour is due to the give and take system they have e.g. if I render you a service you need to render a service to me too.

4) You must be educated or have a lot of money. When you have never been to school, living in Snow will be a danger for yourself and for others. You will always feel lonely, although you are living with people. If you are educated, you can have the chance to be useful somewhere and some how. But if you are not educated, you must have a lot of money in order to pay for your services. The educated are being looked down upon, what more of someone who is not educated.

5) You must clearly know why you're going to Europe. Many people leave the Dust to the Snow without really having a particular purpose. This leads, unfortunately most of the time, to misfortune and confusion. Many people get involved in drug business, not because they want to, but because they do not know what to do.

6) You must know the laws and regulations of your host country. Most of us are used to the chaos of the Dust, where the law is there only for others but not for us. That is why we are more and more underdeveloped. We look at the law only when it is beneficial to us. If not, it does not exist. But in the Snow, every thing is orderly. You are not allowed to do any kind of rubbish you used to do in the Dust. If you don't know the law and regulations, you will find yourself one day where you have never expected, maybe in a cell.

7) You must know the climate of the country. The climate in the Snow is almost the contrary of what we have in our Dust. Being aware is very necessary so we can buy some warm clothes: winter jackets, warm shoes, etc, before coming to the Snow.

The cold oldies Church

What made me sad was that, I realised Sunday is the day people sleep longer and no one cared to go to church, even people who had been strong Christians at home before leaving for Europe. They were ready to find one excuse or the other to stay at home. When I even tried to talk about church, some said, "We did like you when we just came here!" but that with time the desire to go to church died down. I told them it all depended on everyone's personal relationship with God. Europe, my friends, is not paradise, but to a certain degree a graveyard for the Christian faith, if we're not careful. How many still go to church, how many still practice their Christian faith? Only God alone knows.

It is true that some of the church services are boring with mostly old people, especially, when one is new and still learning the language. I also think we could learn the language faster and be a blessing to the members of the congregation we go to. In addition to that, there are some English or French churches around. But since the people are not open to us and don't think that a dusty person can also be a blessing to them, they miss many blessings, for every child of God has a particular gift.

A dusty beggar in the Snow?

The man of the Snow will always look at the one from Dust as a beggar. He's not happy when you really look good, and all what he thinks at that time is that we came to take away their money. They will always want you to tell them you do not have clothes, what to eat, etc, so they can carry their remains and old stuff they want to throw away to give you. This is not true for all of them.

Should our pride of being born in the Dust be questioned because we are in the Snow? A free man like me, a "Munen", has never been a beggar. Through his hard work and sense of life, a Munen builds up his ingenuity to continue to be a free man, while trying to live in harmony with others. A free man is ready to die in poverty, but does not put his dignity in question. Even the poor still have dignity.

Advantages

Of course, not all about the Snow is bad. I was personally touched after seeing the snow for the first time. It showed me, once more, God's greatness and might in creation. The whiteness reminded me of the passage (Isaiah 1:18), where the Lord says, "Come now let us reason together, though your sins are like scarlet, they shall be as white as snow; though they are red like crimson, they shall be as wool."

I love the discipline that exists in the Snow, Europe. People keep to time: for appointments, events, and so on. A program starts at the scheduled time, even if there is only one person.

Those who work, try to do their work as best and honestly as possible. Those who want to work really work hard, but those who don't want to work really don't work. Fortunately, they have a good social system, which takes care of people who have no job, who have lost their job, or don't want to work at all. I find this good and bad. I find it bad because this has made many people to become lazy. They know that at the end of the month, they will receive money that will permit them to live well. I find this good because, at least, every citizen has the possibility of living in a house and feeding himself. For example, in all the places I worked, you will see nobody leaving his place of work before the closing time. I mean, no one will leave even one minute before the normal closing time without permission. That was amazing. That was a big contrast to my country, where some people, especially civil servants, leave as early as 3-4 hours before the closing time. At times, some don't even come to work at all. Take for example, in my country, the day it rains, there are many people who don't go to work. That is different in the Snow. Her people go to work under the rain, sun or snow. The only excuse one could have in the Snow to be absent from work is in case of illness, or some other emergencies one could give enough proof for.

Open corruption is one thing I've not yet seen in the Snow. People may do it secretly in some services, but someone will never take money for the job he or she is supposed to do openly. This is really something I appreciate, not like in the Dust where corruption has become a normal thing: students corrupt teachers, teachers corrupt children; in hospitals, patients have to bribe the doctors before receiving proper attention, not to talk of government offices, the police and Gendarmes. In the Snow, it is first-come first-serve. Be it in the supermarket, or government offices, one must not try to be served before the person who came before.

The treatment at the hospital is special. There, the medical staff values the human life. This aspect of the Snow impressed me. The first time I went for consultation, it was like I should be going every month to the hospital. The doctor was so loving and nice to me. Not like home where you can even die, because you or your family did not motivate the doctor with something. In Germany, you have the most modern equipment. Some of this equipment is so expensive that we cannot afford in our Dust, so we have to die. What are the kinds of instruments we receive back at home? Second hand, old instruments, which are no longer needed in the Snow; that's what we proudly use on our patients, sad but true.

At the university, I was amazed by the fact that in an anatomy laboratory, every student had a microscope at his or her disposal. This gave the opportunity for every student to be responsible. We had enough slides, and each student had the same number for the necessary practical exercise, and had to make sure they don't break them or spoil the preparation. At the beginning, I thought the many slides in my box were for all in my group, but was told that each one of us had as many slides in his or her box as I had. Chemistry, biological, physics, medical, technical laboratories are all well equipped. We don't have this at home. I can remember when I was at the University of Yaoundé; we had to miss some practical sessions because there were no reagents. Then we asked the professor how we were going to write the exams. He said we were going to base ourselves on the theory. Can you imagine doing biochemistry without practical? What a scientist! The science students know better what it means to write an exam based only on the theory. I find studies in Germany far better, and I think if we really study we make it. Another thing is the relatively free education we receive from the German government, until now. I think that is really wonderful.

It's at times funny to talk about such realities, which at times bring shame to us and particularly to our incapacity. It was a big shock for me to see how easy certain things are in Europe. I then understood why their development goes ahead everyday while ours goes backwards. For example, to open a bank account in Germany, you don't need to have money. Something like that is unbelievable to someone who has never imagined he could open one in the Dust. Also, our civil servants know better what it means to get one's money at the end of the month. To get the money one has worked for at the end of the month, you have to line up sometimes for a whole day under the sun or the rain. Worse of all, at times, you have to be ready to give 30% of your money to the banker for rendering you a service he is being paid at the end of the month for. It was really amazing, when I opened an account in the Snow for myself and received a credit card, and my secret code. I could go to the bank or cash dispenser, at any time, to get my money. I could do as many money transactions as possible on the automat (cash dispenser), without necessarily going to the counter. That is development. I find that aspect good. The people of Snow have attained a certain level we need a long time to reach.

During my first month, I suffered from the fact that I always had to keep in mind that I did not have to throw dirt just anywhere. I had to wait to get to a trashcan before throwing my dirt or peeling of whatever I had in hand. I also noticed that, almost all, even some who suffered from mental problems, knew their waste or dirt had to get to the trashcan.

Another aspect of order and discipline I noticed was in the use of public toilets. I was impressed by the fact that almost all were conscious of the fact that the toilets had to remain clean, and the toilet tissue put in there was for everybody and not for one person to take home. That is something we cannot even attempt to compare with home, where people misuse public toilets, mess all around the toilet without shame.

There is also something I admire about the Snow. The people know how to beautify. I am somebody who loves flowers so much, and I think the environment pleases me. At every corner, they try to plant flowers or trees, arrange them, water them in summer, trim them when they grow wild, replace them when they're old. It's not like in the Dust, where the people who pass by destroy even the few flowers that are being planted. In the Dust those who are paid to take care of these flowers or trees do their work at their convenience, and given the amount of sun we have in the Dust, they die or do not grow well.

Something I want to testify about, which to me sounds positive and at the same time negative, is the fact that, in Germany we have little or no spiritual attacks as compared to home. I mean things like witchcraft. I think since I came to the Snow, I've been sleeping all through the night, without having to get up to pray because of spiritual attacks, be it in the form of bad dreams or not. I find it good that one has some peace, but on the other hand it's not also good for it makes us grow cold spiritually. We think all is well, and we relax even in our prayer life and in other domains of our Christian life, which is not good.

Another positive thing I saw in the Snow is the "Tapferkeit" (bravery) and the patriotism of the Germans. A German hates defeat in any national or international competition. The pride of being a German should not be put on shame. That is why they are adepts of perfection.

To summarize, we will say that, nowadays, living in the Dust or in the Snow does not matter. What matters is to acknowledge that we are all passengers of the same ship and that we need the support of each other. The first thing is to recognise that we are all human beings with different values. If we put these values together, we will have a better life. We can only do so if we have the will to face the reality, from which we could then build the future.

[In 2005, Joe completed his PhD in Linguistics at the Martin-Luther-Universität, Halle-Wittenberg. In 2006 Germaine completed her Master's. They dedicate this contribution to their three lovely kids, for sacrificing to be separated from them during their time abroad. It would be a wonderful reunion with them at home in Cameroon.

In 2006 Akongwi Fusi was completing her Pharmacy program in Kiel.]

Chapter 20

My graduate school experience in the U.S.

'Great works are performed not by strength but by perseverance.' - Anon

[FK: Here is the first Asian perspective of being a student in the U.S.]

I grew up in the city of Pune situated near the western coast of India, approximately 115 miles southeast of Bombay. Pune, a city of about 2.3 million, is the seat of North Indian Classical music, and it always has been one of the eminent centres of education in India. However, as a physics student with an interest in theoretical physics, I could not find an appropriate place to foster my studies in Non-linear Dynamics in Pune. During my four years university studies in India, I read a lot of papers in the field, most of them written by scientists at the University of Texas at Austin's Centre for Non-linear Dynamics. My father was a university professor, and my elder sister was married and living in the US. So, I figured, if I wanted to become like my father, the best place to go to was the U.S., and if I had to go to the U.S., the best place to go to was to the University of Texas, Austin.

Basically a lot of things are changing in India, but the number of choices and opportunities in a given field are very limited. So after finishing my master's program, equivalent to 17 years of education, I decided to go after my dreams. I applied and obtained admission to UT Austin. Basically, I had different expectations, but primarily to get a good PhD in one of the most renowned institutions in that area of Non-linear Dynamics. Otherwise, I did not want to leave India, since I could have continued my education there in a good institute closer to home. I was not to know this was the beginning of a completely new chapter in my life. Of course, I knew I would have to live independently away from my parents for the first time. However, I did not know how hard or easy that would be. Moreover, I would be in a different country and doing a PhD in Physics! Today, there are times when I think I would not have done it if I knew what I would have to go through. The PhD is a long and hard process, and I did not really have a good appreciation of that at the inception. At most other times, I feel very fortunate for the wonderful learning experience, the opportunities it opened up for me, and for all the interesting, talented and unusual people I met along the way.

My graduate school experience in the US

It was not too difficult to get the F1 visa from the American embassy in Bombay. There are many Indians who want to travel to the U.S., and so there is often a long queue. However, as far as I met the embassy requirements, everything went well and I got the visa. It was a multiple entry F1 visa for the duration of my PhD, which was a standard 5 years.

I travelled with my parents via Japan, where I stayed for three months. In Japan, I had my first impression of how it was to live in a foreign country. There are not many foreigners there; especially in the small towns, you stand out as a foreigner. Besides, most Japanese in small towns do not speak English. The Japanese language structure (grammar/syntax) seems to have many similarities to my language, Tamil, and my mother and I had fun learning some Japanese. My parents and I lived in a small town called Toyokawa, which is a suburb of Nagoya. We all enjoyed our stay in this quiet and pretty town. We didn't do too much travelling while in Japan, but we did get a chance to travel to Kyoto. It is an ancient and extremely beautiful town with many shrines and also the famous Kyoto palace. It was a nice experience.

We finally reached the U.S. in the summer of 1998. I had grown up basically all my life in my parents' home, and so it was good my Mum travelled with me to Texas. I was very lucky about accommodation. My sister's friend had moved recently to Austin, and she helped me find a roommate who was also from India. My monthly rent was about 300 dollars excluding utilities.

After settling down in the apartment, the next days were spent taking care of paperwork at the department. There were other international graduate students, so most of the bureaucratic procedures were done together with others. There was a lot of paperwork, but the Graduate-Advisor, who was very friendly, arranged for everything to be done as a group.

As soon as my Mum left, I realized I was now on my own, and I missed my parents a lot right away. As a result, I often called home. I had huge phone bills calling India every month. My parents could not keep sending me rupees. I had to learn to be independent and to take care of myself financially. It was good that I had a TA (teaching assistantship) which helped cover my fees and living expenses. As a teaching assistant, the University also took care of my insurance. I was however not allowed to work extra. The students I taught were pretty good, but they were mainly medical students. The main task was to make Physics interesting for them. We TAs had weekly meetings during which the laboratory heads advised us. This was very helpful. Everything was well structured, but my work was not easy initially, since I had no such previous experience. I had to grade lab reports, and I taught 8 hours a week.

One main problem, especially while teaching, was my accent, which the students would complain about. Besides, in India we also have different expressions. Americans would complain about the speed at which an Indian speaks. Actually I do not speak very fast compared to other Indians, but I often had to repeat myself for my students to understand me. This was also true for most of the other international students with accents different from the American. You felt the pressure to try to also migrate into the American accent. On the other hand, the Texan accent is very distinct and can be difficult to understand at times. There were also words used in America that are different from their counterparts in India, where the English is more British. Sometimes I felt rather miserable, and it took the fun or focus away having to think about your accent when speaking. Well, soon I realized I needed to get used to it – get it right; but it was not easy.

I slowly settled into teaching and studies at the university and also to taking care of normal things outside, such as banking and shopping. With regard to banking, what fascinated me most were the ATM machines. I could not understand how they worked and how the money deposited or withdrawn was credited to the right account. I had really never had any dealings with banks in India while living with my parents, and so I am not really sure how things work out there. This is not the case in the U.S., where most kids can already use the ATM. Things have changed in India more recently, and so I am sure more people are familiar with ATMs than when I left.

A relatively big problem in the U.S is, of course, public transport. To do shopping, we had to get on the bus from the university to a mall, and then take a taxi home. In the U.S., most things are sold in large quantities, like milk in gallons. We often bought in bulk so that it would last us a couple of weeks and save us taxi money. I never shopped for food in India, as my parents did that. I did not even have a feeling about the prices of things to see how they would compare with those in the U.S. My roommate was more used to the shopping system. Therefore, she initially showed me how things worked.

One main reason for the relatively poor public transportation system in the U.S. is the fact that most people have cars. So just as many other people did, I took a loan from my bank and got my first car, an Escort. I was supposed to pay the loan gradually per month, naturally with interest. I also had to get car insurance, which is quite expensive when one is young, but it was of course helpful, when I had a very scary car accident. One Sunday morning, I was driving off from my apartment, when I suddenly found myself bashing into the wall of a neighbouring apartment. I could not get out of the car through the door, so they had to pull me out of the shattered windscreen. I called the cops and later went to the hospital, but had no concussions or any internal injuries. My insurance company was obviously not happy about the accident, but they had to pay. I learnt the hard way to be very careful while driving and got better at it as time went by.

All in all, I have had many good experiences in the U.S. I have met a lot of interesting people, which made my graduate life more fun. The graduate program is very tedious; I had to take four exams during the first 18 months. After the first two years, I had to defend a research proposal during a one-hour presentation to my PhD committee, also open to public attendance. But it is mainly the members of the committee who can ask questions. Your advisor does help you to come up with the research proposal after you have done some preliminary research work in his/her lab and become familiar with things. The great thing was that my group members, experimental and theoretical, were very cooperative, interactive and helpful, and it was possible to collaborate with them closely.

In the course of my studies, I got to meet a lot of people from different parts of the world. The university in Austin had about 52000 students, and I made good friends with people from various parts of the world such as Japan, Germany, Russia, Switzerland, Turkey, and U.S.. I got to know about many different cultures in the process. I spent many happy weekends and holidays with these friends. Most of my thanksgiving holidays, I was invited to lunch at either an American friend's or at my advisor's place. I spent most of my Xmas vacations at my sister's home.

One striking difference between the U.S. and India is that, in India, you often know what is going on with your neighbours and 'mind their business'. In the U.S., you lead more isolated independent lives, which I think fosters personal development and growth; being independent, you are forced to be creative and take your own initiatives. On the other hand, being independent also means you have to deal with the enormous stress out in the U.S. by yourself. In India, we do have much closer relationships with our parents, grandparents, and extended family.

I also missed the great cultural richness of Indians: celebrating festivals (such as Diwali) with my family, watching Hindi movies with my friends, and attending other seasonal activities. In a way, I also missed the sight of the Bhindi on the faces of Indian women. The Bhindi (bindi) is a coloured spot worn on the forehead by Hindu women. In the U.S. most Indian women do not wear the Bindi; when they do, some even use red nail polish!

Overall I achieved the expectations I left home with. I got my PhD in the field I like from a reputable university. It was a very challenging experience to manage teaching, research, conferences, talks, publications, etc, and bring all these together to obtain a PhD. The five years of PhD took all I could give, and I am not sure I would want to go through this again. The competition is also intense, especially, in such a high standard environment. I felt like giving up at some stages, but thanks to the encouragement of family, friends and my advisor, I made it. I would encourage others to go for a PhD abroad if they dream to, but they should be prepared for the long challenging road ahead! A very helpful virtue would be perseverance, combined with hard work. I typically worked 12-15 hours a day at the university, in addition to the stuff I did at home.

Most Indians go to the U.S. by choice, not as refugees. A majority may go with the idea of pursuing higher education and a better life, forever hoping to return 'tomorrow' to India. Even after assuming American citizenship, the debate continues in their minds on how much the mix should be – whether one is to remain 'an Indian in America', or 'an American of Indian origin'. My future plans are as yet undecided, and right now, it mainly depends on where I find a suitable and fulfilling job after my post-doctoral training.

[FK: Dr. Revathi Ananthakrishnan is a research associate at the University of California, Davis.]

Chapter 21

Racism against foreigners: Is it natural?

'I look forward confidently to the day when all who work for a living will be one with no thought to their separateness as Negroes, Jews, Italians or any other distinctions. This will be the day when we bring into full realization the American dream.... A dream of equality of opportunity, of privilege and property widely distributed; a dream of a land where men will not take necessities from the many to give luxuries to the few; a dream of a land where men will not argue that the color of a man's skin determines the content of his character; a dream of a nation where all our gifts and resources are held not for ourselves alone, but as instruments of service for the rest of humanity; the dream of a country where every man will respect the dignity and worth of the human personality.' – Martin Luther King Jr.

[FK: *From Germany to Russia, from Denmark and Austria, and from France to Britain, people of color are facing increasing trends in racism that make life far more difficult and hazardous than for the average citizen in any of these countries. In Britain, where a black teen was recently killed with an ax embedded in his skull by white men shouting racist taunts, the focus of government is, as in other European centers, not on endemic racism in society, but on right wing extremism. The tendency to downplay racism against blacks in society is belied by the way officialdom reacts when immigrant minorities are caught on the wrong side of the law. Take the case of Hirsi Ali, the prominent Somali-born former Dutch lawmaker who was stripped of her citizenship for admittedly lying in her immigration application. Her conviction and loss of citizenship led to a copycat case in Germany when a Nigerian was stripped of his German citizenship - held since 2000 - for allegedly lying about his employment record during immigration application.*

The experiences included here highlight some ways for dealing with racism. Remember that a vast majority of citizens of these countries are not racists. Tony the Philosopher begins:]

Carrying any skin colour other than the so-called "white" can be a source of immediate danger in Western European societies to those who are so pigmented. They very often easily become targets of hate motivated attacks by exuberant and misguided youths, as well as other individuals who live on the fringe of the society with a warped perception of it. "Coloured" or "Black" people are endangered species, because of the ideological belief of the far right group, which bother on xenophobia for people of foreign origin. Based on this ideology, they seek to pervade their political space with nationalistic feelings. This agenda attracts a lot of sympathy from European nationals, but only a few are fanatical about it. The fanatical ones are those who go to the extent of showing their hatred for foreigners through the use of violence.

The expression of hatred through violence differs from one country to another. In some, it is done covertly and in isolatable circumstances, (for example, USA), while in others, it is widespread and marked by contemptuous boldness. Germany, to many around the world, represents this extremity. According to one school of thought, the rationale for visiting violence is hinged on harsh recessionary economic realities, which have brought about unemployment, dwindling national and personal incomes, and other unpleasant consequences. However, this reason is reprobated by another school, which wonders what right any group whatsoever has to eliminate others in order to better its economic situation. To this school, such an act is a relic of the barbaric past. Also, they are un-persuaded by the argument of the hate groups that foreigners can stand in the way of employment or other economic benefits of Germans who enjoy citizenship priority in all things. Therefore, they disapprove in its entirety the violent activities of the hate groups.

Despite oppositional hues and cries, the hate groups seem undeterred in their resolution to continue business as usual, which is to hunt and attack or kill immigrants, irrespective of whether they are asylum seekers or of other legitimate categories. That this is the case is substantiated by statistics.

The consequence of the activities of the hate groups is grave and negative to the image of Germany as a country, to the extent that it evokes memories of Hitlerism, and reinforces the perception that Germany is interminably racist. This sort of image in this age of globalisation is nonetheless uncomplimentary, and requires to be polished. Expectedly, both the government and the civil societies share this goal. As a proactive response, the latter organize large demonstrations against Neo-Nazis or Skinheads from time to time. On the part of government, measures are being taken to rein-in these groups, and thereby curb their menace. For instance, there is a program in place to win over the far right politicians with financial and other inducements. The idea is that winning them over would whittle down their size and the considerable influence they wield over their foot soldiers, who carry out the attacks. However, it has met with little success so far. But with time, it might have a desirable outcome.

The fact that the various efforts being made to combat the hate groups have been uncoordinated and less effective does not support the case that government has no political will to combat them. In the area of strict law enforcement and prosecution, the government seems to be up and about. I shall buttress this with a personal testimony.

I am Nigerian, living in Leipzig and doing a PhD research in Philosophy at the University of Leipzig. On September 2002, around 9:00 p.m., I had an encounter with skinheads. I was coming back from Bible study and was in a tram. Along the way, two boys joined the tram. Each of them had a giant bottle of hard drink, from which each sipped frequently as they chattered.

As I was about to alight at Wilhelm Leutschner Platz, they noticed that I am an African, and exchanged grim looks. They dismounted too, and followed my trail. I did not make anything out of it. I wanted to get to Roßplatz and take Tram 16 towards home. Somewhere, between Leutschnerplatz and Roßplatz, they began to say to each other: "You hit him on the head and I will do same. He either wakes up in the hospital or in the grave." It was this comment that saved me. Good Samaritans in the persons of Pastor Toospan of St Peter and his guests, who were going for a walk, over-heard the conversation and courageously intervened. As a result of this, the boys ran ahead to Roßplatz and waited. The Pastor and company approached me and recounted what had transpired behind me, because they saw obviously that I was not at all aware. They decided to wait with me till the tram came. This decision angered the boys and they went wild. They began to damage everything in sight at the Roßplatz tram stop. When they moved towards attacking all of us together, someone called the police. In less than 10 minutes, the police arrived from two different directions, arrested the assailants, and took us with them to their station. At the station, the assailants were remanded, and we gave statements about what happened. After that, they drove me home.

Those I shared the story with, both Germans and non-Germans alike, thanked God that I was not hurt. But in a unanimous sarcastic kind of way, they inundated me with chilling stories of those who, in similar circumstances as mine, lost their lives or suffered bodily injury as a result of police ignoring their distress calls. Beyond that, they said, with cynicism, that even on the few and far between occasions police had showed up and arrested culprits, they were soon released without any prosecution. But in contradistinction to all this, those arrested in my case are being prosecuted in a court of law. However, how adequate and punitive the laws are, to deter the skinheads and others who perpetrate violence against immigrants, is another thing all together. The concern here is to show that the prompt deployment of the instrumentality of law and law enforcement agents, as exemplified in my case, is an indication, at least, that there is some political will on the part of the government to curtail the activities of the hate groups.

I have said all this to be able to say this: that although the attacks against immigrants have neither stopped completely nor have they substantially reduced, going by available statistics, it is left for the intending immigrants to decide whether to come to Germany and pursue their life ambition based on potential opportunities she offers or go elsewhere. However, for those who, like me, will like to study in Germany or accomplish one success or the other, my advice to enable them survive the hate groups is that they should avoid keeping late nights. They should endeavour to be in the midst of crowds, or alternatively move in twos or more when necessary. And when danger lurks, they should call the police. In addition, they should be above board in their dealings with people and institutions. Also, they should prove their mettle with excellence in every contest. Finally, they must be law abiding at all times.

To the hate groups, I humbly plead that they have a change of heart and put an end to their reprehensible activities to ensure the emergence of a robust, liveable and eclectic society. This is a society where different human beings from different walks of life with different skills congregate to give their best to the society for the good of all. It is a melting pot of human finesse and only possible when its potential members have no fear of molestation. Thank you for your attention.

Tony Agwuele

[FK: Africans and other dark-skinned minorities in Europe know too well how deeply rooted the racism in society is. They are also aware of how difficult it is to penetrate the consciousness of the average European with this fact. "All we hear is right wing, right wing, right wing," says Eritrean-German Jonas Endrias, vice president of the International League of Human Rights. "The Germans won't admit there is racism in society." On the other hand, Germany is to be appreciated for all the aid and support for asylum seekers. Half a loaf is better than none. Things can improve from there. Recently,
Angela Merkel, Germany's chancellor, has warned that "Anybody who threatens, attacks or, worse, kills anybody because of the color of his skin or because he comes from another country will face the full force of the law."

'Juldas Etoumbi, a postgraduate international relations student at Moscow's RUDN University, remembers well his first encounter with a Russian. Standing in a Moscow Metro carriage for the first time, the young Gabonese man was thrown forward when the train started with a jolt and he grabbed a pole to keep his balance, brushing the Russian man's hand. Without a word, the Russian withdrew his hand, produced a handkerchief and proceeded to wipe it demonstratively in front of the other passengers.']

I met his ghost at the train station in Paris Gare de l'Est. I was supposed to get a connecting train to Zurich, but missed it due to a delay with my flight. This meant I had 2 hours to freeze in the cold winter twilight, before the next train. As I stood cursing under my breath on the platform, visible steam pouring out of my nostrils, wondering how to burn the time, a very pale and indisposed looking tall black African with short curly dark hair came into the focus of my vision. He was sporting a poorly waxed dirty black moustache, which might never have seen a trim. His overall appearance gave me an eerie feeling. He smiled as if it was all he could muster his energy to do, and stretched out a scraggy dirty hand. On the palm of his hand was something I recognized, to be my wallet! 'It fell out of your pocket as you were running for the train', he said.

I could not believe it! He had followed me to give it back to me. From the way he looked, I would have put it way past him to do that. I picked up the wallet from the open palm and spontaneously moved to examine it. He smiled even more weakly and said, 'The money is all there'. I was moved, confused, and a little embarrassed. As he began to turn away, I finally found some words. I extended my hand, 'I am John, John Chiluba, thank you very...' He froze before I could complete my words; I mean he literally froze. What had I said that had drawn such a reaction?

I invited him to a fast food restaurant near the train station. As we ate he began to talk.

'I woke up early the day I died. I remember everything so vividly as if it were just this morning. My cochleae were reverberating in synch with the noise of shouting people, coming through my window from the street below. Was I dreaming? No, the noise was real! I started out of bed, my adrenalin pumping. I searched for, found and flicked on the switch of my bedside lamp, tripping the glass of water on my bedside table in the process. The glass crashed on the floor and I cursed, ignoring it. The small bedside alarm clock pointed past 2:00 in the morning. As my thoughts sorted out and I began to wonder why there was this shouting, I heard a loud explosion, which lit up the frozen night. This galvanized me into action. I dashed to my wardrobe and removed my passport and wallet, considered my most priced possessions. I shot out of my room just as a fire ball swept through the dormitory No. 6 of PFUR. The five-story building of the foreign student's residence was welling up smoke like a massive volcano. What about the fire alarm? No, there was none!

I raced in the direction of the exit sign and the stairs, the screams of neighbours running for their lives rose from below; oh, may be they were trapped! Two of the three stairwells were blocked, many of the windows were barred, and the only exit descended right into the source of the fire on the second floor. Cries for help in the languages of 39 countries rang out through broken windows. Soon the trapped students began to jump, many aflame and falling to their deaths. I jumped also, landing with a dull thud, bones snapping, breaking through burnt flesh, on the back of a Chinese student, who served as a cushion. This saved my life temporarily. The horizontal component of my desperate jump-force catapulted me forward onto a bicycle rack. I collided with a protruding part of the framework. It felt like my crotch was being ripped completely out. I rolled over ending up in a fetal position, beginning to scream myself, holding my crotch and not being able to feel anything between my legs but pain and wetness. I rolled onto one side, vomited and passed out.

I came to in the ER, strapped to a table, an ice pack between my legs. Someone began to cut through the spandex of my trousers. After a while, the doctor informed me that I had sustained massive tissue damage in my groin. My crushed genitals had to be completely removed. They injected local anaesthetic into my groin. As I drifted into semi-oblivion, I tried to recollect what was happening to me, the heir, the African Prince!

The next 24 hours were a blur, lying on my back with a demoral drip going in one arm. The pain was dull but constant with occasional shots of intense pain, which sent my entire body into spasms. By the afternoon of the second day, the pain was at a more manageable level. A nurse came in to change the dressing on my groin. I watched her pretty face as she saw my wound. I could see she tried to keep her composure with some effort. She had apparently never seen anything like that. I was a Prince in disgrace lane. I asked her to leave me alone for just a moment. She hesitated, and then waited outside. I raised the bed so I could see. Everything was swollen red and black and blue. Everything was gone. My manhood was gone. A clear drainage tube ran from either end of my groin. A yellow catheter ran out from the base of where my scrotum had been.

My real name is John Chiluba. That's why I was shocked to meet someone with my very name. For a moment I thought you were my living version, you know. I am originally prince from a village in Zambia; originally, because I now consider myself dead. I shall never return again to Africa. Why do I consider myself dead? The fire at PFUR's Patrice Lumumba People's Friendship University in Russia was my welcome to hell.

I had travelled to Russia as a student sponsored by my father the king of the village. And now, my manhood was gone, heir, prince, to-be-king, everything was gone. How could I ever return to my kingdom? How? So I decided to die. I died on that day. I lost the few friends I had in the fire accident. I heard forty-three students perished. Over 200 other students were injured – almost all hospitalised – and more died. Not like me though. I am a living ghost! Their spirits are at rest!

In Africa, people hardly, if ever, conduct autopsies. Many deaths are often rather attributed to witchcraft, jealousy or an inability to have fulfilled some customs or rites. Growing up in a palace, I am very aware of that. Out here in Europe they will always do the autopsy. If they did it now on me, they would find that I am alive. But here is my proof that I am dead: My manhood is gone.

I personally do not think that what happened represents the general situation in Russia. There are so many good things about the country itself, but I had had enough. I had lost my manhood. As a prince in Africa, that was tantamount to death. So I thought I could as well start a new life. As soon as I was discharged from Hospital, I took the little compensation they gave, and am headed for England.'

I tried to convince John to reconsider his decision to break away completely from his people in Africa. He said it had not been an easy decision, and that he would disappear forever in England. On my way to Zurich on the train, I felt so bad I could not do anything to help my namesake. I had offered my phone number and e-mail address and he had just smiled thinly back at me, 'Forget me, ok! You never saw me. It was just so odd you have the same name like me.'

Later, I verified John's story. I could not believe it was real. The incident John said he had been in was actually documented. I learned that officials quickly pinned the cause of the fire on the students themselves, claiming either misuse of electrical fixtures or arson by dormitory residents. But they were forced to back off after shock, grief and outrage poured in from the students' homelands around the world. Ambassadors from a number of African countries: Gabon, Angola, Guinea-Bissau, Burundi, Congo, Chad and Algeria, later formed an investigation commission with Russian authorities to determine the cause of the fire, and to monitor the care and compensation of the victims. They also had to install a fire alarm in the dormitories. According to an Amnesty International report, most students described the fire as "a racially-motivated act of arson." A Somali student said skinheads often gathered near the dorm and wrote racist graffiti. A medical student from Mali said Skinheads had long been threatening students there. The fire on 24 November was no accident.

In 1960, the campus had been opened as Patrice Lumumba People's Friendship University. Soviet authorities had named the university after the Congolese leader who was allegedly a victim of racist murder by the CIA and Belgian imperialists in 1961. However, when the Soviet degenerated state was destroyed in 1991-92 by the capitalist counterrevolution led by Boris Yeltsin and U.S. President George Bush Sr., these foreign students became targets of racist terror in capitalist Russia. It is also said that on 11 August 1992, Moscow police marked the first anniversary of Yeltsin's coming to power by shooting dead a Zimbabwean university student. It is foreign students who are the fascists' preferred targets. I heard even the South African ambassador's wife was beaten and burned with cigarettes in broad daylight in the Russian capital. An Ethiopian refugee explained that the police are just as bad. "I run faster from them than I do from the skinheads", he said. Even the emergency crews subjected students to racism on the night of the November 24 blaze. The ambulances took away injured Russians first, leaving half-naked foreign victims to suffer frostbite. They later took the foreign students only after trying to extort money from them. I guess John was lucky he was attended to before.

However, I could not verify John's story about being a prince from a village in Zambia. The last image I have of him was pale and febrile, and it haunts me. Let us pray for John and our other African brethren who may be out there in Europe and America, who may for some reason never ever return to Africa again. Such people who have lost their 'manhood' represent the position of Africa today in the world stage. Let us ponder awhile about this.

[FK: 'Gabriel Kotchofa, head of the Foreign Students' Association in Russia, offers fellow Africans considering an education in Russia two pieces of advice: "Consider your personal safety" and "Make sure your parents can pay your living costs".'

While people like John do not return because they consider themselves dead, others in Europe may be alive and yet not be able to return. According to BBC, in the foothills of the Italian Alps, hidden among row after neat row of wooden-shuttered chalets is the Residence Prealpino, where overcrowded, chaotic Dakar has been recreated in suburban Europe. Several hundred immigrants, mostly Senegalese men, have completely taken over this hostel, with up to 16 sharing a single room. Most of the migrants come to Italy with a single goal - to earn enough money to set themselves up in business back home and then return.

Rent is about 50 euros a month each – more if there are fewer people in the room – and it is obvious that hardly any of this goes on the hostel's upkeep. Some people use earplugs to block out the snores of roommates.

Most would like to return to Dakar, but after spending so long supposedly getting rich in Europe, they cannot bear the shame of going home empty-handed. There is the case of a Burkina Faso citizen who left home ten years ago making the tortuous journey through the Sahara. He tried to make it to Saudi Arabia but found things very difficult there and finally ended up in Brescia. He is quoted as saying that in Burkina Faso, in Saudi Arabia, in Italy or even he thinks in the U.S. it's the same. It's not easy to find what you need and whatever you have, you want more. But it took him travelling abroad to realize this.

The worse is that Police are always conducting raids and checking all the fellows with black skin. They even want to close the slums where these Africans live. The Africans are so homesick at times but there is no turning back. Some have wives and kids they have been separated from for more than a decade always hoping they could be able to bring them over but never quite making it. But the shame of going back home is enormous.

And here is the thing: A study at the University of Santa Barbara suggests that it is not natural that skin colour matters. The intriguing results from tests on racially integrated basketball teams showed that skin colour doesn't always tell you what team a person plays for. The results also suggest that, for all our excuse-making to the contrary, there's nothing inevitable about racism. Rather, racism is learned behavior; it is not natural that you prejudge someone because of his/her skin. To take it one step further: racism can be unlearned!]

Chapter 22

Living as a Muslim abroad

'He who leaves his home, reduces his value' – Sudanese saying

[FK: From Sudan to Europe as a student? Esam tells what a life it can be for a Muslim.]

As the famous saying by Oscar Wilde goes, "Experience is one thing you can't get for nothing". This enlightening quote raises the intriguing question: 'Does experience always demand difficulties?' Time passes, however, with both joys and sorrows and each of them leaves memories. What we are keener to speak of is, to a large extent, dependent on how optimistic we are. And another philosophic question remains: 'Do obstacles come to make life difficult or do they come to give the success the taste of happiness after achievements?'

It has been said in German "Starten ist immer schwere", or starting is always difficult. This declaration is actually a psychologically supporting one rather than just a fact. It generalizes the starting difficulty to be a common matter.

It really took me time to adapt and cope with life in Germany. I did not know why the first days were more than 100 hours! They were so long and tedious. With the change of my natural environment to an extremely different culture, everything about this medium was already known for me virtually from the media, films, public education and net. Nevertheless, being down to earth in such an environment, I felt some sort of peculiarity. I had, honestly speaking, an extreme desire to return home at least for some time. I felt like cards in a game distributed and needed to be collected and organized again.

When I first left Frankfurt Airport, people around me were native speakers of Deutsch. It might be natural to understand nothing, but at that time, I had the hopeless feeling that I would never be able to. My memory then began to flash back, just one day back to the day when I was leaving Sudan. In all of the succeeding difficult situations, I always deliberately remembered it. When I felt aloneness, when I found tremendous difficulties with study and when I lacked money even for the essential demands, I always revert to the memories of that day. And now, after successfully achieving my Masters study and getting a position in the university as a PhD student, I feel adapted to staying in Europe.

Studying for a PhD in a specific promising interdisciplinary field, with mutual contacts and feedbacks with great scientific characters, who were and still are inventing and contributing to knowledge worldwide, always makes one content with life. And the monthly paid salary that I receive withdraws away the mare of poverty and fear not to be able to suffice myself as the case when I was studying for my Masters. With the mutual contacts now, some advances in the language mediate to adapt me more with life also. Wide relations with friends and colleagues from different backgrounds on the basis of religion, culture and social aspects also affirm the concept that "human relations overcome differences and break frontiers between cultures". In this light, I support the concept of culture dialog rather than the culture clash proposed by Samuel Huntington in his famous book (Clash of Civilizations). And the famous sentence 'East is east, and west is west' also seems to be more controversial. However, as a Muslim, lots of situations in the daily life strive to consolidate the sense that I'm different. When for example, I am invited to a party or Christmas celebration, I am, most of the time, the only one that doesn't drink beer or other alcoholic drinks, and avoids meats even if it is not pork, because I cannot assure the way the animal was slaughtered. There is a definite way of slaughtering animals in Islam.

I got used to the style of life, but I still feel relationships are cold, compared to social relations in Sudan. At the same time, I totally understand that cold greetings or cold responses to my greetings are not because I'm of different culture or different skin, but probably, because people are more practical than emotional.

On that day I left Sudan towards Germany, all my friends came to see me off, shared supper, fare-welled me with loud laughter and smiles, congratulating that I got a chance of studying in the first world, encouraging and at the same time warning that I should take care not to face violent discriminating groups. At that time, I had a dubious feeling of being, leaving this calmness mixed with the encouraging feeling that I'm going forward towards a goal of further studying. Some times, I induced my sense in favour of the later feeling, against the opposite feeling of the anxiety.

I expected difficulties in Germany, but really didn't think I would suffer because of eating alone most of the time. Eids (Muslim festivals which comes twice a year) have not that taste of extreme happiness I am used to. When it comes in a weekend, as a matter of luck, we have some sort of celebration in groups of friends and families, but some times the

Eid comes on a working day and one has the sense that he is just a Deutsche machine.

The danger of the violent groups such as Nazis is an exaggerated threat. People in Sudan think that foreigners like me will always be attacked and hence all relatives and friends are advised not to move at night. Also, when you say that you are from Sudan, people in Germany at once remember wars. They ask you immediately whether it is safe to walk in streets there in Sudan! These are too exaggerated images, whereas, peace in Germany even invites to wear the typical national dressing of Sudan (Aljalabia) on the streets.

As time slowly passed, I began to adapt to the rhythm. I got used to eating all my meals alone. There in Sudan, the family meets in at least two of the three meals a day.

From dust to snow or from warm social relations to a cold type of relations, from a relaxing mode of living to a hurry-up, catch time rhythm? Nevertheless the picture is much better than I thought. Before coming, I could not picture how a boy and a girl friend would, after exchanging kisses in a restaurant, pay separately for their meals. I was amazed when I realized that most families provide their sons with a valuable amount of money with which to start life with.

With the help of some students of my nationality, it was easier to find my typical food. However, I am very cautious to read in depth all the ingredients included in the foods, so as not to eat something religiously forbidden. It is good practice to always read on the back of all groceries to know the constituent elements. I found some Arabic and Turkish restaurants and shops, which made it easy to find types of food I need.

I expected difficulties, but couldn't imagine that I would be obliged to leave the city where I'm studying to a far city searching for work. I suffered from not finding a job and was on the verge of having no money at all. When I received my first wages, I had already been experiencing the pangs of hunger for 2 days. The same happened the following summer. The only difference was that I had lesser psychological stress. I had acquired some of the features of the language to the level that I could pretend that I could speak German to enhance my possibilities to fit a vacancy.

I worked for a known shop called Kaufhof. The work office (Arbeitsamt) was really fair in providing me this chance. The job was to pack off books from their cartons, stamp the prices on them and arrange them in a countable manner. Within 7 weeks, I earned money enough to last till the next summer. Again, a new academic semester began with its heavy load but much better conditions of adaptation. I got used to everything, the much quicker rhythms, and better contacts. The presence of some Arabic channels in the student hostels helped relieve the sense of being away from home.

Friday is the day all or most of Muslims meet in 'salat aljomaa', listen to a brief talk about religion and contemporary life affairs, pray and then get acquainted and associate with each other. For me, Fridays had a special taste. When I came back to study I always felt refreshed.

Being a foreigner, it needs special psychology to adapt, as I think. In Sudan, there is a famous saying: 'He, who leaves his home, reduces his value.' Here, you are mostly alone, while people in Sudan always give you the sense of effectiveness to the family and to all people. When you are sick there, you find people around you who are so concerned, even more than you. The first question the physician asks you in Germany is whether you have medical insurance or not. But, on the other hand, you are always confident that you will receive the best quality of treatment, while people in Sudan die of malaria and other out-of-date diseases.

By the way, animals like cats and dogs are lucky if they are born as Deutsch (German) nationals. They will receive food and life style better than majority of African people! One of the most fascinating features of life in Germany is the part of supermarkets that are special for cats and dogs. Most of people in Sudan do not believe it or can not even imagine it! There are things that you can justify and convince yourself why they are so, and also there are some things you can only attribute to difference in mentality. For instance, it was unjustifiable that the costs of the repair of an electronic device such as a radio cassette are higher than its price, as a brand new!

When I'm to return home for a vacation, I always made a checklist of benefits and outcomes of being in Europe. I knew by heart that I had to be realistic, and consider in much more concern the drawbacks and losses, and not to be a false facade of an absolute high scale comer, as most people in Sudan believe that European skies have golden raindrops. The most crucial point in my checklist is the Deutsch practical mentality, which I think I'm gradually acquiring some aspects of it, but cannot guarantee so far. The Deutsch mentality seems to be based on doing your job as best as possible, even with apparently trivial matters – accidents are considered but should always be justified. This is contrary to the system in Sudan. There, there are many things classified as trivial although they may cause fatal consequences, and catastrophes. For us, they are nothing else than 'Algadar'!

In conclusion, life in Germany is well organized, highly civilized. Life in Sudan is not so organized, but is extremely enjoyable, as you live among people who, when they smile, it means that they are smiling.

From Dust to Snow: The African Dream?

As time passes, one needs to checklist every now and then. But, can one checklist for his adaptation of emotional development or regression?

EsamEldin tagElsir AhmedMohamed

Chapter 23

When East Meets West

'Even the mightiest eagle comes down to the tree tops to rest' –
Ugandan saying

[FK: When I first met Nurpur, I could understand why a prominent professor like Dr. Kundu could not resist a beautiful lady like her. But as Nurpur testifies, culture shock knows neither beauty nor prominence. Be inspired by Nurpur's account!]

It was 29th of June 1986.

"Nupur, the horoscope matches very well," said my mom, "Now we have to fix a wedding day!"

This was with respect to the groom, who had come to meet us a couple of days before with his sister. We liked each other, and the families liked each other too. The only criteria before the final "Yes" was to compare the horoscopes to see if the marriage would survive. This was an arranged Indian marriage, where the groom's family had placed an advertisement stating the type of bride they were looking for. My parents had responded with a photograph of me.

Although our marriage was arranged, it was somewhat different from the traditional Indian-arranged marriages. More than fifty years ago, a traditionally arranged marriage was decided by the parents, without the child's consent. In those days, the bride and the groom saw each other for the first time only on the wedding day. But in the present days, the potential bride and groom get to interview each other first before the parents' interference. We interviewed each other, and had the feeling that we could live together, as we had similar mental alignments.

Now, matching a horoscope is not very common; in fact, both my parents and my parents-in-law were married without it; they are happily married to this day. But there was a sad incident, where one of my cousins lost her husband in a car accident at the age of twenty-four. She had been married for four years, and had a two-year old daughter. When she went to the astrologer after this mishap, she was told that this mishap was inevitable. So you see, no parent wants to make this mistake; therefore, this big fuss over the matching of horoscopes.

June 29: my parents-in-law, to-be, were invited over for lunch to decide on the date. Bikram, my husband, to-be, was then an assistant professor at the University of Arizona in Tucson, Arizona, U.S.A. He had come over during the summer vacation, and had to be back by the end of July or the beginning of August. So, the date was fixed for July 12, 1986.

July 12, 1986 was only thirteen days away! Some of you must be wondering, 'How can you plan a wedding in thirteen days?' Well, in India everything is possible. The decorators were contacted to decorate the house with flowers and fabric. The caterers were informed immediately, and the cards were printed the next day. Our relatives were invited within two days by going to each of their houses, because if they were invited simply by mail or over the telephone, they would be so insulted that they would not show up. So my parents, in spite of the scorching heat in July, paid a visit to all the relatives inviting them to this auspicious occasion.

Although I liked Bikram's humble personality, there was still a lot to worry about. First of all, I did not know how to cook. Secondly, I was going to go to a foreign land in a couple of weeks. This land was not close to my motherland, but the farthest possible distance from it. I had been under my parents' roof for twenty years. Now, I could not imagine my life without my family, especially, my mother who was my best friend. I had not spent more than a day without them at any relative's place.

The days were flying; thirteen days seemed like thirteen hours! My father was so disheartened at the thought of my departure from the family that he was debating whether or not to call off the wedding. My mother, having total faith in God, assured my dad that everything would be fine and continued with the wedding plans.

July 12, 1986: my mother woke me up at 4:00 a.m. I had to go through a ceremony, and eat my non-vegetarian meal for the day until the marriage ceremony was over. The house was full of my closest relatives from the previous day. All the married women took part in the ceremony, and fed me. The meal is typically of rice, vegetables, fish, and sweet yoghurt. I felt like a cat eating the obligatory fish on that early morning! I had to make the best use of it, as I had to fast after this meal till the end of the marriage ceremony, late that night.

The wedding music was soon turned on. This music always seemed so joyous when it had been at someone else's house. Today the tune was heartbreaking for me. The house was beautifully decorated with flowers, colourful fabrics and lights. The guests started arriving early in the morning. My friends came too. Since I was the first one to get married among my friends, they had a ball at my wedding!

Our weddings typically last for three days. On the first day, the groom comes to the bride's family with his closest family members, except his mother. Both the bride's and groom's mothers are not allowed to witness the wedding ceremony, as it is believed to bring bad luck on the newly married couple's life!

Bikram came in the evening with his elder brother and his sister-in-law in the decorated car that was sent by my family. The rest of his close family came in a chartered bus. Our wedding ceremony took place very late at night, as it was the only auspicious time of the day. After the ceremony, Bikram and I got some time together in a separate room to rest and relax. My anxious nerves were soothed, while we talked for the rest of the night.

July 13: after some more ceremonies at our place, it was time for me to depart from my family, my home, and start a new life. I still remember the agonizing pain. I was choked for a few hours; I can still feel the sore throat. Although I knew my family would always be mine and their home would always be there for me, it would not be the same as before. The thought of not seeing my mother every morning when I wake up, and not having her at my side through my difficult times, made the departure more painful. I was wondering how I was going to survive not chatting with my family every day! With a heavy heart and acute pain, we started for Bikram's place. I cried so much, before I left, that I fell asleep on the way, as it was about an hour's drive from my place to theirs.

My sister-in-law woke me up when we reached the house, and I started having butterflies in my tummy! Here, I came to a family that I did not know that well. The warm welcome at my in-laws' place made me feel at home instantly, and soon I became very relaxed. There was a small ceremony at their place in the evening. I spent a very relaxing evening with my new family.

July 14 was the reception day at my in-laws' place, where I would be meeting all of Bikram's relatives and family friends. My family and our closest relatives would be there too in the evening. I was looking forward to that time since late morning. I was overjoyed to see the familiar faces of my family in the evening. I tried to make the best use of time with them for the few hours they were there. Soon it was time for them to leave; it was a painful moment. My mother who always covers herself in a strong charade could not fool me. I could see and feel her separation agony too!

Finally, all the guests left, and it was time for Bikram and me to retire to our room. We had been treated like a "King and Queen" for the last three days. Now we got to sleep in a bed that was decorated with roses. "Life is not a bed of Roses", as we know. So in Indian marriages, we get to spend the first night on a bed of roses!!

The next three weeks flew by, as we got to know each other and the families better. I had always preferred an arranged marriage to choosing my own partner, as there is no comparing the person before and after the wedding. Unless two people live under the same roof with a commitment, it is very hard to really know each other. In our case, we grew up together; it was an adventure! We visited the relatives from both sides as a couple now. Before we realised, it was time to leave for U.S.A.

August 10: the flight to U.S.A. by Japan Airlines via Tokyo was to depart from Calcutta in the afternoon. It was another day of heartache for my family and me! Both our families, and some close relatives came to see us off at the airport. My mother tried her best to hold back her tears bidding me a warm farewell, but I failed to do the same. It was a very emotional goodbye for my sisters and I. Reality struck me at this time! Now, I was going so far that it would not be possible to visit my family whenever I wanted! Chills ran down my spine, as the thought of it overpowered my excitement of beginning a new episode of my life!

August 10: the wheels of JAL touched down in Los Angeles, California. 'Here I am in the "Land of Opportunity"!' I thought to myself. I have relatives in the States, and some family friends in California. Therefore, I had some concept of U.S.A. I realized that seeing something in real life is quite different from only reading about it. The gigantic L.A. airport with all its modernization mesmerized me. The people and the officials were very friendly. After the customs and immigration clearance, we went to the domestic terminal from the international terminal where we took our flight to Tucson, Arizona.

The flight reached Tucson in the afternoon. As I came out of the aircraft, it felt like I was diving into a furnace! The month of August is the worst time to arrive in Arizona. With the scorching heat of 105 °F (40.5 °C), and twenty percent humidity, it was a very shocking experience for me! But as soon as we entered the terminal, it was wonderful. All the buildings, cars, houses and stores are air-conditioned, so you do not feel the heat. I was amazed to find that there are people who really love this kind of hot weather; they spend hours in the sun!

Tucson is a pretty place in the valley of the Rocky Mountains. Finally we reached Bikram's and my new home. This is the house that he bought before we got married. It was a nice three-bedroom, two-bathroom house, with a nice backyard and a view of the Rocky Mountains. I had to use my interior designing skills to improve the bachelor interior look of the house.

All of Bikram's friends and students called the next morning to welcome me, and came to meet me in the evening. They were my new friends, and some of them became like my family in the later years. Although they are very nice friends, no one can replace one's own family. I could not sleep at night for the first few weeks, as I was suffering from jet lag. Moreover, as soon as I closed my eyes, I could see my family in Calcutta sitting in the family room watching T.V. and chatting. I felt so nostalgic that I could not fall asleep. Bikram's reaction to this was, "That's good; this way you can visit your family everyday without any expense!"

I started getting used to my new life without my mother being at my side to help me. I had to make my own decisions. The most difficult part was to think up what to eat on my own. This was very difficult for me, since I had always been served prepared meals before I got married! If I asked for Bikram's suggestion on what to eat, he said, "Open the refrigerator and you will find lots of food." But that was not the point; I couldn't decide what to prepare! In my family, we three sisters had been pampered a lot, which is not very common. I guessed it was time to grow up!

The U.S.A. is a place where everybody feels at home. Although I have not had any unpleasant experiences, I have heard that there are a few places in the south and the mid-west where people are not that friendly to coloured people. The west coast of the U.S.A. is newly developed as compared to the northeast. Educated professional immigrants are more common in this part of the country. The west is also more enriched in nature.

One day while we were grocery shopping, I made eye contact with a man who in return smiled at me. I was so upset about this that I informed my husband immediately about the incident. He calmly told me to smile back whenever someone smiles at me, even if it is a man. Talk about culture shock! All this time in India, I grew up knowing that only characterless men smile at unknown women, and the women who smiles back are equally characterless! Feeling a little uncomfortable for the first few days, I took my husband's advice and got used to this custom in no time.

All my life, I have heard that Americans do not speak good English; well that is true, if you consider British English to be the benchmark for good English. One evening while watching the weather report, the meteorologist said, "Rain is falling at the airport." I could not believe my ears! I remembered correcting a sixth grade student, when I was in eighth grade that she was supposed to say, "It is raining" and not "Rain is falling." I still have a hard time digesting the sentence. The American accent was also a little difficult for me to understand at first, as I was more used to the British accent.

Greeting unknown people at the stores or while strolling down the streets is a very common practice in U.S.A. This makes one feel more at home. The smiling faces of the cashiers at the stores, and always being asked about my day or how I was doing, overwhelmed me, as I was still struggling to cope with my new life being in a foreign land and away from my family.

I was impressed by the informal attitude of the people in U.S.A. There were no class distinctions; the janitors and the professors sit at the same table and have their lunch. This is just unthinkable in India even to this day! The vice president of a company treats his employees as his friends, whereas in Indian culture, the employees treat a vice president as a god! A person has to make an appointment, consulting the vice president's secretary in advance in order to speak to him; calling him on his cellular phone or his private office phone is not a common practice in India. Addressing a person by his or her first name is also not a common practice in India. Therefore, I was very uncomfortable with calling the people who were of the same age as my parents and grandparents by their first names. Although I have not mastered this custom yet, two decades later, I am getting better at it. Very close friends are offended when they are not addressed by their first name, no matter how old they are. When two countries are on the two extreme opposite sides of the world, every thing is opposite!

Almost three years after my arrival in the U.S.A., we had the chance to spend fifteen months in Europe when Bikram took his sabbatical. In most American Universities, tenured faculty is given six to twelve months off every six years, to carry out intensive research in the area of their research interest. This is the time when the faculty member does not have to teach, and is free of any departmental obligations, so as to be able to concentrate exclusively on research. This research can be done from home, or collaborating with domestic or foreign researchers. The Chalmers University of Technology, in Gothenburg, Sweden, invited Bikram as a visiting professor. He also received the Humboldt fellowship from Germany to carry out some interdisciplinary collaborative research at the J.W. Goethe University of Frankfurt, West Germany. He decided to stay in Sweden for three months and Germany for twelve months.

We were very excited about this sabbatical, as this would be our first European visit and a long-term stay there. We were not worried about our stay in Sweden, but a little sceptical about our stay in Germany, as we had heard that without the German language, it was hard to survive in Germany. Although my husband is a wizard at mathematics, he does not have the language aptitude, and due to his lack of time, I enrolled myself in a German course at the University of Arizona. I learned the basics of the German language for one semester, and had the knowledge to get along in daily life.

May 31, 1989: we left the U.S.A. for Europe. Travelling in Europe is every American's dream. Our friends did not forget to mention several times how lucky we were to have this opportunity. We were still newly married then, therefore we were looking forward to this extended "Honeymoon". Our Pan Am flight was supposed to take off from JFK International in New York. The colossal JFK overwhelmed us with its sophisticated technology! It looked like we were in a small city and not an airport. The entrance to the aircraft from the terminal was very impressive; we entered a double-decked huge elevator, which moved so smoothly that it was difficult to realize if it moved forward, backward or sideways. Before we knew it, we were at the gate of the aircraft! I felt like "Alice in Wonderland!" I still wonder to this day what had happened. I flew from JFK many times later in my life, but did not witness anything like that again! Maybe I was too young and too excited, such that I was spellbound before the trip!

From JFK, we were supposed to transit at Heathrow International, London, on our way to Gothenburg, Sweden. Since the British colonized India for so long, we knew a lot about this country. I was always fascinated by England's landscape, its rich literature, and most of all "Princess Di"; visiting London was my dream! This time, although we were only transit passengers, we planned to visit London during our stay in Europe, as Bikram was invited to give a lecture at Oxford University.

We landed in Heathrow, and to my incredulity, the airport was too humble compared to JFK. It was interesting, how annoying it was to hear the British accent, even though I had been used to this accent since I was a toddler! Surprisingly, in only three years, the American accent felt more soothing to my ears than the British. It was amazing how my British accent had changed without my conscious effort! The stiff and cold attitude of the people was noteworthy without any doubt. I tried to excuse their attitude, by looking at their inflexible outfits.

Anyway, all the passengers were asked to collect their luggage. Since we were transit passengers, we thought we only needed to identify our luggage. Oh no, you had to collect your luggage, no matter what, and nobody wanted to listen to your excuse! The lady official had a big ruler, and was using it to poke the passengers who were not maintaining a straight queue. It seemed like we were in an elementary school with a stern principal. She made a big fuss over why we did not have a transit visa. We tried to explain to her that we were not planning to stay in this country, but were only passing; but all was in vain! Finally she called her superior to whom we explained our story, showed our Swedish and German residence permits along with our American Green card. The supervisor apologized for any inconvenience, and gave us the transit visa without any hesitation.

From Dust to Snow: The African Dream?

Our next stop was Copenhagen, Denmark, before we reached Sweden. There was a drastic change in the people's attitude. It felt like we were back to U.S.A. The people were very friendly and helpful.

On June 1, 1989, we reached Gothenburg, Sweden, very late at night. Gothenburg looked like a city taken out of a fairytale book. Scandinavian people are generally very friendly. Although the senior citizens are not very tolerant with coloured people, the young generation did not have any hang-ups about it. We enjoyed our three months stay in Gothenburg very much. Among all positive experiences, there is also a very unpleasant memory. This incident occurred at a bus stop. There were four seats at the stop, and three of them were occupied. I took the last available seat, without noticing who was seated next to me. As soon as I sat down, the old lady next to me sprang up and moved to the other end, and since there were no other unoccupied seats, she just stood there. At first I thought she was going to take the bus that was coming. Well, guess what! She was just so scared of me and my colour that she refused to sit by me, and was very indiscreet about her feelings!

September 1, 1989: we reached Frankfurt, Germany. The commercial appearance of the city was not very alluring to me, but it had its own charm. When I went to the grocery store the first day and smiled at the cashier, she gave me a look of, "What is your problem lady? Why are you smiling at me?" Talk about cultural shock! The Germans seemed like they were taxed to smile too! Before the German reunification, they were less tolerant of coloured people. Bikram got a "Hitler Salute" at the University, which was just appalling! One would think that the educated community would act better than this. Anyway, the Germans have changed a lot since the reunification of Germany. Probably now, they believe that the coloured people were better than their eastern brothers. We visited Germany again in 1996 for nine months, 2003 for seven months, and 2004 for three. Each time, the change in attitude of the Germans towards the coloured people was significantly noticeable, positively.

During our stays in Germany in 1989, 1996 and 2003, we travelled a lot in Europe. Each country had its own charm; therefore it is very difficult to crown the "Best country in Europe".

Switzerland is the queen of beautiful nature. It seemed Mother Nature was over generous to Switzerland. Just driving down the freeway can be extremely pleasurable, even if you do not visit their natural parks. Swiss people have the reputation of being very peaceful. They are very friendly and open minded towards coloured people.

Italy, Spain and Portugal are popular among the European tourists for the warm weather. Although I am not very fond of warm weather, I still liked these countries, as the people are friendlier and fun loving in these countries. The physical features and their food have a lot of resemblance to that of the Indians. I am often mistaken as a Spanish or Italian in Europe. One day, when I asked for our hotel direction in Spain, the man started giving the direction in Spanish. When I stopped him and said we could not follow in Spanish but in English, he gave me a look, which said: "Why are you showing off when you are a Spanish woman?" In Italy, people often came up to me and started talking in Italian without any hesitation.

We have heard a lot of stories about the "unfriendly French" people, but we had a very positive experience every time we visited and stayed in France. We had the chance to stay in France for two months every summer, for a few years, as Bikram was collaborating with some French scientists. Most of the time, we lived within ten to fifteen kilometres of Paris. I can crown Paris as "Europe's most beautiful city", due to its unique modern architectural structures, among which the Eiffel Tower is my favourite. The first time we visited France was from Germany, in 1990, as tourists, and the difference was significant! The French, being horrible drivers, were very polite and courteous. The French have a reputation for refusing to speak any other language but theirs. Believe me, this is absolutely misrepresented! Unlike the Germans, they were very polite and did not make a big fuss over their language. Everybody spoke English even though most of them had poor spoken English skills.

In the summer of 1999, we went to France again. We were touched by the French hospitality! The daughter of Bikram's host professor got married that summer, and we were invited to the wedding. After the wedding ceremony, all the guests were invited to the reception at the Professor's place. We thought now was the time to get bored for a few hours, as we did not know any of the guests. Well, to our astonishment, we had a great time! The bride's family paid special attention to us, and each of the guests (though very busy at the party), giving us constant company alternately. They introduced us to all their family members and friends. In fact, they treated us as family members. This kind of behaviour is unimaginable from the Germans!

Having a very negative experience the first time at the London airport, we were very sceptical about our London visit in 1989. Well, the people that you come across in the streets everyday are very different! They are very courteous, helpful and friendly. The British drivers are the best in the world, with unthinkable patience. We had a great time enjoying the countryside of London. While we were visiting Shakespeare's house in Stratford-upon-Avon, Bikram was taking a photo of me with Shakespeare's house in the background, when a gentleman who was walking down the street asked Bikram, "Would you like to be in the picture too? I would be happy to take this picture for you." Well why not? "Sure, I would love that. Thank you", replied Bikram. Now we have a nice photo of both of us in front of the famous writer's house! There were several occasions where we were looking at the map, trying to find our way in the city, when people came up to us and asked, "Can I help you?" This was a very impressive gesture.

Our experiences of Eastern Europe were completely different from those of Western Europe. The Western part of Europe is well travelled by coloured tourists as opposed to Eastern Europe. So, when we visited the countries of the Czech Republic, Hungary and Poland, the reactions of the people were noticeable. They look at coloured people as one would a Museum display! They try to guess, "Why are you here?" Most of the time, they had a suspicious attitude towards coloured people. They tried to protect their valuables very indiscreetly around a coloured person! In the cities of Prague and Budapest, we had an interesting incident while travelling with their metro. Five to six boys surrounded us while we tried to get inside the train compartment from the door. We just could not move. Our daughters, being three and four years old, were almost suffocated by the pressure from all around them. I could feel that they were trying to unzip my purse! I cautioned Bikram immediately in our mother language Bengali to be careful about his camera bag, as we were in the process of being victims to pickpockets. Well, this worked like magic; the boys, not knowing what I had said, got scared and left us alone by moving in different directions of the compartment. I was right! After they moved away, I saw that my purse was unzipped but fortunately nothing was missing. Well I guess they thought: "Since these coloured people are visiting our country they must be rich, so why not steal from them." In spite of a couple of these bad experiences, we enjoyed Prague and Budapest very much.

In Krakow, Poland, we had an experience that will top the list of any unpleasant ones. We were in the grocery store looking for some snack items. Since we did not have much to buy, we did not take the shopping cart. All four of us carried one item, and were looking for some ice cream, when I realized there were two people from the store cash department staring at us. Not caring much about it, we went to a different isle, when one person from the last isle came almost running behind us to spy on us. This time I was really upset with this behaviour. Living in U.S.A. for a while, we have learned to trust people. This action was really insulting to me. We just went to the cashier and paid for the things we needed and left the store. When we returned to the same store after a few hours, we saw a big queue in front of the store and a security person was controlling the queue. We asked what the problem was. He said in the Polish language, with the help of physical gestures, that they were out of shopping carts. We told him we only needed one thing, so we did not need a cart: could we still go in? Oh no, you could not go in without a shopping cart, irrespective of how many things you had to buy! Now it was clear why the people were spying on us a few hours back.

We sometimes faced the same problem in Germany in 2003, even after they were open about coloured people staying in their country. I had security people following me in some stores in fear of shoplifting! This has never happened to me in U.S.A., England or France. In Germany, I have not seen the white Germans behaving like this; we have encountered this kind of behaviour mostly from the security guards of foreign origin.

Before visiting Moscow, Russia in 1995, I thought that there were security guards with rifles at the ground level of each building. I have even heard that they shoot people for no good reason! Guess what! I was completely wrong! Moscow was a very peaceful city. The people were very tolerant of coloured people. We availed their metro till one o'clock in the morning without any problem. The underground metro stations in Moscow are exceptionally beautiful and clean. They are rated five-star in my travel book.

Well, it has been many years now since I moved to the U.S.A. I like the American way of life where there is no unnecessary interference from your neighbours, friends or colleagues. This is just unimaginable in India! Uninvited advice from extended family, friends and neighbours is a part of daily life there, which can be very annoying at times when we visit India.

Life in U.S.A is very fast, even faster than Europe. Everybody is running after time. Because of the punctuality and diligence of the people, the country is so prosperous. You are your own identity; nobody cares whether your father is a janitor or the President. A person has to earn his own identity. The family does not hand it out to him or her. This is the country of equal opportunity and equal rights. I personally support the concept of dignity of labour of this country.

The people in the eastern world are well known for their hospitality and warmth, whereas, the people in the western world usually have a reputation of being cold towards their guests. This is another misconception. The warm behaviour of our American neighbours in Tucson made it very easy to consider them as our close family members. We trust them more than our Indian friends. We had more unpleasant experiences with the people of our own country because of their envious attitude. The colleague in Germany with whom Bikram collaborates is also like our family. Their warmth and hospitality will tarnish any eastern saga. It is true that you do not come across these kinds of families everyday.

When we are in a different culture and society, it is always better to see and choose the positive things of that society, and not have a fixation on what we have learnt all our lives. An adaptive person is always a better achiever. There are always pros and cons of a culture, and we have to exercise our best judgment in what to receive and reject to enjoy a successful and happy life.

[FK: If I ever have a daughter, I will name her Nupur, which means ornament. Thanks Nupur!']

Chapter 24

A graveyard for Christians

'All divorces begin with marriage' - Anon

[FK: For another perspective student experience from outside Africa, let us welcome the always-smiling Mr Lawmsang Van from Burma. Van has learned to ease his difficulties with a smile, rejoicing in every circumstance and trusting God for deliverance. His experience starts with something to smile about!]

I like dog meat a lot, so when I spotted the cans with the dog drawn on the outside, my mouth started to water! The shelf had quite a variety. Apparently, they had different preparations of dog meat. I walked down the aisle, picking up different cans and examining them. They had cat meat too! Wow! I would definitely tell my wife, when I called her next. She would love Deutschland.

I had made a discovery! In Burma dog meat was one of the most expensive – a delicacy. But here, I had just found out the dog meat was cheaper than beef. I scooped several cans off the shelf, and put them in the shopping wagon. My taste buds were really watering, and I could not wait to get home. Besides, I was really hungry. I began to turn over in my mind, what would be the ideal thing to eat the dog with. I wasn't to know I had a big disappointment awaiting me.

I was born in a small village in a remote area called Phunte, Falam Township in Myanmar. Myanmar or 'Union of Myanmar' is the more recent name for Burma. I am the last son in my family, which means I am the heir; it also means I have enormous responsibility. I have to take care of my parents when they are old. I will inherit my parent's house, and the farmland. As soon as I came of age, I experienced how hard it was to be from a family that lived on farming, and had to dig hard into the soil. I did not want to end up like my parents, so I decided to become and educated man, so I could help my family, especially, my parents when they retired. I was not a clever boy, and some of my teachers gave up on me, but I was not a truant and did not dare not to face my problems and difficulties. I was determined and tried to work really hard. Besides, my 7 siblings were not cleverer than me, and did not bother to study, so I had the family's weight on my shoulders.

From Dust to Snow: The African Dream?

After University, I got a chance to apply for a scholarship through the Myanmar Christian council. In the church, I was youth president of the Yangoon circuit for six years, and served in the Sunday school children ministry of the Yangoon society for five years. I was also a local preacher at some point. Because of my involvement in the church, I could apply for the scholarship. It was very difficult to get a scholarship as a civilian. I needed to do a lot. For example, my English and general knowledge had to be really good. I had to take oral test and written English tests (IELTS) at the British Embassy. The exam and course fees were very high for the poor like me: $120 for exam fees, and $150 dollars for 51 hours of lectures.

I had to quit my job, and spent a lot of money for preparation. My wife was then a freshman in university. I had to take care of my family, as we now had a beautiful little girl called Theresa. I had to take care of her schooling, and now, with no income, our days were numbered! We trusted God, and lived one day at a time. I had to borrow from a friend, and finally sold my wedding ring. Till today, when people ask me about my wedding ring, I would be at a loss to answer. Normally, I just said it was at home. I believed someday my wife and I would get us a new pair of wedding rings. My dear wife was so worried, and I watched her beauty slip away. She completely stopped smiling. She also doubted if all the sacrifices would even pay off. 90% of those who applied for the scholarship never got it. I did understand why my wife worried so much. She is 11 years younger than me, and at the time she was 20 and in first year at university, she became my wife, giving up a lot. I did not give up hope, and I hoped someday everything would be fine. I had a clear vision that God could make it happen for us, and give me the opportunity.

I had a big vision, if my scholarship were granted. This was to eventually use my study experience from abroad to set up a project for fighting juvenile delinquency in our society and country. It was sad to see the unemployed and uneducated youth up to the dirtiest and worst form of life and biz.

The scholarship was to fund my study for a Masters degree in Small business/enterprise promotion and training in Deutschland. The application process was going smoothly, but seemed still hopeless. I waited for the results anxiously but hopefully and continued in prayer. One day, while I was taking a nap with my dear wife and daughter, the doorbell rang. When I opened, it was the postman with a post-package for me. I opened it so quickly I tore the envelope in the process. It was the scholarship award from ÖSW (Deutschland), not only for me but also with prospects for my family to eventually join me in Deutschland! You can imagine how happy we were giving thanks to our God.

A graveyard for Christians

From that day onwards, my wife and I changed completely. The way I spoke or thought was completely different, and I walked very fast and light-footedly. I was like a Michael Jackson acquitted after a gruesome trial. But the next challenges were equally difficult. I had to make a passport in Rangoon, and again it was very difficult for civilians. I had to make my passport as a job passport, as I was from a civil organization. I paid money to get an attestation from Korea that I had a job there. I paid a lot under the table.

My scheduled departure was the 1st of April 2002, but my passport was not ready yet. I was so worried again, and I informed my university and sponsor in Germany. Fortunately they still accepted my late arrival. One month late, I got my passport. For the visa, it was not a problem because I had all the documents the embassy wanted. It took a week and no bribe at the German embassy

Two of my friends, my wife and daughter Theresa (only two years old), came to the airport. It was hard to leave them though. I started missing them the moment I stepped into that Lufthansa flight. My wife did not look worried, but felt bad. I think she wanted me to leave my country quickly in good hope for the future. I flew Lufthansa, first landing at Bangkok international airport, then Frankfurt. It lasted around 13 hours from Myanmar.

At the Herder Institute in Lumumbastrasse, Leipzig, I received a very warm welcome, and the staffs were very hospitable and polite. They organized everything and called a taxi to take me to my student hostel. The driver did not speak English, and he dropped me off the back entrance, where I could not see the house number of the hostel, and quickly drove off apparently in search of his next customer. I stood there with my luggage for a long time, about 1 hour, not knowing how to proceed. Finally, one student, who must have noticed me from inside his room through the window standing there for so long, came out and helped me. We got my key from another student called Becker, from Jordan, who had already been in Deutschland for about one month. We then went to the supermarket, and he taught me how shopping was done and we bought kitchenware.

On Monday, I went to German language class for the first time and the teacher asked me how good my German was. I said I knew around 30 words! She was appalled and quickly arranged for me to be sent to a different group. I joined another class made up of DAAD scholarship students, just to have some knowledge and then join the next course (Grundstufe).

It was on the first day I went shopping alone that I found this cheap dog meat. So that day, I returned from the supermarket with my canned dog meat. I had chosen the big cans. I would have a feast. As soon as I shut the door, I curiously decided to look into the dictionary what was written on the can. This was just to clear my conscience, so I could really enjoy. I put up my legs and leaned back on my second-hand 'zum mitnehmen' sofa. Then I got my shock! It was not dog; it was dog's food! They sold dog's food in supermarkets!

I was so disappointed. I could not believe my eyes, and I crosschecked over and over again. But it added up. The price, and the fact I saw a lot of very healthy loose dogs since my arrival. Reluctantly, I decided to return the cans to the supermarket. I took my dictionary along to help me explain. There I explained my problem to the lady at the counter. I had wanted to buy dog meat not dog's food. She was apparently equally appalled that I ate dog! She said she was sorry they could not take it back. I said, 'Then take it!' in my broken German. She, patiently, said she was sorry she had no dog! Irritated, I left the cans there at the counter, and returned dejectedly to my room. Later on, I shared my experience with someone and actually heard that someone had eaten a whole can of dog's food, thinking it was canned dog meat. I had been lucky I had decided to look before eating.

The hardest times came soon. The doctors said my pregnant wife would have to have a C-section. I could hardly sleep, and when I did, I always dreamt I was with them. I found and joined the Leipzig English Church by then. I was even part of a home-group there which met weekly for Bible study and prayer, and they really supported me in the next months. I – we prayed so hard, especially, as I would not be there to take care of my wife. It was so hard having to imagine from a distance and letting others take care of my wife. My wife's sister came to live with her during this period. What could I do but pray and wait. What would happen?

In the meantime, I was getting some more nasty shocks from the cultural discrepancies between Deutschland and Burma. Early on, my German teacher advised me to buy a TV and radio to help improve my German. I bought one for 15 Euro from an Arab who had picked it up from somewhere. That evening, I switched it on and was stunned to find them showing sex scenes. That was at around 11 P.M. I quickly changed channels. After midnight nearly every channel showed some porn! I could not believe it. The next day, I complained to my German language course mates, and they laughed at me saying I would soon get used to it.

Another day, I invited Mimi, also from Burma, and two other friends to watch a movie titled Evi & Adam, which had been highly advertised in my language school. Mimi was Buddhist, and so I thought it was an absolute chance to tell her about Christianity. We went very promptly to watch the movie. To my utter shock and dismay, they started showing offensive sex scenes and ridiculing God and the idea of marriage. I was so red-faced and embarrassed and had to apologize over and over, especially to Mimi, that I did not know it was such a movie! She probably thought I wanted to show her a blue movie to get across to her. I explained to her that it could not have been my intention; otherwise I could have invited her alone.

Soon after the semester began, my apartment mate arrived. We shared the same kitchen and bathroom. In Myanmar, it was often the case that in the toilets there was a towel for wiping your hands after you shit. My apartment mate kept his bath-towel in our common bath, and I used it to wipe my hands everyday, after emptying my bowels or bladder. I think he always wondered why his towel was wet. One day, he gathered enough courage to ask me if I used his towel after my shower. 'No!' I quickly replied. 'Of course not! I only use it to wipe my hands after excreting; not after a shower!' He turned pink and blue before I realized my folly. I apologized emphatically.

During the early days, I needed to extend my visa. So I went to the foreign office to register. There, I sat and waited and waited and waited. People kept coming and going in before me. Normally, I am a calm boy; otherwise I would have really gotten worked up. I had expected to see a queue. After a long time, I did get partially worked up. I realized that you had to press a button on a small machine, built into a wall, to get a number. Then you had to wait for the number to be called before you go in. I just was not used to such stuff.

I really needed a church, so I combed around for one. I knew Martin Luther, who started the reformation, was Deutsch, and had been in Leipzig. So, I expected to find a high level of Christianity here. I soon found the Nikolai and Thomas Kirche (church) where Martin Luther allegedly started the reformation. At these churches, I found they were more of a tourist attraction than a church. At the services, there were no young people, only old people. The young were either in the park, or lake or picnic or somewhere else on Sunday. This was one of my greatest shocks and disappointments, the life style of Germans and their religious poverty.

Here is a typical Sunday in late spring: As soon as the sun is out on the eastern skies, you find the old ones being led by their dogs across the parks and side walks. Then, soon the younger ones and sundry come out and lie in the sun half-naked. But my biggest shock arrived when I went to the Cospudener See (lake), and found an area they called 'Free Body Culture', where people are stark naked. Apart from the fact that I was overwhelmed at seeing completely nude people, men and women and kids, each doing their own thing, I found the lot of shrivelled-up male parts were uncircumcised, as they dangled freely around. This was the west! This was freedom! It was even more disturbing to find the old women (with drooping breasts) as well, showing off 'God knows what', all to my utter disgust. Never have private parts experienced more liberty. I wonder if modernity is not taking us back to early-man days.

Another thing that disturbed me was the fact that a lot of people lived together without being married, and with hardly any child. However, it may be better they do not have children, because the children that are there are out of control with a different advanced type of delinquency. One day I saw two boys, about 12 years old, having a squabble with an elderly house superintendent. After a heated debate, the children picked up sticks and stones and threatened him. 'We are right and want to fight, common!' they shouted at him. The man said he would call the police, and the kids said they were not afraid of the police. The man's wife quickly and nervously called the police, and the kids escaped. I held my head with both hands. 'What was wrong with kids in this country?'

There are many advantages in Deutschland. They take care of the handicapped so well with the technology. Their transportation is one of the best in the world. Other nice things include the freedom – which I think is overdone, living standards, punctuality, city plan, easy internet, phone (which allows me to communicate expensively with family back home).

More disadvantages include the fact that they are a wrong example in beer consumption, as they are amongst the top in the world. Then, there are the lonely old people. A lot of women smoke. Then drugs! As of 2002, Burma was the world's second largest producer of illicit opium, but they do not consume it as in Deutschland. Probably because there is more stress here. People can switch their wives here, or have sex orgies, and the women do not see their role as in the Bible. My teacher said she could not enter her 18-year-old daughter's room without permission. 'If my husband said not to do anything, I don't care; I can go ahead and do it. I am free to go to the nightclub, and have boyfriends outside marriage. What will he do anyway? Divorce me? All divorces begin with marriage anyway.' There is no security in marriage, partly, because of the religious poverty as I term it.

Oh how I missed my wife and family. Everyday, I prayed helplessly. The doctors said it would be another girl. We would have another baby girl, if the C-section went well. All I could do was send money to my family through my cousin-brother in Singapore. Due to the situation back home, I cannot send the money directly.

Finally a miracle happened, as I can say. My wife gave birth to a bouncing baby girl naturally, without a C-section. I thank God so much. We have named the baby Deborah. That is the best thing that has happened to me all this time I have been in Deutschland. Children are a gift from God… Blessed is the man who has such arrows.

The thing that made me most angry in Deutschland is the fact that Germans who have not travelled have a limited painfully fixed picture from the TV about developing countries, especially, negatively. I guess it is the same in the developing countries where the people have a very misleading illusion about the streets of gold out in the developed countries, also mostly from TV. One day, I was really upset with my teacher, when I told her Burma has two main seasons in a year and she adamantly said this could not be true. Even that! I am from Burma!

Let me end by saying that, overall, Germany is very good, especially, for the opportunities. They are also very rich, but riches do not necessarily mean happiness. If you are a Christian travelling to Europe, watch out! If your faith is not strong, then you will lose your religion so fast you will not know what hit you. Also, Deutschland is good for studies. It may not be the best place to seek for jobs or asylum, at the cost of your family. Now I have had the clearance from my scholarship body to invite my family. However, getting the paper work is still a nightmare. I am still dreaming to meet my wife and two daughters some day. I am Van

[We can also smile about this: Van completed his Master's studies in 2005. His lovely wife and daughters Deborah and Theresa got to join him in Germany.]

Chapter 25

There is no place like home!

'This is no time for ease and comfort. It is time to dare and endure.' – Winston Churchill

[FK: The first thing Karen wanted to know on her arrival in England was why the Queen has 2 birthdays. She ended up knowing even more: Why her age-mate from Korea is actually younger than her, and how life can be for a single black female in London. Many times she found herself crying. Why? Let's finds out!]

In a family of four girls, I am the third. Dad was a civil servant but has recently retired, and mum is a dressmaker. Dad was always particular about our education, while mum always wanted us to attain more than she had.

Dad brought my attention to the idea of travelling abroad for further studies while I was still in high school. I wasn't excited, as I knew there was still so much I did not understand about the outside world. After four years, my aunt suggested that I should go to the UK. I talked with dad about it, and a few weeks later, we asked one of my cousins in the UK to send us various college brochures.

We went to the British Council to make enquiries, and were advised on what to do and how to safely send out applications and financial requirements. By this time, I was at University and had heard of many 'not so good' methods through which people travel abroad. Some of these included fake documents and visas. I made up my mind that I would not use an 'unclean' method, or try to do what is not honest in order to obtain a visa. I prayed a lot about the situation and said to myself, "If God wants me to go abroad, I will be given a visa". I prayed so much for God's will to prevail, particularly, because my visa application process disrupted my studies during exams at university; I often had to travel out of town.

At the British High commission, I met a few people who encouraged me, telling me to be myself when I went for the interview. One of the men working there told me the story of a girl who had come in for an interview a few days before me. Because she was very nervous, her visa was turned down. I immediately made up my mind not to be scared or nervous. On the interview day, I met people who where more confident than I was. Being proactive, I told them I was a bit anxious and nervous (just in case someone would say something to encourage me). One of the boys told me to relax. He said he had had several interviews, and that I should just take it as though I was having a conversation with the interviewer. I relaxed and decided to follow his advice. I went in for the interview and was asked to come back later that day for my visa. I was so excited and couldn't wait to go home and tell mum. Dad did not think I would be given the visa that day. He had left some money for me to travel back to school just in case I wasn't granted a visa. When I reached home, my sister immediately asked, "Did they give it to you?" I said, "Yes." She was as excited as though it had been given to her! Mum was overjoyed!

The next day, I made the 6-hour bus journey to collect my things from my aunt's place where I lived while at university in Buea. I also had to let my friends know I was about to leave. It was exam time, so it was hard for me to locate a lot of them who were studying at different quiet corners. I went to the student residential area to see if some were in their rooms. I met a few sitting together, and when I told them I was leaving within days, they all screamed, exclaiming, "Bush girl! So this is the last time I am seeing you." Within a few hours, the news had spread. On my way to my aunt's, I met another friend who had been trying for months to travel too. She was standing at her door. When she saw me, she called out, "Karen!" and signalled me to come. When I walked to her, she said, "I heard something – is it true?" I immediately knew what she was talking about and said, "Yes." She too began screaming and clapping her hands. I just laughed – it was fun! It was our way – when you heard something exciting, you just screamed! She and the others I had met arranged to come and meet me that evening. I also spent time that day with the friends with whom I regularly prayed, and I made sure I ate enough of the meal our hostess had cooked. I still remember what it was, water-fufu and eru, the traditional dish of her area of origin. I knew that it would be one of the last real traditional meals I was going to eat in a long time. I maximised the last hours and minutes I had with my friends.

When evening came, most of those who promised to come and say their final farewell came to my aunt's. It was exciting to see my friends come to show their love, as I was about to leave. Some others had heard and came along too. I felt blessed to see my friends come over to pray with me the night before I left, even though not all of them could make it. We talked, ate our last meal together, laughed and cracked jokes about what I would look like after some time. Many said when I came to visit I would say "Hi", not "Good Morning". I would favour make-up over a natural look, and would wear flimsy clothes. Many feared I would not keep in touch regularly like many 'Bush-fallers' who had gone before me. Close friends shared how we first met, and how our friendship had grown over the period of time we had known each other. Some of them shared their interests of wanting to come over some day as well. Others promised to keep in touch while we were apart. I tried to keep smiling, but the fact that I was leaving and was not sure if and when I would see some of them again made me want to cry.

Friends came in turns. Each time I went and saw off one group, I would see another group coming in! When one group was about to leave, I burst into tears; when the next group was about to leave, I would start crying all over again. Those to whom I was closest cried with me. We hugged, wiped off our tears consoled one another with the assurance that we would meet again soon enough. But the truth was, none of us knew how soon 'soon' would be.

My closest friend Laura stayed late into the night. When all the others had left, we sat staring at each other, not knowing what to say to each other. All of a sudden, we both burst into tears. We both felt a lot of pain, knowing we were going to miss each other terribly. After we thought we had cried all our tears, I went to see Laura off to get a cab to her house. On our way, I started crying all over again. We stopped and prayed together. It was unbelievably hard to say bye to each other.

I made it safely home to my parents. A few hours before we left for the airport, dad encouraged me. My family prayed with me, and I had the confidence that God was going to be with me while I was away from home. Dad said he had a lot of confidence in me, and encouraged me to be focused and keep my eyes on God. Mum assured me of her love for me, and how she was happy that I was going a step ahead. Some of mum's friends had come to see me. They wished me well, and I took a few photos with them, for the last time in a long time. My aunt talked with me about the journey, as she had been to London before. She said I should just read the signs, listen to announcements being made, and follow the crowd.

Everyone in the family including cousins accompanied me to the airport. Not everyone could fit in one car. Our neighbour assisted with his car. On the way to the airport I was in a daze. It all felt so unreal – was I really leaving home? I kept thinking about how much I was going to miss my younger sister. From time to time, there would be complete silence in the car, each person just looking at another. My cousin Tom would sometimes break the silence saying things like: 'So this small sis is leaving for bush!' Then my oldest sister, who is always ready with a response, would answer with something like, "I tell you, now we have one person in the family who is a 'Bush-faller'". When we reached the airport, I took a few photos with everyone, but I could not really smile in them as I was struggling to hold back tears. I was beginning to see how much I would miss everyone. The hour came for me to leave. I hugged everyone and tried not to cry. However, when I came to mum, the tears rolled freely down our faces. It hurt to depart.

In the plane, I sat by the window, beside a stranger from my region who was used to travelling abroad. I asked him many questions such as: "Where are you going?", "How high up are we from the ground?", "How far are we from home?" I thought, because he had travelled before, he knew many things about air travel. I looked out the window to see what it looked like outside. I couldn't see anything except clouds. At first, I didn't realise they were clouds. I wondered what they were, and where we were. I thought perhaps we were in space. I had expected at least to be able to see trees and houses below. I turned and asked the man besides me for clarification. He said they were clouds. I thought, "Oh!" and wished I could touch them. For a long time we remained in the midst of clouds. I began to feel a bit uncomfortable because I began to think, "What am I doing in the midst of clouds? I want to go to earth." I wanted to see trees and houses and what it looks like viewing tall buildings from the top. I wanted to see how big or small people are when you look at them from far above. The man beside me was fast asleep. I looked at him and wondered, "How come he is so comfortable?"

While on the plane, I found it hard to eat what was served. I kept asking the hostess to give me a Sprite, as that was the only drink being served that I was familiar with. I was getting hungry, but I could not eat the sandwiches served because I didn't know what they tasted like, and I was scared to eat strange-looking food. The man right beside me ate everything that was served to him. I looked at him at one point and thought, 'I wish I could eat like he does'.

I had to transit at Charles De Gaulle Airport in Paris. When I arrived in Paris, I pulled my small hand luggage along while looking around. I listened to the announcements, and paid attention to what was happening around me like my aunt had advised. I was thrilled. I was awed that everything around me was very neat and tidy. There was a lot of protocol and everything was in order! I went to where I had to take my next flight to London, my end destination.

I reached London a few hours later. As I disembarked, I thought to myself, "If these many people are coming to London alone, then London must be a great place." I turned around and realised that we were already in a large room, no longer on the plane as I had initially thought.

I couldn't wait to go out and see London for myself! When I was done with customs and security checks, I followed a sign, which said "WAY OUT". I stood at the door. It was raining. I watched a few people pass by. Then I saw one old red bus pass in front of me. I got very disappointed. I could not imagine a bus in London looking so old and not at all clean. I saw many people standing at the airport holding large boards with names on them. I looked at them and wondered what the matter was with them. There were many of them, no one talking to the other, all very serious, looking strictly at those coming off our flight. I really thought something was wrong with them, because I had never seen people just standing and holding boards with names written on them, let alone the fact that no one was talking to the other. Later I realised they where waiting for people they had never met before.

I walked up to a money exchange point called Thomas Cook and changed the French francs dad had given me into Pounds. It felt really good holding pounds Sterling in my hands. When I had finished, I looked round to see if any of my cousins Dibo, Cece or Peter had come to pick me up. It was 20 minutes past my arrival time, but there was no one at the airport I could recognise. I turned and saw a phone booth and thought of making a phone call. I couldn't because I didn't know how to use it. It wasn't like the booths we had in Cameroon. I looked to see if anyone had a 'kind' countenance, so I could walk up to him or her and ask for help. I didn't see anyone who I could boldly walk up to. I stood there with my luggage at my feet, looked round and decided to make enquiries about how to get to my new home. I walked back to the lady who had served me at the money exchange counter. She told me where to go for help. I followed her instructions, made more enquiries, and also listened to instructions on how to get to the nearest train station through the speakers. I went to the station and asked how much it would cost me to go to Leytonstone (where my cousins lived). I couldn't pronounce the Leytonstone properly. I said to the customer service officer, 'I'd like to buy a ticket for Leystoneton.' She looked at me, giggled and said, 'Leytonstone.' I nodded my head in acceptance. She said it would cost two pounds twenty pence. I picked up each coin I had in my hand, examining each in turn to find "2 pounds". I finally found it, placed it on the counter and continued in search of twenty pence!

When I got to the entrance to the trains, everyone I saw walked so fast. At first, I thought something was wrong. I stood for a while and looked, but didn't notice anything out of place. All I could see were people walking very fast in all directions. Well, I decided to join them and start walking quickly too, now grateful that my luggage had not arrived with me and would be delivered to me. I got to the neighbourhood that would be my new home two hours after leaving the airport! Finding the right house was my next problem. I was not far from it. I finally got the right house, but no one was home. I just sat at the door, too tired to try anything else. Dibo came home two hours later and met me sitting at the door of the house. She screamed, "How did you get here?" I, on the other hand, quickly noticed her shoes and said to myself, "Yeah! These are some of those bush shoes!" I thought those were the type of shoes I would have to wear now that I was in London.

Dibo and I had not seen each other in a very long time. With so much joy in us, we just stood there beaming at each other. She finally came to herself, opened the door, and we got into the house. Cece was in sleeping. A few minutes later, Peter came in with his friend. They all gathered around me, asking me to tell them the latest expressions and stories from home. They were all very excited and wanted to know so much about what was happening at home as well as the exciting things that had been happening at UniBu. I was surprised at how much they missed home. I glanced at them and thought, "They are missing home, while those at home want to come over here!" We went further and talked about family members, displaying the things mum had sent: chocolates from home, pictures of mum's 50th birthday party and letters.

As we spoke, I lifted my eyes to see what the living room was like. I wanted to see those beautiful backgrounds that I saw when Cece and Dibo used to send photos back home. The room was empty and there was a lone long sofa inside. I realised that there was no cupboard in the house, and the television was on the floor as there was no television stand.

I realised I was hungry and turned to Cece, "Is there any food? I am hungry." She responded, "There's no food. We haven't cooked but I'm drinking Dr. Pepper." At first I was surprised that there was no food at home, but I decided to keep silent. Then she went on, "Have some, it is very nice". When I heard of the name of the drink, I got scared. I wondered what sort of a drink could be called Dr. Pepper, and what it tasted like. I took the cup and sipped some. 'Yes! Yes!' It was really nice. But then again, I wondered what was "pepperish" about the drink, and most of all why the name Dr. Pepper. I took the cup to pour more of Dr. Pepper into it. Only then, did I notice it was a teacup. I asked her where I could get another cup. She said there were no cups, as there are only three teacups at home. I was a little bit surprised, but I realised that they were comfortable, and were not bothered. I knew that there were many more little surprises I would come across.

Just then, I turned and looked at the clock. It was 7 p.m., but it was still very bright outside. It was as bright as though it was 4 p.m. I looked, and kept still. Later on at about 9 p.m., it was still quite bright outside. Dibo called my parents to tell them I had arrived safely. She passed the phone to me. All I could tell mum was that it was 9 p.m., but still quite bright outside. I was so fascinated with daylight at nighttime.

From Dust to Snow: The African Dream?

Before school started, I would walk round with Dibo, Cece or Peter. They knew the sorts of things that I would find strange and unusual. I had to start school four days after I arrived. I was in the same school as Peter. Dad had paid my fees already from home before I came to Britain, so I did not have much trouble with fees for that year. I started with a Computer course. I knew that it was essential for me to know how to work on a computer, as most assignments would be computer based.

I was very surprised by the college. It wasn't as big as I had expected. I had anticipated large rooms with computer facilities in most of the rooms. I was with Peter most of my first day at college. He showed me around. Sometimes, he stopped to say hello to classmates, most of who were from other African nations. Sometimes he stopped to greet his mates who were from Asia. I found the Asian boys very funny and interesting, especially, when they talked. I stood by and listened keenly to how they spoke. Most of the time, I couldn't make sense of what they were saying. The few words I heard them say were often words that contained an R or an L, which would be greatly stressed. For instance, if they were to say something regarding an envelope, the L in the word envelope would be greatly stressed. I found it very funny and would giggle.

There was no one at College whom I knew besides Peter. It gradually dawned on me that I was actually in a foreign place where a lot of things were different. I met a lot of students from South Africa. Most of them knew one another, especially, those who were in their second year. I noticed most students were more relaxed amidst people or students who were from their own country. I envied those who knew a lot of people and wished my friends where there with me too, so that we could stand in a cluster and have fun talking with one another too.

Peter finally walked me to the door of my class. One of my tutors was in already. I quickly went in and quietly pulled out my notebook. My tutor was from South Africa. He had a different way of talking too, though he was clearer in his speech. First of all, I was happy that I had seen someone from South Africa for I had always liked South Africa. We did not have a proper lesson that day. Our tutor gave us the course syllabus, and explained to us what we would be doing throughout the year. After a while, I turned to look around the class to see if by some coincidence, I would see someone I knew. I looked carefully and saw that most of the students were Asians, and a few were from other African nations. I didn't recognise anyone in the room! I felt very disappointed and tried to keep calm within me. However, more and more, I realised I was in a different part of the world. There was a new feeling within me by this time! Back home, I would have said hello, hugged, laughed and waved at several people before even entering class. But here, I didn't even recognise anyone to say hello to in a familiar style. However, as days went by, I made a few friends and had a small sense of belonging within me.

I found it very hard to get a job; most of the jobs required that I should have had some experience in that field. One day, I went to my friends in church and asked them what I should do regarding work. I told them that I had been having a lot of difficulties trying to get a job. They advised me to ask to do voluntary work in whatever field I was interested in; later on, I should then apply to work using the skills I would obtain. I followed their advice, and went to apply for voluntary work the following week in a hairdressing salon. To my surprise, they decided to offer me the job without any work experience. I was very happy and headed to tell the others at home about it.

I started working one day per week. Later, I was offered three days per week. However, when I received a fixed timetable from college, I could not work three days anymore as some of my college hours clashed with work hours. I had to drop a day and work 2 days only since my studies were my priority. Working just two days a week could only provide part of the money I needed for my rents. I decided to start plaiting hair at home so as to make extra money for rents, food, and transportation to school. At first, I did not have enough clients to plait and raise the necessary amount of money. By this time, I began to realise that I had to fully depend on God for provision. Something interesting kept happening. A friend with whom I went to do evangelism called me one time when I had no transport money and gave me money that would cover my transport for the month. Another time I was short of rents, I went to one of our counselling pastors in church. I told him that I was short of rents and neither of my relations had any money to help me. He immediately went to his office and brought to me an envelope with money to help for my rents. It was interesting to me how people often helped me when I had no money.

However, as time went on, I told my mates at school that I was available to plait. This made many more people to know me, and to come to me for plaiting. I took the plaiting very seriously, sometimes going out of my comfort zone to plait till very late at night, especially, when I knew that I needed extra money for my own leisure.

One funny experience I had was when I started working. My first job was in a hairdressing salon, as I earlier mentioned. Because I had just started working, I was not allowed to do what most of the qualified stylist did. Often, my manager would ask me to go to the next-door shop and get something for her. Each time she pronounced the name of the sweets or whatever she wanted, it sounded different from what it actually was. I would go to the shop, repeat to the sales person exactly what my manager had said, or so I thought. Unfortunately, the sales person would not know what I was talking about, and would say he didn't have what I had asked for. I would come back and tell my manager that what she wanted was unavailable. She would then send another person who knew what she was talking about, and he/she would go to the same shop and come back with what she wanted. I then decided that in order to stop the embarrassment, I would ask her to write down what she wanted. One day she asked me to go and buy her Malteesers. However, as soon as I heard the word Malt, I thought of the Malt drink we have back in Cameroon! Then I said to myself, "You'd better ask her to spell it, and you write it down lest you go and get something different". When I went into the shop, I looked at the piece of paper and read it out to the shopkeeper. I said, 'I want Malteesers.' He gave me a packet of chocolate sweets! I could not believe it. Well, I paid for it and took it to my manager. She took it, said, 'Thank you!' and continued with what she was doing. I was very surprised that Malteesers were sweets, but I was happy I had saved myself from embarrassment this time around.

On the other hand, we had a very difficult experience when Dibo, Cece, Peter and I had to move out from where we were living into a new house. Our landlord had asked us to move out by a certain date, because he wanted to refurbish the house. We had been looking for affordable housing, where we could move into with no success. We often got worried, as we spent time searching through Newspapers and on the Internet for housing to no avail. Dibo, Cece and Peter also let their friends know we were looking for a new place to call home. We found a few and went to look at them. A lot of times, we could only do this in the evenings when we had returned from school, sometimes travelling up to an hour to get to a house. In our tiredness we often travelled in silence. Once, Cece said, "Imagine us sleeping on the street because we were chucked out!" I said I couldn't imagine such a thing. They laughed at me and said, "This is England, it happens." I was appalled. We looked at a nice house in a good neighbourhood with four bedrooms. We were thrilled at the thought of each of us having our own room. We enquired after the reason the present tenants wanted to leave the house, and what they thought about the house. They said it was a very nice house and the main reason why they were leaving was because the rent was a bit too high for them. They said £750, without utilities. When we heard how much the house cost, we immediately knew that if we took it, we would be struggling to pay the rents each month. We felt really bad. To me it looked ideal, nice and comfortable like the houses we used to live in back at home.

Finally, we found a very small 2-bedroom house. We rationalised, saying we were only students and didn't really need a living room. By this time, we had exceeded the date we had been given to leave the former house by two weeks, and the landlord kept threatening to throw us out. During that period, at least one person had to stay indoors when the others went out, just in case. When we paid for the extra two weeks, our deposit for the new house was no longer sufficient. We then had to plead with the new landlord, saying we were students and would pay in good time. There were others with ready cash to take the place. We had just enough money to do necessary things for the new house. We bought food from very cheap shops, because we were saving money towards rents. Ironically, during that period, we all grew fat, particularly me! Anyone at home would have concluded I was fat because I was enjoying the good life. Little would they know the extra kilos were from cheap, high calorie, low nutritional value foods. All this happened a few months after I arrived. Dibo, Cece and Peter knew people, with whom they could live with for some time if there was no other way out, but I knew no one; neither did I know enough to be of much help in finding a solution. All I did was to stand by Dibo, give her moral support and remind her that God would help us.

Finally, we were given the house! Dibo was particularly very happy, because she had strained so much. She came home that afternoon and told us the good news. We moved into our new house at midnight. It was like a dream. The house wasn't what we wanted, but we did not mind at all. We were just grateful that we had a roof over our heads, but that was about it. After we moved in, we realised that the house had no heater. The floor had tiny cracks in it, and one of the windows did not open. During winter, the house would be extremely cold; when the wind blew, it seemed to blow through the cracks in Dibo's room. We complained to the landlord, but he did not bother to do anything about it. When I came back from school or work, I would quickly jump into my bed and wrap myself under the blanket. We were just recovering from the financial strain, and we did not have enough money to buy a proper heater for the house. We had to manage for sometime. Usually when I lay down to sleep, I would wonder whether mum and dad could imagine what I was going through. I would think of times back home when mum and dad would rush to my aid whenever I was in need, or any other relative if they could.

I became aware of a lot of truths through the challenges I faced. The first thing I realised was that you can't afford to be very picky and choosy in the west as at home. There are several opportunities to do what you may want to do, but initially, it is hard to go in for what you want because you are a foreigner, and there are usually a few laws of restriction. Also, I realised that even though there are several opportunities, you need to be careful not to be sidetracked from what you originally wanted to do.

From Dust to Snow: The African Dream?

Unlike at home, where you have a lot of people around you and you can quickly turn to your neighbour and have a nice talk when you are lonely, it is not so in London. I learned early on that your friend could be your neighbour, but if you don't make time for one another, you could spend weeks without seeing your friend. I noticed that everyone is always busy! Whether busy playing or working, they are busy all the same! It is rare to turn around and see people just standing and chatting.

At home, the chances that people will help you when you are stuck in a problem, whether or not they know you, are very high. I discovered a great difference in London. I noticed that there was an air of 'Every man for himself and God for us all'. People are not really bothered about what is going on with you. Most of those who would dare to help you are people with your type of skin colour; so in most cases, you ought to be strong when going through a challenge.

Before I left home, I thought it would be easy for me to pick up a decent job, sustain myself and meet up with my needs. I was a bit disappointed at how hard it was to get a job. I lowered my standards of living as I realised that I had to provide for myself based on the budget I had. I became more responsible and more alert than I have ever been.

What I enjoy most about England is the diversity of people, cultures and opportunities. It is very interesting when you see how people behave differently as a result of their culture. I like it when I look and see beautiful streets, buildings and designer shops.

As a result of diversity in culture and the many different immigrants, there is major diversity in food types. Sometimes you may walk into a shop to buy a food type and end up not buying it, just because they call it something else and you think it is not what you want. Once, my friends and I went into a restaurant to eat. We looked at the menu, and I decided to order what I knew – a plate of potatoes. My two friends ordered rice. When the food was served, I looked at her plate and said, "This is called Jollof rice in my home country." She in turn replied, "Well I was told at the counter that it is Vegetable Jambalia."

There are differences in other areas as well. One evening after school, I was chatting with my mates. Amongst them was a Korean girl. I asked her about Korean culture. The first thing she said was that in Korea, when you are born, you are considered to be a year old. When you are one year old, you are actually two years old. She said for instance, she was 27 in England but 28 in Korea.

Within weeks of my arrival in England, I started missing my family, close friends and even home foods. I emailed friends at least twice a week to tell them what it was like and how I felt. I called my parents once in two weeks, because dad would always say I was spending too much money calling home. I called my sisters and mum more often when dad wasn't home, and told them some of my experiences. As time went on, I missed my family and friends extremely. Sometimes, I would wake up in the middle of the night crying simply because I was homesick. One night, about a year after my arrival, and after my cousins and I had split up, my roommate asked me why I was crying. I told her how I missed everyone at home. She looked at me and said, "I've been there. How long will you keep crying? Give it up!" This challenged me. I gradually began to overcome homesickness. I realised with time that I had to mature fast and accept the realities of the different location in which I was. Once in a while, I still get homesick. I often think of that day, when I will go home to see my family and friends. I miss the atmosphere of love that is so strong at home. I realised that back at home, though a lot of people do not have the luxury they may think they want, they often receive the love they need.

[FK: As of 2006, Karen is a student at the Financial Training Company, London. She found out that the Queen's real birthday is April 21, but that it is celebrated officially on the second Saturday in June – 2 birthdays!

Gosh! Have you seen Karen? Such a pretty woman! And she is – guess what! Single! She got me thinking how it must be like for a single black female in the Diaspora. It's not like they would readily put an ad in the newspaper like their Western counterparts:

"Single Black Female, 24. Petite, but curvy, looking for Single Male over 1.7 m. Must like books, music, and Pinot Noir (the dog). Must be between 23-33, and ambitious."

You see, if Karen put up such an ad, I would respond to it in a hurry. Many, I have interviewed, concur with the fact that it is not easy for females coming from our African background to find a true African Prince Charming while living abroad.

In many western countries, one often attends welcoming parties organized by friends and acquaintances who went to Africa, married and successfully petitioned for their wives to come abroad. The immigration process can be lengthy and frustrating – depending on the petitioner's immigration status. It may require lots of money, ingenuity and perseverance!

But why do African men go home to marry the "unknowns" instead of marrying the women they have wined and dined with abroad? Well, it is purportedly for reasons like the followings: (1) most men are under the illusion that the women back home are innocent, un-spoilt and virginal; (2) it allows some men to mask their "failures and shortcomings" since the women who are already abroad can tell where they are on the social and economic ladder; (3) some men want their women to look up to them since it makes them appear more than what and who they really are (at least in the initial stages); (4) there are those who will tell you African girls abroad have all "gone bad...rotten...too exposed...too independent." Ha, whatever that means! Perhaps, they are really struggling about having to marry a woman who is 'emancipated'. On the other hand, I have seen a really rotten girl give a friend of mine the works of hell.

May be the ladies abroad should also go home. The problem, I fear, is that most guys back home suffer from inferiority complex, to have a wife who earns more than they do or who is 'higher' than them.

It is also true that many men who go back home later find out that those ladies they marry from home may just be interested in becoming bush-fallers themselves. Once they are abroad, they show their true colours; enduring the process of metamorphosis or emancipation with them can be worse. Experiences show that it can be really bad!

By the way, the above was not an ad or description for Karen. She does not need an ad. Excuse me for getting carried away.]

Chapter 26

Footprints in the snow

"The future lies before you, like paths of pure white snow. Be careful how you tread it, for every step will show." Anon

[FK: Abram, when he was called by God to leave his father's house, relatives and country, to the 'Promised Land', did not leave without his wife Sarai. He even took his nephew Lot. Contrast that with Mr. Ambe, who left Cameroon (around the equator) to 'The Land of a thousand lakes' (almost at the North Pole!) without his dear wife Florence and two kids, and without knowing where the control key on the computer keyboard was. So, was it not God's will for Mr. Ambe to leave Cameroon? How would he survive in a cold high-tech society, and living away from his wife and kids not knowing when he would ever see them again?]

In 1992, I lost my job at COTECC. What was so annoying is that the salary I had been receiving was really chicken feed. I had worked so hard, and my reward was exactly that, I was fired; reasons, they wanted to recruit people with degrees. By then, I had only a GCE A-level certificate. It was then that the first impulse to travel abroad hit a high note in my mind. However, coming from a poor family, no uncle and being the eldest of 6 children, the idea was simply fantasy. My parents are peasant farmers.

Luckily I picked up another job at P.S.S Mankon. However, just as it happened in COTECC, I lost my Job in P.S.S (four years later), and for the same reasons.

Finding myself on the street again, I realised I really needed to foster my education. Since what I really loved to study (IT) was not offered at any significant level in Cameroon, this gave more impetus to my dream of travelling abroad. I got admission letters into universities in South Africa, Germany and Finland. Germany was out of question due to the visa requirements, which included blocking up to 6000 euros in a bank account.

I was out for a year trying to explore the other options. I met one bloke who said he could help me secure the visa for South Africa. I gathered all the family savings, which amounted to about 500 euros and gave them to him. Before I knew it, he vanished into thin air. I was completely broken, and it became an extremely difficult time for the family. We accepted it was not God's will that I go to South Africa, just coming out of the apartheid era. So we prayed God to show us another way.

As we prayed, I sat for the entrance exam to the (polytechnic) school in Finland, at the Finnish consulate in Yaoundé. Two of us succeeded. However, the consulate could not issue a visa for Finland. They advised me to go to Paris where I could obtain the visa. I needed, in that case, a transit visa to France. At the French embassy, it was not a big problem to obtain the transit visa. I only needed to show my flight confirmation and my admission letter to the school in Finland.

When I got the visa, I was not all that excited, as it was not easy to 'abandon' my family, knowing it could take many years to ever see them again if ever. There was no other option now, and I believed it was the only way to change our fortunes. I had lost all the money in the South Africa hoax; I could not even leave any money with my wife. Since this door was opened, my dear wife (Florence) and I believed God was going to provide for us. We knew that I was going out there in order to work out a better future for the whole family. It was a big gamble, but we believed if God allowed it, He would also show us how to manage, heads or tails. There was a lot of uncertainty, about what would become of me, or how things would play out. I did not even know what conditions awaited me in Paris. Paying the Air France flight, about 700 euros (student tariff, two-way to cover deportation), took all the resources we had on earth. I did not even have what I would live on in Europe, even if it paid off. I just had to take the bull by the horn.

On the day of my departure, I was in Douala together with Flo. I wanted us to make it a memorable 'au revoir'. We spent some time together, ate grilled fish well spiced with ginger and garlic. It was rainy, so we could not move around a lot, so we just cuddled. At the airport, we greeted each other properly, the way a man and wife should. I told her to take care of the boys. I got my bag and went to the waiting room. I don't think she cried. We both had not come to terms yet with what was happening.

Shortly after 11 p.m. on the 25th of August 1997, as the aeroplane started taxiing down the runway, my feelings were as mixed as rice and sand can be. The unknown challenges ahead bothered me. I sat by the window. The whole night I never slept. I knew nobody in Paris. Nobody would be waiting for me at the airport, and I had no pre-information, just the premonition shared by most Africans that Europe was paradise on earth.

When I arrived Paris, I realised I needed to declare where I would be staying. I did have the address of a Togolese friend of someone I knew, so I called him to tell him I was at the airport. He did not come for 2 days, during which I slept at the airport, in the international zone. To check out, I needed to know where I was going. Besides I had no money to pay for a hotel. I continued to wait. I got phone cards. With one of the phone cards, I tried to call my wife to tell her I had arrived. It was a prepaid card, which meant I had to first dial an 800 number, and give in the pin code on the phone card. It was the first time I had come in touch with such a phone card, so it was difficult to figure out what to do. I struggled and struggled till I instinctively realised what I needed to do.

When my wife finally got on the receiving end, I did not tell her I was still at the airport, so she would not be alarmed and worried. I did not tell her I slept on the couch in the waiting rooms of the airport, using my bag for a pillow. I had some garri, roasted peanuts and other snacks she had prepared for me. This is what I ate. I did not bathe, and I used the toilets in the airport. It was not a good way to begin living in 'paradise'. I had heard some Africans come to Europe and spend the night in train stations, because of no money, or when they travel out of their towns to look for jobs. Here I was, on the very first days in Europe, sleeping in Charles de Gaulle airport. Well, at least it was an airport in Europe!

Finally after two days, the Togolese pastor came. I did not ask him why he had taken so long, and he did not tell me why he had not come earlier. He just said things were difficult. At least he had come! The home he took me to had more or less an African home set-up, but the environment was very different. On the way from the airport I was impressed by the cleanliness of the streets and the paved roads.

After another two days I went to the Finnish embassy and realised immediately it would be very difficult for me to get the study visa. I also had to show proof that my financial status would meet up with my study expenses. So I was stuck in Paris. What would happen to me? What was I supposed to do now? All I could do was pray.

The Togolese Pastor placed me on the preaching roster of his church, since I had some layman preaching experience. So, I spend the next weeks preaching in his congregation and even others. Some people, moved by my sermons, and not even knowing what I was going through, gave magnanimously to me. The most amazing thing was that, with time, I got to save quite some money. For about three months, I preached in English in different churches, thus through a translator to French. In a Ghanaian congregation, they translated to Twi, a tone language spoken in southern Ghana.

Once I finished preaching in one congregation, and a French man walked up to me and said God had prompted him to give me 2000 French francs. I was overwhelmed! With time, the money came up to

From Dust to Snow: The African Dream?

something, and I sent 600 FF to my wife, the first money I sent home after three months. It's amazing how I sent it. There was no Western Union or fast money transfer method at the time, and if there were, they would be way too expensive. So I took some photos, which amounted to an album. I folded the money appropriately and hid it behind some photos in the Album. I then prayed and said: 'LORD you gave me this little money, and you know how much my family needs it'. I put the album in an envelope like a package, and posted it by normal snail mail. The risk was enormous, especially, in Cameroon where they often opened nearly every mail from abroad to see if there was something they could help themselves with. I addressed the letter 'care of' somebody in the P&T (post and telecommunications) delegation in my town. I kept calling to see if the mail had arrived, but it had not. Other mail arrived apart from that. Just to say that all this time in Paris, I was neither registered anywhere, nor insured. I did not even have an address I could use in case they had to return the mail, which was itself not registered or insured. Finally, finally, the mail arrived. I breathed a deep sigh of relief. At least my wife and the boys were covered for a little while.

Once my savings reached something reasonable, my Togolese brother lent me the rest of the money necessary to establish the proof of financial resources. I was then going to send back the money to him as soon as I was in Finland. I was very zealous to move at that time. So I booked the Finair flight.

I had kept communicating with my school in Finland that I was going to come, so they knew I was on my way. Actually, I left towards the end of October, a few weeks late for the winter semester. Apprehensive of the cold climate in Finland, Sister Miriam gave me some winter gear before I left. She actually took me to a philanthropic shop, since I had to save every dime I had. Since Paris was still warmer, I did not really have a feeling of how cold it could be. So, she was the one who selected the necessary jackets, gloves etc that I needed.

Just before landing, they announced the ground temperature in Helsinki. That was when I knew I had changed latitude. At the airport, after stamping my passport, I called my school in Vaasa to announce my arrival and ask for directions. They told me to take a bus to the main train station, from where I could board the train for Vaasa, and that someone would be waiting for me in Vaasa. That was really good. All this conversation took place, of course, in English. After I hung up, I took three steps out of the main entrance of the airport, and quickly recoiled inside. It was frightfully cold. I could never have imagined! I opened my luggage and removed my winter gear and put it on. When I came out again, I realized it was so cold everyone had winter caps with earflaps to cover their ears. So, I also removed my own cap with earflaps and put it on. I now looked like the others. Feeling better, I bought a ticket to the train station where I would buy another one for Vaasa.

As we drove from the airport to the train station, it was amazing to see that the trees had 'dried off'. I wondered what type of hot summer could have dried up the trees. I would have loved to ask someone but I could not speak Finnish or Swedish. It was only later that I learned that the trees shed their leaves in autumn.

There was an international student waiting for me in Vaasa. He took me to the hostel, which would house me for the next months. He showed me our shared kitchen, bath and sitting room and then my room. The first thing I found 'remarkable' in my room was the six-spring spring bed. I was very discouraged to think I would be sleeping in such a small bed. Since I left secondary school, I had never seen such a bed again! I asked the fellow if he could change the bed, and he told me all students used that type of bed. On the first night, I found myself on the floor. You could not share such a bed! I called my wife as I did after making any move to let her know I had arrived. I did not tell her about the bed.

The next day, my roommate took me to the shop for the first time. He spoke English so it was very useful. Nevertheless, I was already used to the European shopping system while in France. However, I had to guess only from the pictures on the packet what they contained, since whatever was written on the packets was in Finnish.

The next days, I did my student registration at the Vaasa Polytechnic. I was three weeks late and had to join the already rolling lectures. The studies were interesting. The school was well equipped, more than any I had ever seen before. In computer classes, every student had a computer to himself. I was impressed, and felt stupid. Why? I left Cameroon without any knowledge of how the keyboard looked like. The teacher would say press 'control' and I would have no idea. I typed like a sick chicken trying to eat maize. When the teacher gave us a task, there were some small boys and girls who were finished even before I had figured out the first key to press. I immediately told myself I had some real catching up to do. It was in Finland that I learned to sleep at 2:00 or 3:00 a.m.

I missed my wife so much and the good food she prepared. I missed eating with my 2 boys. The Finnish government provided free lunch for every student, so I only had to think of supper. I could do without supper, as I had no money. The refectory was opened between noon and 14:00 O'clock. It was a serve yourself style meal, and the ladies who supervised encouraged me to drink lots of milk to get fat, so I could withstand the cold. So I decided there was no point in drinking water. In school I would drink three glasses of milk just at lunch.

I also registered at the town hall, and got my visa extended. I had a social security number, but was allowed to work only 20 hours a week. Still then, there was almost no work I could do. If there was, I needed to speak the language. Most students scrambled for the most frequent job, which was to clean the ships or boats, as there were so many lakes in Vaasa.

Soon I found myself in the midst of acute financial crises. I had to send the money of the Togolese brother, but I also needed to live and take care of my family back home. As usual, I looked up to the heavens for a solution. I came in contact with a Baptist church Pastor who again put me on the preaching roster. I preached almost across Finland. I told God, 'If no work LORD, I work for you.' God was faithful and kept providing somehow for my basic necessities. The Pastor of the Baptist church paid my rents, some people in church gave me material and monetary help.

One morning, I got up, dressed up, took my school bag, and went downstairs on my way to school. I opened the door of the hostel, and it was blocked from outside. I did not find it funny. I pulled back the curtains and looked out. It was all white outside; I knew something extraordinary had happened! First I checked if it was not 'The Rapture' (spoken about in the Bible). No it was definitely not, as I could hear running water and normal activity in neighbouring rooms. So what had happened? I forced the door open and saw something that looked crispy and white. I scooped it up with my fingers, and it was cold. I dashed upstairs to my roommate. 'Maco, Maco! What is this?' I shouted. He grinned knowingly and said it was snow. It had snowed heavily during the night. I went back downstairs, put down my school bag and walked out a distance into the snow, and saw my footprints, like on the beach. I asked Maco to take photos of me. I carried the snow, threw it in the air, made snowballs and shot them against the dried trees. I played like a child! 'At last I had touched heaven's dust!' I had met snow! I had to share this experience with someone. Of course, my wife came to mind first. I picked up my pen and wrote to her, not forgetting to include the photos.

As soon as I returned to ground state, I realised two problems. Firstly, the snow was very cold and could become dangerously slippery. Of course, the roads were being cleared up, but people needed winter tyres, and those who rode bicycles found it very tricky! But, I also realized tears kept running down my eyes. I had never seen such immaculate white, and the sunrays reflecting from the snow were obviously causing havoc with my eyes. Whenever it snowed, I had a lot of problems with my eyes. Good enough, my health insurance covered me to obtain glasses, which I wear to this very day. In addition, I did really need glasses having to work on computers all day.

Soon it was Christmas. The Finnish have a culture that during Christmas all families come together to celebrate as one family. So I found myself very lonely on that day, with my family so far away. Just like in Cameroon, the Baptist Church had a Christmas day service. I am Presbyterian, but as most Africans abroad would testify, denomination is not a big issue when you are there. More important is that services are held in a language you can follow. After Church, I went back to my room. It was so quiet you could hear a pin drop on a carpet two rooms away. Nearly all, if not all students, had gone somewhere. Good enough I had received a Xmas card from my wife, which I read over and over. I hummed some Cameroonian songs and ate Spaghetti in the kitchen while playing Cameroonian music. Later I told myself it was a good time to catch up on the other students e.g. to learn more how to type, to learn more about computers before school began again. I stayed alone in my room for over a week, accompanied by the dead silence in the hostel.

There are some interesting traditional habits of the Finnish. They have a traditional meal every Thursday composed of pancakes and some type of bean soup. One elderly woman in Church prepared it every Thursday for me. I really enjoyed it. The traditional Finn is also very cold, maybe induced by their weather. There is a saying that goes, 'as cold as a Finn'. However, through the church family, I found warmth and nicer people like this woman. Well, actually the cold ones generally open up once they get to know you better.

I had one bad experience to remember at Lahti, which I never expected. Lahti is a vigorous cultural, sports and business centre, amidst the Salpausselkä ridge landscape of great natural beauty. We were invited for a service there, and they built a tent for us. Here, there were mosquito clouds, and it was not funny when they attacked you. The only good thing was that they only feasted on you, but carried no malaria. The most surprising thing was that the Finns did not care. I complained agitatedly, and they laughed at me. They recounted a story about a yearly Mosquito competition where mostly fat people contested. They would go out, lie on their backs and expose their tummies to the mosquito clouds. They termed it 'restaurant period'. The contestants then try to catch the mosquitoes; the winner is the person who caught the most. A mosquito-killing competition!

The other Championship in Finland, Sonkajärvi, is the wife-carrying competition. The competition reminds me of the "ayo", wrestling competitions, in Nigeria, typical of Nigerian village life. This wrestling duel is often associated with marriage when young suitors would be required to prove their physical prowess, to justify their choice of spouse from a particular group. It also used to be a way of identifying young men with strength that could be reckoned with when there was the need for defence from outside attack.

Back to school, the course was quite intensive. One thing that I had to get used to in Finland was the fact that students did not respect their elders. I was really shocked by this. I remember we discussed this problem, compared to African universities, during a project management course I took. Students had no respect for their professors. They could put their legs up on the table during lectures. I told myself if I were the lecturer, the student would either leave or I would.

Classes ran from 8:00 to 18:00 with a one-hour lunch break and a couple of 15-minute breaks. The timetable was flexible though. Since I could not work on the side, I concentrated fully on my studies, taking as many courses as possible. I had exams at the end of each semester. At the end of the first semester, I discovered that, even though I had been late, I could catch up. Part of the syllabus was familiar, so I doubled courses, and took some second year courses. By the end of the second semester I had finished year three courses and mastered the computer.

Well, I really thank God for the blessings, and for how far He has brought me. One thing I really appreciate God for is the ability He has given me to learn fast. I am at times amazed at what I can learn to do within a short while. As I continue to miss my wife and boys, I am determined to leave an African footprint in the snow of Europe.

[FK: Today Mr. Ambe Lucas is a computer guru. He presently holds a M.Sc. in Computer Science. This helped Florence and the kids to reunite with him. He has left an indelible footprint in the European snow.]

Chapter 27

Germany versus Macedonia

'In the morning be first up, and in the evening last to go to bed, for they that sleep catch no fish' – Macedonian proverb

[FK: How does a European student's experience in another European country compare with that of an African in Europe?]

On the day of my departure for Germany, my mother's last gift was to prepare some ready-made food items for me to take with me. She probably sensed it would be tough for me with respect to food in Germany. I would have to cook for myself or go after fast food. Also as a Muslim, I would have to monitor my new environment first before biting into anything.

My fiancée Heriet and her parents came with my parents to the Airport in Skopje. Heriet did not cry at the airport. She trusted me and believed I would come back to marry her and take her with me to Germany. She was probably shy to cry before my parents and hers. My parents looked quite sad, but I was not in a crying mood. Probably I was apprehensive of what awaited me in Germany. I knew virtually no German, and I had just about a thousand euros to take care of me till I could find my own feet. This was clearly going to be very insufficient. I had to find work as soon as I was in Germany.

The Macedonian airlines spring flight from Skopje to Hamburg took off on schedule. It was not my first time to fly, and during the over 2 hours flight I was pre-occupied with how it would be in Germany. I was hoping I would marry Heriet later that year. Everything depended on how fast and successful things worked out for me in Germany.

In Hamburg, I had family friends and an uncle. I spent two days in Hamburg and then caught the train to Leipzig on March 23rd. Then I was on my own. It was my first time to board a train, but my uncle explained everything to me. What bothered me during the trip was the fact that I did not know where I would spend the night. I was also banking on the hope that in East Germany I would find people who could speak and understand English.

It was rainy and windy in Leipzig as I plotted my way to the Studentenwerk. There I met Ms Klimmek. Her English was not very good, and so she sent me to Ms Zaumseil, whose English was much better. She would become my angel in the next days. I showed my admission letter and was matriculated accordingly. They called someone in charge of housing and arranged something immediately for me in Tarostrasse. At least now I had somewhere to stay.

My room was a double bed student room, which meant there were two beds and a set each of furniture. My roommate was a German sports science student. He could speak English but was often not at home. After two weeks, he left and another student could replace him. Our next-door neighbour was also German, reading medicine.

From my first day in Leipzig, my torture began. I could only express myself in English, and contrary to my hopes, very few people understood English. I was lost. It was my first time in a foreign country with different people and different mentality. Even at the foreign office, where I had to extend my visa and obtain a work permit, the officer could not understand English! Even at the foreign office! I had to call Ms Zaumseil from the foreign office to explain things to her, so that she in turn explained to the immigration officer. She served as phone translator everywhere I went. I am very grateful to her to this day. It was a nightmare for me.

I began eating at the student refectory immediately. But I had to make sure what I ate had no pork, so I always asked someone who could understand me. One day I did not find someone. On the menu I found something, which I suspected to have no pork, a type of soup with German sausage. I did not suspect that the sausage had some pork, so I put a piece in my mouth and bit in. The alarms went off, as I smelled pig! Immediately, I spat it out and went home to prepare macaroni. So it became my routine: Mornings, bread and butter; evenings, macaroni with sauce, without meat. Cow meat was expensive, and I had just about 490 euros remaining in my pocket from which even my next month's rents would come from and then... what?

From the first day I began struggling to get a job, just any job that could give me some income. I went to the students' job office and they refused to give me a job because my German was almost inexistent! That was a huge set back for me! I called angel Zaumseil, who translated the reasons why they could not give me the job. I was devastated. Here I was, with my to-be bride waiting for me back home, when I could not even be sure of my next month's rents and insurance. My thoughts were always home. I was stressed. I needed to work out something, and fast.

I had come to study, so I did have to think about that. But how could I concentrate on studies? Good enough, I was familiar with part of the syllabus of the main lectures, having taken similar courses back home. This also meant I could regulate my time to have free days during which I would find ways to remedy my financial situation. I would wonder around the public places, including the train station, hoping I could meet someone who could first understand me, and then help me get whatever job.

One day, at the train station, I ran into someone from Kosovo. I explained my situation to him and he said he knew an Italian who could help. This Italian could not speak German very well. Actually, he had other workers from Albania who could not understand Italian. Then I got really excited. I told him I could understand and speak Italian. So maybe, I could serve simultaneously to translate instructions. However, he warned me that this Italian contractor paid very low, and the work would be hard. These warnings fell on deaf ears. I was off to see him. True enough, the Italian paid really low, and had the foulest mouth I have ever met. I did not know such foul language could actually be used so systematically and frequently all day long. Well, I tried to let the vulgar language bounce off me. The important thing was that I had found a job. I worked really hard from the beginning to impress him and became a regular worker on my free days. This improved my financial situation a bit. I am still very grateful to this Italian for accepting me.

Once I had relief from concerns for my basic needs, I started worrying about Heriet. I had to apply for admission for her to come and study in Leipzig also. She had actually applied to universities in Macedonia for the past three years but was not admitted. At the time, less than 1% of students admitted were from the Albanian minority.

Luckily, she was admitted in Leipzig. She would have to study in German, which meant she had to attend a preparatory course (Studien Kolleg) in the Herder Institute. However, getting the admission was one thing, and getting the visa was another. To me her coming was a do or die. It meant if she could not come, I would go back to Macedonia. I could not bear staying in Germany without her. So when they refused to give her the visa, I was desolated. However, before this, let me share some of my experiences in Germany.

My father had worked in Germany for six years; my Uncle was still presently in Hamburg, and Macedonia's highest exports were to Germany. Hence, I knew a lot about Germany in Macedonia, even before I travelled. However, there were still some things that shocked me a bit. My first impression was that Germans generally come across as cold, especially at first sight. I believe you can only find such cold people in Germany. So I could say the people were really 'German'. But watch out! When you get to know them better, you realize there are very many nice people in Germany. One such person was Prof. W. Grill who initiated the first ever English language Bachelors to PhD International Physics Studies program in which I was. Prof. Grill was particularly very helpful to me psychologically. He is a very positive person who encourages and motivates you even if sometimes he raises your expectations too high. But I needed that, especially at the beginning. Foreign students particularly needed someone like him. Besides, he later on employed me as a student help in the laboratories and even later as research assistant. I also commend him for the way the program and courses where structured. At the beginning, my first concern was how to support myself, not my studies. I was actually interested in Biophysics and was happy Prof. Grill helped to organize that.

One thing that actually grounded the cold impression I had of Germans was when one day, in the tram, an elderly lady, I would consider my grandmother, came on. There were no seats available, so I stood up and respectfully offered her my seat, as I would be expected to do in Macedonia. To my utter surprise and shame, she refused, even though you could see she was struggling to stay on her feet in the moving tram. The worst thing is that at least she could have said 'No, thank you'. No she did not thank me. It made me feel really bad.

I rode my first lift in Germany. It was nice to see how my pulley lessons in Physics could be applied to transfer people from floor to floor. But I had problems with the doors – not the lift doors, but doors to buildings, which often shut automatically, and you had to push or pull to open them. It was polite and nice to hold it open for someone and say 'Bitte'.

I must still say that before coming to Germany, I thought Germans were very hard working people. I came to realize that it was not the case. Most Germans just wait for their 8 working hours to pass. I had also thought that one could easily find jobs and even work during weekends. However, it is even forbidden to work on weekends. Only recently do they even allow normal shops to open till Saturday evenings. I am actually pleased though with the educational system here. One gets quality education virtually for free even if now they plan to institute some sort of fee. It is still chicken feed compared to what they charge you in England and the U.S.

One other thing, that I found interesting, is that there were many Germans working out of their home states. In Macedonia, it was hard to have whole families move from one region to the other. Even marrying someone far from your village was an occasional thing. That is one of the reasons I had to go home in September. My cousin was going to wed, and I was his best man; but even more, I was to repair his public relations image since he was going to marry someone far away from our village. But most of all, I wanted to go home and marry my darling Heriet. I could not wait. I was getting old, and the ages of 25, 26 to 28 come only once in your life! This for me was an ideal period to get married.

Another reason I needed to go home was that my sister was also 'betrothed' and as the senior male in the family, I had to be there. So I travelled home during the summer break, using the money I was able to save while working for the Italian. Because I really needed money, I was home for only two weeks during which three weddings took place: mine, my cousins and last but not least, my sisters. It was tedious and it meant we did not have a real honeymoon.

I had to get back to Germany fast, for school's sake and for money's sake. I worked in Hamburg at a building construction site. The job was easily arranged because my relatives were there. It was there that the problem with my back began. I often have this excruciating pain and despite consistent treatment it is still a problem for me and probably will remain till I die.

One day, I got a letter in my mailbox from the foreign office. I still could not read German well. So, for a whole week I had it with me trying to figure out the contents. Then I realized it was saying they could not issue the visa to my wife with the documents she had submitted. I could not also ask my wife to go to the German Embassy, because we had said she had had about 600 hours of German, when she knew virtually no German. Going there, they could interview her and find out, and that would worsen the situation. So, I called the German attaché at the embassy and explained my predicament to her. I told her I had paid 3100 DM in a language school for my wife and if she could not come, then it meant I would loss all the money. This was true, and worse because I had borrowed the money from my relative in Hamburg. Even the affidavit of support letter made for Heriet had been done by a relation. But the German immigration had rejected these documents. If Heriet was not coming, then all my troubles in Germany would have been in vain. The attaché found the attestation of the 3100 DM payment in Heriet's file and it was what rescued the process.

My highest point in my life in Germany came the day she got that visa! Heavens! I was so excited and happy and could not wait for Heriet to come. It meant I could also continue with my studies in Germany. I worked really hard those days, despite my back, to save as much money in preparation for her coming.

Meanwhile Heriet started preparing to travel. She was going to be the first from her family to travel abroad and away from her parents. She was her parent's favourite child, and it was going to be hard to leave them. Her parents tried to be strong and encouraged her to even go and stay with her in-laws (my parents). When she went there, my parents asked her to return to her parents so she could enjoy her last days better with them! So they tossed her to and fro. Finally the day of her flight arrived. Both sets of parents were also at the airport and Heriet's mother cried, seeing her daughter leave. Heriet said she did not cry because she knew I was waiting at the other end! I specially rented a car to pick up my bride and drive her to Leipzig were we would have our first real honeymoon. I had moved out of my Tarostrasse student housing and found a fairly cheap apartment for my wife and I. It had no furniture, and I did not yet have enough money. So the first day we arrived in Leipzig, we slept on the floor on a mattress. Gradually I earned enough money to buy second-hand stuff for the apartment.

Heriet was visibly really happy to see me again. I imagine how difficult it had been for her, because it had been very difficult for me. I am happy she had trusted me. Heriet spent the first months in the Herder institute studying German and preparing herself for the main university major course. There she met a lot of foreigners. At the beginning it was not funny at all! Oh, I mean it was funny! There were foreign students from Japan, Madagascar, Russia, Mongolia etc. At first they could not understand each other as they had no common language. They had to talk with signs. But with time their German got better and she made a lot of friends.

Heriet's coming transformed my lonely days to glorious ones. I am very happy to have my wife. I looked forward to going home after Baustelle (Building construction site work). Then, I had warm good food waiting and someone to help me survive the autumn and impending winter. We still needed to save money and had to buy cheap things. I had to pay back the debts but the motivation was there. We encouraged one another.

I have gotten to know Germany better, and my German has improved considerably. I am even doing a PhD in a research group where we speak German almost all the time. I have gotten to know many more nice people, dispelling my first impressions.

We both plan to go home after our studies. I already have a position in the University of Tetovo. In November of 2001, the Macedonian Parliament approved a series of new constitutional amendments strengthening minority rights. Now we the Albanian minority have more opportunities. Heriet will also have a Master's degree and will easily get employment and we can together help to give something to our people and contribute to the further development of our country.

Now we are expecting our first baby after over three years of marriage. My parents and parents in-law are so excited they will have a grand child from us. They have been nudging impatiently for sometime now and wondering what was wrong in our household. But we needed to be where we could be able to take care of the baby when the time comes. Soon, very soon we will have a baby! We too are so excited!

[FK: 'Thank you very much Bashkim and Heriet. I am sure many Africans could not possibly imagine the cultural similarities we share with those of Bashkim and Heriet.

Bashkim and Heriet Ziberi now have 2 beautiful daughters. Bashkim completed his PhD in 2006.]

Chapter 28

Nobody is healthy in London

"Nobody is healthy in London, nobody can be." – Jane Austen

[*FK: So you have gotten your UK visa! Just think, soon you will be flying over, trudging through the airport with big heavy bags full of everything you just couldn't leave behind, then having found the bus stop you'll be hopping onto the bus or 'coach' and voilà! You will have arrived at your new home, and new life. Not to mention new city, new culture, new ways of doing things, new friends, new laws…Whew! It's a lot to take in for anyone. You need help!*]

My name is Ndenko Asong. I am an accountancy student in London. I hold GCE A-levels from P.S.S Mankon, and a B.Sc. in Biochemistry from University of Buea, Cameroon. So how did I get here?

I first applied for a visa for the UK when my initial study plans failed, when I 'allegedly' flunked the entrance examinations into medical school (CUSS), after my A-Levels. I may indeed have failed, or not passed well enough, but one never really knows if all those who don't make it, don't deserve to be there. Some qualify, but have neither connections nor money to unlock unseen doors. My dad thought, at least, attempting to travel abroad for studies would cheer me up.

Unfortunately, the British rejected my first student visa application. My dad said we were not going to give up without a fight. We used our right to appeal the rejection. Some succeed to travel abroad with forged certificates; here I was having my genuine documents questioned. A court in London took up the case. My sisters were charged with representing me, and dealing with the proceeding fees.

Well, in a way, it did take my mind off the disappointment of the medical school exams. Having learnt from the mistakes of many others before me, who had put their lives on hold in pursuit of a visa to travel abroad for months, even years, I did not stay at home waiting for things to pull through. I rather continued with my studies at the University of Buea, just in case things didn't work out the way I hoped.

It was while reading at the British council Library in Bamenda to re-sit my final exams towards a Bachelors degree in biochemistry, three years after my A-Levels, that I got this message: "Mr Asong, you are required to contact the British High Commission in Yaoundé for an urgent matter." That was my dad joking about serious stuff! I went out, with butterflies in my stomach, not knowing what was coming. I tried to picture life both ways i.e. if I was granted a visa, and if I wasn't. I was not successful in the latter. I could only picture things one way, being if I got the visa. The corrupted ideas of grandeur portrayed by channels of communication such as the TV, magazines, films, and books would not permit my mind to think that I was not going to be part of that world. With God always at work for our good, I got the visa. I cannot explain what I felt. To the outside world, I appeared normal and fine. But deep inside, I felt like nothing anyone could be able to explain. I told my dad the news very simply, as if I was saying, 'Tomorrow is Tuesday'. My dad could not believe the reaction he saw, or rather the apparent lack of one.

Before I left, I got some pep talk from my family. My Mum knows that if I do not eat well, I never stay healthy. So she kept on repeating, "Stay away from junk food and make sure you eat healthy." A few days before I left, I even went to the doctor and explained to him: "I am going to Europe, and I have been a constant victim of malaria, I don't know if I will be okay in Europe blah blah blah, I need your advice." He gave me full malaria treatment (Asurmax) and a sachet of Doxcycline to take for a while when I got to Europe to clear any other pathogens that I might have brought from home. I had even heard you would be placed in the intensive care unit in Europe if you had malaria. So I felt a lot safer and comfortable taking my own medicine along.

Dad did not want his son to go wayward, so he went on and on about me not ever forgetting school: "Don't let work and money go to your head so much that you forget why you are there" was basically what he said. "I promise dad." was my reverent and honest answer. Till this day, I am keeping that promise and I have no plans of breaking it. My sisters! Yeah, my sisters! They told me lots of things, gave me lots of tips and encouragement. They advised me not to compete with others that were there already, to be very cautious when making friends, to be patient with life, to study, not to disappoint them, to be careful, responsible, to be...

Immigration can be the first hurdle as you step off the plane. It can range from relatively painless to the sort of time-consuming, frustrating experience that will leave you wanting to rip your hair out. Either way, I had learnt that it is important to remain courteous and reasonable throughout the proceedings. Having all proper documentation with you beforehand (passport, visa, etc.) should help expedite the process. Landing at London City Airport was the easiest way through, in comparison to London Heathrow. The congestion was minimal, and I was out of the airport in no time, with no major event.

From Dust to Snow: The African Dream?

Jet lag is one of those unpleasant consequences of travelling across a number of time zones. Typical symptoms include feeling tired, waking up and wanting to sleep at the 'wrong' times of day, and the irritation and feelings of unease that would naturally accompany such symptoms. Probably, some of the best advice is to stay hydrated by drinking plenty of water and trying to get into the pattern of the new time zone as soon as possible. Another tip that sometimes helps people if they are not shifting too many time zones is to try to move their schedule somewhat closer to that of the new country before getting on the plane. I did not suffer too much from the 6-hour jetlag.

My first few weeks in England were what you can call weeks of grace. My sisters just let me see the bright side of things. I mean, they really let me enjoy myself. One of my sisters is a salesperson in Birmingham, the other teaches French at a London college. I was lucky, because not many people have that kind of opportunity. Coming in three months before school starts is so wonderful.

What did I do in three months? Well, it was a time of total mayhem, chaos, call it what you may. There were some major catastrophes. I had problems in the house, getting myself around London, and finding work. Things were very different from what I had ever known. I had done a fair amount of research on where I was going, but I think I missed out on some minor details: like where to turn on the heater when you are left alone in the house, how to do laundry without boiling my sister's clothes until they lose shape in the washing machine. I thought all you needed to do was chuck the clothes in and then push the 'on' button, but then there was more to it than that.

Also I had never encountered a European-style broom before – a vacuum cleaner. This is culture shock in the extreme! Then, there was the gas cooker. I was used to gas cookers, but with pipes connected to bottles not meters. You had to charge a card to put on credit or something. All this fascinated me.

I enjoyed riding the black cab for the first time, though it is very expensive. It was less exciting riding the double cab (cabin) buses characteristic of London. Surprisingly the buses in London are often late. This reminds me of a major problem I had getting around in London. For example, walking can be a huge problem. You laugh, but how many of you despite being told since nursery school to look both ways before crossing a street, actually look one way, step into the street, and then look the other way. This is fine if you can trust that the traffic will be travelling on the same side of the road it always has. However, it can make walking very hazardous in a country such as England where you would already be hit by a double-decker bus by the time you look the other way! Talk about the buses. To take them, I had to know where I was going and how to get there. Even with the map, it was not that easy to figure it out. At this time, I missed the luxury of our taxis at home.

Let me tell you some of the dumbest things I did. I went south with the tubes when I actually wanted to go north. That made it all the more confusing to read the maps, because no matter how much I tried at that time, I kept on forgetting that traffic flows opposite to what I had known. Thus, I would always look for a turn on the right when it was supposed to be on the left. That got me lost a thousand times in this city. Furthermore, all the roads looked the same, and I just couldn't figure out which I was looking for. I always had to walk to one end of the road, check the road name and then walk back to where I wanted to go; that is, if I was in the right place to begin with, which more often than not I wasn't. I always passed my home, and I would only realise that when I saw my landmark, which is a park. I went through a lot of trouble trying to figure out things for myself. I could never ask. I don't know why. Maybe I was afraid, you know, the strange-land syndrome. But then, once I became used to things, I started asking. Then I realised how much time I would have saved if I had done it earlier. People are there to help you, so there is no reason why you should see them as the enemy: the police, traffic warden, the man at the store, just anybody. It saves a tremendous amount of effort and time and sometimes money (that is, when you pay for the wrong bus or train).

Arriving 3 months before school had the setback that I did not have orientation for 3 months. Universities offer that; it is especially useful to foreign students, and is something not to miss. Besides walking and buses, orientation typically covers a variety of issues including an introduction to the program, health and safety information, information on registering with the local embassy, information on housing, personal conduct, travelling, and language training where applicable. Basically, many of the things you desperately want to know, you will be handed if you go to orientation. And probably most of it will be handed to you physically in some written form that you should keep for later reference, since there is little chance you will absorb everything on your first attempt.

After I could find my bearings in London, the next headache I had was finding something to do. It is quite boring to be left alone in the house. I thought the issue was very simple, but on the contrary, it is quite complicated. It can really get you frustrated. I thought the day I walked out to the high street, I would just have a job. I was wrong, very wrong. I had a kind of a chicken and egg situation. Everyone wanted me to have had experience in what I had to do, but no one wanted to give me a try so I could get experience. I couldn't understand what they were talking about. I thought I had so many people around me, but then I realised I was alone on this turf. I was walking the streets alone; I was being rejected alone. That wasn't fun. There were so many things I would have loved to have someone give me a hand with, and I just did not understand why there was no one available to do so. I told my sister what was happening, but all she said was, "You will just have to keep on trying. That is the way life is in England." But then again, she said something that was very interesting. She said, "You should be thankful that you believe in God because at this stage those who do not hold the faith come crashing down."

I did not exactly understand what she was saying, but as the days went by, I came to understand what that meant. I have always thanked my parents for bringing us up in a Christian home; it is really the way to go. Job searching is a job of its own; only you do not make money, you spend it. It is just like going shopping with mums. You go out thinking it won't take long since you know what you are going out for, but you end up spending the whole day and emptying your pockets, returning exhausted. I had always known there is something called the CV, but I had never really known the significance. At this time, I needed much more than just a CV. There is something called the winning CV. I really don't know what it contains, but someday I think mine will be one. If I had a second chance, I would do as much work in Cameroon as possible, before leaving. That gives you what are called references. Even community work will do. These are things we overlook, but which seem to be very important in Europe.

Things were becoming tough; I was beginning to get really frustrated. No one even called me in for an interview. That was not a good sign. It looked like I was just wasting my time. But then, I realised something. I was spending time with the wrong crowd. I was trying to take the second step before the first. What I was doing was what I was told to do by people who had passed my stage many years back, and somehow did not realise that things had changed. It was like trying to use diesel in a petrol car. It couldn't work. I needed to spend more time with people around my age group and limitations, and then I found out just how things can work out.

There was progress. I started getting invited for interviews. For my first interview, I looked like a Lord in my best suit. I expected questions about the royal line, historical dates and so forth. I was shocked at the silly questions that came: 'Where are you from?', 'Why do you want this job?', and so on. After my two months of grace and one month of intense job searching, I got my first job. It was a nine-hour a week job, as a porter in a nursery. I then added a catering job through an agency and steadily climbed to eighteen, then thirty-five hours of work per week during the semester break.

Due to the intensive nature of British courses, there is often little time for work while studying. However, students can obtain part-time employment. A student can work for maximum 20 hours a week. Students are entitled to work full time during the holidays.

When schools resumed, I needed money to be able to take care of my needs, so I kept the thirty-five hour workweek in addition to my studies. My days of looking for things to fill the days were over. Now, I maximise whatever free time I get. This has been a long way, and I really appreciate those who helped me get there. However, though I got a lot of tips by hanging out with my mates, there were a lot of temptations. They always asked me to tell outrageous lies, forge documents, and things like that. I said no to all that, and till today, I really think that was a miracle. I was under a lot of pressure to start working. Thank God, I was not in danger of starving or sleeping on the streets since I live with my sister; but I have to work towards being independent.

One thing I like about Britain is their subsidized health service, which provides free health care and treatment for people who are resident in Britain. If a doctor prescribes any medicines, these are subsidized but there will be a charge made for each. Dental treatment is also subsidized, but everyone has to pay something towards the cost of his or her treatment. Additionally, African immigration has overtaken gay sex as the biggest cause of HIV in Britain. If the millions of HIV-positive Africans can get into Britain, they can obtain "free" treatment for the rest of their lives by appealing under the Human Rights Act. It is said that Third World immigration is doubling the rates of HIV in Britain, tripling the rates of tuberculosis and increasing by twenty-fold the rates of hepatitis. Furthermore, those who get asylum in Britain, which is the most used method, get a pile of benefits which include: housing, full health care (including free plastic surgery) as well as free immigration lawyers who will string your claim out for years. Even when such cases are rejected out of hand, as happens 90 percent of the time, asylum seekers are allowed to stay anyway. But I know life is very very difficult for them.

The British are generally kind to foreigners who behave politely and respect the local culture. However, like in other countries, there are some people who do not like foreigners. Sometimes you may hear people calling you a rude name. These are some of the slang expressions which are sometimes used for foreigners (do not use these, as they usually sound offensive): Japanese: Nip, Jap; Chinese: Chink; Spanish/Italian: Dago; German: Kraut, Hun; French: Frog; Pakistani: Paki; Russian: Rusky; and black African: Nigger. If people call you names, it is usually safer either to ignore them or to report them to the police.

From Dust to Snow: The African Dream?

Being an ethnically diverse and multi-faith country and a confluence of many cultures and communities, international students are able to adapt and assimilate admirably into the larger British culture. African students without a scholarship, though, find it very difficult to pay the tuition fees, and must toil really hard to meet up.

Here are some tips to help you adapt easily if you find yourself in England:

The British queue, whether it is for a bus, at a shop or at the ice cream van. Join the 'end' of the queue and wait your turn.

When you first meet people, especially in a formal situation, you will normally shake hands. Brits are quite personal and generally do not talk about their age, earnings, politics or religion.

When coughing or yawning, it is polite to cover your mouth with your hand, especially, if you are not sure about your breath. And do always carry Tic Tac Mints with you. Since you do not converse as much as at home, you often would develop a foul breath quickly. Also back in Africa, we often do not consider deodorants important, but out in the West, the importance cannot be over-emphasized. A friend shared how she got really embarrassed when she developed foul odour. In Cameroon, she was used to mopping the floor with a wet rag and a bucket of water, using bare-hands, small scale. So on this day, while doing a cleaning job, she found it more complicated using a rag at the end of a 'stick', and went ahead to mop with her hands. Since she had to mop

. the floor for a long time, she perspired profusely. At some point, a colleague complained bitterly that she was stinking. She said she felt really ashamed. So do take care of your scents when in the West. It is a serious matter. Oh, and when sneezing it is polite to have a tissue available. If someone else sneezes, it is a custom to say 'Bless you'.

Brits are very punctual. If a class or meeting starts at 9 am you are expected to be there at 9 am. It is more relaxed with social invitations from friends.

It may seem over the top in your language, but listen to the amount of time a Brit says 'please', 'thank you', 'sorry', or 'excuse me' and try to follow suit.

If you hold a current driving licence from your own country or an international driving licence, then you are able to drive in the UK for 12 months from the date of entry stamped on your passport qualification. If you are intending to stay for more than one year, you should apply for a British Driving Licence.

It is not normal to tip every time as, generally, restaurants add 10% to the bill for service or it is highlighted on the menu - Look out for this. If you cannot see that they have added for service it is expected, where you feel you have received a good service, to give 10% of the price as a tip. Bar staff are not normally tipped, however taxi drivers are, especially if they help you with your luggage. Around 10% is fine or a little less if it is only a short journey.

Sexual attitudes are also different from those in Cameroon. The British are more liberal. You will find that British men and women mix easily. British women are independent, and although they mix freely with men, this does not imply a willingness to enter into sexual relationships.

If you are invited to someone's home for a meal, you may wish to take a small gift (flowers, chocolate or a bottle of wine are the norm), or you could invite him or her to your house in return. It's a nice idea to bring some small things from your home country or some photographs to show to friends or guests - British people will be interested in these.

It is important to stress that culture shock is entirely normal, usually unavoidable and not a sign that you have made a mistake or that you won't manage. In fact there are very positive aspects of culture shock. The experience can be a significant learning experience, making you more aware of aspects of your own culture as well as the new culture you have entered. It will give you valuable skills that will serve you in many ways now and in the future and which will be part of the benefit of an international education. Initially, you will do some things that will also shock the British. I remember the incident of a friend's mum who came to Birmingham and balanced a post office package on her head en route to the post office. Suddenly she became the centre of attraction.

It's clear that Africans in the UK are a formidable force. There are many African shops in London! Nigerian churches and mosques flourish and compete for worshippers. As immigrants fill the pews of churches here in the U.K, like the Anglican Church, they are adding another dimension to the complex debate over gay men and lesbians in the church. Most of us Africans hail from more conservative cultures, where homosexuality is rarely discussed or even acknowledged. Because of that, one finds many Nigerians and other Africans forming their own nondenominational or evangelical churches. Africans and Whites, who stay together, despite the clashes, decide that other aspects of their faith should be the church's main focus. Each group, on its own, has refrained from taking actions that might inflame the other side.

Perhaps that is the best way we should live as foreigners in the west: Try to maintain our own values, while not taking offence or inflaming the society that has welcomed us into their midst. Unfortunately, back home we are already copying a lot of these western 'values'.

There is a Cameroonian saying that "If the person who left to draw water hasn't returned, it means that the water bottles aren't filled up yet" The African immigrants I've come across in the UK are hard working, idealistic, and bright – except for some Nigerians and Cameroonians. Most Africans (like me) want to go home, maybe not today, maybe not tomorrow, but - when their countries are at peace, when they've made a bit of money, when democracy returns - they will return.

[FK: Many students say London exceeded their expectations:
'I expected a dreary city full of proper, aristocratic British people. I expected rain every day, a very rigid and conservative populace, and a very much condescending attitude towards developing nations. When I arrived in London, the weather was gorgeous. Things were in full bloom, the gardens were completely green, the sun was out every day and I didn't experience the infamous London weather until at least a week in, by which time I had already fallen in love with the city. It was a vibrant and brilliant cross between the old and new. The first people I met were extremely friendly and warm, and also quite diverse. If you plan to study in the UK go to a school in London, preferably SOAS because the people (both students and professors) are the coolest. Live in the dorms. Stand by your beliefs, but never close your mind to new ideas. Try to see as much of London as possible. Make the most out of your studies'.]

Chapter 29

Asylum in South Africa

'God is our refuge and strength, a very present help in trouble' –
Bible

[FK: They have become so desperate that they just want to have a change of scene. Go out of their country, away from continual dependence on their parents even in their late twenties. With a Masters degree in chemistry, John Ndi was modest enough to accept any job as an asylum seeker, in another African country – if only he would be permitted.]

In 1990, when I was in the second year in High School, my father decided that I take the Joint Admissions and Matriculation Exams, which was the requisite for admission into Nigerian Universities. Being an only son to my father, it was his wish to see me get to the highest height in academics. That era was also one in which almost every parent wanted to see their children become medical doctors. So around November 1992, my father went to Nigeria himself to seek admission for me at the Ahmadu Bello University, Zaria to study medicine. His mission was unsuccessful as he wasn't able to secure a place for me at the College of Medicine. Admission into medicine then was very competitive, and preference was given to the indigenes. So finally in December 1992, I went to Nigeria again where I was able to secure for myself a place in the Department of Chemistry at Ahmadu Bello University.

The academic climate in Nigeria during that period was nothing to write home about. There were strikes every now and then either by the academic staff, the non-academic staff, or the students themselves; so, every now and then, the Universities were closed down. I can remember in 1995, by a presidential decree, all universities in Nigeria were closed down for 12 months. Finally, I had to get back to Nigeria, and given the instability in the academic and political sectors of Nigeria then, it was not until December 1998 that I had my first degree in Chemistry. All those years, I made a trip once a year to Cameroon, where normally I'd spend about two weeks with my family before returning to Nigeria.

At the end of my B.Sc., I was already used to the system and so decided to go in for a Masters degree. I applied to the University of Ibadan, and was offered a place. In 1999, I then registered for a M.Sc. in

Ibadan, which I finished in January 2001. Not much happened out of the ordinary during the two years I spent in Ibadan. At the end of my M.Sc., though my family had wanted me to continue with a PhD, I felt it was time for me to return home and sell the skills I had so far acquired. So, I returned home and went to Douala where I thought life was easy, and getting a job wouldn't really be much of a problem.

That was the biggest misconception I ever had in life. It was then that I had to come face to face with the realities of Cameroon at that time. Jobs were not obtained by merit. One needed to have a relation, or know someone who was influential enough to recommend one to get a job. I found people who were more qualified than me, roaming the streets everyday in search of jobs. Some of them even did some of the filthiest jobs you could think of. On the other hand, you'd find some who had never even been to school in some of the best positions you could ever imagine. It got to the point, where I told myself, the system in Cameroon wasn't meant for me. I had to find a way out. Fortunately for me, my sister who's in Holland was ready to make any financial sacrifice to get me out of Cameroon. So, somewhere around June 2002, I met someone who promised getting me a visa for the US if I paid him one million francs. He convinced me that he had enabled many people get into the US. The condition was that I give him an advance of 600,000 francs, and then when I get the visa I'll pay up the balance. My sister in Holland then sent me that amount of money, which I paid to this individual. I had thought I would just hand him my passport and wait for him to get me the visa. I didn't know that I would have to go through the normal procedure, which I would normally have gone through if I had applied for a visa myself.

The guy demanded I make a passport to show that I was working for an NGO in Douala, whose main activity was in the area of environmental protection, which I did with his assistance. He then made pay slips for me for a period of about 12 months, made a bank statement showing I had money in the bank to the tune of about 6 million francs (9000 dollars), made some papers to show that I was also partly involved in running a family business, a birth certificate for an inexistent child I had in Cameroon, and several other fraudulent papers. At the helm of it all, he registered me for a conference that was to take place in Georgia that was somewhat related to environmental protection. Well, it looked like a genuine conference. It had a website that could be visited for information, and I was genuinely registered for it, as my name was even on the website amongst the accepted participants for the conference. I had a genuine hotel reservation for the conference period, which was paid for with some fraudulent credit card. After making all these, he

Asylum in South Africa

asked me to meet him in Yaoundé about a week to my appointment for interview at the American Embassy.

Because we had agreed I'd give him the balance of the money immediately after I got the visa, I took the money along with me to Yaoundé. When I got there and he knew that I had come with the money, he told me stories about certain documents he had not yet made, because he had ran out of money, and required me to give him some more money. So eventually, I gave him quite a reasonable amount from the 400,000 francs, which I had to give him at the end. I spent the days prior to the interview with him coaching me and telling me the possible questions that I was going to be asked, and what answers I was expected to give.

When finally I went for the interview, I got quite discouraged by the number of people that were waiting to be interviewed. I was on the queue the whole day, and it only got to my turn late in the evening despite the fact that I got there by 6 a.m. When I got in, the consular officer asked me to present every document I thought was relevant for my application. I gave him the whole file that I had. He studied each document in it. At the end, all he said was, "Mr. Ndi, I can see you're registered for a conference in the U.S., but you don't have enough evidence to show that you're not an intending immigrant to the U.S. I'm therefore sorry to inform you that your application for a visa to the U.S. is turned down. If you have any reason why you think you must go to the U.S., you can file an appeal to this decision."

That was the statement that was to redirect or maybe change my whole life. I felt bitter with myself. I was so bitter. I regretted why I had let someone else compile fraudulent documents for me for the application. I even thought, if I had gone there with my own genuine documents, and had some reason to go to the U.S, I would have had the visa. Obviously, the September 11 attacks also influenced the difficulty to get non-immigrant visas. Worst of it all, I was given a letter, which stated I couldn't reapply for a visa to the U.S before the end of one year. I had lost so much money, I couldn't reapply for a visa to the U.S again until one year after, and I couldn't believe myself staying in Cameroon again for another year. That was 26th August 2002.

With all the frustration and bitterness, I returned to Douala and continued in my misery, counting each day as it went by. A few weeks later, a friend with whom I'd spent my undergraduate days in Nigeria phoned me from South Africa. In the course of our discussion, I told him my ordeal at the American Embassy, and what I was going through in Cameroon. He felt pity for me. He asked if I could raise some money so he could work a way for me to join him in South Africa. Around November, his cousin came to Cameroon from South Africa, and he directed her to contact me for the deal. She came and demanded an advance of 100,000 Frs. to get me a visa for South Africa, after which I'd have to give her 150,000 Frs. She actually even told me she could do it without the advance, but just wanted it for me to show how serious I was about it, because she didn't want a situation where after getting the visa, I might not be able to pay or might change my mind about going to South Africa, and at the end, she would have lost her own money. And so again, I got the money from my sister in Holland, and gave her the advance.

I never had the feeling that I would go to South Africa. One morning in December, when I had even completely forgotten about the fact that I had given her the money, I got a call from her. She told me to meet her at a certain hotel in Douala with the rest of the money and get my visa. I was amazed! I just couldn't believe what she told me. So I went and saw her and saw my visa myself. I wasn't able to give her the money immediately, but a few days later, I got the money and had to go to Bamenda to give her. I also took the advantage to meet my family, and inform them that I was leaving for South Africa for an adventure.

I returned to Douala, bought my ticket, and that was how on 7th of December 2002, at about 5:30 am, I found myself at the JHB international airport in South Africa. My friend was at the airport with some other friends to pick me up. That same day, they drove me around Johannesburg and Pretoria for me to have a feel of South Africa. It was so fascinating and relieving to be out of Cameroon. Later that evening, we drove to Bronkhorstpruit where they live.

My first days in South Africa were okay. At least, I was just new and had to be welcomed nicely. But with time, I had to face some realities. The first of them was how to legalise my residency status in South Africa, because my visa only allowed me three weeks in South Africa. The next was getting something to do, which normally I couldn't without first getting a valid residency status. I got pieces of advice from a lot of friends I had met, whom I knew before.

Finally, I decided to apply for asylum. That had its problems. With that status, I wasn't permitted to work, and so the whole idea was useless. I was already beginning to have the kind of situation I had been facing in Cameroon. I even got to realise that life was not as easy outside Cameroon as I thought. There were people who had been out in South Africa for so long, and were still suffering even worse than what I had been going through in Cameroon. A lot of friends told me about what they went through the first time they had come to South Africa. I knew then that I had been fortunate to have come, and even gotten a place to stay. Most others came and stayed on the streets, before eventually getting a place to stay. Some had to do the meanest jobs, just to be able to feed themselves. Some had to do night security jobs out in the cold during winter, the first time ever in their lives that they experienced winter. The stories were so varied and shocking. Being abroad is not what most people back at home think it is, also not the impressions the people abroad give to those back at home. In fact, despite the difficulties those back at home face, they're sure of their meals everyday.

After applying for asylum in South Africa, I was required to renew my application every month. This is a service that is supposed to be done for free, by the Home Affairs Department in charge of refugee affairs. However, when one gets there, one is always required to tip them a reasonable amount of money before they get it renewed. Unlike in other countries like Germany, where asylum seekers even got the 50 euros or so basic living allowance from the government, the South African government doesn't seem to care about them. The worst part of my asylum-seeker permit was that it prohibited me from studying and working. I got fed-up with the conditions, and began to look for alternatives.

The alternative, which was going to be the best for me, was to marry a South African citizen. That usually costs quite some money, especially, when it has to be done as a contract marriage. So I got advice from friends, and finally I got a lady who accepted to marry me. To get a less expensive choice, I got a lady from the rural areas. In short, just looking at her physical appearance, you'd know categorically that it's not a feasible marriage with me. And so, we made the marriage arrangements. On a fateful day, we went to one of the Home Affairs offices in the rural areas, and did a very low profile marriage, like the Hollywood stars often do. Only four other witnesses, who were all my friends, accompanied us. The marriage was done without the consent of Xola's family.

Within the course of making all these marriage plans, I had met a friend who was in the University in Pretoria, and when he understood that I had a Masters degree, he advised me to apply to a University there. I made him understand that my residency status didn't allow me to study, and he encouraged me to give it a try. After a lot of encouragement from him, late in January 2003, when the academic year had just begun, I went to the Chemistry Department of the University of Pretoria, just for enquiries.

When I got there, I was quite amazed at the reception I had. I was treated with a lot of respect, unlike the kind of treatment I would have gotten in a similar situation in Cameroon. I was directed to one of the professors in the area of my research interests. I made him understand that my asylum-seeker status did not allow me to study, but that I was desperately interested in studying. He accepted to take me under his supervision, reassuring me that we were going to sort out the problem with my status with time. Of course, I made it clear to him that I did not have any means of sponsoring myself. There and then, he proposed to give me some money from his research grant, which was going to be enough for my fees and accommodation, and also to get me some part-time job with the department that was going to give me some living allowance. That was the best day of my life in South Africa. Then something happened!

I had been paying Xola, my wife, a regular allowance. One day, she phoned me and told me her parents had found out about our marriage and needed to see me. I made an appointment with them through her. When I got there on the day of the appointment, her relations from other towns had come for the meeting. I was surprised at what I met there. I was told that, by their culture, I could only discuss with the parents through some intermediary and couldn't see them. They made me understand that the parents were very cross about me getting married to their daughter without their consent. They needed to know whether I did that just for the sake of getting a residency status in the country, or it was a genuine marriage. Of course, it would have been the end of things for me, if I had responded that it was for me to get my papers. And so, I told them that we had actually intended to get married, but that there had been an urgent need for it because I needed to get papers that allowed me to reside legally in South Africa.

Finally, after a long debate, I was levied a fine to pay for getting married to their daughter without their consent, after which they were going to tell me about other obligations I had to fulfil in terms of bride price and so forth. My plan is to drag on with the payment, giving them very little each time until I finally get a full citizenship, which cannot be withdrawn from me, or after I complete my studies. At that point, I can and probably will ask for a divorce.

[FK: John presently has a contract with a South African company financing his studies.

Sometimes and oftentimes, arranged marriages become the only way out for asylum seekers. In Europe and the U.S., there are numerous stories of such arranged marriages, some involving huge financial rewards for the national.]

Chapter 30

At the mercy of a white man

"The most important thing an applicant takes into the asylum process is credibility. When that credibility is damaged, it makes it that much harder." – The New Standard

Entering Europe, I did not know that things would finally turn out to be like this. I did not even know the meaning of asylum, not to talk of how to seek it. I had come on a family visa as wife to my very own brother. I called him 'Husther', from husband and brother. Since we both had the same last name, it had been easy to arrange for a marriage certificate. Unfortunately, my husther's studies were coming to an end in just a little over three months, and according to regulations he had to return to his home country after his studies. This meant I would have to return too. Of course, I wasn't planning to. That was completely out of question. I had not come all this way only to return to the miserable life I had earlier.

I grew up in the Volta Region of Ghana bordering Togo. It is a region of extraordinary scenic beauty, with rolling hills and valleys, rocky outcrops overlooking Lake Volta, and lagoons. The region stretches from the coastal plains on the Atlantic coast right up to the arid lands of the north, and climatic conditions can vary tremendously. From the coastal plain, fringed by sun-dappled beaches and mangrove swamps, through moist deciduous rain forests in the central belt, where Mt. Afadjato at 885 m is the highest point in Ghana, to the arid savannah of northern Ghana, you could experience almost every tropical climate in West Africa including the unemployment climate. As was the case with most graduates, I was unemployed and my dream was to travel abroad! Not abroad to another African country, but to Europe or the U.S. There were lots of things that motivated one to aim for Europe here. The relics of European coastal forts and other structures still remain in Ghana; further north, vestiges of the German colonial era are unmistakable. The regional museum at Ho reminds us of our heritage and History.

When my bachelor brother came home for his last visit before completing his studies in Germany, we 'got married'. We planned I would look for other possibilities once in Europe. The first thing was to get out of Ghana.

From Dust to Snow: The African Dream?

When I arrived, it did not take long to realize things would be very tough! Things were not what I had conjectured they would be, and my brother had not told me. Even if he had warned me, I would not have listened; that's probably why he did not bother. I realized I could not change my visa into another one in Germany. My husther and I became really stressed up! We did not know what to do. He travelled to France, Denmark and Holland to monitor possibilities for me, but wound up spending so much money to no avail. Along the line somebody did suggest prostitution. I was shocked! So when the idea of asylum came up, I readily accepted.

I started to plot out a strategy. The way out of this predicament would be to wipe the slate clean. I would have to delete my past, and start anew. All my certificates, degrees, and names would have to be forgotten as soon as I presented myself to the asylum officer. I would say I was from a different country, false age, and last name. That was hard to imagine. I was a university graduate, and so all the years of my educational life until now would have nothing to show for themselves. I struggled with this a bit. Finally, since I had made up my mind not to return to Ghana, I decided to go all the way and sacrifice everything, if only it would work.

So the next step was to plot out the story I would present. This was a tough nut to crack. I could not imagine ending up in those miserable social conditions, or being deported and then imprisoned. For three whole days, I could not eat. My husther was so stressed he decided to try applying for a visa to England for both of us. At least, his residence permit was still valid for more than 6 months. In fact, in Germany, students do not really get residence permits, but something like 'a residency approval' valid only for study purposes. We thought it would be easier for me to get lost in England, if only I could get there. He travelled to Düsseldorf for the visa, and was granted a visa to England. Unfortunately, mine was rejected for the very reason we feared, that my permit to stay in Germany was less than 6 months.

In any case, I heard asylum seekers were equally facing a very tough time in Britain. According to a BBC report, David Blunkett the British Home secretary at the time had dramatically lined up behind the German definition of a refugee. Germany, along with France and Italy, observed a narrow line, restricting the protection of the 1951 Geneva Convention only to people suffering from state persecution. According to the report, Blunkett said it would help pull the plug on the ruthless organized gangs running illegal migrant smuggling operations.

Truly there was a problem. According to reports, proof had been found that Nigerian and Dutch authorities were involved in the trafficking of women, and the whole affair now put female refugees in an unfavourable light, complicating my case. The past 4 years, about 400 Nigerian girls had disappeared from Dutch asylum-seekers' centres, and most probably ended up in forced prostitution. Women traffickers used voodoo (juju) to hold the girls in their power.

Research of Terre des Hommes, and the Nigerian Democratic Movement in the Netherlands (NDNM) showed how women traffickers get young Nigerian girls in their power. Some of the girls are already shanghaied in Nigeria under the pretence of getting work in Europe in sweatshops, nurseries and restaurants. The girls all come from rural parts of Nigeria, where economic perspectives are bad and information about Europe is scarce. Usually, the trafficker and the girl agree that he will pay in advance an amount, for travelling and mediating expenses. A voodoo priest then seals the agreement. Often, the parents of the girls are present at the ritual, because they are responsible if the girl doesn't pay her debts. For a visa to Europe, the trafficker usually pays about 4.000 to 6.000 euros. The girls are told that they must ask for asylum as soon as they get to the Netherlands. In the asylum-seekers' centre, they then must contact another "work mediator", who picks them up. After that, they are sold for about 28.000 euros to a pimp or a whore madam, or sometimes to some other trafficker. Other girls don't get into contact with women traffickers until they are in the Netherlands. The traffickers usually succeed in winning the girls' confidence, because they speak the same language and come from the same culture. Often these girls start with a cleaning or household job, or they are involved in a 'love affair' with their trafficker. After sometimes they are forced into prostitution.

Also the reports showed the traffickers are often ex-prostitutes themselves. They came to Holland as minor victims or as prostitutes by choice. They paid their debt, and often get a residence permit due to a marriage with a Dutchman. Some of them are operating in the business together with their husbands. Another group consisted of Nigerian drug-dealers and businessmen, who also operate in the trafficking of women. There are many in the Netherlands who get rich in this trade. It is alleged that employees of the Nigerian immigration bureau, and Nigerian officials of the Dutch embassy in Nigeria have granted visas to the traffickers in women; that the Dutch consul in Nigeria had been fired at some point, because he let a similar thing happen earlier in Sri Lanka, when he was in office there.

Another option for me was to get married to a German for papers! I would have to divorce my husther though. But where would I begin? First it would mean I need plenty of money to convince a German to do that, or I would have to convince one to fall in love with me. The prostitution option was made more appealing by someone, who argued it was clean in Germany, and you would get rich fast and then could duck out. Prostitution! My husther said I should rather go home than try it. Finally, after weeks of debate, stress, little food and sleeplessness, I finally decided I would go for asylum. If I were lucky, I would be amongst the few who would be granted asylum. In trying to come up with a convincing story, I read more stuff about female asylum rights.

The definition of a refugee as contained in the 1951 Geneva Convention relating to the Status of Refugees does not specifically recognize that persecution based on gender may constitute grounds for refugee status. However, any of the five grounds included in the definition can and should provide a legal basis for the recognition of women fleeing persecution as refugees. Thus, all claims for refugee status by women should be assessed under each of the definition grounds to see if the harm from which the woman is fleeing amounts to persecution. Each of these grounds, in particular religion, political opinion and social group should be interpreted appropriately so as to encompass gender-related persecution claims.

Two particular forms of gender-related harm frequently arise as an issue in claims by asylum-seeking women. The first is where women have been the targets of sexual violence. Women in such cases have often faced difficulties in showing that they are victims of persecution, rather than targets of random violence, despite the fact that it is widely accepted that rape and sexual violence are commonly used as weapons of war. The difficulties are made worse by the trauma resulting from such experiences, and the cultural factors that may inhibit the woman from speaking freely about her experience. Consequently, States often take great care in dealing with claims involving sexual violence. I liked this form better in making my asylum case, but it would mean I really had to lie.

I found out the following general procedures for asylum-seeking women: Claims by asylum-seeking women were to be assessed on their own merits and independently of male family members. This did not concern me since I was going alone, though legally married. Next, female interviewers along with female interpreters should conduct interviews, since women fleeing persecution may be uncomfortable talking to men about their experiences. If this were not possible at a particular time, the woman should be informed in writing, or through a medium she understands, of her right to postpone the interview to secure a female interviewer and interpreter. Due to the difficulties that asylum seekers may encounter in recalling traumatic experiences and to help build confidence, they were to be given the option of retaining the same interpreter for the duration of the asylum determination procedure. Furthermore, interviews were to be conducted in a non-confrontational, non-adversarial and sensitive manner and in accordance with the ICCL Statement of Best Practice. It was said that procedures for dealing with cases deemed to be manifestly unfounded had the potential to adversely affect asylum-seeking women more than males, because of the difficulties women can experience in disclosing a history of sexual violence. As it is entirely possible that women may not feel able to disclose such events in the initial stages of the asylum procedure, it is essential that extreme caution be exercised in deciding whether or not to deem claims by women as manifestly unfounded. At a minimum, this should be done only where the case clearly meets UNHCR criteria, i.e. where it is clearly fraudulent, or where it is not related to the 1951 Geneva Convention grounds for refugee status.

This last point was appealing to me, and gave me a sense of motivation in coining my story. Deportation of asylum-seeking women was not to take place if a doctor has certified that the woman is unfit to travel. In all cases, women should not be deported where the medical and other services in their countries of origin are clearly inadequate to meet their needs. If a deportation is to take place, it should be carried out, where possible by a female immigration officer, in a humane manner, having regard to any special needs of the woman, and allowing adequate time for arrangements to be made before departure. What I was not sure about was whether Germany followed these procedures.

Finally, after further research and brainstorming, my husther and I had a story. I was going to pay a high prize, beginning with my complete loss of identity. Also, I did not know if I would ever see any of my relatives again. I will never forget the day I finally parted with my brother. At that moment, I really felt he was both my husband and brother. At the train station, we held each other for a long time crying. It was a step into the unknown.

I presented my self to asylum officers, and was sent to Düsseldorf in another state the following day with two other boys. They gave us tickets for the train, and just directed us to the train station. We took off at about 9:00 a.m., and arrived Düsseldorf at about 2:00 p.m. On our way, it seemed we crossed many rivers. I complained to the others that I did not like to see so much water. I am really very much afraid of big bodies of water. I have had a 'water phobia' since I was a kid. I mean, not just water, but any body of water that could drown.

When we arrived the office and presented ourselves, they told us to wait outside beside a bus, and that they were coming to take us to where we would sleep. After 20 minutes, the driver came and drove us to a place, to my greatest dismay, at the seashore. He said that was where we would sleep. Not believing my ears, I asked him again where he meant. He said, 'Inside that ship.' I was stunned for some minutes, and the other boys laughed at me because of what we had been discussing on the way about my fear of water. I took a deep long breath, picked up my bag, and went down to the ship. There was an office there. They registered us, and then took us upstairs to our various rooms. We were six per room. The inside of the ship was not bad, but just the fact that I knew the ship was on the sea kept every sleep impulse from my eyes. I could not sleep. I had the imagination that the ship could sink one night while I was asleep. So I was always out of the ship till late in the night before going in to sleep. But I could not sleep in there. During the day, I would go out to dry land and sleep on the grass somewhere or on a park-bench.

I grew thinner and thinner, an interplay of many factors. I kept wondering what would become of me. Yet when I looked around me, there were many boys and girls of the same status like me. There were mothers and fathers and children also.

I stayed there for about one week and two days, before I had my interview. In the meantime I went over my story denumerable times. I cross-examined myself over and over. Finally the day of the interview arrived.

The interview was conducted in English with a translator as I had read. My translator was a woman. The Interviewer asked me to confirm that I was okay with the translator, and that I could understand her. There was another man with the interviewer. They first explained to me the necessity and objective of the interview. I was asked to confirm that I had provided all personal documents I had. It was explained to me that, during the interview, I had the chance to conceal any information, which could be used to my detriment, and might result in my deportation. My nerves were fluttering; I knew questions would be asked I was unprepared for. Thank God the black pigment I have shields any skin colour change. I told myself I had nothing to loose. The alternate option of prostitution gave me additional wind. Here is how the interview went.

Interviewer: 'Do you speak any language apart from English?'
Answer: 'Besides English I speak Bakwere.'
(As I had searched the Internet, I had found some websites on Cameroon from which I extracted information to build my story. I had decided to build my asylum case on a political-persecution and sexual abuse basis. So I had to come up with a story that could be verified. At that time, the country, which had just had elections in Africa, was Cameroon. I had heard about it on CNN, and researched my story. Apart from the fact that Cameroon had just had elections, it was good to say I was from another country apart from my real country; if they deported me there, the authorities would refuse to admit me. At least, I heard so. Besides, if I was lucky, and my asylum case was passed, I heard they would allow you to visit every other country apart from your own home

country. So since I hoped I would someday visit Ghana again, it was better to lie I was from a different country.)

Interviewer: 'Do you have or have you ever had any other nationality?' *Answer:* 'No.'

Interviewer: 'Do you belong to a particular race or tribe?' *Answer:* 'I belong to the Bakwere group of people in Cameroon.'

Interviewer: 'Can you present to us any personal papers: passport, national ID, or lassez passer?' *Answer:* 'I have no personal papers. I had only a student identity.'

Interviewer: 'Where is this student ID now?' *Answer:* 'The student ID is in the village'.

Interviewer: 'Why did you not bring it with you?' *Answer:* 'It is because I did not travel here from my village. I left in a hurry.'

Interviewer: 'Could you present to me any other documents like Birth certificate, driving license, school certificates etc?' *Answer:* 'No, I have nothing.'

Interviewer: 'Did you have or do you have a visa or residence document for Germany or any other country?' *Answer:* 'No.'

Interviewer: 'Please tell me your last official address in your home country! Did you stay there before your departure? If not, where?' *Answer:* 'I had, till 29th July, been working as a house girl in Yaoundé.'

Interviewer: 'Please tell me the last name, maiden name, birthday, and place of birth of your marriage partner, and date and place of wedding! Can you present proof to that?' *Answer:* 'I am single.'

Interviewer: 'Do you have children? Please give the names fully: last name, first name and place of birth of all children. Could you provide proof for this?' *Answer:* 'I have no children.'

Interviewer: 'Give me the names of your parents and their address!' *Answer:* 'My father died in 1995 due to an illness, and my mum is still living in the village.'

Interviewer: 'Do you have brothers and sisters, grand parents, uncles or aunties who live outside your home country?' *Answer:* 'No.'

Interviewer: 'Are there other relatives living in your home country?' *Answer:* 'A brother of mine is still living in Cameroon.'

Interviewer: 'What type of trade did you learn? With employer did you lastly work? Did you have your own business?' *Answer:* 'I had worked as house-girl.'

Interviewer: 'Since when did you work with this teacher?' *Answer:* 'Since the beginning of 2000.'

Interviewer: 'Until when did you work for this teacher?' *Answer:* 'Till 5th July 2002.'

Interviewer: 'If you were a house-girl for this teacher up to the 5th of July 2002, how then did you stay till the 29th of July 2002?' *Answer:* 'It was so that I went to Douala around the 5th of July 2002.'

(Here was apparently a first inconsistency! My mouth felt dry.)

Interviewer: 'Why then did you say previously that you lived with the teacher up to 29th July, if you left Yaoundé on the 25th?' *Answer:* 'I thought you had asked until when I had lived in Cameroon. I left Cameroon on the 29th of July 2002.'

(The interviewer did not look convinced, but he continued.)

Interviewer: 'Have you ever been to the Federal Republic of Germany before?' *Answer:* 'No.'

Interviewer: 'Have you ever applied for asylum in another country or made such a wish known?' *Answer:* 'No.'

Interviewer: 'Please tell me how and when you came to Germany. Tell me in the process, when and by which means you left your home country, which countries you passed through, and how you got into Europe and Germany.' *Answer:* 'I left Cameroon on the 29th of July 2002 with a ship. The trip lasted 3 weeks. On the 24th of August I arrived Germany through an unknown seaport.'

Interviewer: 'How then did you come here to Düsseldorf?' *Answer:* 'Since I had problems, I had called my father's friend who lived in Douala, and told him my problems. He said he would find a way to help me. He said he knew someone who worked on a ship.'

Interviewer: 'I only really wanted to know how you left the unknown German seaport, and came to Düsseldorf.' *Answer:* 'This man from Douala had taken my photo and said he would send it to someone he knew in Germany. He said this person was supposed to come to the seaport between the 22nd and 25th August to look for me. As I left the ship, someone asked me if I was called so and so. He collected me with a car and took me to Mannheim.'

Interviewer: 'How could you have left the ship despite all the controls there and at the port?' *Answer:* 'A man from the ship took me to a small room with a small bed, and I stayed there the whole time. I was hidden on the ship. After the controls were over, he came and called me and took me off the ship.'

Interviewer: 'And how was it that you passed through the restricted areas of the port without being controlled?' *Answer:* 'I think the man who worked on the ship knew when he should fetch me out of the ship. Then seemingly he waited till the controls were over and he quickly whisked me off the ship to go with him.'

(I was then told that I would have to explain why I think I should be granted asylum due to political reasons. I explained that communal and parliamentary elections were supposed to take place on the 23rd of June

2002 in Cameroon. The elections were however postponed on the very 23rd June at 9 a.m. to June 30th 2002. The day the elections were originally due was a Sunday. Some citizens left very early to go and vote, since they wanted to go to church after. When the election postponement was announced on the radio, the people were upset. The teacher for whom I worked was an active member of a major opposition party.)

Interviewer: 'What really happened to you yourself that was so bad you had to leave your country?' *Answer:* 'As the elections were postponed, the people suspected that the authorities in power wanted to rig the elections. Flyers were produced.'

Interviewer: 'I ask you once again. What happened to you really bad that you yourself had to leave the country?' *Answer:* 'The teacher sent me on the 24th of June with others to distribute the flyers. I shared the flyers with others. We posted the flyers on trees and electric poles, and shared them to people. Then, two men came dressed in civilian clothes and arrested us. We were taken to the police prison.'

Interviewer: 'What then happened there?' *Answer:* 'There, we were beaten and locked up. In the meantime, my boss the teacher was looking for me, and found me there after two days. He requested for my release, but his request was rejected. They said that, if at all, they would only free us after the elections. I was then in prison for another whole week. They beat us everyday.'

Interviewer: 'When were you released?' *Answer:* 'I was not released, but I escaped. A day later, a policeman took me out of the cell to another single cell. There, I was raped over and over by many a police on Tuesday and Wednesday.'

(I began to sob. I thought about my father's death, how I was now disconnected from my family, and all I had gone through, and the tears were flowing profusely. Indeed, I had lost my dad in 1995. I could tell my sobbing had some effect on my interviewers.)

Interviewer: 'Would you prefer to recount the raping incident now to a female person than to me?' *Answer:* 'No, it is not necessary.' (I began to sob even louder.) 'If my dad were alive he could have killed those bastards. Oh daddy, why did you leave me alone in this world!'

(They brought me tissue paper. I was asked to describe my escape – as best as possible)

'On Thursday, a policeman came and called me. He said I should accompany him to the street to buy roasted maize. When we crossed the street, the policeman bought the maize and paid. There were other people there who also wanted to buy the maize. The seller gave me the change. As we were about to cross the street, a car came racing up. The policeman had already crossed the street. If I tried to run across also, the car could have hit me. So, I made a quick decision. The terror of going back to that cell and being raped again – repeatedly, gave me undescribable energy, which propelled me into action. I turned around, and used the split moment to run behind a house by the roadside. I quickly reached another street, and took a taxi with the change I had gotten for the maize to the part of the town where I had been arrested. From there I ran back to the house of the teacher.'

Interviewer: 'When you arrived the house, what did you do?' *Answer:* 'When I came to the house, the teacher was not there. His wife was at home, and she cried and shouted, asking if I had been released. I said, 'No' and that I had absconded. She pulled me into the house, and asked how I had managed to escape. Then she called her husband the teacher. He came and said he would try everything to secure my freedom.'

Interviewer: 'How long did you remain with the teacher then?' *Answer:* 'I reached there around 10:30 p.m., and stayed there till the following day around 10 a.m.'

Interviewer: 'What did you then do the following morning from 10 a.m.?' *Answer:* 'I left the house and travelled to Douala to the friend of my father. The teacher got money from my payments from the bank and gave to me.'

Interviewer: 'How long were you on the way?'
(I flinched. I knew this was a crucial question. They would surely verify on their map the approximate distance.)
Answer: 'About 3 hours with the bus.'

Interviewer: 'What did you then do in Douala?' *Answer:* 'My father's friend picked me from the bus stop and took me to his house.'

Interviewer: 'How long were you at the home of this your father's friend?' *Answer:* 'Around 3 weeks.'

Interviewer: 'I would like to know from you what you did in this house during these 3 weeks. What happened during this period worth mentioning?' *Answer:* 'I did nothing, I did not leave the house.'

Interviewer: 'Did I understand right that you where raped two times by a police man?' *Answer:* 'Yes.'

Interviewer: 'Could you maybe explain how long this lasted?' *Answer:* 'The raping did not last long. It was a few minutes. I was raped by 2 people one after the other.'

Interviewer: 'And the next violation, was it then the following day?' *Answer:* 'Yes, I was violated by the same people. That did not also last for long. Not longer than 10 minutes.'

Interviewer: 'You also said you were beaten up while in prison. Could you give more details?' *Answer:* 'They came as we were together in the cell. They came with rubber clubs and beat us, and marched on us with their heavy boots.'

Interviewer: 'Were you yourself marched upon with the boots?' *Answer:* 'Yes, as we were in the group, we fell down as we were being beaten, and then, they walked on us so we would not stand up again. Since we were in a group, some of us got kicks and others strokes from the clubs. I had no wounds but enormous pain.'

Interviewer: 'How often did the beating take place?' *Answer:* 'It was only during the morning and evenings. They called it morning and evening café everyday we were in jail.'

(I then explained that after I had escaped, my sexual organ began to itch. I had this itching just before I left Cameroon. I also had abdominal pains. On the ship I could not do anything. I was really uncomfortable, but only complained about it on arrival.)

Interviewer: 'To whom did you complain and when was it?' *Answer:* 'It was when I came to this office. I complained on the second floor, at the social office. They sent me to the doctor. He examined me, and prescribed medicine for me.'

(I showed them the medicine, which was then given back to me.)

Interviewer: 'Do you have an explanation, how after such a massive violation by the policeman, he would still ask you to accompany him to buy roasted maize?' *Answer:* 'There, I cannot really explain. I could not refuse to go with him; if I refused, he could have violated me even more or done worse things on me.'

Interviewer: 'You explained that you crossed the street, and the policeman paid for the maize. How come they, instead, returned the change to you?' *Answer:* 'As the policeman paid for the maize and the lady was giving back the change, someone he knew greeted him from behind. He turned to speak to him and since there were other customers, and the lady knew I had come with the policeman, she gave the change to me.'

Interviewer: 'You said that when you finished buying, you could not cross the street after the policeman had already crossed. Is there an explanation why he crossed the street without making sure you were crossing with him?' *Answer:* 'The policeman was already on the street, and if I had followed him the car could have hit me. Things happened so fast.'

Interviewer: 'How was it at the beginning when you just came to the prison? What were the proceedings?' *Answer:* 'We were brought to the office, our particulars were taken and we were photographed.'

Interviewer: 'Have you ever been arrested before, or sentenced to jail, or fined in court?' *Answer:* 'No.'

Interviewer: 'Were you ever before a political activist in your country?' *Answer:* 'No, sometimes when there were campaigns or rallies I went there to listen.'

Interviewer: 'If your asylum application is rejected and you are deported, what do you think would happen then?'
(I felt the sweat running down my armpits.)
Answer: 'I would then be in great danger. I am sure I am being searched for presently, and that the policeman who took me out will do everything to find me and arrest me.'
Interviewer: 'Why then did you finally decide to travel on a ship to an unknown destination instead of going to a neighbouring country?'
Answer: 'I had no person to turn to who could help me, except this my father's friend, and he knew someone who worked on the ship. For me it was just really important to leave the country as soon as possible regardless how.'
Interviewer: 'Have you mentioned all the essential reasons for applying for an asylum, or you still have something to add?' *Answer:* 'I have nothing to add.'
(I then reaffirmed that I had had enough opportunity to state my asylum case to prevent deportation or being sent anywhere else. I was reminded of my duty to inform the office of any changes in address or further information. I also confirmed that I had not had any difficulties to understand during the interview.)

After the interview, I was sent to a transit camp where I had to stay and wait. I was praying everyday in church, because there was a church there for those who are Christians. There we had well prepared food, enough for everybody, and they gave us 9 euros every Tuesday. In this camp, there was a Ghanaian association, which I joined, not realizing this could blow my cover story. The suspense was really much for me. I realized I had had some inconsistencies during my interview.

In the meantime, I could spend time on the Internet exploring new options if I were rejected. There was an Internet Yahoo chat room for asylum seekers. I met a very good Internet friend from Kenya. Her name was Macy, and she shared a true version of my story. She had come to the UK in January 1996, and applied for asylum immediately after arrival. She had fled Kenya because she was politically active in an opposition movement, and was imprisoned, raped several times, tortured mentally and physically; yet, her asylum case was rejected. This story really made me nervous. If a true story was rejected in Britain, what more of mine? And that was the sad thing. It was probably because of people like me, who made it difficult for the true cases to be discerned. She said, in Britain, things got even worse after her claim was rejected. They sent her from one office to another, from the Asylum Team to Social Services to Housing, and all of them said they were not responsible for her. They refused to help even for a few weeks while her situation was being considered by the National Asylum Support Service (NASS). She had been sent away empty-handed, without money for food. She said she was now getting vouchers, which were a nightmare, because she could not pay bills with them, and supermarkets are expensive. She said she was now under a lot of stress and had lost weight, especially, with the threat of homelessness. It was particularly difficult because she was anaemic. The only prescription she could get was for paracetamol, which she couldn't afford to pay for.

I followed Macy's story each time I came online. After a few days, she told me that a colleague of hers had been granted asylum. While in the Democratic Republic of Congo, this colleague had been arrested and detained with her baby son by authorities looking for her husband. Mother and baby were held in a small dark cell for three weeks. Each day, this colleague was systematically gang-raped and sexually assaulted by soldiers, until a family friend helped her escape. Whilst not disputing that this colleague was raped, the British Home Office denied it happened in detention, claiming that the threat of rape is present for women in many parts of Kinshasa, causing women not to leave their homes at night! However, the Adjudicator considering her appeal, found her a credible witness, and she was granted asylum. Some good news at least for Macy's colleague! Would it be good news for me too?

One month after, I received a very large blue envelope from the Bundesamt. I guessed it was my rejection. I rushed to a lawyer, since I could not understand the language. The lawyer was a woman. She read it, and told me it was a positive letter not a rejection, and then explained what the article meant. She asked me to take it to the foreign office, where they would give me a passport. I could not believe my ears. Today I have it, a United Nations passport! I was told that the part of my story they did not believe was how I got into Germany from the seaport.

I have been sent to school, and I now have the right to stay in any town in NordRhein Westfalen. The State will pay for everything until I finish my schooling. I thank all those who gave me ideas to go and start this process. They have also contributed much to my success. It was a bitter experience, but all that has been forgotten since I succeeded, which is not always the case, especially for boys. Being at the mercy of other fellow men in the world can be very hard. I did not decide to be born in an underdeveloped country. I don't believe God planned it for some humans to suffer while others enjoy. I look forward to using my talents to give back what the Germans are investing in me today. At the end, my country is the looser. I pray and hope someday things will change. It's a pity I had to fake a story. I particularly feel bad because there are many others, like Macy, whose cases for asylum are authentic, but have been rejected.

The worst thing is that I have lost all my certificates. I have to begin afresh at 25 years. I have decided to do nursing. First I have to learn German. The state is paying for it, so I may as well take the opportunity. I was lucky to be granted asylum. I have heard things are getting tougher. I hear the European Union plans drastic restraints on rights to asylum.

My name is Ekuwa Addo.

Chapter 31

Deleted 'Scenes' (Experiences)

'I have learned that all over the world, each society is different. Yet, these differences are significant to the advancement of all peoples. Each society has something to give to the next: something to teach, which will spread new light.' – Martin R-Williams, LEC Germany

[FK: Some Experiences and perspectives were 'deleted', but I thought you may still learn something from them, before we conclude. The first one is for fun:]

My name is Eamon. I was born and raised in England. I have also had the privilege to travel to many countries including the U.S. and Germany. Here are some differences I observed, which may help you if you want to travel to England, USA, or Germany.

Some Britons may agree that one remarkable difference between Americans and Germans are that: Germans have a few different standards regarding what constitutes politeness. Americans tend to define politeness in terms of friendliness: smiling, telling white lies to avoid hurting people's feelings, pretending to like people even if they don't. Germans, however, tend to consider respect to be the proper way to show politeness, and respect assumes that the other person wants an honest answer, not some pretty little white lie. Oh, and please use titles in Germany unless distinctly told otherwise. So, unless you really want your ego hurt, don't ask a German, "So, how d'you like my new dress?" You might not like the answer that he gives. Likewise, don't ever say anything to him just to be nice, if you don't really mean it; he is too likely to take you quite literally at your word and then be terribly hurt later when he finds out that you didn't really mean it. Also Americans have an international reputation for being extremely ignorant about the rest of the world - Germans, however, usually are not so ignorant about international politics, news, current events, foreign cultures.

There are many differences between British English and American English, than one actually imagines. Let me share some examples. In America, money is referred to as "bucks" in slang, not "goolies" as in Britain. Prams are called buses in America, and "bumbershoots" are called trains. "Lorries" are called motorcycles and for reasons unknown, the "off-license" is called a "hospital". It's also very important to know that in England a "doctor" only means a PhD holder, not a physician as in America. In the U.S. words such as "colour" have no "U" in them. We do not invent new verbs by adding "-ise", but "-ize". The past tense of "dive" is "dove", not "dived". The past tense of "plead" is "pled" not "pleaded". In Britain, "puff" means homosexual, therefore Puff Daddy translates as "gay father", or possibly as "father of all gays".

We all know in England that gas is the gaseous substance piped into buildings for central heating, cooking and gas fires. Inside houses, there are closets not cupboards. In America, gas is the fuel cars run on. In Britain, "closet" means water closet i.e. the toilet. In America they use somebody's name, John, to mean toilet.

In the U.S., they wear "sweaters" not "jumpers". I thought a "sweater" is a person who perspires a lot. In the U.S. men do not wear a dinner jacket but a tuxedo. "Nike" which rhymes with "bike" in British English, is called "Nigh - key". Americans would be surprised to learn that in Britain "smart" means well dressed, and that if a British says you "look smart today" they are complimenting your choice of clothing, not suggesting you look unusually intelligent.

In the U.S. babies wear diapers not nappies. Baby bottles have nipples not teats. Babies suck pacifiers not dummies, and they go out in strollers, not pushchairs, prams or buggies. An American would be surprised to hear that a stroller is not a baby buggy, but a person who is taking a gentle walk.

Aha! Don't forget that in the U.S. dates are written in the format month-day-year. Americans are surprised to hear that in Britain, if a word starts with an "H", we pronounce the "H" - i.e. "herbs", not "urbs". Americans often joke that if you tell a Brit that you are a Gulf War vet, he will automatically assume you provided medical care to the camels. In America we have "ER" not "A&E" or "Casualty Dept".

In conclusion, I was fortunate to be able to travel to many countries at an early age. As a result, my mind was open to change. Therefore, I feel that such trips to different cultures should be encouraged. It is only through these experiences that the world will be able to appreciate the many advantageous differences that are found in each culture. It is very easy to read a book and learn of cultural differences; yet, a deep and true understanding of a culture only comes from visiting that particular nation. Then, in the future we will begin to see a harmony among cultures, sparked by dialogues among these nations.

****

[FK: Beware!]

Deleted experiences

My name is Lucy. I work with a Geneva-based International Organization for Migration to curb the trafficking of women into Western Europe's brothels. I just want to sound a note of warning. Girls interested in working abroad should be careful because there are organized crime groups that traffic you for sex slavery. In a 2001 migration organization report, 24-year-old Mary (a pseudonym) explains how a friend she'd known for three years offered her a job in Germany. He said he could get her an illegal au pair job with a rich family. Trusting him, she moved to Germany, where her "friend" sold her to a group of Albanians for $1,000. She says she was beaten, raped and later sold a second time and taken to a small Italian town, where she was forced to work as a prostitute for half a year. Mary had never suspected danger because the job tip had come from someone she knew.

A Nigerian girl was just 14 when she was approached at a local market. She was told she would earn big money pleating hair in Italy. She was smuggled across a number of West African countries to the Ivory Coast where she was sold to a Nigerian woman - a "Madame" based in Italy. Like so many other teenage girls, she was forced to become a prostitute.

Generally, a local agent, a sponsor, who pays for their journey abroad, as well as the bribes and false documents necessary to get them there, recruits the teenagers. Voodoo is used to coerce the girls into working for their sponsors. They have to swear not to tell anyone and while they are swearing they are being cut. Some girls have 40 or 50 cuts all over their body. They are forced to drink blood and this all happens in a dark and frightening place.

They are then transported on an often fatal journey through a number of West African countries until they reach their departure point where they are sold on to their "madame". If they realize their ordeal and do not want to cooperate, some are even starved to death by the madams.

Because the Italian authorities have become increasingly alert to direct flights from West Africa, the traffickers now use other European countries like Britain and France as staging posts. Bathed in the orange glow of late-night lights, hundreds of half-naked, high-heeled Nigerian girls and women sell sex. With debts of up to $50,000, it can take two or three years working night and day to pay off the money

Greater police co-operation across borders, harsher sentences for the perpetrators and specific anti-trafficking legislation as well as increased resources would reduce the exploitation and enslavement of young girls from Nigeria.

It's not only in Nigeria! There are growing signs that economic pressures and persistent poverty in Africa are leading to a resurgence of the traffic in child slaves. These children are for sale in West African countries as both domestic and commercial labour and also for sexual exploitation. Until recently, this trade has been largely seen as a phenomenon of war-ravaged societies such as Angola, Sudan, Somalia or Chad - where even 10-year-old girls are servants and concubines at rebel military bases. But now, even in relatively peaceful areas, the traffic is growing. Countries in the front line of this trade include Benin, Burkina Faso, Cameroon, Cote d'Ivoire, Gabon, Nigeria and Togo.

The responsibility of educating children has traditionally been given to the extended family system. In Benin it is known as "videmegon" - an expression of community solidarity. In many cases middle-aged "sugar daddies" provide girls with money for school fees, books or clothes in return for domestic help. However, the increasing need for paid work in modern West Africa is eroding the traditional values of communities that once placed limits on the abuse of children. Brokers scout for children among poor families in rural areas in Benin and Togo. They see their work as a cross-border operation. Some of these brokers kidnap children simply playing outside or who have wandered into urban areas. Others persuade parents that their children will receive a professional training or a good education with a wealthy family. Most of the parents are then corrupted by receiving a little cash. A significant number run away from their employers. Unable to return home and unable to find alternative employment, many of them resort to prostitution, washing cars or collecting fares on mini-buses.

This does not only happen abroad in western countries, but also other African countries. Traders say girls from Benin and Togo are particularly in demand in wealthy families in Lagos in Nigeria and in Libreville in Gabon. Other children are taken as far away as Bangui in the Central African Republic, which itself is a poor country.

****

[FK: Living as a debtor in the US]

I was more comfortable as an African in the U.S, than in European countries, even Britain. However, my accent was a label on me wherever I went. When I spoke, people immediately asked where I was from. They knew I could not be African American with that accent. My first big surprise was the word 'oops'. I had never heard such a word before. There were many more to learn that are peculiar to America. I would pronounce fuel as 'foil' and no one would know what I meant. Still, it is also understandable that a Blackman would feel more at ease in the

U.S. than in the UK. For example, the Black British population is much smaller than the African American population. In the US, there is a significant black middle class, whereas, in the UK there is still no viable black middle class; in British institutions, there is a distinct absence of black people in senior positions. Indeed, a Guardian (UK newspaper) article (May 2000) drew attention to the significant number of Black British academics who had relocated to the US to further their careers. On the other hand, in the States there is a significant body of black intellectuals illustrated by the substantial literature on the black experience originating from the US. Still, it is suggested that the US is a more aggressively racist society than the UK; racism in the US is more 'in your face' than in Britain.

One thing I noticed immediately is that many more blacks in the US had no health insurance. The U.S. health insurance system compares very poorly with that of Britain or Germany. In Britain the health service is relatively free; in Germany, all are required to have heath insurance, and it covers pretty much everything. Arriving in the U.S. we were even told that insurance companies required that you must have been living for two years in the U.S. before they could give you a policy. Things got worse when I had a bacteria infection and had to go to the emergency room. It was then I realized that the 400 dollars a month health insurance I had was good for nothing. After going back and forth between hospital and insurance company, I got a letter that I would be paying $3003 dollars. The insurance had accepted to pay $75! We had to arrange to pay the money gradually $80 a month. We started to live on credit.

That brings me to the greatest culture shock I experienced yet: the credit card. Buying on credit has become synonymous with the "American way of life". Some reports say the average American has 7 credit cards, owing an average of $2500 per card. If you do not have a credit card, you are a dead duck! In almost every financial transaction, they want to check your credit history or report. Credit reports are a detailed record of all of your credit activities from how many credit card accounts you have, how many loans you may have taken out, and it shows whether you are paying your monthly payments on time or have a lot of unpaid bills. If you have a lot of negativity on your credit reports, you will not be able to apply for a loan, buy a house, or even apply for a credit card. Sometimes you are even unable to get a checking account if you have a very negative credit report. Keeping your credit up to par is very important and is the key. As a foreigner or new immigrant, you have no credit, and you are just as screwed (excuse my language) as if you had a bad credit report. I needed good credit history to install a phone, power, get cable TV, furniture and other household stuff. Otherwise we had to pay high deposits or pay up front which was undoable. This is one thing one needs to adjust to, especially, coming from Africa were the concept of credit history is still mostly a foreign thing.

My impression of Americans is that they're also quite rule-bound. You can't even buy a stepladder without reading rules on how to use it. And there's a general compliance with rules both written and unwritten. Things are really very orderly here. Take those irritating left-turn jughandles we have in New Jersey. They make a lot of sense once you get used to them. But in South Africa, you'd simply say, "Stuff it, I'm going to turn left right here and just go."

What we haven't experienced here is a real welcome beyond the superficial level. It's tough getting into social circles. Time is such a huge issue, and Americans try to fit so much into their days. So when they socialize, there is another agenda going on as well. The unspoken question always is, 'How can this contact work for me?'

The main priority in my life is striking a balance between work and non-work. Here, work is an end in itself. But I prefer to leave it as a means to an end. The process is a lot tougher on the spouses. My wife, Miriam, doesn't exist to this country. Because she's not entitled to work; she has no Social Security number. I must come with her whenever she needs to do anything official, such as get a driver's license, and explain everything over and over again. When I'm at work, I worry about her. What this kind of experience does is pull the family together more than ever before. And I'm aware that she is the one who must take care of the kids and cope with all the loose ends. But it's one thing to have a great day at the office, and then go home to someone who has been having an entirely different day. My family is always my priority. Without my family, my work would be meaningless.

We had spoken about moving to another country for a long time. And when I got the job at Warner-Lambert in Cape Town, we were excited about the prospect of possibly being transferred to the United States. But when it did happen, we had to remind ourselves, "This is what we wanted." When we initially discussed doing this, it was before we had children. And when you have children, you come to rely on friends and family quite a bit. The children have made it much harder and much easier at the same time. It's harder to orient yourself to a new place with two little kids in tow. You can only do it in short spurts. On the other hand, with kids you meet people more easily. We've already joined a play group, and Miriam joined an organization of stay-at-home mothers.

Miriam agrees that it didn't start out easily. 'When we first moved in here, no one came over to introduce themselves. I thought, "Well, in order to make this work, I'm going to have to be the one to extend myself." If I don't make the effort, the only person I talk to is the checkout person at the grocery store. I've had a couple of days when I really felt lousy and missed people back home. I miss my rituals. For instance, there was a really great coffee shop in Cape Town that had a playground for kids. A good friend ran it. So I could spend the day there, and I'd know half of the people that walked in and out. But here I don't even have the social network of the corporate world. I worry about my husband's peace of mind. I know he's not focusing on what he's doing at work if he's worrying that I'm miserable. Being the kind of guy he is, I know he'd go the extra mile to make sure I'm happy. I do still get lonely, so I try to keep busy. I plan things. I never go a whole week without doing something special with the kids. I have a calendar stuck on the fridge, and I make sure it's full. If I admit that I'm battling culture shock, then I've lost. It's far better to rationalize it, to intellectualize it, and to remind myself that we just got here and it takes time. And I must be getting better. There was a time when my 4-year-old would ask me 10 times a day, "Are you happy, Mom?" He has stopped doing that now. I'll take that as a good sign.'

If you are traveling to the U.S. with your family, be prepared.

****

[FK: A woman's struggle]

Women from Africa are noted for their beauty, grace, charm and loyalty. With their shy smiles and traditional values, African women possess an inner beauty that many men find irresistible. African women are by their nature family-orientated, resourceful and are highly devoted wives. In Africa, the society generally finds married adults more responsible than singles. Since African women are very family-oriented, those who do not get married by a certain age feel some invisible pressure.

For men, it is not a big problem, since they think they can get married at any age. But for females, it can be a horror when you hit 30 and still do not have a life-partner. Men in their thirties go for women in their twenties, and men in their forties, who are supposed to go for women in their forties or thirties, still go for women in their twenties, or are already comfortably married with kids. Divorce cases are relatively few compared to Europe and America. So as an unmarried lady in the thirties, you find yourself in a serious societal swamp. Though in many areas of Africa, girls still marry in their teens, greater gender equality has brought with it a significant rise in the average age of marriage, especially, in Sub-Saharan Africa. This is more so, as females can now also get well educated, and can take on jobs previously considered male business. Girls who have travelled abroad definitely identify with this. Most men still feel very threatened by women who are equally educated and or have good paying jobs. This seriously compounds the prospects of marriage for such girls, who have already delayed getting married for educational reasons.

This is one of the greatest problems girls face out in the west. The additional fact that you can now date boys without the watchful eyes of parents or family, also leads to many of us losing our African values. We can date as many men as we want, buy a whole chicken and eat it, gizzard and all, etc. This makes African men to look back home for their brides. I was a benefactor of this. My husband had a British passport after having lived and worked in Britain for years. When he came home for a visit, he chose me for his bride. I was already 30, and I would be able to travel abroad, so it was easier to say yes.

Shortly after arrival in London, I realized I needed to work in other to meet up with the demands from my family back home. As a new arrival, one of the easiest jobs one finds is cleaning jobs. It was at one such job that I had one of the experiences, which made my head feel so big I wanted to go right back to Zambia. Back home, we often do not consider deodorants important. But out in the west, the importance cannot be over-emphasized. This is partly because people probably have reason to sweat more in the west, due to the higher stress levels, but it also has to do with the type of job one does. I was used to mopping the floor with a wet rag and a bucket of water, using my bare-hands, small scale. So on this day, I found it more complicated using a rag at the end of a 'stick', and went ahead to mop with my hands. Since I had to mop the floor for a long time, I perspired profusely. At some point, a colleague, or was it the boss, complained that I was stinking. I was very embarrassed. Worse still, a day later, I found out that the skin of my hands was peeling off due to the chemicals I had exposed my hands to during the mopping.

I am family oriented so I noticed a lot of things concerning differences in family and social behaviours out here in England. Here are some things that strike me particularly:

British children look directly at their parents when they rebuke them. They look them in the eye. That doesn't convey the respect we show in Africa. African kids born here could become too westernized…too focused on making money. I'm fearful that they will forget who they are. I want my children to know that Africa is the home of their ancestors, and to maintain the values. I was impressed by a Ghanaian family friend who told his child, 'This house is Ghana. When you go outside, that is England. Inside my house, this is Ghana and you will do according to the Ghanaian culture.'

I noticed that Ghanaians were always together. Even though they mix with everyone else, they try to keep a sense of who they are – through restaurants, churches, and social affairs.

Living abroad also makes it easier to marry across religious lines, exactly what is needed to heal the religious divide that has let to skirmishes in Nigeria. Here in England, a Muslim can date a Christian.

A culture cruncher I found remarkable though, with respect to Muslims, is that their ability to create new business is limited. Those practicing Islam may not pay interest on loans. Thus, they will either have to obtain business loans through grants or fees from some government entity, or borrow it from other Muslims!

Just like in the U.S., Christians in England do find themselves under a church on a cultural divide e.g. with the gay issue. As immigrants fill the pews of churches here in the U.K, like the Anglican Church, they are adding another dimension to the complex debate over gay men and lesbians in the church. Most of us Africans hail from more conservative cultures, where homosexuality is rarely discussed or even acknowledged. Because of that, one finds many Africans forming their own nondenominational or evangelical churches. Africans and whites, who stay together, despite the clashes, decide that other aspects of their faith should be the church's main focus. Each group, on its own, has refrained from taking actions that might inflame the other side.

Perhaps that is the best way we should live as foreigners in the West: Try to maintain our own values, while not taking offence or inflaming the society that has welcomed us into their midst. Unfortunately, back home we are already copying a lot of these western 'values'.

****

Florence Ambe (London): Travelling to Europe has often been the cry of many Africans. Some go with genuine reasons and some just feel: 'Well if I could only cross what ever it takes, I will be far much better than staying here in Africa.' The most striking issue here is the fact that even those who are well-to-do still think it would be better for them to abandon what ever they have and cross so that they can have much more than what they already have. Those who have little or nothing prefer even to borrow, steal, or use dubious means just to buy their way out to Europe. It is rather an unfortunate situation, because many, who just thought they should find themselves in this continent of milk and honey no matter what it takes, have often experienced lots of tragedies.

From Dust to Snow: The African Dream?

Over the years, there have been lots of reports of such cases. For instance, some secretly enter into cargo containers to be transported, and of course can not withstand those extreme conditions, and the only thing is they die. Some are deported immediately on their arrival, some get into drug dealings just to get bold when they are confronted by police. Some, who find it difficult to make it, resort to getting married to their own mothers and fathers just to have a place to stay. Some roam the streets for lack of a place to stay; some get into selling themselves for money just to obtain a living. Those who even report themselves in asylum camps tend to deny their nationalities completely, and will choose other countries to be their country of origin. Some present mystical stories to explain how they got there, e.g. 'A horse came and left me here from an unknown origin, and then went on to an unknown destination'; 'My grandfather robbed saliva in his palms and touched my face with it, and I suddenly discovered myself here.' Some, as a result of their stay in these camps tend to learn how to fabricate lies of all forms from other colleagues seeking asylum. The idea about truthfulness in theses camps is far fetched. Those, who had never known how to live a double-personality life, get into it straight away so as to defend their stay in Europe. This in effect ruins the real personalities of many as time goes on. They loose the voice of truth in themselves; their language changes sooner or later, and they start to live a completely different life. About 95% of these people tend to regret why they left their home countries. On the other hand, those, who even came genuinely, still face so many difficulties because the society is completely different from what they had in mind before coming. Most often than not, many tend to abandon their studies and get into other businesses. Nevertheless, those who know why they came will always make it.

Travelling, this time not only within the country by bus and taxi, but now travelling abroad and by airplane is always very exciting and with lots of expectations. When this idea of travelling abroad first dawns on someone, usually, the individual already begins to imagine him or herself a multi-millionaire, riding in luxurious cars, living in modern houses and above all eating whatever he or she desires as it is going to be all milk and honey.

He will say, 'Let me just cross; all that I have not been able to do for my past life – I give myself, say a couple of months. I am going to acquire a plot and set up a very fantastic modern structure for myself. Within a year, I should already be a landlord of at least two well to do tenants. I should be sending home at least three taxies and two containers of assorted items every year. This will not be long from my arrival. The only thing is – let me first cross.'

Deleted experiences

When you apply for the visa your first fears are that, 'Let me not be rejected at the level of the embassy else this is going to abort all my plans. Secondly, it would therefore mean that I would continue to live in this very poor and unproductive country of ours where you always get a minus, no matter what you put in.' Your first visit to the embassy already creates some anxiety in you as you begin to see yourself already in the process of leaving the country to achieve your goals. Though not very sure you are going to make it, your mentality changes and you begin to think big, see yourself in an imaginary town with streets beyond description, very distinct structures, and a different culture entirely.

As a matter of fact about 90% of the people who travel abroad would want to keep it top secret as possible, but due to excitement, they will just tell their very close family members, who will in turn tell it to their own best friends, and that's where the danger lies; as it has often resulted to loss of many lives. For instance, when I got my visa, I had to wait again for some time due to insufficient finances. According to my understanding, only those I shared with knew about it. But as time went on, they also told their best 'who-so-ever', and it happened to enter the ears of witches and wizards, who attacked me and I was at the point of losing my life. I was almost mad; I was hunted day and night by demonic forces. On the streets, I was moving and praying to myself, quoting the word of God to counter the wicked powers.

I actually experienced the power that is in the word of God. I have known it, and experienced it many times, but not up to this magnitude. If not for the intervention of God Almighty, the story would have been different from what it is today. I have every reason till eternity to keep thanking God for his unfailing love for my family and me. That's why the bible says, 'Those who call upon the name of the Lord shall never be disappointed. Call Him even in times of problems He is there to answer you.' Well, this incident scared me so much that only one or two persons knew exactly when I was leaving. It was not until I entered the plane and took off that I was a bit sure of my life. Inside the plane, was another war completely; fear of plane crash, highjack or terrorist attack was another threat to my life. Each time I looked outside the plane, only a bad thought would come to me, and quite often I preferred to be meditating on the word of God. Above it all, God took perfect control and it came to pass that I arrived safely.

With high hopes and great expectations, one is always anxious to see with true eyes how the new environment, the 'white man country', looks like. There are plenty of surprises awaiting you!

****

From Dust to Snow: The African Dream?

[FK: Third culture kid]

I am: known to my sister as Slimeball, known to my nephews and nieces as Uncle Nits, known to my Mummy as Martipoos. I am known to the uninitiated as odd, to my friends as exasperating. I am known to the congregation of the Leipzig English Church as Martin, and to myself as Earwig. I am known to Interpol as General Sir Charles Snoagey-Borse, but would like to be known as Martin Lipsiensis.

I was born in Africa, and remember very well some kids in prep school in England thought my parents were African, though I have a 'European' skin colour. My father had begun his colonial service in Tanzania in 1951. He had met my Mum in Uganda and they got married in 1960. My elder sister was born just before Uganda had its independence, and I after. We moved to Australia for three years, and then to Fiji for two years and later to Malawi for 3 years and then back to Fiji for about 13 years. So you may call me a third culture kid, born and raised between different cultural worlds, with none to particularly call my own.

No, you would be wrong on the most part, because I spent the significant years of my childhood in England. I always felt British because I actually went to boarding school there and did about 13 years of education there. Over the years though, I have realized I may not be typically British

I was brought up in a Christian home, but I made my own personal commitment at about 11. Later I moved to Germany where with the backing of ICS, the Leipzig English Church was established, which today stands as an unique Gemeinde with Christians from many nations, cultures and confessions. The turnover of Christians from different cultural backgrounds probably reflects my on multicultural background. I am not particularly conscious of any cultural difficulties I face, and do not find it difficult to settle in other places.

However, I have always found that there are things one needs to adjust to when you move to another cultural setting, and one needs to be flexible. I think I am inherently flexible, because even when my Mum just dropped me off in boarding school to return to Fiji, I adapted pretty easily. Whether in Australia or Germany, I have found there are characteristic differences one needs to adjust to. I think particularly that Germany is relatively more organized and planned than England. I would also term Germany the homeland of bureaucracy. I like the levels of organization in Germany but prefer the British level of bureaucracy. The corollary to this may justify why Britain is more stringent on immigration, because, unlike in Germany were you need to carry an id with you, you can just get lost in England. In Germany you have to do all the paper work, lots of copies of certificates and translated versions, and your address is registered and your whereabouts implicitly known at all times.

I also think the notion of a civil servant in Germany is different than that in the U.K. In Britain, there is a more flexible interpretation of the law. Government stays out of your hair as much as possible. The line between state and personal responsibility is more inclined to the state in Germany. Also British workers toil for about 100 hours a year more on average than their counterparts in the rest of the European Union, according to new figures. The average UK employee works for 1,673 hours each year - the equivalent of 32 hours 10 minutes a week - compared to 1,354 in Holland, 1,446 in Germany and 1,453 in France.

However, I do not see my ministry in Leipzig as just a job. I have heard a lot of people comment that most German Pastors take their ministry as just another job. Still, I think Germany has a better cultural understanding, for example, of Christianity, of baptism, and paying church taxes. In England, there is no rigid loyalty to denominations.

As a European worker in another European country, one thing that immediately came to mind was adjusting to the language, German, as is the case in Germany. I think I am naturally gifted in languages, so I did not experience a huge shock with respect to that. Besides, I did have the opportunity earlier in my childhood to study in Heidelberg, which made my later return as a worker easier.

My many experiences, travelling to different countries around the world, have had a tremendous impression on the way that I look at the world. These trips have broadened my horizons on what my culture exactly is, and what my beliefs exactly are. Instead of being narrow-minded – thinking that all people are like my own, I have learned that all over the world, each society is different. Yet, these differences are significant to the advancement of all peoples. Each society has something to give to the next: something to teach, which will spread new light on an old/misconceived notion. Every culture takes a different look at a particular issue, and when all other individuals understand where this difference originates, great progress can be made. Generally, if you are travelling to any part of the world, all I can recommend is that you be flexible, tolerant and ready to learn. For example, in Germany, always remember your friends' birthdays. In fact, people you would consider as friends get rather offended if you don't. Africans and Brits living and/or working abroad, especially, should be flexible enough to drink tea without milk or even sugar. If you are travelling to Germany and happen to come to Leipzig, you are highly welcome to fellowship with us at the Leipzig English Church.

Chapter 32

The African Dream

'I have a dream that one day every valley shall be engulfed, every hill shall be exalted and every mountain shall be made low, the rough places will be made plains and the crooked places will be made straight and the glory of the Lord shall be revealed and all flesh shall see it together." – Martin Luther King, Jr.,

Faced with the crushing effects of a devastating exile on the intellectual, religious, moral, political, social, and economic life of the Judeans in 587 BCE, the Judean prophet, Second Isaiah, envisioned a time when the inequalities of life and the unfortunate twists and turns that throw people off track would be erased and straightened out. Centuries later, King embraced that same poetic and practical vision as he articulated a new dream for segregated America, challenging the intellectual and moral basis of a segregated world. As an African-American, King not only challenged the historical and institutionalized legacy of slavery and segregation, but also the moral complacency of a nation and a world that had failed to live up to its essential creed and profession of faith: that all people are created equal. For Africans on the continent and in the New World, King's dream was an African dream, then a universal dream. King's message of transforming a segregated US into an integrated US found tremendous resonance with the work of African leaders such as Nkrumah, Sankara, Senghor, and Mandela as they engaged in fierce (sometimes tragic) struggles against the legacy of colonial rule and ethnic conflicts, not to mention the horrors of apartheid. In rearticulating and re-contextualizing Isaiah's vision for a noble cause that is still fresh in our memories, these leaders provided us with a rhetorical and philosophical "prototype" for articulating and constructing an African dream. In these leaders, we realize that great dreamers possess the ability to provide a diagnosis of their circumstances and propose solutions that respond to the immediate concerns but also transcend such immediate contexts. The legacy of their dreams continues.

In the compilation of the stories in this book, the "dreams" of many Africans have been explored, as they search for success abroad, and sometimes have to survive or thrive under much duress. So it is that dreams are born and bred in specific circumstances. Sometimes the circumstances that trigger these journeys abroad in search of "dreams" are largely negative and destructive (for example, segregation, apartheid, colonization, economic injustice, corruption), thereby inhibiting the realization of the full potential of humans. At other times, the circumstances are positive (for example, the end of apartheid, colonial rule, and segregation; attractive jobs elsewhere). Irrespective of the immediate causes of these journeys, a basic quality of the contributors is their ability to transcend their contextual struggles and limitations by creating and pursuing noble causes on which to ground the vital need for personal and communal well-being. Accordingly, sometimes the journeys abroad are really not a search for dreams, but attempts to protect inherent dreams from being destroyed, and providing receptacles where they can flourish. That is why successful dreams are those that can appeal to multiple audiences and contexts in ways that, when achieved, would allow different groups to identify with the dream, personalize, fulfill, and defend it without having to justify themselves to others. The African dream thus perceived and envisioned will be such that any African or non-African resident can aspire to and achieve any day, anywhere, anytime on the continent, irrespective of ethnicity, religious affiliation or political leaning. It is a dream of self identity and self fulfillment.

Part of the African Renaissance Ambassador's (ARA, pronounced 'ERA') mission is to create a forum for conversations on what constitutes an African dream, and what would take to realize such dreams, not just for particular persons but for the general public. The stories recounted in this book capture that dream. At this point, to further formulate the conversation, let me present to you three other accounts of success stories and then share a few thoughts on how they affect the three-dimensional character (science, arts, and socio-economic) and *raison d'etre* of an African dream as envisioned by ARA.

In his book *Voyage through Time – Walks of Life to the Nobel Prize*, African Diaspora Nobel Laureate, Ahmed Zewail, partly recounts his experience 'From Dust to Snow.' His family's dream had been to see him receive a high degree abroad and to return to become a university professor. On the door to his study room, a sign was placed reading, "Dr. Ahmed," even though he was still far from becoming a doctor. In other words, he had a 'Dream' to become 'Dr. Ahmed'. After finishing high school, he applied to universities. His desire to become a doctor led him through an intellectual/academic and physical journey across continents to the US. After several years of intensive work, he earned his doctoral degree in science, and eventually became a winner of the Nobel Prize. Ahmed recalls: 'A telephone call at dawn on October 12, 1999, shook my inner being just as an earthquake does in California. In Pasadena, California, I received the news at 5:30 A.M. from the secretary general of the Swedish Academy of Sciences, congratulating me on the award of the 1999 Nobel Prize in Chemistry. He read the citation of the academy and indicated that I was receiving the prize unshared. After three other members of the academy praised the contribution for which the prize was awarded, the secretary-general came back on the line and said: 'In twenty minutes we will be announcing it to the world – these are the last twenty minutes of peace in your life.' The secretary-general was right. My life has changed, and in the years to come there will be opportunities to reflect on these changes following the Nobel Prize.'

The journey from Egypt to America was full of surprises. As a Moeid, Ahmed was unaware of the Nobel Prize in the way he now sees its impact in the West. They used to gather around the TV or read in the newspaper about the recognition of famous Egyptian scientists and writers by the President, and these moments gave him and his friends a real thrill. They dreamed of, maybe, one day being in the position themselves for achievements in science or literature. Some decades later, when President Mubarak bestowed the Order of Merit, first class, and the Grand Collar of the Nile ("Kiladate El Niel"), the highest State honor, on Prof Ahmed Zewail, it brought those emotional boyhood days back to his memory. He never expected that his portrait, next to the pyramids, would be on a postage stamp or that the school he went to as a boy and the road to Rosetta would be named after him. Certainly, as a youngster in love with science, with dreams to become a 'Dr', his dreams were fulfilled beyond his imaginations. What an inspiring experience! Today Dr Ahmed is a model for Africans. He inspires African Scientists to dream! But even more importantly, his initial desire for success is a testament to the powerful effects that positive leadership that proactively affirms and rewards success and hard work can exert on younger generations.

How about African Artists? Consider the inspiration from African Diaspora Oscar Prize Winner Charlize Theron. Theron was born in Benoni, South Africa. She grew up as the only child on her parents' farm near Johannesburg and was sent to a boarding school at the age of thirteen. She had her own fair amount of 'problems' as a child. At fifteen, Theron witnessed the death of her father; her mother shot him in self defense when he attacked her in a drunken rage. No charges were pressed. At the age of sixteen, Theron traveled to Milan, Italy on a one-year modeling contract, after winning a local competition. Her contract ended while she was in New York, and she decided to remain there, attending the Joffrey Ballet, where she trained as a ballet dancer and performed in productions of both Swan Lake and The Nutcracker. A knee injury ended this career path at the age of 18. Unable to dance, she bought a ticket to Los Angeles. After eight months in the city, she was cast in her first film part, a non-speaking role in the direct-to-video film *Children of the Corn III*. She followed this with larger roles in widely released Hollywood films, and her career skyrocketed in the late nineties, with box office successes like *The Devil's Advocate*.

After appearing in a few notable films, Theron starred as serial killer in the film *Monster* in 2003. Receiving praise for her performance (film critic Roger Ebert called it "one of the greatest performances in the history of the cinema"), Theron won the Best Actress Oscar at the 76th Academy Awards in February 2004, as well as the SAG Award and the Golden Globe Award. She is the first African 'African' to win an Oscar for Best Actress.

In 2005, she received her own bronze star on the Hollywood Walk of Fame. Theron tells Africans that they can make it to the top but more importantly, you do not need to be at the top to contribute to Africa's 're-awakening': "I've always been very proud to be a South African and I've always been very honest to people about that. And whatever I can do in my power I promise you I will do. I don't think it's too much pressure. I think it's our duty as citizens of this country. You don't have to win an Oscar to do something good for your country. We all can do that. If I can be an encouragement for that I'll be glad to be that."

After winning her Oscar, she returned to great celebrations in her native South Africa, and she even met former South African President Nelson Mandela. When he praised her for putting their country on the map and gave her a hug, Theron broke into tears (she was guest of honor at the Nelson Mandela Foundation in Johannesburg on March 11th 2004). Theron inspires African Artists.

Should I continue? How about the Social/socio-economic 'Light'? African Diaspora basketball superstar Dikembe Mutombo Mpolondo Mukamba Jean Jacques Wamutombo, a member of the Luba ethnic group in the Democratic Republic of Congo had a 'dream' to grow up and help the society, his people, by being a Doctor. He came to the U.S. in 1987 on an academic scholarship to attend Georgetown. As a premed major, he expected to return to the Congo as a doctor. In his second year, Georgetown basketball coach John Thompson invited the 7-foot-2 Mutombo to try out for the team. He grew up loving soccer, but eventually came around to basketball under Thompson's guidance.

Mutombo became a 4-time NBA Defensive Player of the Year. After 15 years in the NBA, Mutombo had the means to live the life he could only dream of growing up in Kinshasa, capital city of Congo. Mutombo, is able to own multiple homes and drive luxurious cars. But the memories from his youth compel him not to forget his impoverished homeland, the former Zaire. He paid for the Congolese women's basketball team's trip to the 1996 Atlanta Olympics and for the track team's uniforms and expenses. He regularly sends medicines and equipment back home.

But Mutombo's most daunting undertaking has been the construction of the 300-bed Biamba Marie Mutombo Hospital near Kinshasa. Mutombo says the hospital, named in memory of his mother, is in keeping with an African proverb: "When you take the elevator up to reach the top, please don't forget to send the elevator back down so that someone else can take it to the top." 'Mutombo is fulfilling his life-long dream! 'I'm still a doctor, serving the people," Mutombo says. Mutombo inspires Social/Socio-economic 'Light', a passion shared by Africans in Diaspora (those who have traveled abroad) who seek to give back to their home countries. The passion to help their continent is epitomized by the frequent monetary transfers, up to 44 million dollars per year to some African countries alone (e.g. Cameroon and Rwanda).

But what is particularly "African" about these dreams? In a sense, there is nothing "African" about wanting to be successful, have a healthy family, job security etc. But it is the framing of the dream, the prioritizing of what it takes to achieve it, and the translation of such concepts into practical, accessible resources for the masses back on the continent that characterizes the "African-ness" of these dreams. Therefore, even though the stories in this book are individual experiences, they all bear an underlying unifying theme, namely, a persistent and powerful drive in most Africans to be willing to metaphorically of physically "loose" their homeland and accept "exile" as a first step towards realizing their potential and making a better life for themselves, and necessarily by extension for Africa. To dream about success is not the prerogative of any individual people, including Africans. To dream to be a successful African away from "home" is fast becoming an accepted price to pay in order to achieve dreams born from circumstances back on the continent. But most importantly, to dream to be a successful African on the continent and to work for a successful *Africa* is indeed the second and crucial step towards realizing the African dream. The African dream is about Africans, but more importantly about Africa. It is a dream that transcends the ethnicities and languages of the continent, together with the respective political leanings, preferences, and ideologies. This dream is consistent with, and rooted in indigenous African religious, philosophical, and wisdom thought according to which the forces of negativity and destruction that emerge in society must be tamed, neutralized and transformed rather than avoided.

So even though it is true that the "dream" of many Africans is to travel abroad as evident in the anthology of experiences in this book, the more basic question is to ask why? Why do they want to travel abroad? In other words, is the African dream a dream of survival? Do they travel because they have to or because they want to? In a sense, this question may be a matter of semantics, since need creates desire. That is, they want to because they have to. However, pondering this question will help frame the nature and character of the dream. The stories in this book seem to suggest that "survival" is not too far fetched a word to use to describe the underlying mentality of some of those embarking on those journeys. Survival here is used in a dual sense, meaning first of all "escape" from circumstances deemed harmful at worse or non-supportive of one's needs at best; and second, survival is used in the sense of "triumph" over tough circumstances, as people who travel often end up having to face equally tough situations in their new locations. Therefore, it would be quite sensible to argue that those who spend a great deal of effort trying to survive (the psychology of a survivor is quite unique) do not necessarily prioritize and fulfill their potentials as would otherwise be the case. So, not only do we end with brain/resource drain but also significant brain/resource waste, as human and intellectual resources are not only lost in tragic incidences associated with relocation, but also spent not in developing skills but in trying to "fit in" and be accepted in the host cultures. Accordingly, the stories in this book about the struggles of Africans and their search for justice, economic prosperity, peace, good functional governments etc, are not isolated instances but quite pervasive desires shared by many Africans across the continent and abroad. The desires are cross-ethnic and cross-cultural; they transcend any individual location. The dream that is expressed in these stories is that employment, peace, job security, political and economic integrity and freedom are not just socio-political and economic rights; they are permanent non-negotiable human rights! The three success stories recounted above (representing the three wings of ARA) demonstrate a fulfillment of the first step taken by those outside of the continent to realize their dreams. They accomplish the dream away from home. Their stories, however, also have a second component. A crucial underlying current in these three stories, equally reflected in the several stories in this book, is the desire to make the physical, intellectual, and material journey back home after success abroad. What seem to unify and complete the sense of fulfillment in these stories is not the successes but also and more especially the desire to return home to the continent to make the dream accessible and realizable to others.

So what is the African dream? To answer quite simply, it is the African Renaissance. It is remarkable, according to our internal ARA polling, that when presented with the choice of either going abroad in search of their dream or staying at home and working for an African Renaissance, most Africans on the continent prefer to stay at home and

From Dust to Snow: The African Dream?

have an African Renaissance. The desire for an African Renaissance is almost palpable for both Africans on the continent and in the Diaspora. Among Diaspora Africans, this desire is evidenced by their wish to return home. This aspect of the African dream has also been captured and expressed by President Mbeki:

> 'I dream of the day when these: the African mathematicians and computer specialists in Washington and New York, the African physicists, engineers, doctors, business managers and economists, will return from London and Manchester and Paris and Brussels to add to the African pool of brain power, to enquire into and find solutions to Africa's problems and challenges, to open the African door to the world of knowledge, to elevate Africa's place within the universe of research,... education and information' – President Mbeki, at the African Renaissance Conference.

It is perhaps an overlooked truism that the measure and greatness of a dream is not how grandiose it is in "exile" but how relevant, rewarding and transformative it is back home. As is evident in the several folkloric, legendary and epic narratives in Africa and across the world, the journey back home is as important, if not more important than the journey away from home. As the epic of Sundiata from Old Mali indicates, the heroism of an individual is not measured solely by the adversity they face and overcome away from home, but ultimately by their inspiring return home, the homecoming. The African dream thus conceived and advocated must ultimately be a dream that is tailored to respond to the contextual needs and aspirations of Africans on the continent. The question then is this: is there any historical precedent, any anterior cultural prototype, any enduring intellectual tradition that can serve as the foundation and receptacle for the realization of such an African dream, the African Renaissance? In other words, does Africa's history have a place for, and can it accommodate the idea of a renaissance? Or is Africa's image forever seared into our psyche as a place of complacency, mediocrity, corruption, poverty, moral laissez-faire—the personification of "The Wretched of the Earth" in the words of Frantz Fanon?

Let's step back for a moment in history. Recall that Africa is the birthplace of Scientific thought hundreds of years ago, with inventions in science, engineering, medicine and other fields. Nearly a millennium ago, Civilization from Egypt reached Europe and Asia, and certainly became instrumental in the birth of a European Renaissance. Recall that as the European Renaissance burst into history in the 15th and 16th centuries, there was a royal court in the African city of Timbuktu which, in the same centuries, was as learned as its European counterparts. There are spectacular African works of art that encompass the varied artistic creations of the Nubians and the Egyptians, the Benin bronzes of Nigeria and the intricate sculptures of the Makonde of Tanzania and Mozambique. There are centuries-old contributions to the evolution of religious thought made by Coptic Christians of Ethiopia and Muslims of Nigeria. Refer to the architectural monuments represented by the giant sculptured stones of Aksum in Ethiopia, the Egyptian sphinxes and pyramids, the Tunisian city of Carthage, and the Zimbabwe ruins, as well as the legacy of the ancient universities of Alexandria of Egypt, Fez of Morocco and, once more, Timbuktu of Mali. It is therefore clear that the African dream of a renaissance is deeply rooted in the ingenuity, charisma, grace, and creativity of our forebears. The current experience of Africa is therefore a clear and unacceptable mishap, one that must be corrected if Africans are to remain true to their history.

In order to correct this mishap and bring about the realization of the African dream, three factors are here identified as essential building blocks for such a vision advocated in the context of the African Renaissance: (mental) transformation, (global) mobilization, and (structural) reallocation.

First, Africans must demonstrate the mental fortitude to resist the overwhelming and potentially discouraging focus on, and self resignation in the face of tragic events on the continent. It is one thing to face tragedy, but it quite another to be defined and permanently marred by its embodied image. It is true that this created negative self image (the need to prove oneself simply because one is African, or sit back and wait for "someone" from outside to react and respond to tragic circumstances) has a history going back to the colonial period when cultural anthropologists, serving the desires of colonial masters, analyzed Africa from afar and classified her as the Dark Continent in need of external civilization. Although that characterization has now been clearly deconstructed, its legacy still wields its ugly head from time to time. One finds that it is not just bad enough that warring ethnic groups engage in negative and destructive conflicts, they also use derogatory propaganda to dehumanize the other, as is clear from the 1994 conflict in Rwanda. Also, not only are individual nations wrecked by financial corruption, but there are many instances where governments are run with budget crisis and debts that the future generations will have to bear. It is obvious, not only from the effects of colonial rule but also from ethnic conflicts, that a dualistic mindset that categorizes people along exclusive lines and proceeds to create a moral hierarchy privileging one group over another inevitably leads to mutual suspicion, distrust, conflict, exploitation, and corruption. The real danger is that this "unwritten law" of socio-political and economic discrimination (everyone officially denounces it) is still practiced in subtle ways across the board, from administrative decisions to personal interactions on the streets, and is therefore threatening to become a culture. An African Renaissance thus begins with a change in mentality and respect for the other, and the realization that ethnic, political, religious, and national difference does not have to become or degenerate into ethnic, political, and religious danger. Africa must draw on her long standing history of recognizing cultural diversity as integral to her identity as a people.

Accordingly, sensitization at the local levels is crucial. An ARA survey shows that many grassroots-Africans have not yet heard about the African Renaissance, despite the 'talk' at higher levels as in the AU. Recently ARA has been providing incentives for Africans to make pledges, for example, in spreading the AR dream (telling others about it, sharing the candle light), not to give or take a bribe (fight corruption), and to excel in their studies. The Desmond Tutu Foundation's Emerging Leadership program also prepares youth as future leaders – African youths who will choose peace instead of war. Such activities promote an enabling environment for the AR to take root and grow, including attracting foreign investment and support from both the African Diaspora and goodwill Westerners. Such efforts must be elevated to the intensity and need level of HIV/AIDS awareness campaigns in Africa, so that individuals do not sit back and think that change has to come from higher levels or from 'someone' else.

Secondly, Africans have been mobilized and need to continue to mobilize to help the continent. From the experiences recounted in this book, there is a great passion for Africa by Africans abroad that would be an extremely useful ingredient in the realization of the dream for a 'Lighted' Africa. Evidently, Africans in Diaspora work hard to send money (millions of dollars) back home. But more importantly, Africans in the Diaspora have also formed potent networks in cities where they live in North and South America, the Caribbean, Europe, Asia and elsewhere around the globe. According to reports by AFFORD (African Foundation for Development), African Diaspora groups have succeeded in pooling resources to create relationships, networks of trust and co-operation and social capital to provide local communities in Africa with access to financial, material and emotional assets. Furthermore, Africans in Diaspora have begun to wield extraordinary political, cultural, economic, and scientific power, which if properly cultivated, can be effectively leveraged to advance the African Renaissance dream of a 'Light' Africa. At its inaugural in Maputo, the African Union (AU) announced a truly "historic" decision to formally include Africans living in the Diaspora as the Sixth Region of the AU's organizational structure. This decision to open the door to the Diaspora is in part a recognition that today,

The African Dream

perhaps, as many Africans reside outside the continent as live on the continent, and that Africans in Diaspora can significantly contribute to the African Renaissance. The decision dramatically expands the reach of Africa into the power corridors of Washington, New York, London, Paris, Rome, Tokyo and elsewhere. Since announcing this decision, a myriad of ideas have flowed from all corners of the world on how best to define the Diaspora, and how to organize the participation in ways that support sustainable development and economic progress in the continent. Thus, beyond individual contributions to family and individual projects back home, Africans actively seek to support the efforts of organizations working in Africa, either financially, intellectually, materially, or symbolically. An organization like Africare is one such platform by African Americans that rallies support for Africa. Nelson Mandela's remark that Africare is "America's greatest gift to Africa" clearly demonstrates the relevance and need for such organizations on the realization of the African Renaissance.

The third building block of the African dream, the AR, is structural reallocation. Just as Africans traveling abroad need a good social and community network of people who are ready and willing to help them settle and thrive in their new communities, so too it is important for African leadership to provide both the incentives and conditions for both Africans in Diaspora and interested non-Africans to (re)allocate on the continent and bring along their acquired knowledge and skill. Ultimately as seen from the experiences in this book, Africans in Diaspora are more than willing to sacrifice the lure of lucre and return home to put their talents at the service of their continent. A recent survey by the African Renaissance Ambassador (ARA) Corp shows that more than 75% of Africans in Diaspora (neo-Diasporans) want to return home if conditions improve, or if they are assured the appropriate intellectual and economic conditions for flourishing. The good news is that non Africans (people, institutions, and industry or companies) abound with goodwill to support Africa. As an example, a survey by ARA shows that 4 in 5 western scientists, though not very conversant with the situation on the ground in Africa, have an ardent desire to support Africa in its scientific renaissance. They are willing to pledge support in the form of ideological, financial, and equipment resources. Furthermore, U.S, European, Chinese and Japanese funding agencies expressively support science and sustainable development efforts in Africa. Goodwill westerners also abound in supporting education and other renaissance enabling activities. There are a lot of people out there who really care about Africa. There are Peace Corps volunteers, there are former ambassadors, missionaries (e.g. with Campus Crusade and Wycliffe USA). The challenge thus lies with African political leadership to demonstrate not just a rhetorical willingness but a practical policy-driven capacity to encourage and foster such reallocation endeavors and desires. Such leadership that galvanizes human and material resources abroad and at home to transform the socio-political and economic landscape of the continent will not only help Africans in the Diaspora realize their dream of returning home, but will also respond to the latent but real desire of many Africans to remain home and not have to travel abroad in search of dreams.

In this light, consider this African dream, embodied and expressed by Decu. At eight years of age, he has never owned a ball or played a video game. He has never seen a computer or TV. He's never been to school. He is a child, born into poverty in what could be one of the richest places in the World - the Eastern province of Katanga, in the Democratic Republic of Congo. There are vast mineral deposits beneath the soil there, but this treasure trove has always benefited the leaders not the people. The treasure has been used to buy guns for war against fellow Africans.

Decu's day begins at dawn. Usually he does not eat, just drinks a little water. Then he sets off on a two-hour walk with his twin, Kabila. Both have torn sweatshirts and trousers with holes, no shoes, only what nature gave them. By seven or eight each morning, the boys arrive at Ruashi mines, where huge mounds of red, brown and grey soil scar the landscape. They start sifting away soil from mineral deposits. It is heavy work. Decu would like to be like children in Europe. "They go to school." he says. "Who decided that I be born in Africa and they in Europe? They can wear gold rings and I cannot, though I dug up the gold. How come we are so rich and yet poor?"

Decu's apparent rhetorical question is at the same time not rhetorical; it demands and deserves an answer! The good news is that Africans can get rid of the dust. They can move from 'Dust to Gold.' I dream of the day when Africans will not have to leave their continent because they are forced to by circumstances. I dream of an African Rebirth: Sweet Mother Africa bears another Africa, a new Africa. Mother Africa also retains the birthrights, this time! Reflecting on the role of the mother in Africa, John Alphonsus from Nigeria says this: 'A Mother is a new day! New-week! New month! New year! New life! New hope! New strength! New peace! New joy! New song!' – If I may add, 'New ERA!'

There is a Chinese saying that: "Better to light a candle than to curse the darkness." African or not, we can all demonstrate that we care about Africa, and can light a candle for the New ERA. We can light a single candle from the flame already lit by President Mbeki and Mandela and 'prophesied' by Nkrumah, and articulated by other leaders across the continent. Let us reach out to our neighbours and say it is time for change; it is time for a rebirth, for the African Renaissance. There is no doubt that Africans on the ground want a rebirth as evident from the ARA survey. Individual efforts are necessary to inspire, or coerce or complement efforts from the leadership. In addition, non-Africans can help Africans help Africa. A 'Renaissance' Africa will make the world a better place for all. All of us must join hands to make the African Dream a reality. They say there are 3 types of people: those who make things happen, those who watch things happen, and those who do not know what is going on. As you close this book, you will have to make a decision about where history will classify you. Do not procrastinate. If you make a decision to help in making the African Renaissance happen, and is not sure how to go about it or need any support, there is help available at the website below, where many others have been supported in this effort. And remember that, your individual effort counts. I beseech all Africans both within and without the continent, all lovers of Africa, and all people of goodwill, to join together and render the truth of Nelson Mandela's inspirational words which I dare say constitute the 'African Renaissance creed':

"We are all meant to shine, as children do.
We were born to make manifest this glory to God that is within us.
It's not just in some of us; it is in everyone.
And as we let our own light shine, we unconsciously give other people permission to do the same.
As we are liberated from our own fears, our presence automatically liberates others."

With love and appreciation. God bless Mother Africa – and the world!

*Fako Kilimanjaro
African Renaissance Ambassador
(www.africanrenaissanceambassador.com)

♣ Additional Referenced works in this chapter:
- Fanon, Frantz. *The Wretched of the Earth.* New York: Grover, 1963. Translated from the original *Les Damnés de la Terre* (Paris: Maspero, 1961) by Constance Farrington.
- Niane, D. T. *Sundiata: An Epic of Old Mali.* Essex: Longman, 1965
- BBC

The African Anthem

Sweet Mother, by Prince Nico Mbarga *(Voted anthem by BBC readers and listeners in 2004)*

Sweet mother I no go forget you
for the suffer wey you suffer for me.
Sweet mother I no go forget you
for the suffer wey you suffer for me.

When I dey cry, my mother go carry me – she go say,
"'my pikin', wetin you dey cry ye, ye,
stop stop, stop stop make you no cry again oh."

When I want sleep, my mother go pet me,
she go lie me well well for bed,
she cover me cloth, sing me to sleep,
"sleep sleep my pikin oh."

When I dey hungry, my mother go run up and down.
she go find me something when I go chop oh.
Sweet mother I no go forget you for the suffer wey you suffer for me

When I dey sick, my mother go cry, cry, cry,
she go say instead when I go die make she die.
O, she go beg God,
"God help me, God help, my pikin oh."

If I no sleep, my mother no go sleep,
if I no chop, my mother no go chop, she no dey tire oh.
Sweet mother I no go forget you,
for the suffer wey you suffer for me.

You fit get another wife, you fit get another husband,
but you fit get another mother? No!

And if I forget you, therefore I forget my life and the air I breathe.

And then on to you men, forget, verily, forget your mother,
for if you forget your mother you've lost your life.

Country index

A

Algeria, 201
America, 11, 13, 14, 28, 43, 44, 45, 46, 47, 48, 51, 52, 54, 56, 57, 58, 59, 70, 71, 78, 79, 82, 83, 84, 95, 97, 117, 121, 134, 151, 158, 159, 169, 170, 171, 172, 192, 194, 202, 285, 286, 288, 291, 298, 300, 306

B

Benin, 73, 288, 305
Botswana, 123, 125
Burkina Faso, 203, 288
Burma, 221, 224, 226, 227

C

Cameroon, 14, 16, 18, 19, 27, 40, 41, 42, 44, 45, 47, 48, 50, 53, 56, 57, 58, 61, 62, 63, 64, 65, 67, 70, 91, 98, 99, 100, 108, 117, 118, 119, 122, 135, 136, 141, 144, 146, 160, 161, 162, 165, 168, 171, 172, 173, 174, 175, 176, 178, 179, 182, 189, 232, 236, 241, 244, 245, 247, 256, 260, 262, 263, 265, 266, 267, 268, 269, 276, 277, 278, 279, 281, 288, 302
Canada, 43, 47, 82, 114, 127, 128, 129, 130, 131, 132
Central African Republic, 288
Chad, 201, 288
Congo, 86, 97, 201, 283, 301, 308
Cote d'Ivoire, 288
Czech Republic, 218

D

Democratic Republic of Congo, 97, 283, 301, 308
Denmark, 145, 146, 195, 216, 272

E

Egypt, 13, 300, 304
England, 75, 102, 103, 108, 147, 148, 151, 160, 201, 215, 219, 228, 236, 238, 252, 258, 260, 262, 272, 285, 286, 292, 293, 296, 297
Ethiopia, 16, 22, 34, 93, 94, 305

F

Finland, 241, 242, 244, 245, 246, 247, 248
France, 41, 75, 86, 88, 89, 90, 91, 92, 98, 100, 104, 121, 141, 142, 169, 178, 195, 217, 219, 242, 245, 272, 287, 297

G

Gabon, 201, 288
Germany, 14, 15, 16, 17, 18, 19, 20, 22, 24, 25, 26, 27, 28, 30, 31, 32, 33, 34, 35, 38, 40, 42, 43, 49, 55, 91, 98, 100, 102, 103, 106, 107, 121, 123, 125, 126, 128, 129, 133, 139, 141, 142, 143, 144, 145, 146, 149, 150, 153, 154, 155, 156, 157, 161, 163, 164, 165, 166, 167, 168, 173, 174, 175, 176, 178, 179, 180, 182, 185, 187, 188, 189, 193, 195, 196, 198, 204, 205, 206, 207, 214, 216, 217, 219, 223, 227, 241, 249, 251, 252, 253, 254, 269, 271, 272, 273, 275, 277, 278, 283, 285, 287, 289, 296, 297
Ghana, 13, 78, 153, 156, 157, 243, 271, 272, 277, 292
Guinea, 81, 201

H

Holland, 134, 266, 268, 272, 273, 297

Hungary, 98, 121, 218

I

India, 28, 92, 190, 191, 192, 193, 194, 210, 213, 214, 215, 219
Italy, 202, 203, 216, 272, 287, 300

J

Japan, 28, 33, 191, 193, 212, 254

K

Kenya, 16, 20, 21, 28, 30, 43, 94, 96, 158, 159, 282

L

Liberia, 80, 81, 82, 83, 84, 85

M

Macedonia, 27, 249, 251, 252
Malawi, 296
Malaysia, 86, 87
Mali, 90, 91, 202, 304, 305, 309
Morocco, 32, 92, 305
Mozambique, 15, 305

N

Nigeria, 73, 74, 75, 78, 103, 115, 128, 129, 130, 148, 149, 150, 247, 265, 267, 273, 287, 288, 293, 305, 308

P

Poland, 39, 40, 125, 178, 218
Portugal, 216

R

Russia, 27, 28, 125, 193, 195, 201, 202, 219, 254
Rwanda, 302, 305

S

Senegal, 91
Sierra Leone, 169
Singapore, 86, 226
Somalia, 288
South Africa, 14, 28, 29, 89, 106, 109, 121, 152, 166, 202, 234, 241, 242, 265, 267, 268, 269, 270, 290, 300, 301
Spain, 40, 41, 75, 121, 125, 148, 178, 216
Sudan, 94, 97, 170, 204, 205, 206, 207, 288
Sweden, 61, 62, 64, 65, 66, 67, 70, 72, 214, 215, 216
Switzerland, 14, 49, 98, 193, 216

T

Tanzania, 183, 296, 305
Togo, 271, 288

U

U.S., 16, 34, 40, 43, 44, 45, 46, 47, 48, 49, 50, 55, 56, 57, 83, 84, 85, 95, 96, 99, 108, 116, 117, 118, 119, 120, 121, 123, 127, 148, 149, 150, 152, 158, 170, 171, 190, 191, 192, 193, 194, 202, 203, 210, 212, 213, 214, 216, 218, 219, 252, 267, 270, 271, 285, 286, 289, 291, 293, 301
Uganda, 296
UK, 98, 228, 256, 262, 263, 264, 282, 289, 297

Z

Zaire, 301
Zambia, 145, 201, 202, 292
Zimbabwe, 305

www.ingramcontent.com/pod-product-compliance
Lightning Source LLC
Chambersburg PA
CBHW031616160426
43196CB00006B/158